# HOUSING:
# A
# BIBLIOGRAPHY

Also by Virginia Paulus:

HOUSING: 1971-1972, co-edited with George Sternlieb

# HOUSING: A BIBLIOGRAPHY

1960-1972

edited, with an Introduction, by

Virginia Paulus
*Center for Urban Policy Research*
*Rutgers University*

AMS PRESS
New York

 Published in the United States by AMS Press, Inc., 56 East 13th Street, New York, New York 10003.

Library of Congress Cataloging in Publication Data

Paulus, Virginia.
Housing: a bibliography, 1960-1972.

1. Housing–United States–Bibliography.
I. Title
Z7164.H8P38 016.3015'4'0973 73-15863
ISBN 0-404-10537-8

Manufactured in the United States of America.

# TABLE OF CONTENTS

# III. SOCIAL/POLITICAL FRAMEWORK

## IV. DEMOGRAPHIC FRAMEWORK



## V. INFORMATIONAL FRAMEWORK



## VI. GENERAL WORKS AND ANTHOLOGIES ON HOUSING

# INTRODUCTION

The years 1960-1972 represent an era of growing concern with the nation's housing problems as well as a time of vigorous experimentation and research in the housing field. *Housing, 1960-1972: A Bibliography* is a selective listing of materials of research value issued during this time period and is intended as a reference source for those studying various aspects of housing—faculty, students, planners, developers, government officials, etc. Included in the bibliography are a number of major works published before 1960 but reprinted during 1960-1972. More adequate coverage of publications prior to 1960 can be found in several of the bibliographies listed in this book, specifically, in *Housing, Renewal and Development Bibliography*, by Wheaton, Baer and Vetter (3550); *60 Books on Housing and Community Development*, by the U.S. Housing and Home Finance Agency Library (3549); *Bibliography on Housing, Building and Planning*, by the U.S. Department of Housing and Urban Development Library (3542). In addition, several housing volumes contain extensive bibliographies of earlier materials, such as, *Urban Housing*, by Wheaton, Milgram and Meyerson (3625); *Housing, People, and Cities*, by Meyerson, Terrett and Wheaton (3611); and *Housing: A Factual Analysis*, by Glenn H. Beyer (New York: Macmillan, 1958).

Given the vastness of the housing literature, this bibliography is largely limited to items published in the United States and dealing with housing concerns in this country. Within that context, the subject areas of architecture and vacation homes are considered beyond the scope of this work. Due to the existence of numerous bibliographies on new towns, the new town literature was not listed; only bibliographies on the topic have been included. For information on new towns, the reader may also consult an extensive 1973 Urban Land Institute publication, *New Towns Planning and Development: A World-Wide Bibliography*.

An attempt was made to include a variety of sources: books, journal articles, government documents, technical reports, conference proceedings, dissertations, and unpublished papers. These are drawn from the literature of numerous fields such as urban planning, economics, sociology, law, regional science, and public administration. In order to cover a broad range of materials, a variety of sources were consulted in the literature, including *Housing and Planning References, PAIS, Social Sciences and Humanities Index, Index to Legal Periodicals, Business Periodicals Index, Journal of Economic Literature, Dissertation Abstracts,* and *Library of Congress Catalog: Books: Subjects.* In addition, publication lists, bibliographies, and library catalogs were consulted.

The bibliography is organized into six major categories: Economic Framework, Legal Framework, Social/Political Framework, Demographic Framework, Informational Framework, and General Works and Anthologies on Housing. This categorization undoubtedly reflects a subjective conceptualization of the field. A detailed table of contents is provided to facilitate the location of specific topics. In addition, a brief Subject Finding Guide, following the Author Index, lists subjects alphabetically and gives their location within the bibliography. Since materials are only listed once and are cross-referenced when subjects overlap, the reader should consult the cross-references given at the ends of sections.

It is hoped that this bibliography fills a gap in the literature by gathering within one source major works on the varied aspects of housing in this country during 1960-1972.

—Virginia Paulus
*Center for Urban Policy Research*
*Rutgers University*

# I. ECONOMIC FRAMEWORK

## A. RESIDENTIAL DEVELOPMENT AND THE HOMEBUILDING INDUSTRY

### 1. GENERAL

1. Borden, Philip S. "The Home Building Industry – Present and Future: Sales, Production, Financing, Organization and Management, and Land Development." *University of Washington Business Review*, October 1965, pp. 64-83.

2. Briloff, Abraham J. "The Home Builders' House Is Not in Order." *Real Estate Review*, Fall 1972, pp. 69-76.

3. Burns, Leland S. and Frank Mittelbach. "Efficiency in the Housing Industry." In U. S. President's Committee on Urban Housing. *Report: Technical Studies, Volume II.* Washington, D.C.: Government Printing Office, 1968, pp. 75-144.

4. Catanese, Anthony James *et al. The Residential Development of New Jersey: A Regional Approach.* Trenton, N. J.: Division of State and Regional Planning, Department of Conservation and Economic Development, 1964. 144pp.

5. Collier, Robert Wesley. *An Analysis of the Large Scale Single-Family Residential Builder in Los Angeles, Orange and Ventura Counties.* Ann Arbor, Mich.: University Microfilms, 1967 (Ph.D. dissertation, University of Southern California, 1967). 229pp. (order #67-13,738).

6. Daly, Grover and D. Robert Papera. "The Sale and Financing of On-the-Lot Housing." *Land Economics*, November 1964, pp. 433-437.

7. Debro, J. "Minority Builder." *Labor Law Journal*, May 1970, pp. 298+.

8. Donelson, Lewis R. "Multicorporation Home Builders: Three Cases Deciding Important Issues in the Multicorporation Operation." *Illinois Taxes*, October 1960, pp. 789-795.

9. Eisenberg, Lawrence D. "Uncle Tom's Multi-Cabin Subdivision: Constitutional Restrictions on Racial Discrimination by Developers." *Cornell Law Review,* January 1968, pp. 314-324.

10. Evans, Richard H. "The Future Demand for Building Materials in Residential Construction in the United States." *University of Washington Business Review,* Summer 1967, pp. 48-56.

11. "Exploring Restrictive Building Practices." *Monthly Labor Review,* July 1969, pp. 31-39.

12. Gillies, James. "Some Preliminary Observations on the Publicly Held Company and Management in the Light Construction Industry." In *Essays in Urban Land Economics.* Los Angeles, Calif.: Real Estate Research Program, University of California, 1966, pp. 287-300.

13. Herzog, John P. "Analysis of the Dynamics of Large-Scale Housebuilding." Unpublished Ph.D. dissertation, University of California, Berkeley, 1962.

14. Herzog, John P. *The Dynamics of Large-Scale Housebuilding.* Berkeley, Calif.: Real Estate Research Program, University of California, 1963.

15. Herzog, John. "Structural Change in the Housebuilding Industry." *Land Economics,* May 1963, pp. 133-141.

16. "Housing Enters the Era of the Superbuilder." *Business Week,* December 26, 1970, pp. 50-53.

17. "The Housing Industry: How Firm a Foundation?" *First National City Bank of New York, Monthly Economic Letter,* August 1971, pp. 9-13.

18. "How to Build Volume in the Big – But Difficult – Rural Market." *House & Home,* June 1972, pp. 74-79.

19. Kaiser, Edward J. and Shirley F. Weiss. "Public Policy and the Residential Development Process." *Journal of the American Institute of Planners,* January 1970, pp. 30-37.

20. Kaiser, Edward J. and Shirley F. Weiss. "Local Public Policy and the Residential Development Process." *Law and Contemporary Problems,* Spring 1967, pp. 232-249.

21. Keegan, J. E. and W. Rutzick. "Private Developers and the New Communities Act of 1968." *Georgetown Law Journal.* June 1969, pp. 1119+.

22. Kniffen, F. and H. Glassie. "Building in Wood in the Eastern United States: A Time-Place Perspective." *Geographical Review*, January 1966, pp. 40-66.

23. Larson, C. Theodore. "The Emerging Superindustry of Building." *Michigan Business Review*, January 1968, pp. 25-32.

24. Lefcoe, George and Thomas W. Dobson. "Savings Associations as Land Developers." *Yale Law Journal*, July 1966, pp. 1271-1299.

25. Lilley, William III. "Home Builders' Lobbying Skills Resulting in Successes, 'Good Guy' Image." *National Journal*, February 27, 1971, pp. 431-445.

26. Maisel, Sherman J. *Housebuilding in Transition*. Berkeley, Calif.: University of California Press, 1961, c1953.

27. Mittelbach, Frank G. "Home Building in the California Economy." In California Governor's Advisory Commission on Housing Problems. *Appendix to the Report on Housing in California*. San Francisco, 1963, pp. 469-533.

28. National Association of Business Economists. Housing Seminar, Los Angeles, 1970. *The Housing Industry in Flux; Proceedings of the NABE Housing Seminar, March 12, 1970, Los Angeles, California*. Washington, D.C., 1970. 117pp.

29. National Planning Association. *The Construction Industry and Its Capital Goods Requirements*. Washington, D.C., 1963. 34pp.

30. "The New Multi-Market Builders." *American Builder*, February 1969, pp. 26-31.

31. Pryor, Lorna Stokenbury. *A Source of New Single-Family Homes*. Ann Arbor, Mich.: University Microfilms. 1966 (Ph.D. dissertation, University of Arkansas, 1966). 132pp. (order #66 – 11,633)

32. "Restrictive Building Practices." In U. S. National Commission on Urban Problems. *Building the American City*. Washington, D.C.: Government Printing Office, 1969, pp. 465-475.

33. Roberts, John. "Home-Building U. S. A.: A Systems Analysis." *Industrialization Forum*, April 1970, pp. 35-40.

34. Sims, Christopher A. "Efficiency in the Construction Industry." In U. S. President's Committee on Urban Housing. *Report: Technical Studies, Volume II*. Washington, D.C.: Government Printing Office, 1968, pp. 145-176.

35. Stastny, John A. "Homebuilding in the Seventies." *Real Estate Review*, Spring 1971, pp. 40-42.

36. Sumichrast, Michael and Sara A. Frankel. *Profile of the Builder and His Industry*. Washington, D.C.: National Association of Home Builders, 1970. 222pp.

37. Sussna, Stephen and Jack Kirchhoff. "The Problem of Premature Subdivision." *Appraisal Journal*, October 1971, pp. 592-601.

38. Swan, Craig. "Homebuilding: A Review of Experience." *Brookings Papers on Economic Activity*,Volume 1, number 1, 1970, pp. 48-70.

39. Swan, Craig. "Recovery for Homebuilding?" *Brookings Papers on Economic Activity*. No. 2, 1970, pp. 313-318.

40. U. S. Department of Commerce. *The Housing Industry: A Challenge for the Nation: Report of the Panel on Housing Technology to the Commerce Technical Advisory Board*. Washington, D.C.: Government Printing Office, January 1970. 36pp.

41. Urban Land Institute. *Innovations vs. Traditions in Community Development: A Comparative Study in Residential Land Use*. Washington, D.C., December 1963 (ULI Technical Bulletin #47).

42. Urban Land Institute. *New Approaches to Residential Land Development*. Washington, D.C., 1961. 151pp. (ULI Technical Bulletin no. 40).

43. Winger, Alan R. and John Madden. "The Application of the Theory of Joint Products: The Case of Residential Construction." *Quarterly Review of Economics and Business*, Summer 1970, pp. 61-69. Also in George Sternlieb and Lynne B. Sagalyn (eds.). *Housing: 1970-1971; An AMS Anthology*. New York: AMS Press, 1972, pp. 299-306.

44. Wittausch, William K. *Housing as a Consumer Product; An Emerging New Industry*. Washington, D.C.: Chamber of Commerce of the U. S., 1968. 46pp.

45. Wittausch, William K. "New Concepts for the Housing Industry." *Urban Land*, May 1966, pp. 11-12.

46. Wyatt, George Lee. *Residential Construction and the Composition Decision: An Empirical Analysis, 1960-68*. Ann Arbor, Mich.: University Microfilms, 1972 (Ph.D. dissertation, University of Kentucky, 1971). 220pp. (order #72-9430).

47. Young, A. H. and C. M. Ball. "Industrial Impacts of Residential Construction and Mobile Home Production." *Survey of Current Business, October 1970, pp. 14-17.*

*See also: 229, 679, 794; Liability in Purchase of Defective Home: 1082+.*

2. BIBLIOGRAPHIES

48. D'Ambrosi, Joan Wirth. *The Housing Industry: A Bibliography.* Monticello, Ill.: Council of Planning Librarians, 1970(Exchange Bibliography #148).

49. National Association of Home Builders. *Basic Texts and Reference Books on Housing and Construction: A Selected Annotated Bibliography.* 2d ed. Washington, D.C., September 1965. 42pp.

50. U. S. Department of Labor. Library. *The Construction Industry: Selected References, 1960-1969.* Washington, D.C., March 1970.

3. FACTORS IN THE CHOICE OF THE DEVELOPMENT SITE

51. Carlson, Eric D. *Operational Aspects of a Probabilistic Model for Residential Growth.* Chapel Hill, N.C.: Center for Urban and Regional Studies, University of North Carolina, 1968 (Environmental Policies and Urban Development Thesis Series #10). 89pp.

52. Chapin, F. Stuart, Jr. "A Model for Simulating Residential Development." *Journal of the American Institute of Planners,* May 1965, pp. 120-125.

53. Chapin. F. Stuart, Jr. and Shirley F. Weiss. *Factors Influencing Land Development.* Chapel Hill, N.C.: Center for Urban and Regional Studies, University of North Carolina, 1962. 101pp.

54. Chapin, F. Stuart, Jr. and Shirley F. Weiss. *Some Input Refinements for a Residential Model.* Chapel Hill, N.C.: Center for Urban and Regional Studies, University of North Carolina, July 1965.

55. Donnelly, Thomas G., F. Stuart Chapin, Jr. and Shirley F. Weiss. *A Probabilistic Model for Residential Growth.* Chapel Hill, N.C.: Center for Urban and Regional Studies, University of North Carolina, 1964. 65pp.

56. Eldridge, Mark T. *Explorations into Decision Factors in the Rental Housing Market.* Chapel Hill, N.C.: Center for Urban and Regional Studies, University of North Carolina, 1967 (Environmental Policies and Urban Development Thesis Series #9). 121pp.

57. Kaiser, Edward J. "Locational Decision Factors in a Producer Model of Residential Development." *Land Economics,* August 1968, pp. 351-362.

58. Kaiser, Edward J. *A Producer Model for Residential Growth.* Chapel Hill: Center for Urban and Regional Studies, Institute for Social Science Research, University of North Carolina, 1968. 77pp.

59. Kaiser, Edward J. *Toward a Model of Residential Developer Locational Behavior.* Ann Arbor, Mich.: University Microfilms, 1966 (Ph.D. dissertation, Department of City and Regional Planning, University of North Carolina at Chapel Hill, 1966). 302pp. (order #67-1007).

60. Kaiser, Edward J. *Toward a Model of Residential Developer Locational Behavior.* Chapel Hill, N.C.: Center for Urban And Regional Studies, University of North Carolina, 1966. 291pp. (Environmental Policies and Urban Development Thesis Series #4).

61. Kaiser, Edward J. and Shirley F. Weiss. "Decision Agent Models of the Residential Development Process – A Review of Recent Research." *Traffic Quarterly*, October 1969, pp. 597-632.

62. Kaiser, Edward J. *et al.* "Developer Behavior: A New Dimension in Urban Growth Research." *Research Preview* (Institute for Research in Social Science, University of North Carolina), March 1965, pp. 29-40.

63. Kenney, Kenneth B. "Locational Decisions of Residential Development and Building Firms in the Greensboro Urban Area." Unpublished research memorandum, Center for Urban and Regional Studies, Institute for Research in Social Science, University of North Carolina, September 17, 1964.

64. Kenney, Kenneth B. *The Residential Land Developer and His Land Purchase Decision.* Chapel Hill, N.C.: Center for Urban and Regional Studies, University of North Carolina, 1972 (Environmental Policies and Urban Development Thesis Series #16). 262pp.

65. Massie, Ronald Wayne. *A System of Linked Models for Forecasting Urban Residential Growth.* Chapel Hill, N.C.: Center for Urban and Regional Studies, University of North Carolina, 1969. 99pp. (Environmental Policies and Urban Development Thesis Series #13).

66. Stollenwerk, Donald A. *Cost Factors in the Choice of Subdivision Locations by Residential Developers.* Chapel Hill, N.C.: Center for Urban and Regional Studies, University of North Carolina, 1964. 90pp. (Environmental Policies and Urban Development Thesis Series #2).

67. Twin Cities Metropolitan Planning Commission. *Determinants of Residential Development.* St. Paul, March 1962.

68. Weiss, Shirley F., Raymond J. Burby and Newton W. Andrews. *Lake-Oriented Residential Subdivisions in North Carolina: Decision Factors and Policy Implications for Urban Growth Patterns.* Chapel Hill, N.C.: Institute for Research in Social Science, University of North Carolina, November 1967.

69. Weiss, Shirley F. *et al. Residential Developer Decisions: A Focused View of the Urban Growth Process.* Chapel Hill, N.C.: Center for Urban and Regional Studies, University of North Carolina, April 1966.

70. Wolfe, Myer R. "Locational Factors Involved in Suburban Land Development." Unpublished report to the Weyerhauser Company prepared in the College of Architecture and Urban Planning, University of Washington, 1961.

## 4. PLANNED RESIDENTIAL DEVELOPMENTS: CLUSTER HOUSING AND PLANNED UNIT DEVELOPMENT

71. Ahrens, Clifford H. "Planned Unit Development." *Missouri Law Review,* Winter 1970, pp. 27-38.

72. American Society of Planning Officials. *Cluster Subdivisions.* Chicago, Ill., June 1960. 35pp. (Planning Advisory Service Report #135).

73. Burchell, Robert W. with James W. Hughes. *Planned Unit Development: New Communities American Style.* New Brunswick, N.J.: Center for Urban Policy Research, 1972. 254pp.

74. Federation of Home Owners Associations. *The Developers Guidebook for the Successful Formulation and Implementation of a Home Owners Association in a Planned Unit Development.* Berkeley, Calif.: Federation of Home Owners Associations; Associated Home Builders of the Greater Eastbay, 1972. 1v.

75. Hubert, Curt C. "Planned Unit Development." *Jersey Plans,* Spring 1967, pp. 36-47.

76. Huntoon, M. C., Jr. *PUD – A Better Way for the Suburbs.* Washington, D.C.: Urban Land Institute, 1971. 72pp.

77. Krasnowiecki, Jan. *Legal Aspects of Planned Unit Development.* Washington, D.C.: Urban Land Institute, 1965 (ULI Technical Bulletin #52).

78. Krasnowiecki, Jan. "Planned Unit Development: A Challenge to Established Theory and Practice of Land Use Control." *University of Pennsylvania Law Review,* November 1965, pp. 47-97.

79. Krasnowiecki, Jan. *Planned Unit Residential Development with a Homes Association: A Comparison of ULI and FHA-VA Legal Forms.* Washington, D.C.: Urban Land Institute. 1965. 7pp.

80. Lansing, John B., Robert W. Marans and Robert B. Zehner. *Planned Residential Environments.* Ann Arbor, Mich.: Survey Research Center, Institute for Social Research, University of Michigan, 1970. 269pp.

81. Lloyd, Gerald D. *et al.* "Symposium: Planned Unit Development." *University of Pennsylvania Law Review*, November 1965, pp. 3-170.

82. Mandelker, Daniel R. *Controlling Planned Residential Developments.* Chicago, Ill.: American Society of Planning Officials, 1966. 66pp.

83. New Jersey Department of Conservation and Economic Development. *Planned Unit Development: A New Tool for Achieving a More Desirable Environment.* Trenton, N.J., July 1966.

84. Norcross, Carl. *Open Space Communities in the Market Place; A Survey of Public Acceptance.* Statistics by Sanford Goodkin. Washington, D.C.: Urban Land Institute, 1966. 97pp. (ULI Technical Bulletin #57).

85. Pope, Joseph C. *Home Owners Associations in Planned Unit Developments: An Evaluation of their Current Problems and Future Feasibility.* Berkeley, Calif.: Associated Home Builders of the Greater Eastbay, 1971.

86. Scattergood, Roger. "Planned Unit Development."*New Jersey Municipalities,* Vol. XLVII, pp. 8-9, 28-29. Also in George Sternlieb and Lynne B. Sagalyn (eds.). *Housing: 1970-1971; An AMS Anthology*. New York: AMS Press, 1972, pp. 144-149.

87. Sternlieb, George, Robert W. Burchell and James W. Hughes. "Planned Unit Development: Environmental Suboptimization." *Environmental Affairs,* March 1972, pp. 694-715.

88. Sternlieb, George, Robert W. Burchell and James W. Hughes. *Planned Unit Development: Theoretical Origins, Evolutionary Framework*. Monticello, Ill.: Council of Planning Librarians, February 1972. 51pp. (Exchange Bibliography #256).

89. Sussna, Stephen. "Blending Housing and Open Space – The Case for Planned Unit Development." *Current Municipal Problems,* November 1971, pp. 203-210.

90. "Town Houses: Planned-Unit Development with a Homes Association." *Urban Land,* September 1963, pp. 3-7.

91. U. S. Department of Housing and Urban Development. *Planned Unit Development with a Homes Association.* Washington, D.C.: Government Printing Office, 1970.

92. U. S. Federal Housing Administration. *Planned-Unit Development with a Homes Association.* Washington, D.C.: Government Printing Office, December 1963. 64pp.

93. Urban Land Institute. *The Homes Association Handbook; A Guide to the Development and Conservation of Residential Neighborhoods with Common Open Space and Facilities Privately Owned and Maintained by Property-Owners Associations Founded on Legal Agreements Running with the Land.* Washington, D.C., 1964. 406pp. (ULI Technical Bulletin #50)

94. Whyte, William H. *Cluster Development.* New York: American Conservation Association, 1964. 130pp.

95. Wolffe, Lenard L. *New Zoning Landmarks in Planned Unit Development.* Washington, D.C.: Urban Land Institute, 1968. (ULI Technical Bulletin #62).

See also: 1278.

## 5. FACTORS INFLUENCING CONSTRUCTION VOLUME

96. Atkinson, L. Jay. "Long-Term Influences Affecting the Volume of New Housing Units." *Survey of Current Business,* November 1963, pp. 8-19.

97. Dilbeck, Harold. "The Response of Local Residential Construction to Changes in National Credit Conditions, 1953-1959." *Journal of Business,* July 1964, pp. 295-308.

98. Dilbeck, Harold R. "The Structure of the Mortgage Market as a Determinant of the Stability of Residential Construction in Several Metropolitan Areas, 1953-1959." Unpublished Ph.D. dissertation. University of California, Los Angeles, 1961.

99. Fukushima, Hajime. *The Analysis of New Housing Construction.* Washington, D.C.: The Urban Institute, 1972. 36pp. (Urban Institute Working Paper #208-2).

100. Grebler, Leo and Sherman J. Maisel. "Determinants of Residential Construction: A Review of Present Knowledge." In *Impacts of Monetary Policy. Research Study Prepared for the Commission on Money and Credit.* Englewood Cliffs, N.J.: Prentice-Hall, 1963, pp. 475-620. Also in Alfred N. Page and Warren R. Seyfried (eds.). *Urban Analysis: Readings in Housing and Urban Development.* Glenview, Ill.: Scott, Foresman, 1970, pp. 60-72.

101. Maisel, Sherman J. "The Relationship of Residential Financing and Expenditure on Residential Construction." In *Proceedings of Conference on Savings and Residential Financing.* Chicago, Ill.: United States Savings and Loan League, May 1965, pp. 1-11.

102. Schaaf, A. H. "Effect of Federal Mortgage Underwriting on Residential Construction." *Appraisal Journal*, January 1967, pp. 54-69.

103. Tsagris, Basilios Estathios. *The Economic Impact of Savings and Loan Associations on Residential Constructions.* Ann Arbor, Mich.: University Microfilms, 1964 (Ph.D. dissertation, University of Southern California, 1964). 383pp. (order #64-9627).

104. Winger, Alan R. "Demand and Residential Construction." Unpublished paper, 1970.

105. Winger, Alan R. "Local Construction Response to National Credit-Market Changes: A Comment." *Journal of Business*, October 1966, pp. 505-11.

## 6. FLUCTUATIONS IN RESIDENTIAL CONSTRUCTION

106. Alberts, William. "Business Cycles, Residential Construction Cycles and the Mortgage Market." *Journal of Political Economy*, June 1962, pp. 263-81. Also in Alfred N. Page and Warren R. Seyfried (eds.). *Urban Analysis: Readings in Housing and Urban Development.* Glenview, Ill.: Scott, Foresman, 1970, pp. 89-105.

107. Beeman, W. *et al. The Contribution of Fiscal Policy to the Housing Problem.* Washington, D.C.: U. S. Board of Governors of the Federal Reserve System, 1971. 30pp. (Studies of Short Term Cycles in Housing Production #2).

108. Brady, Eugene. "Regional Cycles of Residential Construction and the Inter-Regional Mortgage Market: 1954-59." *Land Economics*, February 1963, pp. 15-30.

109. Campbell, Burnham Orlando, Jr. *The Housing Life Cycle and Long Swings in Residential Construction: A Statistical and Theoretical Analysis.* Ann Arbor, Mich.: University Microfilms, 1961 (Ph.D. dissertation, Stanford University, 1961). 442pp. (order #61-4123).

110. Campbell, Burnham O. "Long Swings in Residential Construction: The Postwar Experience." *American Economic Review, Papers and Proceedings*, May 1963, pp. 508-518.

111. Campbell, Burnham, O. *Population Change and Building Cycles.* Urbana, Ill.: University of Illinois, 1966. 199pp. (University of Illinois Bureau of Economic and Business Research Bulletin Series #91).

112. Federal Reserve System. Board of Governors. *Ways to Moderate Fluctuations in Housing Construction.* Washington, D.C., December 1972. 487pp.

113. Fisher, R. M. and C. J. Siegman. "Patterns of Housing Experience during Periods of Credit Restraint in Industrialized Countries." *Journal of Finance,* May 1972, pp. 193-205 and 222-226 (with discussion).

114. Frazer, William J., Jr. "Instability in the Home Construction Industry and Monetary Policy." *Business & Economic Dimensions,* November 1970, pp. 1-7.

115. Gramley, Lyle E. *Short-Term Cycles in Housing Production: An Overview of the Problem and Possible Solutions.* Washington, D.C.: U. S. Board of Governors of the Federal Reserve System, 1971. 160pp. (Studies of Short Term Cycles in Housing Production #22).

116. Guttentag, Jack M. "The Short Cycle in Residential Construction, 1946-59." *American Economic Review,* June 1961, pp. 275-298. Also in Alfred N. Page and Warren R. Seyfried (eds.). *Urban Analysis: Readings in Housing and Urban Development.* Glenview, Ill.: Scott, Foresman, 1970, pp. 73-88.

117. Habakuk, H. J. "Fluctuations in House-Building in Britain and the United States in the Nineteenth Century." *The Journal of Economic History,* June 1962, pp. 198-230.

118. "Homebuilding – Another Boom-Bust Cycle?" *Morgan Guaranty Survey,* June 1972, pp. 4-11.

119. "Housing's Cyclical Behavior: A Shift from Government-Aided to Conventional Mortgages Has Reversed the Industry's Contracyclical Pattern." *Conference Board Record,* December 1962, pp. 9-11.

120. Maisel, Sherman J. "A Theory of Fluctuations in Residential Construction Starts." *American Economic Review,* June 1963, pp. 359-383. Also in Alfred N. Page and Warren R. Seyfried (eds.). *Urban Analysis: Readings in Housing and Urban Development.* Glenview, Ill.: Scott, Foresman, 1970, pp. 122-139.

121. Melnyk, M. "The Problem of Long Cycles in Residential Construction." *Land Economics,* November 1968, pp. 480-491.

122. Page, Alfred N. "Regional Residential Construction Cycles." *Land Economics,* February 1965, pp. 66-69.

123. Sparks, Gordon. "An Econometric Analysis of the Role of Financial Intermediates in Postwar Residential Building Cycles." In R. Feber (ed.).

*Determinants of Investment Behavior.* New York: National Bureau of Economic Research, 1967, pp. 301-331.

124. Stern, A. "Fluctuations in Residential Construction: Some Evidence from the Spectral Estimates." *Review of Economics and Statistics,* August 1972, pp. 328-331.

125. "Ways to Moderate Fluctuations in the Construction of Housing." *Federal Reserve Bulletin,* March 1972, pp. 215-225.

126. Winger, Alan R. "Fluctuations in Residential Construction." *Mississippi Valley Journal of Business and Economics,* Spring 1970, pp. 39-51.

127. Winger, A. R. "Short-Term Activity in Residential Construction Markets: Some Regional Considerations." *Southern Economic Journal,* April 1970, pp. 390-403.

128. Winger, A. R. "Short-Term Fluctuations in Residential Construction: An Overview of Recent Research." *Mississippi Valley Journal of Business and Economics,* Spring 1970, pp. 39-51.

See also: 417, 938.

## 7. CONSTRUCTION TRENDS AND STATISTICS

129. "Advance in Housing Construction." *Survey of Current Business,* December 1961, pp. 9-11.

130. Burnham, James B. "Housing Starts, 1966 and 1969: A Comparison Using an Econometric Model." *Land Economics,* February 1972, pp. 88-89.

131. Cloos, George W. "Housing Leads Construction Rise." *Federal Reserve Chicago, Business Conditions: A Review,* May 1971, pp. 2-12.

132. "Construction Activity: Review and Outlook." *Federal Reserve Chicago, Business Conditions: A Review,* January 1971, pp. 9-11.

133. "Construction and Housing." *Federal Reserve Bulletin,* December 1961, pp. 1383-1389.

134. Converse, Muriel Judith Weiser. *An Analysis of Housing Starts in the United States, 1953-1963.* Ann Arbor, Mich.: University Microfilms, 1966 (Ph.D. dissertation, University of Michigan, 1966). 170 pp. (order no. 66-14,503).

135. Daniel, Caldwell III. "The Volume of Nonfarm Residential Construction: An Analytical Framework." *Land Economics,* May 1960, pp. 202-207.

136. Edwards, R. Gordon, Jr. *Residential Construction Industry Outlook, 1966-1975.* New York: Institutional Research Department, Oppenheimer, 1967.

137. "F. W. Dodge Forecasts Construction Outlook for 1980." *Architectural Record,* March 1969, pp. 83-87.

138. Freedman, Bernard N. *Private Housing Completions – A New Dimension in Construction Statistics.* Washington, D.C.: Board of Governors of the Federal Reserve System, 1972. (Staff Economic Studies no. 66).

139. Gottlieb, Manuel. *Estimates of Residential Building, United States 1840-1939.* New York, N.Y.: National Bureau of Economic Research, 1964. 99pp.

140. Hale, Carl W. "Residential Construction in the Southwest." *Federal Reserve Dallas, Business Review,* June 1965, pp. 7-10.

141. Hanson, Bruce. "Single-Family Construction: A Reversal of Its Downward Trend." *Federal Home Loan Bank Board Journal,* August 1971, pp. 7-11.

142. "Housing and Business Expansion." *Federal Reserve Richmond, Monthly Review,* August 1962, pp. 2-5.

143. "Housing Production and Finance." *Federal Reserve Bulletin,* March 1969, pp. 228-234.

144. King, Donald A. "Homebuilding Activity in 1969." *Survey of Current Business,* October 1969, pp. 16-22.

145. Kinzie, George R. "New Construction in 1970." *Construction Review,* May 1971, pp. 4-8, 16-19. Also in George Sternlieb and Lynne Sagalyn (eds.). *Housing: 1970-1971; An AMS Anthology.* New York: AMS Press, 1972, pp. 35-55.

146. Lipsey, Robert E. and Doris Proston. *Source Book of Statistics Relating to Construction.* New York: National Bureau of Economic Research, distributed by Columbia University Press, 1966. 307pp.

147. "Multifamily Construction Rises: Number of New Dwelling Units Provided by Building Permits." *Real Estate Analyst,* June 17, 1963, pp. 197-223.

148. National Industrial Conference Board, Inc. *Regional Construction Trends.* New York, April 15, 1970. 4pp.

149. National Industrial Conference Board, Inc. *Residential Construction in the 1960's.* New York, April 1, 1970. 4pp.

150. "New Housing Units in 226 Metropolitan Areas Decreased in 1969." *Real Estate Analyst,* April 24, 1970, pp. 149-200.

151. "New Housing Units in 226 Metropolitan Areas Increased in 1971 by More than 40%." *Real Estate Analyst, Construction Bulletin,* April 1972, pp. 121-173.

152. Page, Alfred N. "Residential Construction: Exploration of the Statistical Series." *Journal of Business,* January 1967, pp. 36-43. Also in Alfred N. Page and Warren R. Seyfried (eds.). *Urban Analysis: Readings in Housing and Urban Development.* Glenview, Ill.: Scott, Foresman, 1970, pp. 139-145.

153. "Postwar Patterns in Homebuilding and Financing." *Federal Reserve Cleveland, Economic Review.* August 1961, pp. 2-9.

154. "Residential Construction – 1961 and 1962." *Real Estate Analyst,* October 31, 1962, pp. 437-444.

155. Richey, Clyde Warren. *A System of Forecasting Residential Construction for Use by the Residential Builder.* Ann Arbor, Mich.: University Microfilms, 1970 (Ph.D. dissertation, University of Wisconsin, 1969). 258pp. (order no. 70-3678).

156. Snyder, Christopher Lynam. *Forecasting Residential Construction.* Ann Arbor, Mich.: University Microfilms, 1970 (Ph.D. dissertation, Lehigh University, 1969). 150pp. (order no. 70-1747).

157. "The Solid Foundation under Housing." *Fortune,* April 1972, pp. 19+.

158. Stolzer, A. "Construction in 1969." *Construction Review,* April 1970, pp. 4-14.

159. U. S. Bureau of the Census. Social and Economic Statistics Administration. *Construction Reports: Housing Authorized by Building Permits and Public Contracts: States and Selected Standard Metropolitan Statistical Areas.* Washington, D.C.: Government Printing Office, published monthly, with annual summary (C40 series).

160. U. S. Bureau of the Census and U. S. Department of Housing and Urban Development. *Construction Reports: Housing Completions.* Washington, D.C.: Census Bureau, published monthly (C22 series).

161. U. S. Bureau of the Census. Social and Economic Statistics Administration. *Construction Reports: Housing Starts.* Washington, D.C.: Government Printing Office, published monthly (C20 series).

162. U. S. Bureau of the Census and U. S. Department of Housing and Urban Development. *Construction Reports: New One-Family Homes Sold and for Sale.* Washington, D.C.: Bureau of the Census, published monthly with quarterly supplements and annual edition (C25 series).

163. U. S. Bureau of the Census. Social and Economic Statistics Administration. *Construction Reports: Value of New Construction Put in Place.* Washington, D.C.: Government Printing Office, published monthly with annual supplement (C30 series).

164. U. S. Bureau of the Census. *Housing Construction Statistics, 1889 to 1964.* Washington, D.C.: Government Printing Office, 1966. 805pp.

165. U. S. Bureau of the Census. *New One-Family Homes – Contractor Built 1963 to 1967.* Washington, D.C.: Government Printing Office, 1969. 50pp.

166. U. S. Bureau of the Census and U. S. Department of Housing and Urban Development. *New One-Family Homes Sold and for Sale: 1963 to 1967.* Washington, D.C.: Government Printing Office, July 1969. 293pp.

167. Wallace, A. "Forecasting Housing Starts: A Disaggregated Model." *Business Economics,* May 1969, pp. 29-31.

8. MANPOWER IN THE HOMEBUILDING INDUSTRY – MANPOWER REQUIREMENTS, UNIONS, WAGES

168. Ball, Robert and Larry Ludwig. "Labor Requirements for Construction of Single-Family Houses." *Monthly Labor Review,* September 1971, pp. 12-14.

169. Burck, Gilbert. "The Building Trades versus the People." *Fortune,* October 1970, pp. 94-97, 159-160. Also in George Sternlieb and Lynne B. Sagalyn (eds.). *Housing: 1970-1971; An AMS Anthology.* New York: AMS Press, 1972, pp. 273-287.

170. Burke, William. "Calibrating the Building Trades: 1. The Industry. 2. The Wage Issue." *Federal Reserve San Francisco, Monthly Review,* June 1971, pp. 101-114.

171. Dunlop, J. T. and D. Q. Mills. "Manpower in Construction: A Profile of the Industry and Projections to 1975." In U. S. President's Committee

on Urban Housing. *Report: Technical Studies, Volume II.* Washington, D.C.: Government Printing Office, 1968, pp. 239-286a.

172. Finn, J. T. "Labor Requirements for Public Housing." *Monthly Labor Review,* April 1972, pp. 40-42.

173. Foster, Howard G. "Unions, Residential Construction, and Public Policy." *Quarterly Review of Economics and Business,* Winter 1972, pp. 45-55.

174. Givens, Richard A. "Job Security in the Building Industry – and High Quality Low-Rent Housing." *Labor Law Journal,* August 1967, pp. 468-477.

175. Hahn, William F. "Construction Manpower Needs by 1980." *Monthly Labor Review,* July 1971, pp. 12-18.

176. Iden, George. "A Test of Union Power in the Construction Industry." *Annals of Regional Science,* June 1972, pp. 116-123.

177. "Industrialized Building: Resolving the Labor Conflicts." *Columbia Journal of Law and Social Problems,* Summer 1972, pp. 493+.

178. Mandelstamm, Allan B. "The Effects of Unions on Efficiency in the Residential Construction Industry: A Case Study." *Industrial and Labor Relations Review,* July 1965, pp. 503-521.

179. Miller, Stanley Frederick and Philip Jaynes. *Labor and Material Requirements for Public Housing Construction.* Prepared for Bureau of Labor Statistics, U. S. Department of Labor. Washington, D.C.: Government Printing Office, 1964, 42 pp. (Bureau of Labor Statistics Bulletin No. 1402). Summarized in S. F. Miller. "Labor and Material Requirements for Public Housing." *Monthly Labor Review,* September 1964, pp. 1029-1032.

180. Mills, D. Q. "Housing and Manpower in the 1970's." In U. S. Congress. House. Committee on Banking and Currency. *Papers Submitted to Subcommittee on Housing Panels on Housing Production, Housing Demand, and Developing a Suitable Living Environment: Part 1.* Washington, D.C.: Government Printing Office, 1971, pp. 287-314.

181. Mills, D. Q. *A Study of Problems of Manpower Utilization in the Construction Industry; Intermittency of Employment, Unemployment and Labor Shortages.* Washington, D.C.: Manpower Administration, U. S. Department of Labor, 1969. 113pp.

182. O'Hanlon, Thomas. "The Unchecked Power of the Building Trades." *Fortune,* December 1968, pp. 102-106+.

183. "The Philadelphia Plan vs. the Chicago Plan: Alternative Approaches for Integrating the Construction Industry." *Northwestern University Law Review*, September-October 1970, pp. 642-670.

184. Pohlman, J. E. "Hard-Core Unemployment, Public Housing Construction and the Davis-Bacon Act." *Labor Law Journal*, April 1971, pp. 195-203.

185. Swan, Craig. "Labor and Material Requirements for Housing." *Brookings Papers on Economic Activity*, No. 2, 1971, pp. 347-381.

186. U. S. Department of Labor. Bureau of Labor Statistics. *Labor and Material Requirements for Construction of Private Single-Family Houses.* Washington, D.C.: Government Printing Office, 1972. 30pp. (BLS Bulletin no. 1755).

187. U. S. Department of Labor. Bureau of Labor Statistics. *Labor and Material Requirements for Private One-Family House Construction.* Washington, D.C.: Government Printing Office, 1964. 37pp. (BLS Bulletin 1404). Summarized in Herman J. Rothberg, "Labor and Material Requirements for One-Family Housing." *Monthly Labor Review*, July 1964, pp. 797-800.

188. "Why Construction Won't Get Thousands of New Trainees." *American Builder*, September 1968, pp. 14+.

See also: 274, 280, 2537, 2538.

## 9. TECHNOLOGY

### a. General

189. "A Boom That Didn't Come Off – Factory Built Houses. *U. S. News and World Report*, July 31, 1972, pp. 64-66.

190. "Breaking our Marketing Bottleneck." *Automation in Housing*, March 1971, pp. 46-55.

191. National Academy of Sciences – National Research Council. Building Research Advisory Board. *New Technologies in the Development of Housing for Lower-Income Families.* A Special Advisory Report to the Office of Urban Technology and Research, Dept. of Housing and Urban Development. Washington, D.C.: National Research Council, National Academy of Sciences; National Academy of Engineering, 1969. 26pp.

192. Cornell University. Center for Housing and Environmental Studies. *The New Building Block: A Report on the Factory-Produced Dwelling Module.* Ithaca, N.Y., 1968.

193. Dietz, Albert G. H. "Building Technology: Potentials and Problems." *American Institute of Architects Journal,* November 1969, pp. 69-76.

194. Dietz, Albert George Henry. *Dwelling House Construction.* Cambridge, Mass.: MIT Press, 1971. 396pp.

195. Dietz, Albert George Henry and Laurence S. Cutler (eds.). *Industrialized Building Systems for Housing.* Cambridge, Mass.: MIT Press, 1971. 260 pp.

196. Dixon, John Morris. "Industrialized Housing: Can It Happen Here?" *Architectural Forum,* July/August 1969, pp. 100-108.

197. "Factory Methods Applied to Custom Housing." *Systems Building News,* June 1972, pp. 26-29.

198. Gonzales, Bennie M. "Design and Production of Housing." In U. S. Congress. House. Committee on Banking and Currency. *Papers Submitted to Subcommittee on Housing Panels on Housing Production, Housing Demand, and Developing a Suitable Living Environment: Part 1.* Washington, D.C.: Government Printing Office, 1971, pp. 229-241.

199. Grubb, Clarence A. and M. I. Phares. *Industrialization: A New Concept for Housing.* New York: Praeger, 1972. 128pp.

200. Guy, R. B. *et al. The State of the Art of Prefabrication in the Construction Industry.* Columbus, Ohio: Battelle Memorial Institute, 1967. 236pp.

201. Hanson, Bruce. "Issues in Determining Impacts of Industrialized Housing." *Federal Home Loan Bank Board Journal,* April 1971, pp. 1-7.

202. "How do We Reach Our Market?" *Automation in Housing,* June 1971, pp. 32-43.

203. "How Will We Break Our Marketing Bottleneck?" *Automation in Housing,* February 1971, pp. 48-63.

204. Hudson, James W. "A Systems Approach to the High-Rise Apartment . . . within the Community Complex." *Systems Building News,* June 1972, pp. 14-17+.

205. I.I.T. Research Institute. *Application of Component Construction to Low-Income Housing.* Chicago, Ill.: I.I.T. Press, 1968. 3 vols.

206. *Industrialized Housing; Materials Compiled and Prepared for the Subcommittee on Urban Affairs of the Joint Economic Committee, Con-*

*gress of the United States.* Washington, D.C.: Government Printing Office, 1969. 257pp.

207. "Industrialization and the Architect." *American Institute of Architects Journal,* Jan. 1972, pp. 48-49.

208. "Leaders in Housing – 1972, Including the 5th Annual AIH 100." *Automation in Housing,* April 1972, pp. 23-46.

209. Little (Arthur D.), Inc. *Technology in Connecticut's Housing Delivery System; Report to the Department of Community Affairs.* Cambridge, Mass., 1969.

210. McQuade, Walter. "An Assembly-Line Answer to the Housing Crisis: The Cities Are Desperate for a Way to Get More Housing Built; Advocates of 'Systems Building' Say They Have One." *Fortune,* May 1969, pp. 99-133+.

211. "Manufactured Buildings 1971: AIH's Annual Industry Report." *Automation in Housing,* December 1970-January 1971, pp. 44-51.

212. National Academy of Sciences – National Research Council. Building Research Advisory Board. "An Historical Evaluation of Industrialized Housing and Building Systems in the United States." In U. S. President's Committee on Urban Housing. *Report: Technical Studies, Volume II.* Washington, D.C.: Government Printing Office, 1968, pp. 177-189.

213. National Homes Corp. *Industrialized Housing.* Lafayette, Ind., 1972.

214. Pearson, Karl G. *Industrialized Housing.* Ann Arbor, Mich.: Industrial Development Division, Institute of Science and Technology, University of Michigan, 1972. 94pp.

215. "Shell Home Boom Cools Off: Industry Is Feeling Impact of Excessive Competition, Limited Markets, Inadequate Financing." *Business Week,* October 14, 1961, pp. 120+.

216. "Solution for the Shelter Shortage? Factory-Built Houses." *Morgan Guaranty Survey,* August 1969, pp. 6-9+.

217. Swaback, Vernon D. "Production Dwellings: An Opportunity for Excellence." *Land Economics,* November 1971, pp. 321-338.

218. Trevino, Alberto F. "Some Insights into Systems Building." *Urban Land,* July-August 1970, pp. 3-10.

219. "Union Restrictions on the Use of Prefabrication in the Housing Industry." *Iowa Law Review,* October 1969, pp. 270+.

220. U. S. Congress. Joint Economic Committee. Subcommittee on Urban Affairs. *Industrialized Housing: Hearings, July 9-24, 1969.* Washington, D.C.: Government Printing Office, 1969. 2 vols., 354pp.

221. U. S. Department of Housing and Urban Development. *An Analysis of Twelve Experimental Housing Projects.* Washington, D.C.: Government Printing Office, 1969. 79pp.

222. U. S. Department of Housing and Urban Development. Office of International Affairs. *Industrialized Housing,* by Ian Donald Terner and John F. C. Turner. In Conjunction with OSTI, the Organization for Social and Technical Innovation, Cambridge, Mass. Prepared for the U. S. Agency for International Development. Washington, D.C., 1972. (Ideas and Methods Exchange no. 66).

223. U. S. Executive Office of the President. Office of Science and Technology. *Better Housing for the Future: A Report to the Panel on Civilian Technology.* Washington, D.C.: Government Printing Office, April 1963. 15pp.

224. U. S. Federal Housing Administration. *Fredella Village; A Housing Demonstration; a Report.* Washington, D.C., 1968. 11pp.

225. U. S. Panel on Housing Technology. *The Housing Industry: A Challenge for the Nation; Report of the Panel on Housing Technology to the Commerce Technical Advisory Board.* Washington, D.C.: Government Printing Office, 1970. 36pp.

226. Ural, Oktay *et al.* "Technique and Technology." In U. S. Congress. House. Committee on Banking and Currency. *Papers Submitted to Subcommittee on Housing Panels on Housing Production, Housing Demand, and Developing a Suitable Living Environment: Part 1.* Washington, D.C.: Government Printing Office, 1971, pp. 203-227.

See also: 276, 282, 286, 1100, 1109, 1110; Operation Breakthrough 2654+.

b. Bibliographies

227. Kessler, Mary Z. *Industrialized Housing.* Monticello, Ill.: Council of Planning Librarians, 1970 (Exchange Bibliography no. 137).

228. Sanoff, Henry. *A Bibliography and Critical Review of Industrialized Housing.* Monticello, Ill.: Council of Planning Librarians, 1970 (Exchange Bibliography no. 158).

c. Modular Coordination

229. Eacret, David Theodore. *The Economics of Industrialized Housing: Effects of Modular Production on the Residential Construction Industry.* Ann Arbor, Mich.: University Microfilms, 1972 (Ph.D. dissertation, Colorado State University, 1972). 169pp. (order no. 72-22, 570).

230. Lalli, F. "Modular Housing; The Phantom That Parades as an Industry." *House & Home*, June 1970, pp. 64-75.

231. Lorimer, Chiodo and Associates. *Automated Total Housing Systems in the United States, 1970, As Applied to the State of Minnesota.* St. Paul, Minn.: Research Division, Minnesota Department of Economic Development, 1970. 296pp.

232. "Modular Housing Program Fades Away: Detroit Project Bogs Down in Administrative Bungling and Poor Communications." *Business Week*, March 14, 1970, p. 55+.

233. Reidelbach, J. A. *Modular Housing in the Real; A Study of the Industry and the Product – Focusing on the Wood Framed Sectional Unit.* Annandale, Va.: Modco, 1970. 213pp.

234. "Second Annual Modular Survey – Profile of a Sub-Industry in Ferment." *House & Home*, March 1972, pp. 72-87.

235. "Who's Building the Modulars and How Many?" *House and Home*, June 1971, pp. 46-59.

236. "Who's Who in Modulars." *Professional Builder*, November 1970, pp. 88-96.

See also: 857

## B. HOUSING COSTS

### 1. GENERAL

237. Atkinson, L.J. "Factors Affecting the Purchase Value of New Homes; with Charts and Tables." *Survey of Current Business*, August 1966, pp. 20-36.

238. Bhatia, Kul B. "A Price Index for Nonfarm One-Family Houses, 1947-64." *Journal of the American Statistical Association*, March 1971, pp. 23-32.

239. Brown, Samuel Lovitt. *Price Variation in New FHA Houses: 1959-1961: A Report of Research in Methods of Constructing Price Indexes.* Washington, D.C.: Government Printing Office, 1971 (U.S. Department of Commerce, Bureau of the Census Working Papęr no. 31).

240. Burnham, Bruce O. and Ted L. Jones. *Housing Costs: Rural-Urban Comparisons.* Wooster, Ohio: Ohio Agricultural Research and Development Center, 1969. 23pp.

241. Case, Fred E. *Cash Outlay and the Economic Costs of Home Ownership.* Los Angeles, Calif.: University of California Press, 1960.

242. "Changes in Cost of New Houses." *Real Estate Analyst, Real Estate Trends*, May 1972, pp. 229-233.

243. Cicarelli, James and Clifford Landers. "The Cost of Housing for the Poor: A Case Study." *Land Economics*, February 1972, pp. 53-57.

244. Eaves, Elsie. *How the Many Costs of Housing Fit Together.* Prepared for the National Commission on Urban Problems. Washington, D.C.: Government Printing Office, 1969 (National Commission on Urban Problems Research Report no. 16).

245. Economic Consultants Organization, Inc. *Factors Affecting the Cost and Supply of Housing.* White Plains, N.Y., 1970 (Interim Report no. 2).

246. Goldfinger, Nathaniel. "The Myth of Housing Costs." *American Federationist*, December 1969, pp. 1-6.

247. "Homeownership Cost in 23 Metropolitan Areas." *Real Estate Analyst*, September 16, 1970, pp. 385+.

248. Jackson, Elmo L. "The Inflation in Housing Costs." *Business & Economic Dimensions*, May 1970, pp. 1-6.

249. Joiner, Robert C. "Trends in Homeownership and Rental Costs." *Monthly Labor Review*, July 1970, pp. 26-31.

250. Levitt & Sons, Inc. "Material Prepared for the President's Committee on Urban Housing." In U. S. President's Committee on Urban Housing. *Report: Technical Studies, Volume II.* Washington, D.C.: Government Printing Office, 1968, pp. 65-74.

251. Lozano, Eduardo E. "Housing Costs and Alternative Cost Reducing Policies." *Journal of the American Institute of Planners*, May 1972, pp. 176-181.

252. McDonald J. "Where's the Ceiling on New Homes?" *Fortune*, June 1963, pp. 128-132+.

253. Muth, Richard F. and Elliot Wetzler. *Effects of Constraints on Single-Unit Housing Costs.* Arlington, Va.: Institute of Defense Analyses, 1968.

254. New York (City) Housing and Redevelopment Board. Bureau of Planning and Program Research. *Rising Rents and Housing Costs in the City-Financed Limited-Profit Housing Companies Program: 1957-1967.* New York, September 1967.

255. New York (State) Executive Department. Division of Housing. *Research Study in the Cost of Housing.* Albany, 1960. 49pp.

256. Perron, Robert P., Douglas Anawalt, and G. James Scoggin. *Low Cost Medium Density Housing Study: A Design Proposal in Fremont, California.* Berkeley, Cal.: Institute of Urban and Regional Development, Center for Planning and Development Research, University of California, 1965. 70pp.

257. "Reducing Housing Costs." Part V in U.S. National Commission on Urban Problems. *Building the American City.* Washington, D.C.: Government Printing Office, 1969, pp. 417-485.

258. "Rental-Ownership Cost Gap." *Real Estate Analyst,* December 1972, pp. 463-471.

259. "SBAM Reprot Cites Rising Housing Costs." *Savings Bank Journal,* July 1972, pp. 14-15+.

260. Shelton, John P. "The Cost of Renting Versus Owning a Home." *Land Economics,* February 1968, pp. 59-72.

261. Shohan, L.B. "Estimating Costs by Use of Census Data; Intercity Differences in Housing Costs." *Conference Board Business Record,* September 1960, pp. 6-9.

262. Shohan, Leo B. *Intercity Comparisons of Housing Costs.* New York: National Industrial Conference Board, 1962. 32pp.

263. Smith, Thomas W. *Housing Cost Reduction and the Housing Investment Calculator.* Baltimore, Md: Baltimore Regional Planning Council, 1969. 52pp.

264. U.S. Department of Housing and Urban Development. Office of Urban Technology and Research. *Cost and Time Associated with New Multifamily Housing Construction in New York City.* Washington, D.C., June 1969. 86pp.

265. Vidger, L.P. "Analysis of Price Behavior in San Francisco Housing Markets: The Historical Pattern (1958-1967) and Projections (1968-1975)." *Annals of Regional Science*, June 1969, pp. 143-155.

266. York, H.G.A. "Rent Increases during Phase II." *Los Angeles Bar Bulletin*, March 1972, pp. 179+.

See also: 1129, 1760, 2172, 2228, 2505, 2641, 2642, 2962; Housing Costs in Public Housing 2754+.

2. LAND COSTS

267. Gaffney, Mason and Richard F. Muth. *Land as an Element of Housing Costs; The Effects of Public Policies and Practices; The Effects of Housing Demand.* Two papers by M. Gaffney and R.F. Muth. Arlington, Va.: Institute for Defense Analyses, 1968. 66pp.

268. Frankel, Sara A. "Rising Land Costs Are Burying the Home Builders." *Real Estate Review*, Winter 1972, pp. 88-90.

269. Kamm, Sylvan. "Curbing Inflation in Residential Land Prices." *Urban Land*, September 1971, pp. 3-16.

270. "Land Value as a Percentage of Total Sales Price of Residences." *Real Estate Analyst*, June 13, 1962, pp. 251-254.

271. Maisel, Sherman J. "Background Information on Costs of Land for Single Family Housing." In California Governor's Advisory Commission on Housing Problems. *Appendix to the Report on Housing in California.* San Francisco, 1963, pp. 221-281.

272. Milgram, Grace. *U.S. Land Prices – Directions and Dynamics.* Prepared for the consideration of the National Commission on Urban Problems. Washington, D.C.: Government Printing Office, 1968. 77pp. (National Commission on Urban Problems Research Report no. 13).

3. BUILDING COSTS (Including Development, Materials and Labor Costs)

273. Association of Bay Area Governments. *Development Regulations and Housing Costs.* Berkeley, Calif., 1970. 101pp.

274. Behman, Sara and Donald Codella. "Wage Rates and Housing Prices." *Industrial Relations*, February 1971, pp. 86-104. Also in George Sternlieb and Lynne B. Sagalyn (eds.). *Housing: 1970-1971; An AMS Anthology*. New York: AMS Press, 1972, pp. 255-272.

275. California Department of Housing and Community Development. *Demonstration in Low-Cost Housing Techniques.* Sacramento, Calif., 1970. 60pp.

276. de Leeuw, Frank *et al. Housing Costs and the Industrialization of Housing Production.* Washington, D.C.: The Urban Institute, 1969. 54pp. (Urban Institute Working Paper 112-1).

277. Duncan, Joseph W. "New Approaches to Low-Cost Housing." *Business Economics*, January 1969, pp. 53-56.

278. Edgerton, William H. "Building Costs and Trends." *Appraisal Journal*, January 1971, pp. 118-125.

279. Fisher, Gerald M. "Low Cost Housing Systems." *Urban Lawyer*, Spring 1970, pp. 146-174.

280. Goldfinger, Nat. "Labor Costs and the Rise in Housing Prices." *Monthly Labor Review*, May 1970, pp. 60-61.

281. "Housing Construction Costs." In U.S. National Commission on Urban Problems. *Building the American City*. Washington, D.C.: Government Printing Office, 1969, pp. 417-450.

282. Isler, Morton L. *et al. How Housing Costs May Be Affected by Greater Industrialization.* Washington, D.C.: The Urban Institute, 1969.

283. Johnson, Ralph J. "Housing Technology and Housing Costs." In U.S. President's Committee on Urban Housing. *Report: Technical Studies, Volume II*. Washington, D.C.: Government Printing Office, 1968, pp. 53-64.

284. McGraw-Hill, Inc. "A Study of Comparative Time and Cost for Building Five Selective Types of Low-Cost Housing." In U.S. President's Committee on Urban Housing. *Report: Technical Studies, Volume II.* Washington, D.C.: Government Printing Office, 1968, pp. 1-52.

285. Pereira, Percival E. "Building Costs and Trends." *Appraisal Journal*, January 1972, pp. 144-149.

286. Petro, Sylvester. "Unions, Housing Costs, and the National Labor Policy." *Law and Contemporary Problems*, Spring 1967, pp. 319-348.

287. Saleh, Hussein Ali. *A Dynamic Model for the Construction of Low Cost Housing: Optimum Performance & Cost Efficiency.* Ann Arbor, Mich.: University Microfilms, 1971 (Ph.D. dissertation, University of Pennsylvania, 1970). 244pp. (order no. 71-19,280)

288. U.S. Congress. House. Committee on Banking and Currency. *Rising Costs of Housing: Lumber Price Increases: Hearings, March 24-28, 1969.* Washington, D.C.: Government Printing Office, 1969. 894pp.

289. U.S. Congress. Senate. Committee on Banking and Currency. Subcommittee on Housing and Urban Affairs. *Effect of Lumber Prices and Shortages on the Nation's Housing Goals: Report, June 16, 1969.* Washington, D.C.: Government Printing Office, 1969.

290. Urban Systems Research and Engineering, Inc. *A Systems Analysis of Housing Development Cost Information: Policy Implications.* Boston, 1969.

291. Weiner, Neil S. *Supply Conditions for Low-Cost Housing Production.* Arlington, Va.: Institute for Defense Analyses. 1968. 115pp.

292. "Will Building Costs Shatter Housing Boom Hopes?" *Savings and Loan News,* May 1971, pp. 30-35.

See also: 66, 2874, 2881, 2901.

## 4. OPERATING COSTS

293. Eisenstadt, Karen M. *Factors Affecting Maintenance and Operating Costs in Private Rental Housing.* New York: The New York City Rand Institute, 1972. 136pp.

294. U.S. Department of Labor. Bureau of Labor Statistics. Middle Atlantic Regional Office. *A Price Index of Operating Costs for Uncontrolled Apartment Houses in New York City.* New York, 1971. 70pp. (Its Regional Reports no. 17)

See also: 2755, 2757, 2758, 2773, 1439, 1440.

## 5. MORTGAGE FINANCE AND SETTLEMENT COSTS

295. Ducey, John McMullen and Kenneth R. Berliant. *Loan Closing Costs on Single-Family Homes in Six Metropolitan Areas.* Prepared for the U.S. Housing and Home Finance Agency. Washington, D.C.: Government Printing Office, 1965. 59pp.

296. "Finance and Closing Costs." In U.S. National Commission on Urban Problems. *Building the American City.* Washington, D.C.: Government Printing Office, 1969, pp. 451-464.

297. Hall, Florence T. and Evelyn Freeman. "Survey of Home Buyers' and Sellers' Closing Costs in the Seattle, Washington, Area." *Journal of Home Economics,* January 1972, pp. 20-26.

298. Horn, Robert J. "Outlook: HUD-VA Settlement Cost Regulation." *Title News*, Vol. 51, no. 4, 1972, pp. 4-5+.

299. Mandala, Andrew R. "The Closing Cost Dilemma." *National League Journal*, September 1972, pp. 6-7+.

300. Nevada Legislative Counsel Bureau. *Incidental Charges to the Purchasers of Dwellings under FHA and VA Insured or Guaranteed Mortgages.* Carson City, Nevada, 1962. 272pp.

301. Schaaf, A.H. "Regional Differences in Mortgage Financing Costs." *Journal of Finance*, March 1966, pp. 85-94.

302. U.S. Congress. House. Committee on Banking and Currency. Subcommittee on Housing. *Real Estate Settlement Costs, FHA Mortgage Foreclosures, Housing Abandonment, and Site Selection Policies. Hearings, Ninety-Second Congress, Second Session, on H.R. 13337 . . . February 22 and 24, 1972.* Washington, D.C.: Government Pringing Office, 1972. 2 vols.

303. U.S. Congress. Senate Committee on Banking, Housing and Urban Affairs. Subcommittee on Housing and Urban Affairs. *Mortgage Settlement Costs. Hearings, Ninety-Second Congress, Second Session . . . March 1,2, and 3, 1972.* Washington, D.C.: Government Printing Office, 1972. 241pp.

304. U.S. Congress. Senate. Committee on Banking, Housing and Urban Affairs. *Mortgage Settlement Costs: Reprort of Department of Housing and Urban Development and Veterans' Administration.* Washington, D.C.: Government Printing Office, 1972. 139pp.

305. U.S. Department of Housing and Urban Development. *Bibliography Prepared for HUD-VA Closing Cost Study.* Washington, D.C., 1971.

306. U.S. Department of Housing and Urban Development. Housing Production and Mortgage Credit - Federal Housing Administration and The Veterans Administration. *Report on Mortgage Settlement Costs.* Washington, D.C., January 1972.

307. U.S. Department of Housing and Urban Development. Housing Production and Mortgage Credit — Federal Housing Administration and the Veterans' Administration. *Report on Mortgage Settlement Costs; Supplement.* Prepared by American University persuant to HUD-VA contract no. H-1578. Springfield, Va.: National Technical Information Service, 1972. (PB208020).

308. "What's Ahead for Settlement Costs?" *HUD Challenge*, May 1972, pp. 4-7.

309. "Why Does It Cost So Much to Sell a House?" *Forbes*, October 15, 1972, pp. 35-43+.

## 6. HOUSING EXPENDITURES AS A FUNCTION OF INCOME

310. Alston, Jon Paul. *Housing Status and Expenditure Patterns among Middle-Income Occupations.* Ann Arbor, Mich.: University Microfilms, 1972 (Ph.D. dissertation, University of Texas at Austin, 1971). 105pp. (order no. 72-11,300).

311. Duker, Jacob M. "Housewife and Working-Wife Families: A Housing Comparison." *Land Economics*, May 1970, pp. 138-145.

312. Ekanem, Nkanta F. *The Demand for Housing: An Analysis by Family Type*. Washington, D.C.: The Urban Institute, 1972.

313. Lee, Tong Hun. *Housing Expenditure Analysis: A Decision Unit Model.* Ann Arbor, Mich.: University Microfilms, 1961 (Ph.D. dissertation, University of Wisconsin, 1961). 143pp. (order no. 61-2968).

314. Lee, T.H. "Housing and Permaneent Income: Tests Based on a Three-Year Reinterview Survey." *Review of Economics and Statistics*, November 1968, pp. 480-490.

315. Maisel, Sherman J. and Louis Winnick. "Family Housing Expenditures: Elusive Laws and Intrusive Variances." In *Proceedings of the Conference on Consumption and Saving, Volume I.* Philadelphia, Pa.: University of Pennsylvania, 1960, pp. 359-435.

316. Malone, J.R. "Capital Expenditure for Owner-Occupied Housing: A Study of Determinants." *Journal of Business*, July 1966, pp. 359-366.

317. de Leeuw, Frank. *Income and the Cost of Rental Housing*. Washington, D.C.: The Urban Institute, 1970 (Urban Institute Working Paper 112-11). 44pp.

318. Morgan, James N. "Housing and Ability to Pay." *Econometrica*, April 1965, pp. 289-306.

319. Newman, Dorothy K. "Housing the Poor and the Shelter to Income Ratio." In U.S. Congress. House. Committee on Banking and Currency. *Papers Submitted to Subcommittee on Housing Panels on Housing Production, Housing Demand, and Developing a Suitable Living Environment: Part 2.* Washington, D.C.: Government Printing Office, 1971, pp. 555-578.

320. Reid, Margaret G. *Housing and Income*. Chicago, Ill.: University of Chicago Press, 1962.

321. White, Elizabeth Doris. *The Effects of Income and Other Characteristics on Outlays for Housing of Single Heads of Households, 1960.* Ann Arbor, Mich.: University Microfilms, 1966. (Ph.D. dissertation, University of Illinois, 1966). 206pp. (order no. 66-15,082)

322. Winger, Alan R. "Housing And Income." *Western Economic Journal,* June 1968, pp. 226-232.

323. Winger, Alan R. "Trade-Offs in Housing." *Land Economics,* November 1969, pp. 413-417.

See also: 751, 926, 928.

## 7. RACE AS A FACTOR IN HOUSING COSTS

324. Kau, James Burchel. *Price Discrimination in the Housing Market.* Ann Arbor, Mich.: University Microfilms, 1971 (Ph.D. dissertation, Unviersity of Washington, 1971). 53pp. (order no. 71-28,432)

325. Lapham, Victoria. "Do Blacks Pay More for Housing?" *Journal of Political Economy,* November 1971. pp. 1244-1257.

326. Lapham, Victoria Cannon. *Price Differences for Black and White Housing.* Ann Arbor, Mich.: University Microfilms, 1971 (Ph.D. dissertation, Southern Methodist University, 1970). 120pp. (order no. 71-19,603).

327. Neufield, J.L. and K.B. Kenny. *The Lack of Relation between Race and Housing Costs: A Case Study of Knoxville, Tennessee.* Oak Ridge, Tenn.: Oak Ridge National Laboratory, 1971. 39pp.

328. New York (State) Commission for Human Rights. *Comparative Cost of Housing for White, Nonwhite, and Puerto Rican Families in the New York Metropolitan Area.* New York, 1967.

329. Rapkin, Chester. "Price Discrimination against Negroes in the Rental Housing Market." In *Essays in Urban Land Economics.* Los Angeles, Calif.: Real Estate Research Program, Univerity of California at Los Angeles, 1966, pp. 333-345.

330. Stengel, Mitchell. "Racial Price Discrimination in the Urban Rental Housing Market." Unpublished Ph.D. dissertation, Harvard University, 1970.

331. Wihry, David Francis. *Racial Price Discrimination in Metropolitan Housing Markets.* Ann Arbor, Mich.: University Microfilms, 1972 (Ph.D. dissertation, Syracuse University, 1972). 236pp. (order no. 72-20,379)

See also: Minorities and Housing Markets: 1023+

## C. HOUSING FINANCE

### 1. GENERAL

332. Arnold, Scott. "Service Corporations and the National Corporation for Housing Partnerships." *Federal Home Loan Bank Board Journal,* March 1971, pp. 21-24.

333. Brimmer, Andrew F. "The Federal Reserve and the Subeconomy of Real Estate." *Real Estate Review*, Fall 1971, pp. 15-21.

334. Curzan, Myron P. "Housing and the Role of the Large Corporate Enterprise." In U.S. Congress. House. Committe on Banking and Currency. *Papers submitted to Subcommittee on Housing Panels on Housing Production, Housing Demand, and Developing a Suitable Living Environment: Part 1.* Washington, D.C.: Government Printing Office, 1971, pp. 183-201.

335. Diamond, Arnold H. "Motivations of Investors in Multifamily Housing." *Real Estate Appraiser*, May/June 1972, pp. 17-24.

336. Downs, Anthony and M. Leanne Lachman. "The Current Investment Climate and Strategies in Real Estate." *Real Estate Review*, Summer 1972, pp. 10-14.

337. Freidberg, Sidney. "For NHP, Everything Is Coming Up Roses." *Real Estate Review*, Fall 1972, pp. 32-37.

338. Gillies, James and Leo Grebler. "Financing of Nonfarm Housing in California." In California Governor's Advisory Commission on Housing Problems. *Appendix to the Report on Housing in California.* San Francisco, Calif., 1963, pp. 375-468.

339. Heimann, John G. "Housing and the Private Capital Market." Unpublished paper, September 1966.

340. Hoagland, Henry Elmer and Leo D. Stone. *Real Estate Finance*. 3d ed. Homewood, Ill.: R.D. Irwin, 1965. 628pp.

341. "Housing Partnerships Corporation Reports a Big First Year – 20 Projects Under Way." *House & Home*, March 1971, pp. 28+.

342. "Increasing Sources of Housing Funds." *HUD Challenge*, May 1972, pp. 20-25.

343. "Is There a Fair Profit to Be Made in Subsidized Rental Housing?" *House and Home*, January 1969, pp. 84-89.

344. Jensen, Harold S. "The Changing World of Real Estate Finance." *Urban Land*, June 1971, pp. 3-10.

345. Kalchbrenner, John H. *Theoretical and Empirical Specifications of the Housing Sector*. Washington, D.C.: U.S. Board of Governors of the Federal Reserve System, 1971. 54pp. (Studies of Short Term Cycles in Housing Production no. 16)

346. "Low-Income Housing Gets a Shot in the Arm." *Savings and Loan News*, August 1971, pp. 54-57.

347. Maisel, Sherman J. *Financing Real Estate: Principles and Practices*. New York, New York: McGraw-Hill, 1965.

348. Martin, Preston. "Funds For Housing." *HUD Challenge*, June 1971, pp. 17-19.

349. National Corporation for Housing Partnerships. *National Corporation for Housing Partnerships . . . a Key to Ending the Low and Moderate Rent Housing Problems*. Washington, D.C., 1970. 12pp.

350. "The National Housing Partnership." *Urban Lawyer*, Spring 1972, pp. 259-261.

351. Newcomb, Robinson N. *Financing Housing for the Next Decade*. Washington, D.C.: Homebuilding Press (National Association of Home Builders), 1967.

352. Palmer, Michael. *An Investigation of Factors Associated with Variations in the Relative Importance of Commercial Bank Residential Real Estate Loans*. Ann Arbor, Mich.: University Microfilms, 1967 (D.B.A. dissertation, University of Washington, 1967). 163pp. (order no.67-14,206)

353. Pierce, James L. and P.A. Tinsley. *A Proposal for a Policy Instrument to Effect Business Investment*. Washington, D.C.: U.S. Board of Governors of the Federal Reserve System, 1971. 25pp. (Studies of Short Term Cycles in Housing Production no. 12)

354. Poole, William. *Housing Finance under Inflationary Conditions*. Washington, D.C.: U.S. Board of Governors of the Federal Reserve System, 1971. 57pp. (Studies of Short Term Cycles in Housing Production no. 11)

355. Pyhrr, Stephen Anthony. *A Proposed Model to Simulate Internal Rate of Return and Risk Characteristics of Investments in Multi-Family*

*Rental Housing.* Ann Arbor, Mich.: University Microfilms, 1972 (Ph.D. dissertation, University of Illinois at Urbana-Champaign, 1972). 267pp. (order no. 72-19,910)

356. Stockwell, Eleanor J. *Quantitative Controls.* Washington, D.C.: U.S. Board of Governors of the Federal Reserve System, 1971. 30pp. (Studies of Short Term Cycles in Housing Production #7)

337. Suttles, Clyde Travers. *Accounting Standards for Investments in One- to Four-Family Urban Residential Mortgages.* Ann Arbor, Mich.: University Microfilms, 1968 (Ph.D. dissertation, University of Southern California, 1968). 455pp. (order no. 68-5881)

358. Taylor, Stephen P. *Long-Term Prospects for Housing Finance: A Projection to 1980.* Washington, D.C.: U.S. Board of Governors of the Federal Reserve System, 1971. 53pp. (Studies of Short Term Cycles in Housing Production no. 6)

359. U.S. Congress. House. Committee on Banking and Currency. *Increased Flexibility for Financial Institutions. Hearings.* Washington, D.C.: Government Printing Office, 1964. 1078pp.

360. U.S. Congress. House. Committee on Banking and Currency. *Loans by Savings and Loan Associations on Multifamily Housing: Report, September 14, 1962. . . .* Washington, D.C.: Government Printing Office, 1962. 9pp.

361. U.S. Congress. House. Committee on Banking and Currency. *Rental Housing Loans by Savings and Loan Associations. Hearing. . . .* Washington, D.C.: Government Printing Office, 1962. 20pp.

362. U.S. Congress. House. Committee on Banking and Currency. Ad Hoc Subcommittee on Home Financing Practices and Procedures. *Report and Recomendations. . . .* Washington, D.C.: Government Printing Office, 1970. 31pp.

363. U.S. Congress. Senate. Committee on the District of Columbia. *Housing – Financing and Development: Hearing. . . .* Washington, D.C.: Government Printing Office, 1970. 108pp.

364. U.S. Congress. Senate. Committee on Banking and Currency. *Loans by Savings and Loan Associations on Multifamily Housing; Report. . . .* Washington, D.C.: Government Printing Office, 1962. 9pp.

365. U.S. Congress. Senate. Committee on Commerce. *Utility Participation in Housing for Persons of Low and Moderate Income. Hearings. . . .* Washington, D.C.: Government Printing Office, 1972.

366. U.S. Housing and Home Finance Agency. *Capital Funds for Housing in the United States.* Washington, D.C., 1960. 32pp.

367. Vidger, L.P. "The Performance and Potentials of Non-Institutional Lenders in Financing Urban Real Estate." *Annals of Regional Science*, June 1967, pp. 152-165.

368. Weill, S. Douglas. "Land Leasebacks Move Up Fast as Financing Technique." *Real Estate Review*, Winter, 1972, pp. 65+.

369. Wendt, P.F. and S.N. Wong. "Investment Performance; Common Stocks Versus Apartment Houses." *Journal of Finance*, December 1965, pp. 633-646. Also in *Appraisal Journal*, January 1972, pp. 123-129.

370. Wendt, Paul F. *et al. California Net Income Valuation Tables; One Step Internal Rate of Return Valuation and Analysis.* Berkeley, Calif.: Center for Real Estate and Urban Economics, Institute of Urban and Regional Development, University of California, 1970. 357pp.

371. Wittausch, William K. "The Housing Corporation: A Proposed Innovation in Consumer Home Financing." *Urban Land*, April 1969, pp. 3-9.

372. Wittausch, William K. "New Technology in Financing Homes." *SRI Journal*, November 1967, pp. 7-10.

373. Woodworth, G. Walter. "Monetary Policies and Investment in Housing." *Current Economic Comment*, August 1960, pp. 33-46.

See also: 101, 1444, 1445, 1450-1453, 1495, 1499 1503; Liability in Purchase of Defective Home: 1082+; Mobile Homes – Finance no: 1651-1662; Inner-City Housing – Finance no: 2256+.

## 2. REAL ESTATE INVESTMENT TRUSTS

374. ALI-ABA Monday Forum: Syndication of Low and Middle Income Housing: A New Approach to Real Estate Investment, New York, 1971. *ALI-ABA Monday Forum: Syndication of Low and Middle Income Housing; A New Approach to Real Estate Investment; Study Materials.* Philadelphia, Penn.: Joint Committee on Continuing Legal Education of the American Law Institute and the American Bar Association, 1971. 177pp.

375. Augustine, Don and Ronald R. Hrusoff. "The Growing Pains of Public Real Estate Syndicates." *Real Estate Review*, Fall 1971, pp. 22-27.

376. "Big Business Moves into Housing." *Savings and Loan News*, January 1970, pp. 32-37.

377. "Blind Pool." *Professional Builder*, May 1972, pp. 106-107.

378. "The Boom in Real Estate Investment Trusts: Good News or Bad." *Savings and Loan News*, October 1970, pp. 34-40.

379. Campbell, Kenneth D. "The Real Estate Investment Trust – New Wonderchild." *Real Estate Review*, Winter 1972, pp. 25+.

380. Creamer, Ronald E. and Michael R. Deutschman. "FHA Syndications under the Microscope." *Real Estate Review*, Fall 1972, pp. 5-25.

381. Fass, Peter M. "The Regulated World of the Real Estate Syndicates." *Real Estate Review*, Winter 1972, pp. 52+.

382. Faulkner, Phillip G. "REIT'S – Equity Returns in a Fish Bowl." *Appraisal Journal*, October 1970, pp. 485-494.

383. Gale, Fredric G. "The New Economic Plan: What Effect on REIT's?" *Real Estate Review*, Winter 1972, pp. 37+.

384. Hershman, A. "High Costs of Real Estate Syndications." *Dun's*, December 1972, pp. 53-55.

385. Kahn, Sanford Richard. *An Evaluation of the Real Estate Investment Trust*. Ann Arbor, Mich.: University Microfilms, 1967 (Ph.D. dissertation, University of Cincinnati, 1967). 134pp. (order no. 67-15,966)

386. Kearns, Thomas J. "Analyzing REITs." *Appraisal Journal*, January 1972, pp. 129-132.

387. Korobow, L. and R.J. Gelson. "Real Estate Investment Trusts: An Appraisal of Their Impact on Mortgage Credit." *Federal Reserve New York, Monthly Review*, August 1971, pp. 188-195. Also in *Appraisal Journal*, January 1972, pp. 42-54.

388. Korobow, Leon and Richard J. Gelson. "REITs: Impact on Mortgage Credit." *Appraisal Journal*, January 1972, pp. 42-54.

389. Leik, James E. "Activity of REITs in Intermediate-Term Lending." *Mortgage Banker*, October 1972, pp. 84-90.

390. Oppenheimer, Martin J. "REIT's Seeking Equity Kickers Travel a Perilous Sea." *Real Estate Review*, Winter 1972, pp. 31+.

391. Pearson, Karl G. "Real Estate Investment Trusts." *Appraisal Journal*, January 1972, pp. 127-128.

392. "Real Estate and Mortgage Investment Trusts." *Mortgage Banker*, September 1970, entire issue.

393. Roulac, Stephen E. (ed.). *Notable Syndications Sourcebook.* New York: Practising Law Institute, 1972. 2 vols., 1237pp.

394. Roulac, Stephen R. "What's Inside Those Shiny New Syndication Packages?" *Real Estate Review*, Summer 1972, pp. 74-80+.

395. Schulkin, Peter A. "Recent Developments in the REIT Industry." *New England Economic Review*, September 1972, pp. 3-12.

396. Schulkin, Peter A. "Real Estate Investment Trusts in an Era of Innovation." *Real Estate Review*, Fall 1972, pp. 48-58.

397. "Selling Syndications Shares Successfully: A Professional's Approach." *Real Estate Review*, Fall 1972, pp. 38+.

398. Tunitis, Edmund J. *Real Estate Investment Trusts.* Boston, Mass.: Financial Publishing Co., 1972. 121pp.

See also: 676, 687, 690, 691.

3. CONSTRUCTION AND HOME IMPROVEMENT LOANS

399. Fisher, Robert Moore and Bernard N. Freedman. "Construction Loans at Commercial Banks." *Federal Reserve Bulletin*, June 1972, pp. 533-544.

400. Fisher, Robert Moore. *The Availability of Construction Credit for Housing.* Washington, D.C.: U.S. Board of Governors of the Federal Reserve System, 1970. 20pp. (Studies of Short Term Cycles in Housing Production no. 4)

401. Gail, Donald R. "Savings and Loan Association Industry and Multi-Family 'Home' Development." *Southern California Law Review*, Fall 1965, pp. 594-607.

402. Jung, Allen F. "Terms on Home Improvement Loans: Results of a First-Hand Study of Home Improvement Loans by Commercial Banks and Savings and Loan Associations in the Chicago Area." *National Banking Review*, September 1964, pp. 51-60.

403. LeBeau, E.C. "Interim Financing on Housing Projects." *Arizona Law Review*, Winter 1960, pp. 212+.

404. "Property Improvement Lending: Several Problem Cases and the One Big Lesson They Teach: Associations Invite Trouble if They Don't

Operate It Strictly as a Consumer Credit Business." *Savings & Loan News*, April 1962, pp. 58-69.

405. Schulkin, Peter A. "Construction Lending at Large Commercial Banks." *Real Estate Review*, Spring 1971, pp. 54-60. Also in *New England Economic Review*, July-August 1970, pp. 2-11.

See also: Liability in Purchase of Defective Home: 1082+; 3267.

## 4. MORTGAGE FINANCE

### a. General

406. "Allocating Priority between Open-End Mortgages and Federal Tax Liens: A Suggested Modification of the ABA Proposal." *Yale Law Journal*, January 1961, pp. 461-468.

407. American Institute of Banking. *Home Mortgage Lending*. New York, 1963. 440pp.

408. "Annual Survey of Savings Banks Mortgage Lending Activity Showing Comparisons with Savings and Loan, Life Insurance Industries." *Savings Bank Journal*, July 1960, pp. 38-43.

409. Ashley, Thomas L. "A Look at Housing in the '70's." *Mortgage Banker*, March 1971, pp. 46-50.

410. Bentley, A.R. and A. Macbeth. "Mortgage Lenders and the Housing Supply." *Cornell Law Review*, January 1972, pp. 149+.

411. Bolten, Steven Edward. *An Investigation into the Characteristics of the Mutual Savings Bank Residential Mortgage*. Ann Arbor, Mich.: Univeristy Microfilms, 1969 (Ph.D. dissertation, New York University Graduate School of Business Administration, 1969). 218pp. (order no. 69-18,494)

412. Break, George F. *et al. Federal Credit Agencies; A series of Research Studies.* Englewood Cliffs, N.J.: Prentice-Hall, 1963. 491pp.

413. Brennan, J. William. "Mortgage Loans Packaged as Securities." *Real Estate Review*, Spring 1971, pp. 65-69.

414. Brigham, Eugene F. "Recent Developments in the Savings and Loan Industry." *California Management Review*, Summer 1967, pp. 71-78.

415. Brophy, David J. "The Usury Law: A Barrier to Home Financing." *Michigan Business Review*, January 1970, pp. 25-31.

416. Bryant, Willis Rooks. *Mortgage Lending: Fundamentals and Practices. 2d Ed.* New York: McGraw-Hill, 1962. 423 pp.

417. Burnham, James B. "Asset Diversification and the Housing Cycle." *Federal Home Loan Bank Board Journal*, March 1972, pp. 17-21.

418. Burnham, James B. *Private Financial Institutions and the Residential Mortgage Cycle, with Particular Reference to the Savings and Loan Industry*. Washington, D.C.: U.S. Board of Governors of the Federal Reserve System, 1971. 40pp. (Studies of Short Term Cycles in Housing Production no. 1)

419. Case, Fred E. "Unexploited Mortgage Lending Potentials: An Analysis." *Land Economics*, August 1968, pp. 283-293.

420. Colean, Miles L. "40 Year Mortgages: Unsound, Self-Defeating." *Mortgage Banker*, May 1961, pp. 33-35.

421. Colean, Miles L. "Policy Considerations for 1971." *Mortgage Banker*, January 1971, pp. 16-21.

422. Conway, Lawrence V. *Mortgage Lending*. Chicago, Ill.: American Savings and Loan Institute Press, 1962. 836pp.

423. Cox, John Robert. *Institutional Mortgage Lending in the Los Angeles Metropolitan Area, 1953-54 and 1957-58*. Ann Arbor, Mich.: University Microfilms, 1963 (Ph.D. dissertation, University of Southern California, 1962). 390pp. (order no. 63-2145)

424. Craine, R.N. *et al. Some Evidence on a Fiscal Instrument to Alter Business Investment.* Washington, D.C.: U.S. Board of Governors of the Federal Reserve System, 1971. 45pp. (Studies of Short Term Cycles in Housing Production no. 19).

425. Daniel, Coldwell, III. "General Credit Conditions and Nonfarm Residential Mortgage Credit." *Atlanta Economic Review*, August 1960, pp. 9-12.

426. Davis, Irving F. *Current Problems in Financing Older Homes in Fresno*. Fresno, Calif.: Bureau of Business Research and Service, School of Business, Fresno State College, 1968. 67pp.

427. "Decline in Home Mortgage Credit Quality?" *Federal Reserve Chicago, Business Conditions: A Review*, September 1963, p. 10-16.

428. Deming, Frederick W. "The Federal Government and the Mortgage Lender." *Real Estate Review*, Summer 1971, pp. 47-50.

429. Edwards, Edward E. "The Home Mortgage: A Prime Case for Product Improvement." *Indiana Business Review*, July-August 1970, pp. 17-20.

430. Engleman, David S. "95% Loans." *Federal Home Loan Bank Board Journal*, March 1972, pp. 1-5.

431. "The Expanding World of the Service Corporation." *Savings and Loan News*, April 1971, pp. 33-39.

432. Federal Reserve Bank of Boston. *Policies for a More Competitive Financial System: A Review of the Report of the President's Commission on Financial Structure and Regulation.* (Reed O. Hunt, Chm.): *Proceedings of a Conference Held at Nantucket, Massachusetts, June 1972.* Boston, 1972. 221pp.

433. "Financing Report Disappointing on Mortgages." *NAHB Journal of Homebuilding*, February 1972, pp. 27-28.

434. Fisher, Robert Moore. "Monetary Policy: Its Relation to Mortgage Lending and Land Economics." *Land Economics*, November 1969, pp. 418-424.

435. Fisher, Robert M. "Mortgage Lending Commitments and Monetary Policy." Unpublished paper, February 1969.

436. Fisher, Robert Moore. *Mortgage Repayments As a Source of Loanable Funds.* Washington, D.C.: Board of Governors of the U.S. Federal Reserve System, 1972 (Staff Economic Studies no. 64). 42pp.

437. Forest City Enterprises. *Pension Fund Investment for Home Ownership; Interim Technical Report.* Cleveland, Ohio, 1972. 62pp.

438. Freedman, Bernard N. *Contingent Participation Mortgages on Single-Family Homes.* Washington, D.C.: U.S. Board of Governors of the Federal Reserve System, 1970. 27pp. (Studies of Short Term Cycles in Housing Production no. 18).

439. Gillies, James and Jay S. Berger. *Profile of the Los Angeles Metropolis, Its People and Its Homes. Part 4, Financing Homeownership: The Borrowers, the Lenders, and the Homes.* Los Angeles, Calif.: Real Estate Research Program, Graudate School of Business Administration, University of California, 1965. 77pp. (Research Report no. 7)

440. Goldberg, S.A. "What to do about Mortgages in the Sale of Real Property." *Practical Lawyer*, November 1971, pp. 13+.

441. Graaskamp, James. "Development and Structure of Mortgage Loan Guarantee Insurance in the United States." *Journal of Risk and Insurance*, March 1967, pp. 47-68.

442. Grebler, Leo. "The 'New System' of Residential Mortgage Finance." *Appraisal Journal*, July 1972, pp. 434-448.

443. Grebler, Leo. "A Searching Analysis of the Quality of Mortgage Credit." *Mortgage Banker*, February 1964, pp. 32-36.

444. Grebler, Leo and James Gillies. *Junior Mortgage Financing in Los Angeles County, 1958-1959.* Los Angeles, Calif.: Real Estate Research Program, Division of Research, Graduate School of Business Administration, University of California, December 1960. 71pp.

445. Greene, Raleigh *et al.* "Mortgage Financing Outlook." *Mortgage Banker*, June 1972, pp. 34-40.

446. Gunning, Francis P. "The Wrap-Around Mortgage ... Friend or U.F.O.?" *Real Estate Review*, Summer 1972, pp. 35-48.

447. Guttentag, Jack M. and Morris Beck. *New Series on Home Mortgage Yields Since 1951.* New York: National Bureau of Economic Research; dist. by Columbia University Press, 1970. 357pp.

448. Haar, Charles M. *Federal Credit and Private Housing: the Mass Financing Dilemma.* New York: McGraw-Hill, 1960. 408pp.

449. Halper, John B. "The Influence of Mortgage Lenders on Building Design." *Law and Contemporary Problems*, Spring 1967, pp. 266-273.

450. Hanc, George. "Mortgage Lending Nationwide by Mutual Savings Banks." *Savings Bank Journal*, May 1971, pp. 17+.

451. Harth, Jean G. "Piggyback Mortgage Financing." *Legal Bulletin*, Jan. 1972, pp. 1-10.

452. Healey, Edward F. "A Legal View: Wrap-Around Mortgages." *Title News*, August 1972, pp. 6-7+.

453. Hood, E.T. and J.A. Kushner. "Real Estate Finance: The Discount Point System and Its Effect on Federally Insured Home Loans." *University of Missouri at Kansas City Law Review*, Autumn 1971, pp. 1+.

454. Huang, David. "The Short-Run Flows of Non-Farm Residential Mortgage Credit." *Econometrica*, April 1966, pp. 433-459. Errata, October 1966, p. 909.

455. Johnston, Verle. "Help for Housing?" *Federal Reserve San Francisco, Monthly Review*, July 1967, pp. 139-145.

456. Johnston, Verle. "What Next for the S & L's?" *Federal Reserve San Francisco, Monthly Review*, June 1965, pp. 111-114.

457. Jones, Oliver H. "Mortgage Banking Is Regulated!" *Mortgage Banker*, July 1972, pp. 6-10.

458. Kaminow, Ira. "Should Housing Be Sheltered from Tight Credit?" *Federal Reserve, Philadelphia*, November 1970, pp. 24-35.

459. Kendall, Leon T. *Anatomy of the Residential Mortgage: Loan, Property, and Borrower Characteristics.* Chicago, Ill.: U.S. Savings and Loan League, 1964. 80pp.

460. Kendall, Leon T. "The Quality of Mortgage Credit in Real Estate Adjustments." *Mortgage Banker*, June 1964, pp. 24-27.

461. King, Boyd F. "Savings and Loan Associations in a Changing Economy." *Federal Reserve Bank of Atlanta, Monthly Review*, May 1972, pp. 74-81.

462. Klaman, Saul B. "Outlook for Savings, Housing, and Mortgage Finance." *HUD Challenge*, April 1972, pp. 20-23.

463. Klaman, Saul B. "Public/Private Approaches to Urban Mortgage and Housing Problems." *Law and Contemporary Problems*, Spring 1967, pp. 250-265.

464. Knight, R.E. "The Quality of Mortgage Credit." *Federal Reserve Kansas City, Monthly Review*, March 1969, pp. 13-20 and April 1969, pp. 10-18.

465. Korshak, Jack. "Processing FHA Multi-Family Loans." *Mortgage Banker*, February 1971, pp. 24-30+.

466. Leibold, Arthur W. "The S & L Service Corporation – Its History and Future." *National League Journal*, July 1971, pp. 10-11+.

467. "Liability under the Federal False Claims Act of Fraudulent Party in FHA Loan Transaction." *George Washington Law Review*, March 1960, pp. 642+.

468. Lindsay, Robert. *Rate Risk Insurance for Mortgage Lenders.* Washington, D.C.: U.S. Board of Governors of the Federal Reserve System, 1971. 52pp. (Studies of Short Term Cycles in Housing Production no.21).

469. Litterer, Oscar F. "Mortgage Credit and Home Building." *Federal Reserve, Minneapolis*, June 1961, pp. 1-5.

470. Mao, James C.T. *Residential Mortgage Financing: A Long-Range Projection.* Ann Arbor, Mich.: Bureau of Business Research, School of Business Administration, University of Michigan, 1960. 39pp.

471. Martin, Preston. "New Credit Policies for the 1970's." *Federal Home Loan Bank Board Journal*, December 1970, pp. 1-5+.

472. Martin, Preston. "New Financial Tools Readied for Housing." *Federal Home Loan Bank Board Journal*, July 1970, pp. 1-24.

473. Martin, Preston. "Savings and Loan Challenge." *National League Journal*, April 1972, pp. 10+.

474. Martin, Preston. "A Return to Fundamentals." *Federal Home Loan Bank Board Journal*, May 1972, pp. 1-5.

475. McFarland, M. Carter. "Major Developments in the Financing of Residential Construction since World War II," *Journal of Finance*, May 1966, pp. 382-94.

476. Meininger, Carl R. "Percentage Limitations on Lending." *Federal Home Loan Bank Board Journal*, May 1972, pp. 16-18.

477. Messner, S.D. and B.N. Boyce. "Calculation of Amortization Schedules and Mortgage Balances." *Appraisal Journal*, January 1972, pp. 76-82.

478. Mortgage Bankers Association of America. *Mortgage Banking Survey of Single-Family Loan Operations, 1967.* Washington, D.C., 1969 (Research Committee Operations Report no. 1).

479. Mortgage Bankers Association of America. *Mortgage Banking Survey of Single-Family Loan Operations, 1969: Income and Costs for Origination and Servicing of Single-Family Loans.* Washington, D.C., 1972. 27pp. (Research Committee Operations Report no. 2).

480. "National Mortgage Survey," *Real Estate Analyst*, June 1971, pp. 241-264.

481. "National Mortgage Survey." *Real Estate Analyst*, June 1972, pp. 235-258.

482. New Jersey Legislature. Joint Commission to Study and Investigate Certain Allegedly Unfair Practices in Connection with the Making of Loans Secured by Mortgages on Residential Properties. *Final Report.* Trenton, 1960.

483. New York (State) Legislature. Assembly. Committee on Mortgage and Real Estate. *Report*. Albany, N.Y., 1961. 46pp.

484. Nicol, Robert E.G., B. Schwab and P. Lusztig. "An Alternative in Mortgage Lending." *Quarterly Review of Economics and Business*, Spring 1972, pp. 31-42.

485. "95% Lending: The Extra Edge." *Savings and Loan News*, June 1972, pp. 47-50.

486. Rapkin, Chester, *et al. The Private Insurance of Home Mortgages*. Philadelphia: Institute for Environmental Studies, University of Pennsylvania, 1967.

487. "Recommendations of the President's Commission on Financial Structure and Regulation." *Mortgage Banker*, February 1972, pp. 35-47.

488. Ricks, R. Bruce. "Housing Finance and Competition for Savings and Flows." *Federal Home Loan Bank Board Journal*, September 1970, pp. 1-5.

489. Ricks, R. Bruce. "Housing Goals and Breakthroughs in Housing Finance." *Federal Home Loan Bank Board Journal*, May 1972, pp. 10-18.

490. Ricks, R. Bruce. "An Overview of Residential Mortgage Financing." *National League Journal*, Aug. 1972, pp. 5+.

491. Rubinson, Jack. "Savings Bank Mortgage Activity in 1970." *Savings Bank Journal*, June 1971, pp. 63+.

492. "Saving Flows and Mortgage Lending, 1966-1967." *Federal Reserve Cleveland, Economic Review*. February 1968, pp. 12-19.

493. Schecter, Henry B. *The Residential Mortgage Financing Problem*. Washington, D.C.: Government Printing Office, 1971. 55pp.

494. Schecter, Henry B. and Milton B. Davis. "Residential Mortgage Capital: Mortgage Fund and Housing Construction; Investment Practices of Lenders." *Construction Review*, August 1960, pp. 5-10 and October 1960, pp. 5-10.

495. "Service Corporations – New Approach and Expanded Range of Activities." *Federal Home Loan Bank Board Journal*, October 1970, pp. 14-19.

496. Sharav, Itzhak. *New York City Multifamily Rental Housing with Mortgage Insurance under Section 207 of the National Housing Act: An Analysis of the Record for the Years 1964-1968*. Ann Arbor, Mich.: University Microfilms, 1972 (Ph.D. dissertation, City University of New York, 1971). 294pp. (order no. 72-5079)

497. Smith, Halbert C. "Institutional Aspects of Inter-Regional Mortgage Investment." *Journal of Finance*, May 1968, pp. 349-58.

498. Sonnenblick, Jack E. "High-Ratio Mortgage Financing." *Bankers Magazine*, Autumn 1969, pp. 82-91.

499. Spelman, Everett C. "Mortgage Banking in the Seventies." *Real Estate Review*, Spring 1971, pp. 30-33.

500. Stevenson, Eric. "Should Mortgage Loans Be Socially Significant?" *Real Estate Review*, Winter 1972, pp. 72+.

501. Stiles, Lynn A. "Needed: Adaptable Home Mortgages." *Federal Reserve Chicago, Business Conditions: A Review*, April 1970, pp. 13-16.

502. "There's Money in Mortgage Banking." *Savings and Loan News*, May 1971, pp. 49-53.

503. "Truth-in-Lending: Here's How Savings Associations Can Live with the New Rules through the Systematic Application of Procedures Required in Mortgage Disclosures." *Savings & Loan News*, June 1969, pp. 26-33.

504. von Furstenberg, George M. "The Investment Quality of Home Mortgages." *Journal of Risk and Insurance*, September 1970, pp. 437-446.

505. U.S. Congress. House. Committee on Banking and Currency. *Second Mortgages, Land Sale Contracts, and Other Financing Devices Employed in Conventional Mortgage Lending. Staff Report. . . .* Washington, D.C.: Government Printing Office, 1960. 94pp.

506. U.S. Congress. Senate. Committee on Banking and Currency. Subcommittee on Financial Institutions. *Deposit Rates and Mortgage Credit: Hearings. . . .* Washington, D.C.: Government Printing Office, 1969. 241pp.

507. U.S. Congress. Senate. Committee on Banking and Currency. Subcommittee on Housing and Urban Affairs. *Mortgage Credit: Hearings. . . .* Washington, D.C.: Government Printing Office, 1967. 286pp.

508. U.S. Congress. Senate. Committee on Banking and Currency. *Mortgage Discounts: A Report. . . .* Washington, D.C., 1967. 41pp.

509. U.S. Congress. Senate. Committee on Banking and Currency. Subcommittee on Housing and Urban Affairs. *A Study of Mortgage Credit*, Washington, D.C., 1967. 467pp.

510. U.S. Congress. Senate. Committee on Banking and Currency. *Study of Mortgage Credit. Does the Decade 1961-70 Pose Problems in Private*

*Housing and Mortgage Markets Which Require Federal Legislation by 1960?* Washington, D.C.: Government Printing Office, 1960. 481pp.

511. U.S. Congress. Senate. Committee on Banking and Currency. Subcommittee on Housing. *Study of Mortgage Credit; Does the Decade 1961-70 Pose Problems in Private Housing and Mortgage Markets Which Require Federal Legislation? Recommendations of Federal Agencies.* Washington, D.C.: Government Printing Office, 1961. 255pp.

512. U.S. Congress. Senate. Committee on the Judiciary. *Competition in Real Estate and Mortgage Lending. Hearing. . . .* Washington, D.C.: Government Printing Office, 1972, pt. 1.

513. Vernon, Jack. "Savings and Loan Association Response to Monetary Policies, 1953-61: A Case Study in 'Availability'." *Southern Economic Journal,* January 1965, pp. 227-37.

514. von Furstenberg, George. "Should Equity Kickers Be Permitted in Home Mortgages?" *Indiana Business Review,* July-August 1972, pp. 23-31.

515. Winger, Alan R. *Mortgage Characteristics and Lender Mortgage Acquisitions during Periods of Monetary Restraint: An Economic Analysis.* Washington, D.C.: U.S. Board of Governors of the Federal Reserve System, 1970. 73pp. (Studies of Short Term Cycles in Housing Production no. 5)

516. Yoon, Iee Nee. *The Conventional Mortgage Loans of Savings and Loan Associations.* Ann Arbor, Mich.: University Microfilms, 1968 (Ph.D. dissertation, University of Minnesota, 1967). 96pp. (order no. 68-7441)

See also: 296, 300, 929, 941, 2430, 3567.

b. Mortgage Investment Trusts

517. Campbell, Kenneth D. *Mortgage Trusts, Lenders with a Plus: An Investment Analysis of the Past and Future of Mortgage Real Estate Investment Trusts.* New York, N.Y.: Audit Publications, Inc., 1969. 177pp.

518. Hines, M.A. "The Economic Role of the Mortgage Trust." *Ohio State University Bulletin of Business Research,* March 1972, pp. 5-6.

519. Sonnenblick, Jack E. "The Future of the Mortgage Trust Industry." *Real Estate Review,* Spring 1971, pp. 1-3.

520. Thomas, Dana L. "Renewed Interest: Mortgage Investment Trusts Have Attracted Big Money." *Barron's,* August 24, 1970, pp. 3+.

c. Mortgage Markets

521. Bentley, Allen R. and Angus Macbeth. "Mortgage Lenders and the Housing Supply." *Cornell Law Review*, Jan. 1972, pp. 149-177.

522. Boorman, John T. and Manfred Peterson. "The Hunt Commission and the Mortgage Market: An Appraisal." *Journal of Bank Research*, Autumn 1972, pp. 155-165.

523. Cacy, J.A. "Financial Intermediaries and the Postwar Home Mortgage Market." *Federal Reserve, Kansas City. Monthly Review*, January/February 1967, pp. 12-21.

524. Cacy, J.A. and Linda Moore. "Financial Intermediaries in the Residential Mortgage Market, 1966-1969." *Federal Reserve Kansas City, Monthly Review*, September/October 1970, pp.3-10.

525. Cacy, J.A. "Specialized Mortgage Marketing Facilities." *Federal Reserve Kansas City, Monthly Review*. July/August 1967, pp. 3-13.

526. Case, Fred E. "California's Continuing Need for Mortgage Capital: Recent Efforts to Reduce Interest Rate Differentials throughout the United States Threaten the Ability of California to Attract the Out-of-state Funds Which It Needs." *California Management Review*, Winter 1967, pp. 80-90.

527. Chase, Samuel B. *The Use of Supplementary Reserve Requirements and Reserve Credits to Even Out the Flow of Mortgage Funds*. Washington, D.C.: U.S. Board of Governors of the Federal Reserve System, 1971. 31pp. (Studies of Short Term Cycles in Housing Production no. 3)

528. Clauretie, Terrance Michael. *Monetary Growth Rates, the Business Demand for Funds and the Residential Mortgage Market*. Ann Arbor, Mich.: University Microfilms, 1972 (Ph.D. dissertation, Washington State University, 1971). 124pp. (order no. 72-7639).

529. Davidson, Philip H. "Structure of the Residential Mortgage Market." *Federal Reserve Richmond*, September 1972, pp. 2-6.

530. Fischer, Donald E. and Keith B. Johnson. *The Residential Mortgage Market in Southeastern Connecticut: A Survey*. Storrs, Conn.: Center for Real Estate and Urban Economic Studies, School of Business Administration, University of Connecticut, 1969. 85pp. (Real Estate Reports: No. 9)

531. "Flow of Funds and the Mortgage Market." *Real Estate Analyst*, October 31, 1962, pp. 445-451.

532. Golembe (Carter H.) Associates. "An Appraisal of the Availability of Funds for Housing Needs 1969-78." In U.S. President's Committee on Urban Housing. *Report: Technical Studies, Volume II.* Washington, D.C.: Government Printing Office, 1968, pp. 191-238.

533. Grebler, Leo. *Broadening the Sources of Funds for Residential Mortgages.* Washington, D.C.: U.S. Board of Governors of the Federal Reserve System, 1971. 187pp. (Studies of Short Term Cycles in Housing Production no. 17).

534. Guttentag, Jack M. "Changes in the Structure of the Residential Mortgage Market: Analysis and Proposals." Unpublished paper, 1969.

535. Hershman, Mendes. "Usury and the Tight Mortgage Market – Revisited." *Business Lawyer,* July 1969, pp. 1121-1141.

536. Honea, Hiram J. "New Dimensions in the Mortgage Market." *Federal Reserve Atlanta, Monthly Review,* August 1963, pp. 1-3.

537. "Housing and Residential Mortgage Markets in 1967." *Federal Reserve Bulletin,* September 1967, pp. 1471-1485.

538. Huang, David and Micheal D. McCarthy. "Simulation of the Home Mortgage Market in the Late Sixties." *Review of Economics and Statistics,* November 1967, pp. 441-50.

539. "Impediments to Free Flow of Funds in Mortgage Market." *Real Property, Probate & Trust Journal,* Summer 1971, pp. 215+.

540. Johnson, Alfred P. "Anatomy of a Mortgage Market: A Decade of Financing Home Building in the South." *Federal Reserve Atlanta, Monthly Review,* October 1960, pp. 1-4.

541. Jones, Oliver H. "Must Monetary Policy Discriminate Against the Mortgage Market?" *Mortgage Banker,* June 1971, pp. 16-22.

542. Jung, Allen F. "Terms on Conventional Mortgage Loans: 1965 vs. 1960." *National Banking Review,* March 1966, pp. 379-84.

543. Kessel, Reuben A. "The Allocation of Mortgage Funds." Unpublished paper, 1969.

544. Klaman, Saul B. *The Postwar Residential Mortgage Market.* Princeton, N.J.: Princeton University Press, 1961. 301pp.

545. Martin, Preston. "Changing Scene in Mortgage Markets." *National League Journal,* May 1972, pp. 9-11+.

546. "Monetary Policy and the Residential Mortgage Market: Residential Mortgage Credit and the Activities of the Federal Reserve Board in Carrying Out Its Monetary Policy." *Federal Reserve Bulletin,* May 1967, pp. 728-740.

547. Morrissey, T.F. "Demand for Mortgage Loans and the Concomitant Demand for Home Loan Bank Advances by Savings and Loan Associations." *Journal of Finance,* June 1971, pp. 687-698.

548. "The Mortgage Market." *National Real Estate Investor,* October 1972, pp. 47-49+.

549. "Mortgage Survey for 167 Cities." *Real Estate Analyst,* July 29, 1963, pp. 273-304.

550. National Association of Real Estate Boards. Committee on Real Estate Economy and Research. *The Mortgage Market, Spring 1970: A Market Research Study.* Washington, D.C., 1970. 25pp.

551. Nelson, Jane F. "Federal Housing Agencies and the Residential Mortgage Market." *Federal Reserve Richmond. Monthly Review.* January 1970, pp. 9-11.

552. "The Residential Mortgage Market in 1959." *Federal Reserve, Kansas City. Monthly Review,* April 1960, pp. 3-8.

553. "Residential Mortgage Survey by Cities." *Real Estate Analyst,* May 31, 1962, pp. 219-250.

554. Sarkar, Asit Kumar. *The Institutional Dominance Hypothesis Reexamined: A Case Study of the Houston Residential Mortgage Market.* Ann Arbor, Mich.: University Microfilms, 1969 (Ph.D. dissertation, University of Houston, 1969). 222pp. (order no. 69-13,338)

555. Schaaf, A.H. *The Supply of Residential Mortgage Funds in the San Francisco Bay Area, 1950-1960.* Berkeley, Calif.: Center for Real Estate and Urban Economics, University of California, 1962. 73pp.

556. "The Supply of Mortgage Funds." *Federal Reserve, Richmond. Monthly Review,* August 1966, pp. 7+.

557. Swan, Craig Eliot. *The Behavior of Financial Institutions: An Econometric Analysis with Special Attention to Mortgage Markets and Residential Construction.* Ann Arbor, Mich.: University Microfilms, 1970 (Ph.D. dissertation, Yale University, 1970). 196pp. (order no. 70-26,826)

558. Waldron, William D. "Participatory Investment Reviewed." *Mortgage Banker,* August 1971, pp. 44-49.

559. Winger, Alan R. "Future Residental Mortgage Demands and Supplies." *Financial Analyst Journal*, September-October 1968, pp. 1-8.

560. Winger, A.R. "Regional Growth Disparities and the Mortgage Market." *Journal of Finance*, September 1969, pp. 659-662.

See also: 98, 106, 108, 603-639, 1782.

d. Mortgage Interest Rates

*1) General*

561. Alberts, William W. and Allen F. Jung. "Some Evidence of the Intra-Regional Structure of Interest Rates on Residential Mortgage Loans." *Land Economics*, May 1970, pp. 208-213.

562. Anderson, Paul S. and Robert W. Eisenmenger. "Structural Reform for Thrift Institutions: The Experience in the United States and Canada." *New England Economic Review*, July/August 1972, pp. 3-17.

563. Aspinwall, Richard C. "Market Structure and Commercial Bank Mortgage Interest Rates." *Southern Economic Journal*, April 1970, pp. 376-384.

564. Brimmer, Andrew F. "Statutory Interest Rate Ceilings and the Availability of Mortgage Funds." *Federal Reserve Philadelphia, Business Review*, June 1968, 10-page supplement.

565. "Flaws in the Ceiling." *Barron's*, August 16, 1971, pp. 7+.

566. Guttentag, Jack. "Credit Availability, Interest Rates, and Monetary Policy." *Southern Economic Journal*, January 1960, pp. 219-228.

567. Holden, Arthur C. "The Interest Rate, Mortgage Debt, and Rent." *Land Economics.* February 1966, pp. 103-107.

568. Huang, David. "The Role of FHA–VA Ceiling Rates in the Home Mortgage Market." Unpublished paper, March 1969.

569. Jones, Oliver H. "Mortgage Interest Rate Controls Hurt Low Income Housing Market." *Mortgage Banker*, March 1969, pp. 33-37.

570. "Mortgage Interest Rates." *Real Estate Analyst*, May 31, 1963, pp. 165-168.

571. Jung, Allen F. "Terms on Conventional Mortgage Loans on Existing Houses." *Journal of Finance*, September 1962, pp. 432-443.

572. Muth, Richard F. "Interest Rates, Contract Terms, and the Allocation of Mortgage Funds." *Journal of Finance,* March 1962, pp. 63-80.

573. Opper, Barbara Negri. *Interest Equalization on Home Mortgages.* Washington, D.C.: U.S. Board of Governors of the Federal Reserve System, 1971. 34pp. (Studies of Short Term Cycles in Housing Production no. 13)

574. Please, Robert H. "Money, Mortgages and Interest Rates." *Title News,* January 1971, pp. 14-18.

575. Samuelson, P.A. "The Current State of the Theory of Interest Rates, with Special Reference to Mortgage Rates." In *Conference on Savings and Residential Financing, 1960 Proceedings.* Chicago, Ill.: U.S. Savings and Loan League, 1960.

576. Schaaf, A.H. "Mortgage Interest Rate Controls and the Veteran's Housing Market." *Mississippi Valley Journal of Business and Economics,* Fall 1969, pp. 11-22.

577. "The Strange Case of the Declining Interest Rates." *Mortgage and Real Estate Executives Report,* June 16, 1971, pp. 1-2.

578. "Terms of Home Mortgage Loans." *Federal Reserve Chicago, Business Conditions: A Review,* June 1960, pp. 7-14.

579. U.S. Commission on Mortgage Interest Rates. *Report to the President of the United States and to the Congress.* Washington, D.C.: Government Printing Office, 1969. 141pp.

580. U.S. Congress. House. Committee on Banking and Currency. *To Extend for One Year the Authority for More Flexible Regulations of Maximum Rates of Interest or Dividends, Higher Reserve Requirements and Open Market Operations in Agency Issues: Hearings. . . .* Washington, D.C.: Government Printing Office, 1969. 172pp.

581. U.S. Congress. House. Committee on Banking and Currency. *To Extend Standby Powers of the President to Stabilize Wages and Prices and the Authority of the Federal Reserve Board and the Federal Home Loan Bank Board to Establish Flexible Interest Rates on Time Deposits. Hearings. . . .* Washington, D.C.: Government Printing Office, 1971. 226pp.

582. U.S. Congress. Senate. Committee on Banking and Currency. *Interest Rates and Mortgage Credit: Hearing. . . .* Washington, D.C., 1966. 128pp.

583. U.S. Congress. Senate. Committee on Banking and Currency. *Mortgage Interest Rate Commission Report: Hearings, September 25—October*

*1, 1969, on the Report of the Commission on Mortgage Interest Rates to the President and to the Congress.* Washington, D.C.: Government Printing Office, 1969. 231pp.

584. Weaver, Robert C. "FHA-FNMA Policy and Mortgage Interest Rates." In *Essays in Urban Land Economics.* Los Angeles, Calif.: Real Estate Research Program, University of California, 1966, pp. 234-260.

585. Weber, G.I. "Interest Rates on Mortgages and Dividend Rates on Savings and Loan Shares." *Journal of Finance,* September 1966, pp. 515-521.

*2) Variable Rate Mortgages*

586. Candilis, Wray O. *Variable Rate Mortgage Plans. A Research Paper Prepared for the Mortgage Finance Committee.* Washington, D.C.: American Bankers Association, 1971. 40pp. (Research Paper no. 7)

587. Fisher, Robert M. *Variable-Rate Mortgages.* Washington, D.C.: Board of Governors of the Federal Reserve System, March 1967 (Staff Economics Studies 30).

588. Garrison, Charles P. "A New Plan for Variable Mortgage Rates." *Savings & Loan News,* January 1967, pp. 26-31.

589. Hahn, Herbert R. "Some Implicatoins of Variable Interest Rate Mortgages for the Small Saver and the Potential Home Owner." *Business and Economic Review,* May/June 1971, pp. 2-7.

590. "In Simulation and Real Life: Variable Rates Really Work." *Savings & Loan News,* January 1971, pp. 21-26.

591. Krupnick, Alan J. "Variable-Rate Mortgages: Boon or Bane?" *Federal Reserve Philadelphia, Business Review,* September 1972, pp. 16-23.

592. McManus, R.P. "Variable Mortgage Note: Route to Increased Housing." *American Bar Association Journal,* June 1969, pp. 557+.

593. Page, Alfred N. "The Variation of Mortgage Interest Rates." *Journal of Business,* July 1964, pp. 280-294.

594. Poole, William *et al. The Variable Rate Mortgage on Single-Family Homes.* Washington, D.C.: U.S. Board of Governors of the Federal Reserver System, 1971. 51pp. (Studies of Short Term Cycles in Housing Production no. 10).

595. Quakenbush, Stanley G. "Why Not the Variable Rate Mortgage? But What about the Index?" *Savings Bank Journal,* October 1972, pp. 27-28+.

596. Roth, Dennis and Verle Johnson. "Variable-Rates on Mortgages?" *Federal Reserve San Francisco, Monthly Review*, April 1972, pp. 11-19.

597. Smith, Halbert C. "The Variable Rate Mortgage on Single-Family Homes." *Federal Home Loan Bank Board Journal*, September 1972, pp. 1-7.

598. Spolan, Harmon S. "The Case for Variable Rate Mortgages." *Real Estate Review*, Summer 1971, pp. 15-18. Also in George Sternlieb and Lynne B. Sagalyn (eds.). *Housing: 1970–1971; An AMS Anthology*. New York: AMS Press, 1972, pp. 242-245.

599. "Variable Rates on Mortgages: Their Impact and Use." *New England Economic Review*, March/April 1970, pp. 3-20.

600. von Furstenberg, George M. "The Economics of Variable Interest Rate Mortgages." *Federal Home Loan Bank Board Journal*, June 1972, pp. 8-11.

601. Wetmore, John M. "Variable Rate Mortgages." *Mortgage Banker*, March 1971, pp. 16-26.

602. "Why a Push for Home Loans with Flexible Interest Rates." *U.S. News & World Report*, Aug. 21, 1972, pp. 67-70.

e. Secondary Mortgage Markets

603. Bartke, Richard W. "Fannie Mae and the Secondary Mortgage Market." *Northwestern University Law Review*, March-April 1971, pp. 1-78.

604. Bartke, R.W. "Home Financing at the Crossroads – A Study of the Federal Home Loan Mortgage Corporation." *Indiana Law Journal*, Fall 1972, pp.1+.

605. Breckenfeld, Gurney. "Nobody Pours It Like Fannie Mae." *Fortune*, June 1972, pp. 86-89+.

606. Burns, D.E. "Federal Home Loan Mortgage Corporation – The First 400 Days and Beyond – A Legal View." *Federal Bar Journal*, Fall 1971, pp. 393+.

607. Clarke, T.H. "Regulatory and Housing Functions of the Federal Home Loan Bank Board." *Busniess Lawyer*, September 1970, pp. 37+.

608. Derrickson, G.F. "Role of FNMA in the Financing of Residential Construction." *Construction Review*, January 1962, pp. 9-10.

609. "Evaluating the Secondary Market." *California Savings and Loan Journal*, April 1971, pp. 10-11+.

610. "FHLMC – Its Financing, Functioning and Goals." *Federal Home Loan Bank Board Journal,* August 1971, pp. 1-6.

611. "FNMA and the Rights of Private Investors: Her Heart Still Belongs to Daddy." *Georgetown Law Journal,* November 1970, pp. 364-392.

612. Hunter, Oakley. "Fannie Mae – Lady on a Tightrope." *Title News,* January 1971, pp. 12-14.

613. Hunter, Oakley. "The Federal National Mortgage Association: Its Response to Critical Financing Requirements of Housing." *George Washington Law Review,* May 1971, pp. 818-834.

614. Hunter, Oakley. "Presenting 'Fannie May'." *Journal of Housing,* November 1970, pp. 524-526.

615. Hunter, Oakley. "Two Secondary Markets for Conventional Loans." *Savings Bank Journal,* April 1972, pp. 30-32+.

616. Jones, Oliver. "The Development of an Effective Secondary Mortgage Market." *Journal of Finance,* May 1962, pp. 358-370.

617. Jones, Oliver. "Private Secondary Market Facilities." *Journal of Finance,* May 1968, pp. 359-66.

618. Jones, Oliver and Leo Grebler. *The Secondary Mortgage Market; Its Purpose, Performance, and Potential.* Los Angeles, Calif.: Real Estate Research Program, Graduate School of Business Administration, Division of Research, University of California, 1961. 281pp.

619. Kingman, Woodward. "Attracting New Money into Housing." *HUD Challenge,* June 1971, pp. 4-8.

620. Kwon, Jene K. and Richard M. Thornton. "An Evaluation of the Competitive Effect of FHLB Open Market Operations on Savings Inflows at Savings and Loan Associations." *Journal of Finance,* June 1971, pp. 699-712.

621. Kown, J.K. and R.M. Thornton. "Federal Home Loan Bank and Savings and Loan Associations: An Examination of the Financing of Federal Home Loan Bank Advances." *Review of Economics and Statistics,* February 1972, pp. 97-100.

622. Leibold, Arthur W., Jr. "The Secondary Market: An Idea Whose Time Has Come." *Federal Home Loan Bank Board Journal,* May 1971, pp. 12-14.

623. "Loan Fund Liquidity Gets a Lift." *Savings and Loan News,* April 1971, pp. 52-57.

624. Mandala, Andrew R. "Secondary Markets: They're All Around Us." *National League Journal*, Feb. 1972, pp. 4-5.

625. Martin, Preston. "Chairman Martin Talks About the FHLMC and the Secondary Market." *California Savings and Loan Journal*, April 1972, pp. 15-16+.

626. Martin, Preston. "Heavy Advances Use Promised in '71." *National League Journal*, December 1970, pp. 6-8.

627. Martin, Preston. *Support for the Mortgage Market: Advances Policy and FHLMC Policy*. Washington, D.C.: Federal Home Loan Bank Board, 1970. 22pp.

628. Massaro, Vincent. "The Expanding Role of Federally Sponsored Agencies: A New Force Develops in U.S. Credit Markets and Policy." *Conference Board Record*, April 1971, pp. 14-20.

629. "Meet Ginnie Mae." *Dun's*, March 1971, pp. 72-73.

630. Murray, James E. "Fannie Mae Goes Shopping for Conventional Mortgages." *Real Estate Review*, Fall 1971, pp. 54-60.

631. National Association of Home Builders. *The Federal National Mortgage Association: Your New Opportunity*. Washington, D.C., 1970. 30pp.

632. "Oakley Hunter Discusses Fannie Mae." *California Real Estate Magazine*, May 1971, pp. 4-8.

633. "Special Issue Covering the GNMA Mortgage-Backed Security." *Mortgage Banker*, May 1971, Entire issue.

634. Trubac, Edward Richard. *The Impact of FNMA on the Mortgage Sector and Monetary Policy*. Ann Arbor, Mich.: University Microfilms, 1965 (Ph.D. dissertation, Syracuse University, 1965). 223pp. (order no. 65-7984).

635. U.S. Congress. Senate. Committee on Banking and Currency. Subcommittee on Housing and Urban Affairs. *Secondary Mortgage Market and Mortgage Credit: Hearings. . . .* Washington, D.C.: Government Printing Office, 1970, 355pp.

636. U.S. Federal National Mortgage Association. *Background and History of the Federal National Mortgage Association*. Washington, D.C., 1969.

637. U.S. Federal National Mortgage Association. *FNMA*. Washington, D.C., 1972. 15pp.

638. U.S. General Accounting Office. *Examination of Financial Statements of the Government National Mortgage Association for Fiscal Year 1972.* Washington, D.C., 1972.

639. Widmer, Raymond Francis. *An Appraisal of the Housing Assistance Program of the Federal Home Loan Bank System.* Ann Arbor, Mich.: University Microfilms, 1972 (Ph.D. dissertation, University of Arkansas, 1972). 115pp.

See also: 584, 2405, 2512.

f. Mortgage Delinquency and Foreclosure

640. Andelman, D.R. "Mortgage Foreclosure: Effects upon Mortgagor, Mortgagee, Receiver in Possession: Deed in Lieu of Foreclosure." *New York University Institute of Federal Taxation,* 1972, pp. 309+.

641. "Causes of Foreclosure." *Banking,* February 1963, pp. 47+.

642. "The Causes of Foreclosure." *Real Estate Analyst,* October 1972, pp. 387-390.

643. Creedon, John J. "On Mortgage Foreclosures and Federal Tax Liens (the Lender's Defeat in Victory)." *Business Lawyer,* July 1963, pp. 1117-1151.

644. "Defaults and Foreclosures: The Problem and the Cure." *Mortgage Banker,* Aug. 1972, pp. 18-23+.

645. Fisher, Robert M. "Foreclosures and Delinquencies: Dimensions of a Problem." *Mortgage Banker,* April 1964, pp. 24-28.

646. "The Foreclosure Outlook." *Real Estate Analyst,* July 20, 1962, pp. 323-337.

647. "Foreclosures in 140 Metropolitan Areas." *Real Estate Analyst,* March 31, 1966. pp. 93-108.

648. Herzog, John P. and James S. Earley. *Home Mortgage Delinquency and Foreclosure.* New York: National Bureau of Economic Research, distributed by Columbia University Press, 1970. 170pp.

649. Hoitz, A.L. and T.L. Griem. "Mortgage Foreclosures — New Procedures under P.A. 104 of 1971." *Michigan State Bar Journal,* March 1972, pp. 164+.

650. Megee, Mary. "Statistical Prediction of Mortgage Risk." *Land Economics,* November 1968, pp. 461-470.

651. "1969 Foreclosures in Metropolitan Areas." *Real Estate Analyst*, March 24, 1970, pp. 101-116.

652. "1970 Foreclosures in Metropolitan Areas." *Real Estate Analyst*, March 1971, pp. 107-122.

653. "The Relationship of Unemployment to Mortgage Foreclosures." *Monthly Labor Review*, December 1963, pp. 1421-1425.

654. Theiss, William R. "Default Provisions in Mortgages." *Appraisal Journal*, January 1972, pp. 133-134.

655. Tiderington, Robert H. "Federal Courts – Refusal to Apply State Redemption Statute to FHA-Insured Mortgage Foreclosure." *Wayne Law Review*, January-February 1971, pp. 178-189.

656. von Furstenberg, George M. "Default Risk on FHA-Insured Home Mortgages as a Function of the Terms of Financing: A Quantitative Analysis." *Journal of Finance*, June 1969, pp. 459-477.

657. von Furstenberg, George M. *Technical Studies of Mortgage Default Risk; An Analysis of the Experience with FHA and VA Home Loans during the Decade 1957-66.* Ithaca, N.Y.: Center for Urban Development Research, Cornell University, 1971. 80pp.

658. U.S. Congress. House. Committee on Government Operations. *Defaults on FHA-Insured Home Mortgages, Detroit, Michigan. Fifteenth Report by the Committee on Government Operations.* Washington, D.C.: Government Printing Office, 1972.

659. U.S. Congress. House. Committe on Government Operations. *Defaults on FHA-Insured Mortgages, (Detroit). Hearings.* Washington, D.C.: Government Printing Office, 1972.

660. U.S. Congress. Senate. Committee on Banking and Currency. *FHA Mortgage Foreclosures.* Washington, D.C.: Government Printing Office, January 1966.

661. U.S. Federal Housing Administration. *Experience with Mortgage Foreclosures and Property Acquisitions.* Washington, D.C., January 1963. 81pp.

662. U.S. Housing and Home Finance Agency. Office of Program Policy. *Mortgage Foreclosures in Six Metropolitan Areas.* Washington, D.C., 1963. 192pp.

See also: 302.

g. Mortgage Finance Legislation

663. Holmes, Lee B. "From MBA's Legislative Counsel: A Legislative Outlook for 1972." *Mortgage Banker*, Jan. 1972, pp. 38-44.

664. "Housing – Public Purpose – Legislation Establishing Agency to Finance Mortgage Loans without Restriction on Income of Recipients Serves a Public Purpose." *Harvard Law Review*, June 1971, pp. 1921+.

665. McLaughlin, Robert L. "Banks and Banking – Housing and Home Finance – Scope of Insurance Coverage of Banks under National Housing Act." *Michigan Law Review*, February 1960, pp. 586-588.

666. U.S. Congress. House. Committee on Banking and Currency. *Emergency Home Finance Act of 1970. Report Together with Additional Views and Individual Views to Accompany H.R. 17495.* Washington, D.C., 1970. 34pp.

667. U.S. Congress. House. Committee on Banking and Currency. *Emergency Home Financing: Hearings, February 2-25, 1970.* Washington, D.C.: Government Printing Office, 1970. 777pp.

668. U.S. Congress. Senate. Committee on Banking and Currency. *The Emergency Home Financing Act of 1970; Report. . . .* Washington, D.C.: Government Printing Office, 1970. 52pp.

669. U.S. Congress. Senate. Committee on Banking, Housing and Urban Affairs. Subcommittee on Housing and Urban Affairs. *Housing Institutions Modernization Act of 1971. Hearings, Ninety-second Congress, First Session, on S. 1617 . . . October 13, 14, and 15, 1971.* Washington, D.C.: Government Printing Office, 1971. 280pp.

See also: 2332, 2382.

## D. TAXATION AND HOUSING

### 1. GENERAL

670. Genung, George R., Jr. *Taxes, Housing, and Urban Renewal.* Washington, D.C.: National Association of Housing and Redevelopment Officials, 1969. 22pp.

671. Rusoff, L.R. "Rent Determination and Its Tax Treatment." *Fordham Law Review*, December 1960, pp. 211+.

672. Stocker, Frederic D. "Effects of Taxation on Urban Land Use." *Appraisal Journal*, January 1971, pp. 57-69.

673. Sunley, Emil M., Jr. "Tax Advantages of Homeownership Versus Renting: A Cause of Suburban Migration?" In National Tax Association. *Proceedings of the Sixty-Third Annual Conference on Taxation, Honolulu, Hawaii, September 20-25, 1970.* Columbus, Ohio: National Tax Association, 1971, pp. 377-392.

See also: 1443, 1583; Condominiums–Taxation: 1569+; Mobil Homes–Taxation: 1663+.

2. TAX INCENTIVES

674. Citizens' Housing and Planning Council of New York, Inc. Committee on Tax Policies. *How Tax Exemption Broke the Housing Deadlock in New York City: A Report of a Study of the Post World War I Housing Shortage and the Various Efforts to Overcome It, with Particular Emphasis on the Four-Year Period of 1921–1924, during which Limited Exemption was Granted from Local Taxation for all New Buildings Intended Exclusively for Dwelling Purposes.* New York, 1960. 82pp.

675. "Depreciation Deduction on Used Residential Housing, Turnover Rates in Slum Housing Ownership, and the Tax Reform Act of 1969." *University of Cincinnati Law Review*, Summer 1969, pp. 539+.

676. Gabinet, L. and R.J. Coffey. "Housing Partnerships: Shelters from Taxes and Shelters for People." *Case Western Reserve Law Review*, August 1969, pp. 723+.

677. Gilhooly, J.R. "Low Income Housing Projects: Sales and Taxfree Reinvestments; The New Rules." *New York University Institute on Federal Taxation*, 1971, pp. 1069+.

678. Grey, Francis J. "Real Estate Shelters and Tax Reform." *Real Estate Review*, Summer 1971, pp. 19-25.

679. Groom, Theodore R. "Capital Gains for Builders of Residential Subdivisions." *Maryland Law Review*, Spring 1961, pp. 99-122.

680. Guido, K.J., Jr. "Impact of the Tax Reform Act of 1969 on the Supply of Adequate Housing." *Vanderbilt Law Review*, March 1972, pp. 289+.

681. Halperin, J.Y. and S.F. Tucker. "Low Income Housing (FHA 236) Programs; One of Few Tax Shelter Opportunities Left." *Journal of Taxation*, January 1972, pp. 2-7.

682. Halperin, J.Y. and S.F. Tucker. "Tax Consequences of Operating Low Income Housing (FHA 236) Programs." *Journal of Taxation*, February 1972, pp. 80-87.

683. Karp, Arnold L. "Tax Advantages for the Apartment House Investor." *National Real Estate Investor*, March 1972, p. 50.

684. Kroncke, Charles O. and Karel J. Clettenberg. "Depreciating Residential Property under the New Tax Rules." *Real Estate Review*, Summer 1972, pp. 49-51.

685. Laidler, D. "Income Tax Incentives for Owner Occupied Housing." In Arnold C. Harberger and Martin J. Bailey (eds.). *Taxation of Income from Capital.* Washington, D.C.: The Brookings Institution, 1969, pp. 50-76.

686. Lewis, Jerome Russell. *The Effects of Housing Tax Incentive Schemes on the Housing Market and Revenues of the City of New York.* Ann Arbor, Mich.: University Microfilms, 1969 (Ph.D. dissertation, New York University, 1968). 145pp. (order no. 69-11,822)

687. Malkan, Willard. "Who Gets What in a Tax-Shelter Syndicate." *Real Estate Review*, Fall 1972, pp. 26-31.

688. McKenna, William F. "Tax Reform and Depreciation Allowances." *National League Journal*, October 1969, pp. 9-11+.

689. Ritter, C. Willis and Emil Sunley, Jr. "Real Estate and Tax Reform: An Analysis and Evaluation of the Real Estate Provisions of the Tax Reform Act of 1969." *Maryland Law Review*, Winter 1970, pp. 5-48.

690. Robinson, Gerald J. "The Syndication of Low- and Moderate-Income Housing – Federal Tax Aspects." *The Practical Lawyer*, February 1972, pp. 15-36.

691. Schwartz, Sheldon. "How to Find Tax Shelter as a Limited Partner." *Real Estate Review*, Summer 1971, pp. 54-60.

692. Sexton, J.J. "Working with the New Tax Deferral Provision on Low-Income Housing." *Journal of Taxation*, June 1970, pp. 370+.

693. *Subsidized Housing: Tax and Profit Opportunities in Selling and Buying.* Lewis R. Kaster and Stanley Berman, chairmen. New York: Practising Law Institute, 1971. 544pp.

694. U.S. Congress. Senate. Committee on Finance. *Tax Incentives to Encourage Housing in Urban Poverty Areas. Hearings. . . .* Washington, D.C.: Government Printing Office, 1967. 478pp.

695. Wallace, James Edward. "A Critique of Federal Income Tax Incentives in the Development and Operation of Subsidized Rental Housing." Unpublished Ph.D dissertation, Massachusetts Institute of Technology, 1972. 400pp.

696. Wallace, James E. "Federal Income Tax Incentives in Low- and Moderate-Income Rental Housing." In U.S. Congress. Joint Economic Committee. *The Economics of Federal Subsidy Programs: A Compendium of Papers Submitted to the Joint Economic Committee: Part 5 – Housing Subsidies.* Washington, D.C.: Government Printing Office, 1972, pp. 676-705.

697. Watson, Norman V. *Financial Incentives and HUD Assisted Housing.* Washington, D.C.: U.S. Department of Housing and Urban Development, 1971. 17pp.

See also: 2621; Rehabilitation – Tax Incentives: 2977+.

3. THE INCOME TAX AND HOUSING

698. Aaron, Henry. "Income Taxes and Housing." *American Economic Review,* December 1970, pp. 789-806. Also in George Sternleib and Lynne Sagalyn (eds.). *Housing: 1970–1971; An AMS Anthology.* New York: AMS Press, 1972, pp. 503-519.

699. Askari, Hossein. "Federal Taxes and the Internal Rate of Return on Owner Occupied Housing." *National Tax Journal,* March 1972, pp. 101-105.

700. Blum, Walter J. and Allison Dunham. "Income Tax Law and Slums: Some Further Reflections." *Columbia Law Review,* April 1960, pp. 447-453. Sporn, Arthur D. "Slums and the Income Tax: A Brief Rejoinder," pp. 454-457.

701. Brown, Robert Kevin. "Basic Tax Aspects of Real Estate Investments." *Business and Economic Review,* November 1970, pp. 2-10.

702. "Effect of Federal Income Taxation on Housing." *Notre Dame Lawyer,* Fall 1969, pp. 107+.

703. Feder, Arthur. "How Real Estate Is Faring under the Federal Income Tax." *Real Estate Review,* Spring 1972, pp. 44-51.

704. "Federal Income Taxation and Urban Housing." In U.S. National Commission on Urban Problems. *Building the American City.* Washington, D.C.: Government Printing Office, 1969, pp. 399-407.

705. Goode, Richard. "Imputed Rent of Owner Occupied Dwellings under the Income Tax." *Journal of Finance,* December 1969, pp. 504-530.

706. Higgins, J. Warren. *Impact of Federal Taxation on Real Estate Decisions.* Storrs, Conn.: Center for Real Estate and Urban Economic Studies, University of Connecticut, 1971. 66pp. (CREUES Real Estate Report No. 11)

707. Kindahl, J.K. "Housing and the Federal Income Tax." *National Tax Journal,* December 1960, pp. 376-382.

708. Laidler, David. "The Effects of Federal Dwellings." Unpublished Ph.D. dissertation, University of Chicago, 1964.

709. Lindholm, Richard W. "Home Ownership and the Income Tax: A Proposed Change." *Oregon Business Review,* September 1969, pp. 1-3.

710. Merz, Paul E. "The Income Tax Treatment of Owner-Occupied Housing." *Land Economics,* August 1965, pp. 247-255.

711. Schoenfeld, M. and S. Steinberg. "Federal Income Tax in Relation to Housing: A Commentary." *The Tax Lawyer,* Winter 1971, pp. 347+.

712. Slitor, Richard E. *The Federal Income Tax in Relation to Housing.* Prepared for the consideration of the National Commission on Urban Problems. Washington, D.C.: Government Printing Office, 1969 (U.S. National Commission on Urban Problems Research Report no. 5).

713. Soelberg, Peer and Norbert Stafaniak. "Impact of the Proposed Tax Reform Bill on Real Estate Investment." *Appraisal Journal,* April 1970, pp. 188-211.

714. Tinney, R.W. "Taxing Imputed Rental Income on Owner-Occupied Homes." In A.B. Willis (ed.). *Studies in Substantive Tax Reform.* Chicago, Ill.: American Bar Foundation, 1969.

715. "Treatment of Gain from Disposition of Rental Property." *Columbia Law Review,* June 1968, pp. 1174-1191.

716. White, Melvin and Anne White. "Horizontal Inequality in the Federal Income Tax Treatment of Homeowners and Tenants." *National Tax Journal,* September 1965, pp. 225-239.

717. Woodbury, Wallace R. "Trends in Property Tax Reform – Effect on Decision Making." *Appraisal Journal,* October 1972, pp. 556-564.

## 4. THE PROPERTY TAX AND HOUSING

718. Barley, Benzion. *The Effects of the Property Tax on Investment in Urban Residential Construction (A Case Study of Manhattan).* Ann Arbor, Mich.: University Microfilms, 1970 (Ph.D. dissertation, New York University Graduate School of Business, 1969). 160pp. (order no. 70-8001).

719. Beck, Morris. *Property Taxation and Urban Land Use in Northeastern New Jersey: Interaction of Local Taxes and Urban Development in the Northeastern New Jersey Metropolitan Region.* Washington, D.C.: The Urban Land Institute, 1963. 72pp.

720. "Better Assessment for Better Cities." *Nation's Cities,* May 1970, pp. 17-47.

721. Bird, Frederick L. *The General Property Tax: Findings of the 1957 Census of Governments.* Chicago, Ill.: Public Administration Service, 1960.

722. Black, David E. "The Nature and Extent of Effective Property Tax Rate Variation within the City of Boston." *National Tax Journal,* June 1972, pp. 203-210.

723. Chen, Yung-Ping. "Present Status and Fiscal Significance of Property Tax Exemptions for the Aged." *National Tax Journal,* June 1965, pp. 162-174.

724. Clettenberg, Karel J. "Multiple Regression Analysis as Applied to the Equalization Process: Case Study." *Land Economics,* February 1972, pp. 90-92.

725. Clettenberg, Karel Joseph. *Real Property Assessment Practices: An Empirical Accuracy Test for Single-Family Residences in Madison Wisconsin, 1970.* Ann Arbor, Mich.: University Microfilms, 1971 (Ph.D. dissertation, University of Wisconsin, 1970). 281pp. (order no. 71-3452).

726. "Coming: Tax Relief for Homeowners." *U.S. News & World Report,* March 27, 1972, pp. 51-54.

727. Cook, B.D. *et al.* "Old Aged Homestead Relief; The Wisconsin Experience." *National Tax Journal,* September 1966, pp. 319-324.

728. David, E.L. and Roger B. Skurski. "Property Tax Assessment and Absentee Owners." *National Tax Journal,* December 1966, pp. 421-426.

729. Davis, Otto and Kenneth Wertz. "The Consistency of the Assessment of Property: Some Empirical Results and Managerial Suggestions." *Applied Economics,* Vol. 1, 1969, pp. 151-157.

730. DeSalvo, J.S. *Effects of the Property Tax on Operating and Investment Decisions of Rental Property Owners.* New York: The New York City Rand Institute, August 1970. 10pp.

731. Gaffney, Mason. "Land Planning and the Property Tax." *Journal of the American Institute of Planners,* May 1969, pp. 178-183. Also in Michael A. Stegman. *Housing and Economics: The American Dilemma.* Cambridge, Mass.: MIT Press, 1970, pp. 186-197.

732. Gottlieb, Manuel. "The Burden of Property Taxation on Homeowners in Milwaukee, Wisconsin." *Marquette Business Review,* Summer 1966, pp. 68-78.

733. Hamilton, Bruce Walton. *The Impact of Zoning and Property Taxes on Urban Structure and Housing Markets.* Ann Arbor, Mich.: University Microfilms, 1972 (Ph.D. dissertation, Princeton University, 1972). 116pp. (Order no. 72-29,789)

734. Heilbrun, James. *Real Estate Taxes and Urban Housing.* New York: Columbia University Press, 1966. 195pp.

735. Hendon, William S. "Discrimination Against Negro Homeowners in Property Tax Assessment." *American Journal of Economics and Sociology,* April 1968, pp. 125-132.

736. Lewis, Henry W. *The Property Tax: An Introduction.* Chapel Hill, N.C.: Institute of Government, University of North Carolina, 1972. 88pp.

737. Lindholm, Richard W. (ed.). *Property Taxation; Proceedings of a Symposium Sponsored by the Committee on Taxation, Resources and Economic Development (TRED) at the University of Wisconsin, Milwaukee, 1965.* Madison, Wisc.: University of Wisconsin Press, 1967. 315pp.

738. Netzer, Dick. *The Economics of the Property Tax.* Washington, D.C.: The Brookings Institution, 1966.

739. Netzer, Richard. *Impact of the Property Tax: Its Economic Implications for Urban Problems.* Research report supplied by the National Commission on Urban Problems to the Joint Economic Committee of Congress. Washington, D.C.: Government Printing Office, 1968. 48pp.

740. Oldman, O. and Henry Aaron. "Assessment-Sales Ratios under the Boston Property Tax." *National Tax Journal,* March 1965, pp. 36-49.

741. Orr, L.L. "The Incidence of Differential Property Taxes on Urban Housing." *National Tax Journal,* September 1968, pp. 253-262. Heinberg,

John D. and Wallace E. Oates. "The Incidence of Differential Property Taxes on Urban Housing: A Comment and Some Further Evidence." March 1970, pp. 92-98. Coen, Robert M. and Brian J. Powell. "Theory and Measurement of the Incidence of Differential Property Taxes on Rental Housing." June 1972, pp. 211-216. Reply (Orr), pp. 217-220. Addendum (Heinberg & Oates), pp. 221-222.

742. Paglin, Morton and Michael Fogarty. "Equity and the Property Tax: A New Conceptual Focus." *National Tax Journal*, December 1972, pp. 557-565.

743. "The Painful Squeezes of Property Taxes." *Savings and Loan News*, October 1971, pp. 39-46.

744. Pickard, Jerome. *Taxation and Land Use in Metropolitan and Urban America*. Washington, D.C.: The Urban Land Institute, 1966. 40pp.

745. Pleydell, A. "New York City's Tax Policies and the Housing Shortage." *American Journal of Economics and Sociology*, April 1960, pp. 225-229.

746. Quindry, K.E. and B.D. Cook. "Humanization of the Property Tax for Low Income Households." *National Tax Journal*, September 1969, pp. 357-367.

747. Rackham, John B. "Valuation of Land: Priority Problem in Assessment Administration." *Assessor's Journal*, October 1969, pp. 3-15.

748. Raine, Jesse E. "Variation in Property Taxation in Tulsa." *Annals of Regional Science*,June 1972, pp. 135-144.

749. Richman, Raymond L. "The Incidence of Urban Real Estate Taxes under Conditions of Static and Dynamic Equilibrium." *Land Economics*, May 1967, pp. 172-180.

750. Rosett, Richard N. "Inequity in the Real Property Tax of New York State and the Aggravating Effects of Litigation." *National Tax Journal*, March 1970, pp. 66-73.

751. Rostvold, Gerhard N. "Property Tax Payments in Relation to Household Income: A Case Study of Los Angeles County." *National Tax Journal*, June 1963, pp. 197-199.

752. Rybeck, Walter (ed.). *Property Taxation, Housing and Urban Growth: With Attention to Tax Reform and Assessment Modernization*. Washington, D.C.: The Urban Institute, 1970. 72pp.

753. Schaaf, A.H. "Effects of Property Taxation on Slums and Renewal: A Study of Land-Improvement Assessment Ratios." *Land Economics*, February 1969, pp. 111-117.

754. Schreiberg, Sheldon L. "Home Ownership for Tenants: A Program to Use Tax-Foreclosed Properties." *Harvard Journal on Legislation*, November 1969, pp. 67+.

755. Shannon, John. "Federal Assistance in Moderninzing State Sales and Local Property Taxes." *National Tax Journal*, September 1971, pp. 379-388.

756. Shenkel, William M. "Computer Assisted Assessments: Potentialities and Implications for the Organizational Structure of Property Administration." In National Tax Association. *Proceedings of the Sixty-Third Annual Conference on Taxation, Honolulu, Hawaii, September 20-25, 1970.* Columbus, Ohio: National Tax Association, 1971, pp. 66-86.

757. Smith R. Stafford. "Property Tax Capitalization in San Francisco." *National Tax Journal*, June 1970, pp. 177-193.

758. Smith, Theodore Reynolds. *Real Property Taxation and the Urban Center: A Case Study*. Hartford, Conn.: The John C. Lincoln Institute, January 1972. 126pp.

759. Solomon, Arthur P. and George E. Peterson. *Property Taxes and Populist Reform.* Cambridge, Mass.: Joint Center for Urban Studies of the Massachusetts Institute of Technology and Harvard University, October 1972. (Joint Center Working Paper no. 16).

760. Stegman, Michael. *Variations in Property Taxes and Investment in Owner-Occupied Housing*. Washington, D.C.: International City Managers' Association, 1968. 44pp.

761. Tax Institute of America. *The Property Tax: Problems and Potentials.* Princeton, N.J., 1967. 494pp.

762. U.S. Bureau of the Census. *Trends in Assessed Valuations and Sales Ratios, 1956-1966.* Washington, D.C.: Government Printing Office, 1970. (State and Local Government Special Studies no. 54).

763. Wittman, Dennis L. "Property Tax Relief: A Viable Adjunct to Housing Policy?" *Urban Law Annual 1972*. St. Louis, Mo.: School of Law, Washington University, 1972, pp. 171-196.

764. Woodbury, Coleman. "National Commission on Urban Problems: Property Tax Recommendations." In National Tax Association. *Proceedings of the Sixty-Second Annual Conference on Taxation, Boston, Mass.,*

*September 29–October 3, 1969*. Columbus, Ohio: National Tax Association, 1970, pp. 89-104.

See also: 833, 2911.

5. COST AND COST-REVENUE ANALYSIS BY HOUSING TYPE

765. Arcadia, California, Planning Department. *A Statistical Comparison of Multiple-Family Dwelling Units and Elementary School Enrollment.* Arcadia, California, 1970.

766. Barton-Aschman Associates. *The Barrington, Illinois Area: A Cost-Revenue Analysis of Land Use Alternatives.* Chicago, Ill., 1970. Summarized in Darwin G. Stuart and Robert B. Teska. "Who Pays for What: A Cost-Revenue Analysis of Suburban Land Use Alternatives." *Urban Land*, March 1971, pp. 3-16. Also in George Sternlieb and Lynne B. Sagalyn (eds.). *Housing: 1970–1971; An AMS Anthology*. New York: AMS Press, 1972, pp. 120-143.

767. Clark, William H. "Apartments and Local Taxes: Are Apartment Projects Really Good Ratables?" *New Jersey Municipalities*, October 1963, pp. 17+. and November 1963, pp.39+.

768. Del Guidice, Dominic. "Cost-Revenue Implications of High-Rise Apartments." *Urban Land*, February 1963, pp. 3-5.

769. Fairfax County, Virginia, Planning Department. *The Housing Study for Fairfax County, Virginia.* Fairfax City, Virginia, 1964.

770. Georgia Institute of Technology. Graduate City Planning Program. *Report of a Study of Housing Developments and Their Effect on County Fiscal Capacity*. Atlanta, 1970. 102pp.

771. Holley, Paul. *School Enrollment by Housing Type*. Chicago, Ill.: American Society of Planning Officials, May 1966. 19pp. (Planning Advisory Service Report no. 210).

772. Kaplan, Ethan Z. *Multi-Family Housing in St. Louis County; A Survey and Evaluation Report.* Clayton, Mo.: St. Louis County Planning Commission, 1965. 53pp.

773. Mace, Ruth L. and Warren J. Wicker. *Do Single-Family Homes Pay Their Way? A Comparative Analysis of Costs and Revenues for Public Services.* Washington, D.C.: Urban Land Institute, 1968 (Research Monograph no. 15). 47pp.

774a. Melamed, Anshel. "High-Rise Apartments in the Suburbs." *Urban Land*, October 1961, pp. 3-8.

774b. Muller, Thomas and Grace Dawson. *The Fiscal Impact of Residential and Commercial Development: A Case Study*. Washington, D.C.: The Urban Institute, 1972. 140pp.

775. Newton, Massachusetts, Planning Department. *Apartment Study*. Newton, April 1971.

776. Passaic Valley Citizens Planning Association. *Garden Apartment Study, Little Falls Township, Passaic County, New Jersey*. Clifton, N.J.: Passaic Valley Citizens Planning Association, 1965. 41pp.

777. Prince George County, Maryland, Economic Development Committee. *A Study of Income and Expenditures by Family Dwelling, Apartment and Business Units and Individual School Children for the Fiscal Year 1963–1964.* Hyattsville, Maryland, 1963.

778. Rolde (L. Robert) Company. *Garden Apartments and School Age Children.* Washington, D.C.: National Association of Home Builders, 1962.

779. Sternlieb, George. *The Garden Apartment Development: A Municipal Cost-Revenue Analysis.* New Brunswick, N.J.: Bureau of Economic Research, Rutgers – The State University, 1964. 26pp. Summary in *Urban Land*, September 1964, pp. 1+.

780. Westchester County, New York, Department of Planning. *School Taxes and Residential Development.* White Plains, November 1971. 87pp.

## E. LAND AND PROPERTY VALUES

### 1. GENERAL

781. Brigham, Eugene F. "The Determinants of Residential Land Values." *Land Economics,* November 1965, pp. 325-334.

782. Brigham, Eugene F. *A Model of Residential Land Values.* Santa Monica, Calif.: The Rand Corporation, August 1964. 91pp.

783. Brodsky, Harold, "Residential Land and Improvement Values in a Central City." *Land Economics,* August 1970, pp. 229-247. Reply (C.T. Haworth and D.W. Rasmussen) with rejoinder, May 1972, pp. 196-198.

784. Gottlieb, Manuel. "Influences on Value in Urban Land Markets, U.S.A., 1956–1961." *Journal of Regional Science*, Summer 1965, pp. 1-16.

785. Hoyt, Homer. "Changing Patterns of Land Values." *Land Economics*, May 1960, pp. 109-117.

786. King, Alvin Thomas. *Land Values and the Demand for Housing: A Microeconomic Study*. Ann Arbor, Mich.: University Microfilms, 1972 (Ph.D. dissertation, Yale University, 1972). 310pp. (order no. 72-22,391).

787. McQuiston, John Mark. *Social Components of Housing Cost in the Western Metropolics.* Ann Arbor, Mich.: University Microfilms, 1970 (Ph.D. dissertation, University of Southern California, 1970). 228pp. (order no. 70-26,530).

788. Mittelbach, Frank G. "Residential Land Values in Los Angeles County." In California Governor's Advisory Commission on Housing Problems. *Appendix to the Report on Housing in California.* San Francisco, 1963, pp. 283-289.

789. Musgrave, John. "Trends in Valuation per Square Foot of Building Floor Area, 1956-68." *Construction Review*, November 1969, pp. 4-12.

790. Papageorgiou, G.J. and E. Casetti. "Spatial Equilibrium Residential Land Values in a Multicenter Setting." *Journal of Regional Science*, December 1971, pp. 385-389.

791. Rubinfeld, Daniel. *Urban Land Prices: Empirical and Theoretical Essays.* Cambridge, Mass.: Joint Center for Urban Studies of the Massachusetts Institute of Technology and Harvard University, June 1972. (Joint Center Working Paper no. 13).

792. Seyfried, Warren K. "The Centrality of Urban Land Values." *Land Economics*, August 1963, pp. 275-284.

793. Urban Land Research Analysts Corp. *Urban Land Value as It Relates to Policy*. Lexington, Mass., 1969. 331pp. (Final Report no. 5)

794. Weiss, Shirley F., Thomas G. Donnelly and Edward J. Kaiser. "Land Value and Land Development Influence Factors: An Analytical Approach for Examining Policy Alternatives." *Land Economics*, May 1966, pp. 230-233.

795. Wenzlick, Roy. "Fifty Years of Land Values." *Real Estate Analyst*, August 1972, Entire issue, pp. 327-342.

See also: Residential Location: 3372+.

## 2. EFFECTS OF RACE ON PROPERTY VALUES

796. Bailey, Martin J. "Effects of Race and Other Demographic Factors on the Value of Single-Family Homes." *Land Economics,* May 1966, pp. 215-220. Also in Alfred N. Page and Warren R. Seyfried (eds.). *Urban Analysis: Readings in Housing and Urban Development.* Glenview, Ill.: Scott, Foresman, 1970, pp. 320-325.

797. Bruner, John M. *The Effect of Racial Integration on Property Values and Real Estate Practices.* Los Angeles, Calif.: Research Institute for Business and Economics, University of California, 1970. 35pp.

798. "Do Nonwhites Really Lower Property Values?" *House & Home,* March 1960, pp. 79+.

799. Dobson, Allen. "Price Changes of Single Family Dwelling Units in Racially Changing Neighborhoods." Unpublished Ph.D. dissertation, Washington University, 1970.

800. Downs, Anthony. "An Economic Analysis of *Property Values and Race* (Laurenti)." *Land Economics,* May 1960, pp. 181-188.

801. Favor, Homer Eli. *The Effects of Racial Changes in Occupancy Patterns upon Property Values in Baltimore.* Ann Arbor, Mich.: University Microfilms, 1960 (Ph.D. dissertation, University of Pittsburgh, 1960). 186pp. (order no. 60-6178)

802. Galchus, Kenneth. "Property Values in an Integrated Neighborhood." *Real Estate Appraiser,* November/December 1972, pp. 15-20.

803. Guttentag, Jack M. "Effects of Integration on Neighborhood Home Prices: The Case of West Mt. Airy." *Federal Home Loan Bank Board Journal,* January 1971, pp. 17-19+. Also in George Sternlieb and Lynne B. Sagalyn (eds.). *Housing: 1970–1971; An AMS Anthology.* New York: AMS Press, 1972, pp. 309-314.

804. Kentucky Commission on Human Rights. *Property Values in Louisville's Changing Neighborhoods: Analyzing the Effect of Minority Entry on Real Estate Values.* Frankfort, Ky., 1967.

805. Ladd, W.M. "The Effect of Integration on Property Values." *American Economic Review,* September 1962, pp. 801-808. Also in Alfred N. Page and Warren R. Seyfried (eds.). *Urban Analysis: Readings in Housing and Urban Development.* Glenview, Ill.: Scott, Foresman, 1970, pp. 310-315.

806. Laurenti, Luigi M. "Effects of Nonwhite Purchases on Market Prices of Residences." In Alfred N. Page and Warren R. Seyfried (eds.). *Urban*

*Analysis: Readings in Housing and Urban Development.* Glenview, Ill.: Scott, Foresman, 1970, pp. 275-288. (Reprinted rrom *Appraisal Journal,* July 1952, 314-329.)

807. Laurenti, Luigi. *Property Values and Race; Studies in Seven Cities.* Berkeley, Calif.: University of California Press, 1960. 256pp.

808. Lomax, D.A. "Valuation in an Infiltrated Neighborhood." *Appraisal Journal,* April 1971, pp. 247-253.

809. Marcus, Matiyahu. "Racial Composition and Home Price Changes: A Case Study," *Journal of the American Institute of Planners,* September 1968, pp. 334-338.

810. Martin, Galen. *A Study of Housing Sale Values in a Changing Neighborhood.* Frankfort, Ky.: Kentucky Commission on Human Rights, 1970.

811. Mullendore, Walter E. and Kathleen M. Cooper. "Effects of Race on Property Values: The Case of Dallas." *Annals of Regional Science,* December 1972, pp. 61-72.

812. Osenbaugh, C.L. "Integrated Housing and Value." *Appraisal Journal,* January 1967, pp. 17-20.

813. Page, A.N. "Race and Property Values." *Appraisal Journal,* July 1968, pp. 334-341.

814. Palmore, Erdman. "Integration and Property Values in Washington, D.C." *Phylon,* Spring 1966, pp. 15-19

815. Palmore, Erdman and John Howe. *Residential Integration and Property Values.* New York: Anti-Defamation League of B'nai B'rith. 1962. (Also in *Social Problems,* Summer 1962, pp. 52-55.)

816. Phares, Donald. "Racial Change and Housing Values: Transition in an Inner Suburb." *Social Science Quarterly,* December 1971, pp. 560-573.

817. Phares, Donald. "Racial Transition and Residential Property Values." *Annals of Regional Science,* December 1971, pp. 152-160.

818. Schietinger, E. Frederick. "Racial Succession and Changing Property Values in Residential Chicago." In E.W. Burgess and D.J. Bogue (eds.). *Constributions to Urban Sociology.* Chicago, Ill.: University of Chicago Press, 1964.

819. Wheeler, Raymond H. *The Relationship between Negro Invasion and Property Prices in Grand Rapids, Michigan.* Ann Arbor, Mich.: University Microfilms, 1962 (Ph.D. dissertation, University of Michigan, 1962). 207pp. (order no. 62-2805).

820. Yarmolinsky, Adam. "Reassuring the Small Homeowner." *The Public Interest,* Winter 1971, pp. 106-110.

3. EFFECTS OF OTHER VARIABLES ON PROPERTY VALUES

821. Anderson, R.J. and T.D. Crocker. "Air Pollution and Residential Property Values." *Urban Studies,* October 1971, pp. 171-180.

822. Bruhn, John A. "Zoning – Its Effect on Property Value." *Appraisal Journal,* October 1969, pp. 555-561.

823. Burns, Leland S. and Frank G. Mittelbach. "Location – Fourth Determinant of Residential Value." *Appraisal Journal,* April 1964, pp. 237-246.

824. Davis, Frederick W. "Proximity to a Rapid Transit Station as a Factor in Residential Property Values." *Appraisal Journal,* October 1970, pp. 554-572.

825. Ingram, David, Jr. "The Effect on Value of Noise Factors." *Appraisal Journal,* July 1972, pp. 420-424.

826. Jaksch, J.A. "Air Pollution: Its Effects on Residential Property Values in Toledo, Oregon." *Annals of Regional Science,* December 1970, pp. 43-52.

827. Kennedy, John and Dennis Hill. "Economic and Environmental Effects of One-Way Streets in Residential Areas." *Appraisal Journal,* October 1971, pp. 562-567.

828. Marcus, Matityahu and Michael K. Taussig. "A Proposal for Government Insurance of Home Values Against Locational Risks." *Land Economics,* November 1970, pp. 404-412. Also in George Sternlieb and Lynne B. Sagalyn (eds.). *Housing: 1970–1971; An AMS Anthology.* New York: AMS Press, 1972, pp. 535-543.

829. Mills, W. Raymond. "House Prices near a Planned Community Center." *Journal of the American Institute of Planners,* May 1968, pp. 192-195.

830. Nourse, Hugh O. "The Effect of Air Pollution on Housing Values." *Land Economics,* May 1967, pp. 181-189.

831. Nourse, Hugh O. "The Effect of Public Housing on Property Values in St. Louis." Unpublished Ph.D. dissertation, University of Chicago, 1962.

832. Nourse, Hugh O. "The Effect of Public Housing on Property Values in St. Louis." *Land Economics,* November 1963, pp. 433-441.

833. Oates, W.E. "The Effects of Property Taxes and Local Public Spending on Property Values: An Empirical Study of Tax Capitalization and the Tiebout Hypothesis." *Journal of Political Economy,* November-December 1969, pp. 957-971.

834. Pleeter, Saul. *The Effects of Public Housing on Neighboring Property Values and Rents in Buffalo, New York.* Ann Arbor, Mich.: University Microfilms, 1972 (Ph.D. dissertation, State University of New York at Buffalo, 1971). 175pp. (order no. 72-10,507)

835. Ridker, Ronald C. and J.A. Henning. "The Determinants of Residential Property Values with Special Reference to Air Pollution." *The Review of Economics and Statistics,* May 1967, pp. 246-257.

836. Schafer, Robert. "The Effect of BMIR Housing on Property Values." *Land Economics,* August 1972, pp. 282-286.

837. Steele, Robert A. "The Impact of Civil Disobedience on Property Values." *Appraisal Journal,* July 1968, pp. 342-352.

838. Vickrey, William. "The Impact on Land Values of Taxing Buildings." In National Tax Association. *Proceedings of the Sixty-Second Annual Conference on Taxation, Boston, Mass., September 29–October 3, 1969.* Columbus, Ohio: National Tax Association, 1970, pp. 86-89.

839. Wall, Norbert F. "Do High-Tension Lines Adversely Affect Surrounding Property Values?" *Public Utilities Fortnightly,* August 31, 1972, pp. 15-20.

## 4. APPRAISAL

840. American Institute of Real Estate Appraisers. *The Appraisal of Real Estate.* 5th ed. Chicago, Ill., 1967.

841. American Institute of Real Estate Appraisers. *Appraisal Terminology and Handbook.* 5th ed. Chicago, Ill., 1967.

842. Bailey, John B. "Market Analysis – Fundamental to Defensible Valuations." *Appraisal Journal,* October 1972, pp. 644-649.

843. Becker, Boris W. "On the Reliability of Multiple Listing Service Data." *Appraisal Journal*, April 1972, pp. 264-267.

844. Benedict, Norman R. "Statistical Analysis – Significance for the Appraiser." *Appraisal Journal*, October 1972, pp. 618-629.

845. Berger, Jay S. "Resolving Confusion in Percentage Adjustment Techniques." *Appraisal Journal*, April 1971, pp. 272-276.

846. Boatwright, Ronald Olan. *The Appraisal of Urban Residential Property: A Theoretical and Empirical Model of Price Determination.* Ann Arbor, Mich.: University Microfilms, 1972 (Ph.D. dissertation, University of Florida, 1971). 196pp. (order no. 72-21,046).

847. Carney, John J. "The Development and Use of Gross Income Multipliers." *Appraisal Journal*, April 1963, pp. 221-227.

848. Dilmore, Gene. "Multiple Regression Analysis as an Approach to Value." *Appraisal Journal*, July 1972, pp. 459-461.

849. Emerson, Frank C. "Valuation of Residential Amenities: An Econometric Approach." *Appraisal Journal*, April 1972, pp. 268-278.

850. Gibbons, James E. "The Appraiser: An Economic Generalist." *Appraisal Journal*, January 1972, pp. 55-67.

851. Gibbons, James E. "A View of the Changing Appraisal Scene." *Appraisal Journal*, October 1972, pp. 529-544.

852. Glaze, B.T. "Relationship of Market Value and Rent; A Market Sample of Single-Family Homes." *Appraisal Journal*, October 1966, pp. 574-580.

853. Guthrie, R. David. "Use of the Income Approach with Known Mortgage or Equity Amounts." *Appraisal Journal*, April 1972, pp. 257-263.

854. Kinnard, William N., Jr. "Counseling Investor-Clients through Mortgage-Equity Analysis." *Appraisal Journal*, July 1972, pp. 356-368.

855. Kinnard, William N., Jr. *Income Property Valuation.* Lexington, Mass.: D.C. Heath & Co., 1971. 510pp.

856. Lessinger, Jack. "A 'Final' Word on Multiple Regression and Appraisal." *Appraisal Journal*, July 1972, pp. 449-458.

857. Love, T.L. "Modular Housing's Impact upon Real Estate Appraisal." *Appraisal Journal*, April 1972, pp. 208-216.

858. McCormack, J.E. "Appraisal of Urban Renewal Property for Moderate-Income Low-Rent Public Housing." *Appraisal Journal*, January 1967, pp. 70-81.

859. Miller, George H. *et al.* *California Real Estate Appraisal: Residential Properties.* Englewood Cliffs, N.J.: Prentice-Hall. 1972.

860. Morrison, D.J. "Cash Flow Valuation and Yield Valuation." *Appraisal Journal*, January 1972, pp. 83-95.

861. Nelson, Roland D. and Arthur J. Pollakowski. "The Effect of Financing on Value." *Appraisal Journal*, April 1972, pp. 279-285.

862. Nowicki, Joseph A. "Appraising in the Ghetto." *Real Estate Appraiser*, September—October 1969, pp. 5-9.

863. Randall, William J. *Appraisal Guide for Mobile Home Parks.* Chicago: Mobile Homes Manufacturers Association, 1966. 57pp.

864. Ratcliff, Richard U. "Don't Underrate the Gross Income Multiplier." *Appraisal Journal*, April 1971, pp. 264-271.

865. Ratcliff, Richard U. "Is There a 'New School' of Appraisal Thought." *Appraisal Journal*, October 1972, pp. 522-528.

866. Ratcliff, Richard U. and Dennis G. Swan. "Getting More from Comparables by Rating and Regression." *Appraisal Journal*, January 1972, pp. 68-75.

867. Ritter, F.A. "An Appraisal of Measures of Residential Land Values." *Economic Geography*, April 1971, pp. 185-191.

868. Shade, P.A. "The Income Approach in Appraising Single-Family Dwellings." *Appraisal Journal*, July 1970, pp. 384-395.

869. Smith, Theodore Reynolds. "Multiple Regression and the Appraisal of Single-Family Residential Properties." *Appraisal Journal*, April 1971, pp. 277-284.

870. Spaeth, Robert L. "Measuring the Cost of Airport Noise: Formulas and Pitfalls." *Appraisal Journal*, July 1972, pp. 412-419.

871. Wendt, Paul F. "Highest and Best Use — Fact or Fancy." *Appraisal Journal*, April 1972, pp. 165-174.

872. White, John Robert. "Values and Valuation Techniques in the Seventies." *Appraisal Journal*, October 1972, pp. 545-555.

See also: 808, 1446, 1447, 1449; Condominiums – Appraisal: 1520-1524.

## F. HOUSING AND RESIDENTIAL LAND MARKETS

### 1. GENERAL

873. Brueggman, William Bernard. *The Impact of Private Construction and Government Housing Programs in a Local Housing Market.* Ann Arbor, Mich.: University Microfilms, 1971 (Ph.D. dissertation, Ohio State University, 1970). 252pp. (order #71-17,968).

874. Cain, Charles E. "The Prospects and Problems for Housing in the 1970's." *Title News,* January 1971, pp. 60-64.

875. Case, Fred E. *Real Estate Market Behavior in Los Angeles – A Study of Multiple Listing Data.* Los Angeles, Calif.: Real Estate Research Program, Graduate School of Business Administration, 1963 (Research Report no. 10).

876. Clifton, Charles Wade. *Toward a Model of the Housing Market.* Ann Arbor, Mich.: University Microfilms, 1971 (Ph.D. dissertation, University of Michigan, 1970). 303pp. (order no. 71-4583).

877. Connett, Russell. "Market Imperfections in the Resale of Residential Real Estate in Park Forest, Illinois." Unpublished Ph.D. dissertation, University of Chicago, 1963.

878. Coons, Alvin E. and Bert T. Glaze. *Housing Market Analysis and the Growth of Nonfarm Home Ownership.* Columbus, Ohio: Bureau of Business Research, College of Commerce and Administration, Ohio State University, 1963. 174pp.

879. Crecine, J.P., O.A. Davis and J.E. Jackson. "Urban Property Markets: Some Empirical Results and Their Implications for Municipal Zoning." *Journal of Law and Economics,* October 1967, pp. 79-100.

880. de Leeuw, Frank and Nkanta F. Ekanem. *Time Lags in the Rental Housing Market.* Washington, D.C.: The Urban Institute, 1970 (Urban Institute Working Paper 112-19). 57pp.

881. Deming, Frederick W. "Restoring the Housing Market." *HUD Challenge,* June 1971, pp. 24-25.

882. "Differences in Tomorrow's Housing Market." *House and Home,* June 1968, pp. 82-89.

883. Fair, R.C. "Disequilibrium in Housing Models." *Journal of Finance,* May 1972, pp. 207-221, 226-230 (with discussion, R.B. Ricks, L. Smith).

884. Farb, Warren Edward. *An Estimate of the Relative Supply and Demand for Substandard Rental Housing in Major U.S. Cities.* Ann Arbor, Mich.: University Microfilms, 1971 (Ph.D. dissertation, Washington University, 1971). 130pp. (order no. 71-19,815)

885. Gat, Daniel. *The Market for Houses: Simple Models of Supply and Demand.* Ann Arbor, Mich.: University Microfilms, 1971 (Ph.D. dissertation, Yale University, 1971). 155pp. (order no. 71-22,167).

886. Goldstein, Gerald S. *Household Behavior in the Housing Market: A Cross-Section Study of Households in the San Francisco Bay Area, 1965.* Ann Arbor, Mich.: University Microfilms, 1971 (Ph.D. dissertation, Princeton University, 1970). 250pp. (order no. 71-14,375).

887. Grigsby, William G. *Housing Markets and Public Policy.* Philadelphia, Pa.: University of Pennsylvania Press, 1963. 346pp.

888. Harris, Britton, *Basic Assumptions for a Simulation of the Urban Residential Land Market.* Philadelphia, Penn.: Institute for Environmental Studies, University of Pennsylvania, 1966.

889. "The Housing Market." *Conference Board Business Record,* April 1962, pp. 6-8.

890. Huntoon, Maxwell C., Jr. and John Kirk. "It's Time to Take the Low-Price Market from the Mobiles." *House and Home,* April 1971, pp. 62-71.

891. Ingram, Gregory K. "A Simulation Model of a Metropolitan Housing Market." Unpublished Ph.D. dissertation, Department of Economics, Harvard University, September 1971.

892. Kaplan, Marshall A. "The Economy and the Housing Market." *Federal Home Loan Bank Board Journal,* May 1972, pp. 22-25.

893. Kirwan, R.M. and D.B. Martin. "Some Notes on Housing Market Models for Urban Planning." *Environment and Planning,* Volume 3, number 3, 1971, pp. 243-252.

894. Klaassen, Leo H. "Some Theoretical Considerations for the Structure of the Housing Market." In *Essays in Urban Land Economics.* Los Angeles, Calif.: Real Estate Research Program, University of California, 1966, pp. 68-75.

895. Koenker, Roger. "An Empirical Note on the Elasticity of Substitution Between Land and Capital in a Monocentric Housing Market." *Journal of Regional Science,* Aug. 1972, pp. 299-305.

896. Lindeman, John Bruce II. *Economic Effects of Low-Income Housing Subsidies upon the Housing Market.* Ann Arbor, Mich.: University Microfilms, 1969 (Ph.D. dissertation, Duke University, 1968). 180pp. (order no. 69-11,947)

897. Lindeman, Bruce. *Low-Income Housing Subsidies and the Housing Market: An Economic Analysis.* Atlanta, Ga.: Bureau of Business and Economic Research, Georgia State University, 1969. 33pp.

898. Meyers, Carol S. *Housing Market Trends: A Brief Commentary.* Washington, D.C.: Washington Center for Metropolitan Studies, 1970. 22pp.

899. Meyers, Carol S. *Housing: Recovery and Need.* Washington, D.C.: Washington Center for Metropolitan Studies, 1970. 18pp.

900. Meyers, Carol S. *Inflation and Housing Opportunities; A Market Analysis with Special Emphasis on the Metropolitan Washington Area.* Washington, D.C.: Washington Center for Metropolitan Studies, 1970. 52pp.

901. Miller, G.H., Jr. "Housing in the 60's: A Survey of Some Nonfinancial Factors." *Federal Reserve Kansas City, Monthly Review,* May 1969, pp. 3-10.

902. Mittelbach, F.G., A. Saxer, and L. Klaasen. "Interregional Differences in Housing Market Acitivities." *Annals of Regional Science,* June 1967, pp. 114-126.

903. Muth, Richard. "Urban Residential Land and Housing Markets." In H.S. Perloff and L. Wingo (eds.). *Issues in Urban Economics.* Baltimore, Md.: Johns Hopkins Press, 1968.

904. Naylor, Thomas H. "The Impact of Fiscal and Monetary Policy on the Housing Market." *Law and Contemporary Problems,* Summer 1967, pp. 384-396.

905. "New Kind of Housing Market?" *Forbes,* October 15, 1968, pp. 27-29.

906. Newman, D.K. "The Low-Cost Housing Market: The Present Decline in Housing Activity Could Be Relieved by an Expanded Program of Low-Cost Housing Construction." *Monthly Labor Review,* December 1966, pp. 1362-68.

907. Ogur, Jonathan David. *The Impact of Colleges and Universities on Local Rental Housing Markets.* Ann Arbor, Mich.: University Microfilms, 1971 (Ph.D. dissertation, Cornell University, 1970). 154pp. (order no. 71-13,813)

908. Olsen, E.O. *The Effects of a Simple Rent Control Scheme in a Competitive Housing Market.* New York: New York City Rand Institute, December 1969.

909. Olsen, Edgar O. "Competitive Theory of the Housing Market." *American Economic Review,* September 1969, pp. 612-622. Reply (Gordon Tullock) with rejoinder, March 1971, pp. 218-224.

910. Racster, Ronald Leon. *The Effect of Public Housing on the Housing Market of a Small Community.* Ann Arbor, Mich.: University Microfilms, 1968 (Ph.D. dissertation, University of Illinois, 1967). 206pp. (order no. 68-8200).

911. Racster, Ronald L., Halbert C. Smith, and William B. Brueggeman. "Federal Housing Programs in the Local Housing Market." *Appraisal Journal,* July 1971, pp. 396-414. Also in George Sternlieb and Lynne Sagalyn (eds.). *Housing: 1970–1971; An AMS Anthology.* New York: AMS Press, 1972, pp. 214-234.

912. *Rental Housing in New York City.* New York: New York City Rand Institute, 1970-. 2 vols. Contents: V. 1. Confronting the Crisis, edited by I.S. Lowry; v. 2. The Demand for Shelter, by I.S. Lowry, J.S. DeSalvo and B.M. Woodfill.

913. Robins, Philip Kenneth. *A Theory and Test of Housing Market Behavior.* Ann Arbor, Mich.: University Microfilms, 1972 (Ph.D. dissertation, University of Wisconsin, 1972). 162pp. (order no. 72-13,106).

914. Schaaf, A.H. "Some Theory and Policy Implications of the Postwar Housing Boom." *Land Economics,* May 1966, pp. 179-187.

915. Schechter, H.B. "Changing Nature of Housing Market and Future Outlook." *Commercial and Financial Chronicle,* January 14, 1965, pp. 170+.

916. Sears, David W. *The WCNY Model: Simulation of a Housing Market.* Ann Arbor, Mich.: University Microfilms, 1971 (Ph.D. dissertation, Cornell University, 1971). 189pp. (order no. 17-667).

917. Smith, George Cline. "Housing in the Seventies: Realism vs. Euphoria." *Real Estate Review,* Spring 1971, pp. 34-39. Also in George Sternlieb and Lynne B. Sagalyn (eds.). *Housing: 1970–1971; An AMS Anthology.* New York: AMS Press, 1972, pp. 57-61.

918. Spelman, Everett C. "The Housing Market – 1971." *Title News,* February 1971, pp. 4-5+.

919. Sumichrast, Michael. "Coming Up – Accelerated Change in the Housing Market." *Real Estate Review*, Summer 1972, pp. 52-56.

920. Sweeney, James Lee. *A Dynamic Theory of the Housing Market.* Ann Arbor, Mich.: University Microfilms, 1972 (Ph.D. dissertation, Stanford University, 1971). 176pp. (order no. 72-6008).

921. "The Twilight of New York's Private Housing Market." *First National City Bank/Monthly Economic Letter*, July 1969, pp. 80-83.

922. U.S. Department of Housing and Urban Development. *Housing Surveys: Parts 1 and 2. Occupants of New Housing Units and Mobile Homes and the Housing Supply*. Washington, D.C.: Government Printing Office, 1968. 152pp.

923. Wullkopf, U. "Leo Klaassen's Model for the Structure of the Housing Market Reconsidered." *Annals of Regional Science*, June 1969, pp. 107-114.

See also: 733, 1215, 1217, 1228, 1636, 3571; Residential Location: 3372+; Apartments – Market Analysis: 1454+; Condomimiums – Market Analysis: 1565-1568.

2. BIBLIOGRAPHIES

924. Kroll (Seymour) and Associates. *The U.S. Housing Market; Bibliography*. Chicago, 1970. 134pp.

925. U.S. Department of Housing and Urban Development. Library. *Housing Markets: Selected References.* Washington, D.C., 1968. 40pp.

3. ANALYSIS OF DEMAND

926. Atkinson, L.J. "Factors in the Housing Market; Income Effects on Housing Demand." *Survey of Current Business*, April 1960, pp. 16-22.

927. Barth, Richard Carl. *A Study of the Demand for Housing.* Ann Arbor, Mich.: University Microfilms, 1966 (Ph.D. dissertation, University of Wisconsin, 1966). 123pp. (order no. 66-1261).

928. Bedrosian, Sarah G. *An Analysis of Demand for Housing with Special Reference to Margaret Reid's Hypothesis of the Housing-Income Relationship.* Ann Arbor, Mich.: University Microfilms, 1966 (Ph.D dissertation, University of Southern California, 1966). 412pp. (order no. 66-11,562).

929. Break, George. "The Sensitivity of Housing Demand to Changes in Mortgage Credit Terms." In *The Economic Impact of Federal Loan*

*Insurance*. Washington, D.C.: National Planning Association, 1961. Also in Alfred N. Page and Warren R. Seyfried (eds.). *Urban Analysis: Readings in Housing and Urban Development*. Glenview, Ill.: Scott, Foresman, 1970, pp. 105-122.

930. Collins, G. Rowland. "Financial Factors in the Demand for Housing." *Residential Appraiser*, April 1960, pp. 3-10.

931. de Leeuw, Frank. "The Demand for Housing: A Review of Cross-Section Evidence." *The Review of Economics and Statistics*, February 1971, pp. 1-10. Also in George Sternleib and Lynne B. Sagalyn (eds.) *Housing: 1970–1971; An AMS Anthology*. New York: AMS Press, 1972, pp. 177-185. Reply (Sherman J. Maisel *et al.*), *Review of Economics and Statistics*, November 1971, pp. 410-413.

932. de Leeuw, Frank and Nkanta F. Eklanem. *The Demand for Housing: a Review of Cross-Section Evidence*. Washington, D.C.: Urban Institute, 1970 (Urban Institute Working Paper 112-14). 42pp.

933. Downs, James C., Jr. "Demand and Market for Housing: The Balance of the Decade." *Appraisal Journal*, Jan. 1972, pp. 103-113.

934. G.E. Tempo. "United States Housing Needs, 1968-1978." In U.S. President's Committee on Urban Housing. *Report: Technical Studies, Volume I*. Washington, D.C.: Government Printing Office, 1967, pp. 1-36.

935. Gervis, Guy. "Toward the Fulfillment of Housing Demand." *Building*, May 14, 1971, pp. 82-85.

936. Gladstone (Robert) and Associates. "The Outlook for United States Housing Needs." In U.S. President's Committee on Urban Housing. *Report: Technical Studies, Volume I*. Washington, D.C.: Government Printing Office, 1967, pp. 37-102.

937. Goulet, Peter Gregory. *Discriminant Analysis of Low-Cost Housing Alternatives: A Study of Non-Price Factors Influencing Choice Decision*. Ann Arbor, Mich.: University Microfilms, 1971 (Ph.D. dissertation, Ohio State University, 1970). 129pp. (order no. 71-18,011).

938. Grebler, Leo and Tom Doyel. "Effect of Industry Structure and Government Policies on Housing Demand and Cyclical Stability: Study of 1966 Experience." Unpublished paper, 1969.

939. Hartman, Robert W. "Demand for the Stock of Non-Farm Housing." Unpublished doctoral dissertation, Harvard University, 1964.

940. Hinshaw, Mark and Kathryn Allott. "Environmental Preferences of Future Housing Consumers." *Journal of the American Institute of Planners*, March 1972, pp. 102-107.

941. Huang, David. "Effects of Different Credit Policies on Housing Demand." Unpublished paper, 1969.

942. Jones, Oliver H. "Housing Requirements of the 1970's." *Business Economics*, September 1970, pp. 44-46.

943. Hartman, Arthur E. "New Evidence on the Demand for Housing." *The Southern Economic Journal*, April 1972, pp. 525-530.

944. Keith, Nathaniel S. "An Assessment of National Housing Needs." *Law and Contemporary Problems*, Spring 1967, pp. 209-219.

945. Kenshaw, Edward F. "The Demand for Housing in the Mid-1970's." *Land Economics*, August 1971, pp. 249-255.

946. Kristof, Frank S. *Urban Housing Needs through the 1980's: An Analysis and Projection.* Prepared for the consideration of the National Commission on Urban Problems. Washington, D.C.: Government Printing Office, 1968. 92pp. (National Commission on Urban Problems Research Report no. 10).

947. Lange, Irene. *Potential Market for New Housing.* Fullerton, Calif.: School of Business Administration and Economics, California State College at Fullerton, 1968. 81*l*.

948. League of Women Voters. *Needed: Six Million Homes.* Washington, D.C., 1968.

949. Lee, T.H. "Demand for Housing: A Cross-Section Analysis." *Review of Economics and Statistics*, May 1963, pp. 190-196.

950. Lee, T.H. "The Stock Demand Elasticities of Non-Farm Housing." *Review of Economics and Statistics*, February 1964, pp. 82-89. Discussion (R.F. Muth), November 1965, pp. 447-449. Rejoinder, November 1967, pp. 640-642.

951. Maisel, Sherman J. "Changes in the Rate and Components of Household Formation." *Journal of the American Statistical Association*, June 1960, pp. 268-283.

952. Maisel, Sherman J. "Rates of Ownership, Mobility and Purchase." In *Essays in Urban Land Economics.* Los Angeles, Calif.: Real Estate Research Program, University of California, 1966, pp. 76-107.

953. Marcin, Thomas C. *Projections of Demand for Housing by Type of Unit and Region.* Washington, D.C.: Government Printing Office, May 1972 (Agricultural Handbook no. 428).

954. Marcin, Thomas Casimer. *Simulated Long-Run Housing Requirements by Type and Region.* Ann Arbor, Mich.: University Microfilms, 1971 (Ph.D. dissertation, Michigan State University, 1970). 199pp. (order no. 71-2113).

955. Martin, Preston. "Aggregate Housing Demand: Test Model, Southern California." *Land Economics,* November 1966, pp. 503-513.

956. McAllister, D. "The Demand for Rental Housing: An Investigation of Some Demographic and Economic Determinants." *Annals of Regional Science,* June 1967, pp. 127-142.

957. "Meet the Market: Sales Booming under $25,000." *Professional Builder,* September 1970, pp. 89-93.

958. Menchik, M. "Residential Environmental Preferences and Choice: Empirically Validating Preference Measures." *Environment and Planning,* Vol. 4, no. 4, 1972, pp. 445-458.

959. Michelson, W. "Potential Candidates for the Designers' Paradise, A Social Analysis from a Nationwide Survey." *Social Forces,* December 1967, pp. 190-196.

960. Miller, Glenn H., Jr. "Some Demographic Influences on the Future Market for Housing." *Federal Reserve Kansas City, Monthly Review,* November 1969, pp. 3-9.

961. Muth, Richard F. "The Demand for Non-Farm Housing." In Arnold C. Harberger (ed.). *The Demand for Durable Goods.* Chicago, Ill.: University of Chicago Press, 1960, pp. 29-96. Also in Alfred N. Page and Warren R. Seyfried (eds.). *Urban Analysis: Readings in Housing and Urban Development.* Glenview, Ill.: Scott, Foresman, 1970, pp. 146-165.

926. Muth, Richard F. "The Derived Demand for Urban Residential Land." *Urban Studies,* October 1971, pp. 243-254.

963. Muth, Richard F. *Permanent Income, Instrumental Variables, and the Income Elasticity of Housing Demand.* St. Louis, Mo.: Institute for Urban and Regional Studies, Washington University, 1970. 40pp.

964. Ohls, James C. *A Cross Section Study of Demand Functions for Housing and Policy Implications of the Results.* Ann Arbor, Mich.: University Microfilms, 1972 (Ph.D. dissertation, University of Pennsylvania, 1971). 194pp. (order no. 72-17,407).

965. Peterson, George L. "A Model of Preference: Quantitative Analysis of the Perception of the Visual Appearance of Residential Neighborhoods." *Journal of Regional Science,* Summer 1967, pp. 19-32.

966. Pratt, Robert J.A. "Demand for Housing – 1963." *Residential Appraiser*, November 1962, pp. 8-12.

967. Rapkin, Chester and William G. Grigsby. *Residential Renewal in the Urban Core; an Analysis of the Demand for Housing in Center City Philadelphia, 1957 to 1970, with Reference to the Washington Square East Redevelopment Area.* Philadelphia, Pa.: University of Pennsylvania Press, 1960.

968. Renshaw, Edward F. "The Demand for Housing in the Mid-1970's." *Land Economics*, August 1971, pp. 249-255. Also in George Sternlieb and Lynne Sagalyn (eds.). *Housing: 1970–1971; An AMS Anthology.* New York: AMS Press, 1972, pp. 235-241.

969. Rich, Stuart U. "New Consumer Profiles and the Changing Housing Market." *Forest Products Journal*, Feb. 1972, pp. 9-12.

970. Ritley, Roger D. "Measuring Demand for Multi-Unit Housing." *Journal of Property Management*, November-December 1972, pp. 269-276.

971. Schechter, Henry B. and Marion K. Schlefer. "Housing Needs and National Goals." In U.S. Congress. House. Committee on Banking and Currency. *Papers Submitted to Subcommittee on Housing Panels on Housing Production, Housing Demand, and Developing a Suitable Living Environment: Part 1.* Washington, D.C.: Government Printing Office, 1971, pp. 1-139.

972. Smith, Wallace F. "The Income Level of New Housing Demand." In *Essays in Urban Land Economics.* Los Angeles, Calif.: Real Estate Research Program, University of California, 1966, pp. 143-178.

973. Straszheim, Mahlon. *The Demand for Residential Housing Services.* Cambridge, Mass.: Harvard Institute for Economic Research, Harvard University, June 1971 (Discussion Paper no. 192).

974. Sumichrast, Michael and Maury Seldin. *Components of Future Housing Demand.* Washington, D.C.: National Association of Home Builders, 1967. 70pp.

975. "The Tremendous Demand for Housing in the Next Few Decades." *Real Estate Analyst*, June/July 1963, pp. 249-259.

976. Uhler, Russell Shelby. *The Demand for Housing: A Comparison of Bayesian and Regression Analysis.* Ann Arbor, Mich.: University Microfilms, 1968 (Ph.D. dissertation, Claremont Graduate School and University Center, 1967). 102pp. (order no. 68-10,552).

977. Uhler, Russell S. "The Demand for Housing: An Inverse Probability Approach." *Review of Economics and Statistics,* February 1968, pp. 129-134.

978. "Underlying Demand Factors in the Housing Market." *Federal Reserve San Francisco, Monthly Review,* November 1961, pp. 230-240.

979. Valentini, John Joseph. *Single Family Housing Investment: A Regional and National Analysis.* Ann Arbor, Mich.: University Microfilms, 1970 (Ph.D. dissertation, University of California at Berkeley, 1969). 122pp. (order no. 70-17,676).

980. Weimer, Arthur M. "Future Factors in Housing Demand: Some Comments." In *Essays in Urban Land Economics.* Los Angeles, Calif.: Real Estate Research Program, University of California, 1966, pp. 179-187.

981. "What the Public Is Buying and Renting in 44 Top Markets." *House & Home,* December 1964, pp. 90-98+.

982. Wieler, Verner Jacob. *Market Responses to Life Stage Needs: A Study of Mid–Life Housing Preferences.* Ann Arbor, Mich.: University Microfilms, 1971 (Ph.D. dissertation, University of Washington, 1970). 214pp. (order no. 71-1039).

983. Williams, J.A. "The Multifamily Housing Solution and Housing Type Preference." *Social Science Quarterly,* December 1971, pp. 543-549.

984. Winger, Alan R. "An Approach to Measuring Potential Upgrading Demand in the Housing Market." *The Review of Economics and Statistics,* August 1963, pp. 239-244.

985. Winger, Alan Richard. *An Approach to the Problem of Measuring Upgrading Demand in the Housing Market.* Ann Arbor, Mich.: University Microfilms, 1961 (Ph.D. dissertation, University of Michigan, 1961). 176pp. (order no. Mic61-2807)

986. Winger, Alan R. "Housing Space Demands: A Cross Section Analysis." *Land Economics,* February 1962, pp. 33-41.

987. Winger. A.R. "Housing Tenure Preferences in the 1970s." *Economic and Business Bulletin,* Winter 1971, pp. 32-36.

988. Zehner, Robert B. "Neighborhood and Community Satisfaction in New Towns and Less Planned Suburbs." *Journal of the American Institute of Planners,* November 1971, pp. 379-385.

See also: 104, 912, 2140, 2142, 2173; Residential Location: 3372+.

## 4. ANALYSIS OF SUPPLY

### a. General

989. Brady, E.A. "A Sectoral Econometric Study of the Postwar Residential-Housing Market." *Journal of Political Economy*, April 1967, pp. 147-158. Reply (L.B. Smith) with rejoinder, March 1970, pp. 268-278.

990. Case, F.E. "Construction and Real Estate Market Interrelationships." *Annals of Regional Science*, June 1967, pp. 143-151.

991. de Leeuw, Frank and Nkanta F. Ekanem. "The Supply of Rental Housing." *American Economic Review*, December 1971, pp. 806-817. Also in George Sternlieb and Lynne B. Sagalyn (eds.). *Housing: 1970–1971; An AMS Anthology*. New York: AMS Press, 1972, 186-201.

992. Gold, Neil N. and Paul Davidoff. "The Supply and Availability of Land for Housing for Low- and Moderate-Income Families." In U.S. President's Committee on Urban Housing. *Report: Technical Studies, Volume II*. Washington, D.C.: Government Printing Office, 1968, pp. 287-409.

993. Howrey, E. Philip. "Simulation and Projection of Metropolitan Housing Conditions." *Socio-Economic Planning Sciences*, October 1969, pp. 219-227.

994. Kamm, Sylvan. "Land Availability for Housing and Urban Growth." In U.S. Congress. House. Committee on Banking and Currency. *Papers Submitted to Subcommittee on Housing Panels on Housing Production, Housing Demand, and Developing a Suitable Living Environment: Part 1.* Washington, D.C.: Government Printing Office, 1971, pp. 263-286.

995. Mayer, Lawrence A. "The Housing Shortage Goes Critical." *Fortune*, December 1969, pp. 86-89+.

996. Mittelbach, Frank G. *The Changing Housing Inventory: 1950-1959.* Los Angeles: Real Estate Research Program, Graduate School of Business Administration, University of California, 1963. 33pp.

997. Mittelbach, F.G., D.M. McAllister, and D.D. Gasparis. "The Role of Removals from the Inventory in Regional Housing Markets." *Annals of Regional Science*, June 1970, pp. 38-48.

998. Olsen, E.O. *Can Public Construction and Rehabilitation Increase the Quantity of Housing Service Consumed by Low-Income Families?* New York: The New York City Rand Institute, December 1969.

999. Powers, Mary G. "Age and Space Aspects of City and Suburban Housing." *Land Economics,* November 1964, pp. 381-387.

1000. Smith, Wallace F. *Aspects of Housing Demand – Absorption, Demolition, and Differentiation.* Berkeley, Calif.: Center for Real Estate and Urban Economics, Institute of Urban and Regional Development, University of California, 1966. 89pp.

1001. Sumichrast, Michael and Norman Rarquhar. *Demolition and Other Factors in Housing Replacement Demand.* Washington, D.C.: Homebuilding Press of the National Association of Home Builders, 1967. 98pp.

1002. Vuchich, Millan I. *Housing Improvement as a Market Process.* Ann Arbor, Mich.: University Microfilms, 1966. (Ph.D. dissertation, University of Pittsburhg, 1965). 139pp. (order no. 66-10,097)

See also: 1605, 1608, 1629; Factors Influencing Residential Construction Volume: 96+; Fluctuations in Residential Construction: 106+.

b. Measuring the Quality of the Housing Stock

1003. Fuchs, R.J. "Intraurban Variation of Residential Quality." *Economic Geography,* October 1960, pp. 313-325.

1004. Kain, John F. and John M. Quigley. "Evaluating the Quality of the Residential Environment." *Environment and Planning,* Volume 2, number 1, 1969, pp. 23-32.

1005. Kain, John F. and John M. Quigley. *Measuring the Quality and Cost of Housing Services.* Cambridge, Mass.: Program on Regional and Urban Economics, Harvard University, 1969. 31pp. (Program on Regional and Urban Economics Discussion Paper no. 54).

1006. Kain, John F. and John M. Quigley. "Measuring the Value of Housing Quality." *Journal of the American Statistical Association,* June 1970, pp. 532-548.

1007. Morris, Earl W., Margaret E. Woods and Alvin L. Jacobson. "The Measurement of Housing Quality." *Land Economics,* November 1972, pp. 383-387.

1008. U.S. Bureau of the Census. *Measuring the Quality of Housing: An Appraisal of Census Statistics and Methods.* Washington, D.C., 1967. 92pp. (Working Paper no. 25).

1009. Wellar, Barry S. and Thomas O. Graff. *Introduction and Selected Bibliography on the Quality of Housing and Its Environment.* Monticello, Ill.: Council of Planning Librarians, 1972 (Exchange Bibliography no. 270).

c. Vacancy Analysis

1010. "Apartment Market Review: A 15-city Report: Vacancies Plague Many Areas." *National Real Estate Investor*, August 1972, pp. 35-37+.

1011. "Does the U.S. Need More Vacancies: Today's Vacancy Situation, by Metropolitan Areas." *House and Home*, March 1962, pp. 52-55.

1012. Farrell, P.J. "The Occupancy Gap." *Journal of Property Management*, July-August 1971, pp. 174-177.

1013. "Housing Units, Vacancies, and Rents by Metropolitan Areas." *Real Estate Analyst*, August 25, 1961, pp. 421-436.

1014. Martini, Catherine E. "Vacancy Rates and the Outlook for the Rental Market." *Journal of Property Management*, Fall 1962, pp. 6-11.

1015. Moore, Robert C. "The Meaning of Vacancy." *Journal of Property Management*, August 1971, pp. 190-191.

1016. "Residential Vacancy Dropping Rapidly." *Real Estate Analyst*, September 13, 1968, pp. 384-394.

1017. Ryan, Caroline Jean. *Intra-City Patterns of Residential Vacancy Rates.* Ann Arbor, Mich.: University Microfilms, 1964 (Ph.D. dissertation, Clark University, 1964). 122pp. (order no. 64-13,157).

1018. U.S. Bureau of the Census. Social and Economic Statistics Administration. *Current Housing Reports: Housing Vacancies.* Washington, D.C.: GovernmentPringing Office, published quarterly with annual edition (H111 series).

1019. U.S. Bureau of the Census. Housing Division. *Vacant Housing Units in the United States: 1956 to 1965.* By Aneda E. France. Washington, D.C.: Government Printing Office, 1966. 38pp.

1020. "Vacancy Dropping and Rents Still Rising." *Real Estate Analyst*, August 31, 1962, pp. 359+.

1021. Wenzlick, Roy. "New Residential Vacancy Figures." *Real Estate Analyst Housing Bulletin*, March 1972, pp. 85-92.

1022. Winger, Alan R. "Inter-Area Variations in Vacancy Rates." *Land Economics*, February 1967, pp. 84-90.

See also: 1038, 3555, 3567, 3568.

5. MINORITIES AND HOUSING MARKETS

1023. Ball, H.V. and D.S. Yamamura. "Ethnic Discrimination and the Marketplace; A Study of Landlords' Preferences in a Polyethnic Community." *American Sociological Review,* October 1960, pp. 687-694.

1024. Boston, John *et al.* "The Impact of Race on Housing Markets: A Critical Review." *Social Problems,* Winter 1972, pp. 382-393.

1025. Haugen, Robert A. and A. James Heins. "A Market Separation Theory of Rent Differentials in Metropolitan Areas." *Quarterly Journal of Economics,* November 1969, pp. 660-672.

1026. Kain, John F. "Effect of Housing Market Segregation on Urban Development." In *Savings and Residential Financing, 1969 Conference Proceedings.* Chicago, Ill.: United States Savings and Loan League, 1969, pp. 88-113.

1027. McEntire, Davis. "The Housing Market in Racially Mixed Areas." In Alfred N. Page and Warren R. Seyfried (eds.). *Urban Analysis: Readings in Housing and Urban Development.* Glenview, Ill.: Scott, Foresman, 1970, pp. 288-296. (Reprinted from *Residence and Race.* Berkeley, Calif.: University of California Press, 1960, pp. 157-171.)

1028. McKenna, Joseph P. and Herbert D. Werner. "The Housing Market in Integrating Areas." *Annals of Regional Science,* December 1970, pp. 127-133. Also in George Sternlieb and Lynne Sagalyn (eds.). *Housing: 1970–1971; An AMS Anthology.* New York: AMS Press, 1972, pp. 315-321.

1029. "Minority Housing: a Puzzling Market Starts to Shape Up." *House & Home,* February 1965, pp. 76-83.

1030. Rapkin, Chester and William G. Grigsby. *The Demand for Housing in Eastwick; A Presentation of Estimates and Forecasts, Including Methods and Techniques for Analyzing the Housing Market in a Large Scale Open Occupancy Redevelopment area.* Philadelphia, Pa.: Redevelopment Authority of the City of Philadelphia, 1960. 83pp.

1031. Rapkin, Chester and William G. Grigsby. *The Demand for Housing in Racially Mixed Areas: A Study of the Nature of Neighborhood Change.* Berkeley, Calif.: University of California Press, 1960. 177pp.

1032. Rapkin, Chester. "The Heart of the Matter: More Housing for Negroes: Appraisal of the Growth of the Negro Middle Class and the Great Market for Housing Which It Represents." *Mortgage Banker,* February 1964, pp. 21-25.

1033. Rhode Island Commission Against Discrimination. *Study of Housing Needs of Non-White Families in Rhode Island.* Providence, 1960.

1034. Smolensky, Eugene, Selwyn Becker and Harvey Molotch. "The Prisoner's Dilemma and Ghetto Expansion." *Land Economics,* November 1968, pp. 419-430. Cohen, Benjamin. "Another Theory of Residential Segregation." *Land Economics,* August 1971, pp. 314-315.

1035. Zelder, R.E. "Racial Segregation in Urban Housing Markets." *Journal of Regional Science,* April 1970, pp. 93-105. Reply (Thomas A. Reiner) with rejoinder, April 1972, pp. 137-153.

See also: 1698, 3415; Race as a Factor in Housing Costs: 324+.

## 6. SURVEYS OF SPECIFIC GEOGRAPHIC AREAS

1036. ACTION-Housing, Inc. *The Demand for Lower-Middle Income Houses for Sale in Pennsylvania.* Pittsburgh, Pa.: ACTION-Housing Inc., 1965. 16pp. (Technical Report no. 2).

1037. Anderson, Richard T., David A. Johnson, and Dick Netzer. "Housing Opportunities: An Analysis of New York City and Its Northern and Eastern Suburbs for the New York State Urban Development Corporation." *Regional Plan News,* September 1969, entire issue.

1038. Carman, James M. *Vacancy and Turnover in Alameda County – Characteristics of Rental Housing and Population Mobility 1967-1968.* Berkeley, Calif.: Center for Real Estate and Urban Economics, University of California, 1969. (Center for Real Estate and Urban Economics Technical Report no. 2).

1039. Fischer, Robert B. and Michael H. Ballot. *Chico Housing Market: An Economic Analysis of Factors Affecting the Supply and Demand for Housing in the Greater Chico Area.* Chico, Calif.: Center for Business and Economic Research, Chico State College, 1970. 96pp.

1040. Hammer and Company Associates. *Analysis of the Housing Market of the Baltimore Region.* Washington, D.C., 1964. 64pp.

1041. Hoffman (Morton) and Company. *Housing Market Analysis, Baltimore City, 1964-1980.* Baltimore, Md.: Morton Hoffman and Company, 1965. 142pp. Prepared for Baltimore Urban Renewal and Housing Agency.

1042. Manheim, Uriel. *The Pittsburgh Housing Market at Mid-Decade.* Pittsburgh, Pa.: ACTION-Housing, Inc., 1965. 30pp. (Technical Report no. 3).

1043. Manni, Vicki Lee and Russell L. Connett. *Multifamily Inventory and Vacancy Study, Arcata, Eureka, Fortuna & McKinleyville, 1966.* Arcata, Calif.: Division of Business, Humboldt State College, 1966. 45pp.

1044. Market Metrics. *Analysis of the Montgomery County Housing Stock.* By Eugene B. Sieminski. Silver Spring, Md., 1970.

1045. Maryland Planning Department and Baltimore Regional Planning Council. *Analysis of the Housing Market of the Baltimore Region.* Baltimore, Md., December 1964.

1046. Metropolitan Council on Housing. *A Citizens' Survey of Available Land.* New York, 1964.

1047. Portland Metropolitan Planning Commission. *Portland-Vancouver SMSA Housing Analysis.* Portland, Ore.: Metropolitan Planning Commission, 1965. 88pp.

1048. Smith, Wallace. *Housing Market Data from Census Materials – A Study of California and the Bay Area.* Berkeley, Calif.: Real Estate Research Program, Institute of Business and Economic Research, University of California, 1963. 104pp.

1049. Tsagris, B.E., A. Coskun Samli and Robert M. Roesti. *Housing Market Analysis, Sacramento Metropolitan Area, 1962-1965.* Sacramento, Calif.: Real Estate Research Bureau, Sacramento State College, 1963. 175pp.

1050. Ukeles, Jacob. *An Analysis of Current City-Wide Housing Need.* New York: Community Renewal Program, Department of City Planning, 1965. 72pp.

1051. Vidger, Leonard P. *San Francisco Housing Markets: a Study of Price Movements in 1958-1967 with Projections to 1975.* San Francisco, Calif.: Real Estate Research Program, School of Business, San Francisco State College, 1969. 37pp. California State College, San Francisco. Real Estate Research Program. Occasional Research Report, no. 2.

See also: 900. The Federal Housing Administration has also issued numerous reports on housing markets in specific geographical locations. The HUD field offices distribute reports on areas within their jurisdictions.

## 7. HOUSING MARKET ANALYSIS TECHNIQUES

1052. Associated Home Builders of the Greater Eastbay. *Marketing Research for New Homes and Apartments; Including Comprehensive Case Studies.* Berkeley, Calif., 1971. 97pp.

1053. Cannon, Douglas V. *Market Alert – How the San Francisco Bank Monitors the Urban Housing Market.* San Francisco, Calif.: Federal Home Loan Bank of San Francisco, 1971.

1054. Hardin, David K. "The Home Builders Discover Market Analysis." *Real Estate Review,* Fall 1972, pp. 44-47.

1055. Lippold, Richard W. *Urban Housing Market Analysis.* Prepared for the U.S. Department of Housing and Urban Development. Washington, D.C.: Government Printing Office, 1967. 100pp.

1056. "Market Research." *House & Home,* May 1972, pp. 102-105.

1057. U.S. Department of Housing and Urban Development. Federal Housing Administration. *FHA Techniques of Housing Market Analysis.* Reprinted and revised August 1970. By Stanley W. Kadow and Frank A. Mucha. Washington, D.C.: Government Printing Office, 1970. 299pp.

## G. HOUSING WITHIN THE NATIONAL ECONOMY

1058. Burns, Leland S. *et al. Housing: Symbol and Shelter.* Los Angeles, Calif.: International Housing Productivity Study, Graduate School of Business Administration, University of California, 1970. 148pp.

1059. Burns, Leland S. "Housing as Social Overhead Capital." In *Essays in Urban Land Economics.* Los Angeles, Calif.: Real Estate Research Program, University of California, 1966, pp. 3-30.

1060. Federal Reserve Bank of Boston. *Housing and Monetary Policy: Proceedings of the Monetary Conference, Melvin Village, New Hampshire, October 1970.* Boston, 1970. 139pp.

1061. Fergusson, Donald A. and Raymond F. Valenti. "Housing in a Growth Economy." *Land Economics,* February 1962, pp. 9-19.

1062. Grebler, Leo. *Housing Issues in Economic Stabilization Policy.* New York: National Bureau of Economic Research, 1960. 129pp. (Occasional Paper no. 72).

1063. "How Housing Can Cope with Permanent Inflation." *House & Home,* October 1970, pp. 64-72.

1064. Johnson, Byron L. "Is Housing Productive?" *Land Economics,* February 1964, pp. 92-94.

1065. Kaplan, Marshall A. "Prospects for Housing and the Economy." *Federal Home Loan Bank Board Journal,* January 1971, pp. 5-8.

1066. Keyserling, Leon H. *The Coming Crisis in Housing and Its Adverse Impact upon Economic Growth and Employment.* Washington, D.C.: Conference on Economic Progress, December 1972.

1067. Keyserling, Leon H. "The Economy and Housing – Tomorrow and the Next Day." *Title News,* January 1971, pp. 17-21.

1068. Maisel, Sherman J. "Economic Problems of Housing." *International Social Science Journal,* no. 4, 1965, pp. 693-696.

1069. Pierce, James L. and Mary Graves. *Insulating Housing: The Effects Upon Economic Stabilization Policy.* Washington, D.C.: U.S. Board of Governors of the Federal Reserve System, 1971. 22pp. (Studies of Short Term Cycles in Housing Production no. 23)

1070. Young, Allan H. *et al.* "Residential Capital in the U.S. 1925-70." *Survey of Current Business,* November 1971, pp. 16-27.

## II. LEGAL FRAMEWORK

### A. GENERAL

1071. Bartke, R.W. "Organized Bar in Housing and Urban Development." *Urban Lawyer,* Spring 1972, pp. 206+.

1072. Bourdeaux, T.D. "Representing the Subsidized Housing Sponsor." *Mississippi Law Journal,* Summer 1971, pp. 346+.

1073. *Handbook on Housing Law.* Chicago, Ill.: National Institute for Education in Law and Poverty, Northwestern School of Law, 1969. 987pp.

1074. Lashly, J.H. "The Role of the Lawyer in Urban Housing." *Urban Lawyer,* Fall 1969, pp. 330-335.

1075. "The Lawyer in Housing, Urban Development: Selected Edited Proceedings, American Bar Association National Seminar: St. Louis, Missouri, April 21-22, 1971." *Urban Lawyer,* Spring 1972, pp. 223-340.

1076. Morris, E.J. "Role of the Lawyer in Housing and Urban Development." *Oklahoma Bar Journal,* December 25, 1965, pp. 2345+.

1077. National Housing and Development Law Project. *Handbook on Housing Law.* Berkeley, Calif.: National Housing and Development Law Project, Earl Warren Legal Institute, University of California, 1969. 2 vols.

1078. Krasnowiecki, Jan Z. *Cases and Materials on Housing and Urban Development.* St. Paul, Minn.: West Publishing Co., 1969. 697pp.

1079. Krasnowiecki, Jan. *Model State Housing Societies Law.* Prepared for the Environmental Control Administration. Washington, D.C.: Government Printing Office, 1970. 62pp. (Public Health Service Publication no. 2025)

1080. Rosenstein, Barney. "The Title I Housing Program: An Instrument for Social Progress and Lawyers Role in It." *Lawyers Guild Review,* Spring 1960, pp. 18-23.

1081. U.S. Congress. House. Committee on Banking and Currency. Subcommitttee on Housing. *Basic Laws and Authorities on Housing and Urban Development.* Washington, D.C.: Government Printing Office. Revised annually.

## B. LIABILITY IN PURCHASE OF DEFECTIVE HOME

1082. Bixby, Michael B. "Let the Seller Beware: Remedies for the Purchaser of a Defective Home." *Journal of Urban Law,* February 1972, pp. 533-564.

1083. "Expanding Scope of Enterprise Liability." *Columbia Law Review,* June 1969, pp. 1084-1105.

1084. "Expanding Scope of Liability in the Home Construction Enterprise." *Land & Water Law Review,* Vol. 5, 1970, pp. 637+.

1085. "Extension of Strict Liability to the Construction and Sale of Buildings in Oregon." *Oregon Law Review,* June 1969, pp. 411+.

1086. "Financing of Building Construction: Liability for Structural Defects." *Boston College Industrial & Commercial Law Review,* Summer 1969, pp. 932+.

1087. Lascher, E.L. "Lending-Institution Liability for Defective Home Construction." *Journal of the State Bar of California,* May-June 1970, pp. 338+.

1088. "Lender Liability for Discovering Structural Defects in New Tract Housing." *De Paul Law Review,* Winter 1969, pp. 394+.

1089. "Liability of the Institutional Lender for Structural Defects in New Housing." *University of Chicago Law Review,* Summer 1968, pp. 739-761.

1090. "Miller v. DeWitt: Architect's Liability for Failure to Supervise Contractor's Methods." *Dickinson Law Review*, Spring 1968, pp. 506+.

1091. "Negligence Liability in Construction Lending: Connor v. Great Western Savings and Loan Association ([Cal.] 447 P 2d 609) and Its Sequel, Bradler v. Craig (264 Adv. Cal App. 507)." *University of San Francisco Law Review*, October 1969, pp. 188+.

1092. Pfeiler, T.A. "Construction Lending and Products Liability." *Business Lawyer*, July 1970, pp. 1309+.

1093. "Products Liability – Real Property – Builder-vendors – The Court of Appeals of California Has Held that the Doctrine of Strict Liability Applies to Home Builders and That Privity of Contract Is No Longer Required to Maintain the Action." *Duquesne Law Review*, Summer 1970, pp. 407+.

1094. Schwartz, W. "Defective Housing: The Fall of Caveat Emptor." *American Trial Lawyers Journal*, Vol. 33, 1970, pp. 122+.

1095. "Torts – Lender Liability for Defects in Home Construction." *Dickinson Law Review*, Summer 1969, pp. 730+.

1096. "Torts – Negligence – Construction Financer Held to Have Duty to Protect Purchasers of Defective Homes against Loss." *New York University Law Review*, May 1969, pp. 639+.

1097. U.S. Congress. Senate. Committee on Banking and Currency. Subcommittee on Housing. *Payment of Claims for Defects in FHA Homes: Hearings, October 17 and 18, 1963. . . .* Washington, D.C.: Government Printing Office, 1963. 157pp.

1098. Valore, J.A. "Product Liability for a Defective House." *Insurance Law Journal*, July 1969, pp. 395+.

## C. HOUSING STANDARDS AND CONTROLS

### 1. BUILDING CODES

1099. American Insurance Association, Building Officials and Code Administrators International, Conference of Building Officials, and Southern Building Code Congress. *One and Two Family Dwelling Code.* Chicago, Ill.: Building Officials and Code Administrators International, 1971. 228pp.

1100. "Analysis of the Probable Impact of the California Factory-Built Housing Law." *Standard Law Review*, May 1971, pp. 978+.

1101. "Barriers Down: The Battle to Modernize the Nation's Building Codes Begins to Pay Off." *House & Home*, January 1972, pp. 30+.

1102. "The Building Code Dilemma: Pros and Cons of Building Codes." *HUD Challenge*, November/December 1970, pp. 21-24.

1103. Building Codes." In U.S. National Commission on Urban Problems. *Building the American City*. Washington, D.C.: Government Printing Office, 1969, pp. 254-272.

1104. "Building Codes and Residential Rehabilitation: Tilting at Windmills." *Columbia Journal of Law and Social Problems*, August 1969, pp. 88-98.

1105. Building Officials Conference of America. *BOCA Basic Building Code. 5th Ed. 1970*. Chicago, Ill., 1969. 483pp. With annual supplements.

1106. Chamber of Commerce of the U.S. Construction and Community Development Department. *Building Codes for Community Development and Construction Progress*. Washington, D.C., 1963. 20pp.

1107. "Closing the Low-Cost Housing Gap: The California Factory-Built Housing Law." *Columbia Journal of Law & Social Problems*, Summer 1972, pp. 469+.

1108. "A Code Writer Discusses Approval Housing." *Modular Housing Industry*, September 1970, pp. 19-21.

1109. "Factory-Built Housing: Statutory Solutions." *University of Chicago Law Review*, Summer 1971, pp. 788-806.

1110. Field, Charles Gersten. "Home Manufacturing and Building Codes: The Confrontation between Technology and Institutional Regulation." Unpublished Ph.D. dissertation, Harvard University. 1971.

1111. Field, Charles. "How Local Building Codes Help Perpetuate the Housing Crisis." *Ripon Forum*, April 1970, pp. 11-16.

1112. International Conference of Building Officials. *Analysis of Revisions to the Uniform Building Codes*. Pasadena, Calif., 1970, 47pp.

1113. International Conference of Building Officials. *Uniform Housing Code*. Pasadena, Calif., 1964.

1114. Knott, Hal. "A State Residential Building Code for Colorado." *Colorado Municipalities*, March 1972, pp. 50-51+.

1115. Lehman, Warren. "Building Codes Housing Codes and the Conversion of Chicago's Housing Supply." *University of Chicago Law Review*, Fall 1963, pp. 180-203.

1116. "The Problem of Codes Is Holding Back the Real Modular Breakthrough." *House and Home*, October 1971, pp. 88-89.

1117. Rhyne, Charles S. "Workable Program – A Challenge for Community Improvement." *Law and Contemporary Problems*, Autumn 1960, pp. 685-704.

1118. Richardson, Ambrose. "Building Codes: Reducing Diversity and Facilitating the Amending Process." *Harvard Journal on Legislation*, May 1968, pp. 587-611.

1119. Robbins, Patricia V. *State Steps to Better Housing: A Look at Uniform Building Codes.* Madison, Wisconsin: Legislative Reference Bureau, 1971. 36pp.

1120. Sanderson, Richard L. *Codes and Code Administration: An Introduction to Building Regulations in the United States.* Chicago, Ill.: Building Officials Conference of America, 1969.

1121. Sanderson, Richard. "Is a Federal Building Code Necessary?" *Building Official and Code Administrator*, January 1971, pp. 12-20.

1122. Sanderson, Richard L. "The Role of HUD and Other Federal Agencies." *Building Official and Code Administrator*, February 1971, pp. 17-20.

1123. Sussna, S. "Building Codes, and Housing." *Kentucky Bar Journal*, December 1971, pp. 401+ and January 1972, pp. 63+.

1124. "Systems Building: Will It Thrive under 13,000 Different Codes?" *Systems Building News*, May 1970, pp. 45-57.

1125. U.S. Advisory Commission on Intergovernmental Relations. *Building Codes: A Program for Intergovernmental Reform.* Washington, D.C.: Government Printing Office, January 1966. 103pp.

See also: 1307.

## 2. HOUSING CODES

1126. ABA National Institute on Housing Code Enforcement, Washington, D.C., 1970. *ABA National Institute on Housing Code Enforcement; Outlines of Presentations.* Chicago, Ill.: American Bar Association, 1970. 30*l*.

1127. Alpern, Anne X. "The Judicial Process in Housing Code Enforcement." *The Urban Lawyer,* Fall 1971, pp. 574-576.

1128. Boggan, Carrington E. "Housing Codes as a Means of Preventing Urban Blight: Constitutional Problems." *Wake Forest Intramural Law Review,* March 1970, pp. 255-266.

1129. Boston, Mass., Municipal Research Bureau. *Costs and Other Effects on Owners and Tenants of Repairs Required under Housing Code Enforcement Programs.* Boston, Mass., 1968. (Background Paper no. 32 for the U.S. National Commission on Urban Problems)

1130. Boston Urban Observatory. *The Impact of Housing Inspectional Services on Housing Maintenance in the City of Boston: A Preliminary Evaluation.* Boston, 1971. 143pp.

1131. Bross, James L. "Law Reform Man Meets the Slumlord: Interactions of New Remedies and Old Buildings in Housing Code Enforcement." *The Urban Lawyer,* Fall 1971, pp. 609-628.

1132. Burke, Barlow, Jr. "Redrafting Municipal Housing Codes." *Journal of Urban Law,* June 1971, pp. 933-954.

1133. Carlton, Richard E. *et al.* "Enforcement of Municipal Housing Codes." *Harvard Law Review,* February 1965, pp. 801-860.

1134. Castrataro, G.J. "Housing Code Enforcement: A Century of Failure in New York City." *New York Law Forum,* Spring 1968, pp. 60-75.

1135. Curry, S. Leigh, Jr. "The Federal Role in Housing Code Enforcement." *The Urban Lawyer,* Fall 1971, pp. 567-573.

1136. Davis, Richard P. "Computer Put to Work to Speed and Improve Housing Code Inspection." *Journal of Housing,* December 1971, pp. 596-598.

1137. Dick, Brett R. and John S. Pfarr. "Detroit Housing Code Enforcement and Community Renewal: A Study in Futility." *Prospectus: A Journal of Law Reform,* December 1969, pp. 61-93.

1138. Economic Consultants Organization, Inc. *Code Enforcement in Westchester County, New York.* White Plains, N.Y., September 1969, 62pp.

1139. "Enforcement of Municipal Housing Codes." *Harvard Law Review,* Fall 1965, pp. 801+.

1140. "Enforcement of the New Orleans Housing Code — An Analysis of Present Problems and Suggestions for Improvement." *Tulane Law Review*, April 1968, pp. 604+.

1141. Ermer, Virginia Boyle. *Street-Level Bureaucracrats in Baltimore: The Case of Housing Code Enforcement.* Ann Arbor, Mich.: University Microfilms, 1972 (Ph.D. dissertation, Johns Hopkins University, 1972). 203pp. (order no. 72-24,961)

1142. Ewing, Edgar M. "Baltimore's Housing Clinic: Substitutes Teaching for Fining Housing Code Violators." *Journal of Housing*, August 10, 1962, pp. 321-324.

1143. "Federal Aid for Enforcement of Housing Codes." *New York University Law Review*, November 1965, pp. 948+.

1144. Gilhool, Thomas K. "Social Aspects of Housing Code Enforcement." *The Urban Lawyer*, Fall 1971, pp. 546-550.

1145. Goldberg, Larry. "Receivers Certificates — Valid First Liens for Slum Rehabilitation." *University of Illinois Law Forum*, No. 3, 1970, pp. 379-391.

1146. Grad, Frank. *Legal Remedies for Housing Code Violations.* Prepared for the Consideration of the National Commission on Urban Problems. Washington, D.C.: Government Printing Office, 1968. 264pp. (U.S. National Commission on Urban Problems Research Report no. 14).

1147. Grad, Frank P. "New Sanctions and Remedies in Housing Code Enforcement." *The Urban Lawyer*, Fall 1971, pp. 577-591.

1148. Greenstein, Abraham J. "Federally Assisted Code Enforcement: Problems and Approaches." *The Urban Lawyer*, Fall 1971, pp. 629-642.

1149. Gribetz, Judah. "Housing Code Enforcement in 1970: An Overview." *Urban Lawyer*, Fall 1971, pp. 525-532.

1150. Gribetz, Judah. "New York City's Receivership Law Seen as Essential Code Enforcement Weapon." *Journal of Housing*, July 1964, pp. 297-300.

1151. Gribetz, Judah and Frank Grad. "Housing Code Enforcement: Sanctions and Remedies." *Columbia Law Review*, November 1966, pp. 1254-1290.

1152. Grigsby, William G. "Economic Aspects of Housing Code Enforcement." *The Urban Lawyer*, Fall 1971, pp. 532-536.

1153. Hill, George. "Housing Code Enforcement and the Courts." *Connecticut Government*, August 1968, pp. 1-3+.

1154. "Housing Codes." In U.S. National Commission on Urban Problems. *Building the American City.* Washington, D.C.: Government Printing Office, 1969, pp. 273-307.

1155. "Housing Codes: Court Determination of Reasonableness." *University of Florida Law Review*, Fall 1970, pp. 195+.

1156. "Housing Codes and a Tort of Slumlordism." *Houston Law Review*, January 1971, pp. 522+.

1157. "Housing Codes and the Prevention of Urban Blight – Administrative and Enforcement Problems and Proposals." *Villanova Law Review*, February 1972, pp. 490+.

1158. "Housing Violations Void Lease – A New Tenant's Remedy." *Washington & Lee Law Review*, Fall 1968, pp. 335+.

1159. Jackson, Schuyler. "Housing Code Inspection Subjected to Some Critical Comments and Some Suggestions for the Future." *Journal of Housing*, November 1970, pp. 530-533.

1160. Jackson, S. "Housing Inspection: A Critical Essay." *Building Official and Code Administrator*, January 1971, pp. 4-8.

1161. Lieberman, Barnet. "The Administrative Process – Housing Code Enforcement." *The Urban Lawyer*, Fall 1971, pp. 551-558.

1162. Lieberman, Barnet. *Local Administration and Enforcement of Housing Codes: A Survey of 39 Cities.* Washington, D.C.: National Association of Housing and Redevelopment Officials, 1969. 73pp.

1163. Mandelker, Daniel R. "Housing Codes, Building Demolition, and Just Compensation: A Rationale for the Exercise of Public Powers Over Slum Housing." *Michigan Law Review*, February 1969, pp. 635-678.

1164. Mandelker, Daniel R. "The Local Community's Stake in Code Enforcement." *The Urban Lawyer*, Fall 1971, pp. 601-608.

1165. Marco, R.J. and J.P. Mancino. "Housing Code Enforcement – A New Approach." *Cleveland-Marshall Law Review*, May 1969, pp. 368+.

1166. Massachusetts State Legislative Research Council. *Report Relative to Housing and Code Enforcement.* Boston, 1970. 116pp.

1167. Mileski, Maureen Ann. *Policing Slum Landlords: An Observation Study of Administrative Control.* Ann Arbor, Mich.: University Microfilms, 1971 (Ph.D. dissertation, Yale University, 1971). 216pp. (order no. 71-29,704)

1168. Moses, Herman. "The Enforcement Process – Housing Codes." *The Urban Lawyer,* Fall 1971, pp. 559-566.

1169. Nassau-Suffolk Regional Planning Board. *New Tools and Agencies for Housing Code Enforcement.* Hauppague, N.Y., 1970. 71pp.

1170. National Association of Housing and Redevelopment Officials. *Housing Code Bibliography.* Washington, D.C., 1972.

1171. Nelson, Lowell. "California Housing Code: Strengthened, Expanded by 1961 Legislative Action." *Journal of Housing,* January 1962, pp. 39-41+.

1172. New York Community Service Society. Committee on Housing and Urban Development. Department of Public Affairs. *Code Enforcement and Housing Maintenance in New York City: A Strategy for Change.* New York, December 1972.

1173. New York (State) Division of Housing. Bureau of Urban Renewal and Community Services. *Housing Codes: The Key to Housing Conservation.* New York, 1960. 3 volumes.

1174. "Nonprofitability as a Defense for Noncompliance with Minimum Housing Codes." *Washington University Law Quarterly,* Spring 1972, pp. 374+.

1175. Novick, Robert E. "The Physical and Mental Health Aspects of Housing Code Enforcement." *The Urban Lawyer,* Fall 1971, pp. 538-545.

1176. Odell, Carolyn J. *Code Enforcement for Multiple Dwellings in New York City.* New York: Community Service Society of New York, 1965. 2 Vols.

1177. "Private Enforcement of Municipal Housing Regulations." *Iowa Law Review,* February 1969, pp. 580+.

1178. Quandolo, Joseph *et al. The Constitutionality of Housing Codes: A Summary of the United States Supreme Court and State Supreme Court Decisions on the Constitutionality of Various Provisions of Housing Codes, with Suggestions Designed to Safeguard the Housing Code in the Event of Litigation.* Washington, D.C.: National Association of Housing & Redevelopment Officials, 1961. 72pp.

1179. "Receivers' Certificates – Valid First Liens for Slum Rehabilitation." *University of Illinois Law Forum,* 1970, pp. 379+.

1180. "Rent Receivership: An Evaluation of Its Effectiveness as a Housing Code Enforcement Tool in Connecticut Cities." *Connecticut Law Review,* Spring 1970, pp. 687+.

1181. Rosen, A. "Receivership: A Useful Tool for Helping to Meet the Housing Needs of Low Income People." *Harvard Civil Rights – Civil Liberties Law Review,* Spring 1968, pp. 311+.

1182. Rosenblatt, Joel. *Discretion as a Variable in Housing Code Enforcement.* Washington, D.C.: Urban Institute, 1970. 40pp.

1183. Santa Clara County, California, Planning Department. *Housing Codes.* San Jose, Calif., November 1970.

1184. Segal, Elliot A. "A Slum Landlord Program – An Essential Ingredient in a Housing Code Enforcement Program." *American Journal of Public Health and the Nation's Health,* March 1968, pp. 446-451.

1185. Slavet, Joseph S. and Melvin R. Levin. *New Approaches to Housing Code Administration.* Prepared for the consideration of the National Commission on Urban Problems. Washington, D.C.: Government Printing Office, 1969. (U.S. National Commission on Urban Problems Research Report no. 17).

1186. Struyk, Raymond J. and Gene A. Hartin. *Systematic Code Enforcement in Houston: A Case Study.* Washington, D.C.: The Urban Institute, November 27, 1972. 51pp.

1187. Teitz, M.B. and S. Rosenthal. *Housing Code Enforcement in New York City.* New York: The New York City Rand Institute, May 1971. 58pp.

1188. U.S. Department of Health, Education, and Welfare. Community Environmental Management Bureau. *Basic Housing Inspection.* Washington, D.C.: Government Printing Office, 1970. 173pp.

1189. U.S. Department of Housing and Urban Development. *Code Enforcement.* Washington, D.C., 1972. 38pp. (Community Development Evaluation Series no. 5).

1190. U.S. Environmental Control Administration. Bureau of Community Environmental Management. *Housing Code Administration and Enforcement.* By Spencer Parratt. Washington, D.C.: Government Printing Office, 1970. 182pp.

1191. U.S. General Accounting Office. *Enforcement of Housing Codes: How It Can Help to Achieve Nation's Housing Goals.* Washington, D.C.: Government Printing Office, 1972.

1192. U.S. National Commission on Urban Problems. *Housing Code Standards: Three Critical Studies.* Washington, D.C.: Government Printing Office, 1969. 108pp. (National Commission on Urban Problems Research Report no. 19) Contents: "The Development, Objective, and Adequacy of Current Housing Code Standards," by E.W. Mood; "Administrative Provisions of Housing Codes," by B. Lieberman; "Inadequacies and Inconsistencies in the Definition of Substandard Housing," by O. Sutermeister.

1193. Van Hoorn, Elisabeth. *Code Enforcement for Multiple Dwellings in New York City: A Survey with Recommendations.* New York: Committee on Housing and Urban Development, Community Service Society of New York, March 1962. 41+pp.

1194. Wall, N.L. "Developments in Municipal Housing Codes." *Public Management,* May 1960, pp. 107-109.

1195. "Warrant Procedure Applicable to Municipal Code-Enforcement Inspections of Private Dwellings and Commercial Structures." *Utah Law Review,* December 1967, pp. 589+.

1196. Watkins, Kent. *Housing Code Standards, Administration and Enforcement.* Washington, D.C.: International City Management Association, 1971. 19pp.

1197. Wendell, Frana Summa. *Code Enforcement: Patterns and Consequences of Landlord Response to Housing Codes.* Ann Arbor, Mich.: University Microfilms, 1971 (Ph.D. dissertation, Fordham University, 1971). 344pp. (order no. 71-27,002)

1198. Westchester County, N.Y. Department of Planning. *Residential Analysis for Westchester County, New York: Interim Report 1, Code Enforcement in Westchester County.* White Plains, N.Y., September 1969. 62pp.

1199. Women's Club of New York, Inc. *Maintaining Decent Dwellings: A Study of Code Enforcement in Five New-law Tenements.* New York, 1963. 20pp.

1200. Wool, Sanford E. "Initiation of Receivership Proceedings in Housing Code Enforcement." In *Urban Law Annual 1968.* St. Louis, Mo.: School of Law, Washington University, 1968, pp. 157-163.

See also: 1115, 1366, 1396, 2170, 2171, 3590; Housing Codes within the Landlord-Tenant Relationship: 1398+.

## 3. RENT CONTROL AND RENT STABILIZATION

1201. Ball, H.V. "Social Structure and Rent-Control Violations." *American Journal of Sociology*. May 1960, pp. 598-604.

1202. DeSalvo, Joseph S. "Reforming Rent Control in New York City: Analysis of Housing Expenditures and Market Rentals." *Regional Science Association Papers, Volume Twenty-Seven, 1971*. Philadelphia, Pa.: Regional Science Association, 1971, pp. 195-227.

1203. Fisher, Ernest M. "Twenty Years of Rent Control in New York City." In *Essays in Urban Land Economics*. Los Angeles, Calif.: Real Estate Research Program, University of California, 1966, pp. 31-67.

1204. Knight, Willys R. "The Postwar Rent Control Controversy." *Atlanta Economic Review*, February 1963, pp. 3-7.

1205. Kristof, Frank S. *People, Housing and Rent Control in New York City*. New York: City Rent and Rehabilitation Administration, June 1964. 209pp.

1206. Kristof, Frank S. "The State's New Rent Control Proposals for the Restoration of Private Residential Construction." *Real Estate News*, May 1971, pp. 14-15.

1207. Lowry, Ira S. *Reforming Rent Control in New York City: The Role of Research in Policy-Making*. New York: The New York City Rand Institute, November 1970. Also in *Regional Science Association Papers, Volume Twenty-Seven, 1971*. Philadelphia, Pa: Regional Science Association, 1971, pp. 183-193.

1208. Lukashok, Edward. "There Is a Way to Stabilize Residential Rents." *Real Estate Review*, Spring 1972, pp. 96-99.

1209. Moorhouse, J.C. "Optimal Housing Maintenance under Rent Control." *Southern Economic Journal*, July 1972, pp. 93-106.

1210. New York (City) Housing and Development Administration. *Report to the Mayor on an Investigation into Rental Increases in the Non-Controlled Housing Market*. New York, February 1969. 109pp.

1211. New York (City) Mayor's Rent Control Committee. *Rent Control and Its Impact on Housing in New York City: Report*. New York, December 1969. 36pp.

1212. "New York Rent Stabilization Law of 1969." *Columbia Law Review*, January 1970, pp. 156-177.

1213. New York (State) Governor's Special Committe to Study the Sales Price Basis and Evictions for New Housing under the Emergency Housing Rent Control Law. *Report.* Albany, 1961.

1214. New York (State) Temporary Commission to Make a Study of the Governmental Operation of the City of New York. *The Management of the Maximum Base Rent (MBR) Administration of New York City – from June 1970 to October 1972.* New York, 1972.

1215. Niebanck, Paul L. *Rent Control and the Rental Housing Market, New York City, 1968.* New York: New York City Department of Rent and Housing Maintenance, Housing and Development Administration, 1970. 213pp.

1216. Olsen, Edgar O. "An Econometric Analysis of Rent Control." *Journal of Political Economy,* November/December 1972, pp. 1081-1100.

1217. Rapkin, Chester. *The Private Rental Housing Market in New York City, 1965: A Study of Some Effects of Two Decades of Rent Control.* New York: New York City Rent and Rehabilitation Administration, 1966. 134pp.

1218. Rasch, Joseph. *Landlord and Tenant, New York City Rent Control, with All Amendments through January 1, 1972.* Rochester, N.Y.: Lawyers Co-operative Pub. Co., 1972. 204pp.

1219. "A Reinstatement of Rent Control." *The Real Estate Analyst,* September 8, 1970, pp. 381-384.

1220. "Rent Control Blight: It Is Threatening to Spread throughout the Nation." *Barron's,* December 1, 1969, pp. 1+.

1221. "Rent Stabilization Law Amended: The Code is Extended to Cover Housing in Residential Hotels." *Real Estate News (New York),* November 1969, pp. 350-353.

1222. "Rent Stabilization Law of 1969." *Brooklyn Law Review,* Winter 1970, pp. 307+.

1223. "Residential Rent Control: Stoneridge Apartments v. Lindsay (303 F Supp 677)." *University of Pittsburgh Law Review,* Spring 1970, pp. 457+.

1224. "Residential Rent Control in New York City." *Columbia Journal of Law and Social Problems,* June 1967, pp. 30-65.

1225. Sardy, Hyman. *Achieving Excellence in New York City's Housing: An Investigation into the Problem of Rent Control.* New York, N.Y.: Community Housing Improvement Program, Inc., 1967. 34pp.

1226. Schwartz, Jeffrey B. "Phase II Rent Stabilization." *The Urban Lawyer,* Summer 1972, pp. 417-432.

1227. Siekman, Philip. "The Rent-Control Trap: The City (New York, N.Y.) Is Caught in a Law That Distorts Its Housing Market and Creates New Slums." *Fortune,* February 1960, pp. 123+.

1228. Sternlieb, George. *The Urban Housing Dilemma: The Dynamics of New York City's Rent Controlled Housing.* New York: New York City Housing and Development Administration, 1972. 748pp.

1229. Walther, James Victor. *Analysis of Rent, Housing and OPA Rent Control with Special Reference to the Residential Housing Occupancy Markets in the City of Denver 1940 to 1960.* Ann Arbor, Mich.: University Microfilms, 1963 (Ph.D. dissertation, University of Colorado, 1962). 330pp. (order no. 63-2025)

See also: 908.

## D. LAND-USE CONTROLS

### 1. GENERAL

1230. American Society of Planning Officials. *New Techniques for Shaping Urban Expansion.* Chicago, Ill., July 1962 22pp. (Planning Advisory Service Report no. 160).

1231. American Society of Planning Officials. *Problems of Zoning and Land-use Regulations.* Washington, D.C.: Government Printing Office, 1968. (U.S. National Commission on Urban Problems Research Report no. 2)

1232. American Society of Planning Officials. *Regulatory Devices: Papers Presented at the Regulatory Devices Short Course Held at the 1969 ASPO National Planning Conference.* Chicago, Ill., 1969. 68pp.

1233. American Society of Planning Officials. *Toward a More Effective Land-Use Guidance System: Summary and Analysis of Five Major Reports.* Chicago, Ill., September/October 1969. 120pp. (Planning Advisory Service Report no. 250).

1234. American Society of Planning Officials. *Toward a Regulatory System: For Use, Occupancy, and Construction.* Chicago, Ill., Feburary 1969. 12pp. (Planning Advisory Service Report no. 243).

1235. Anderson, Robert M. *American Law of Zoning – Zoning, Planning, Subdivision Control.* San Francisco, Calif.: Bancroft Whitney, 1968. 4 vols. + supplements.

1236. Babcock, Richard F. "Suburban Zoning, Housing and the Courts." *Record of the Association of the Bar of the City of New York,* April 1972, pp. 230-235.

1237. Bell, Christopher, Jr. "Controlling Residential Developments on the Urban Fringe: St. Louis County, Missouri." *Journal of Urban Law,* Vol. 48, no. 2, 1971, pp. 409-447.

1238. Bellman, Richard F. and Alice Baker. *Summary of Recent Court Challenges to Exclusionary Land-Use Practices.* Washington, D.C.: National Committee Against Discrimination in Housing, September 1972. 27pp.

1239. Bosselman, Fred P. *Alternatives to Urban Sprawl: Legal Guidelines for Government Action.* Prepared for the consideration of the National Commission on Urban Problems. Washington, D.C.: Government Printing Office, 1968 (National Commission on Urban Problems Research Report no. 15).

1240. Coke, James G. and John J. Gargan. *Fragmentation in Land-Use Planning and Control.* Prepared for the consideration of the National Commission on Urban Problems. Washington, D.C.: Government Printing Office, 1969 (National Commission on Urban Problems Research Report no. 18).

1241. Davidoff, Linda, Paul Davidoff and Neil Gold. "The Suburbs Have to Open Their Gates." *New York Times Magazine,* November 7, 1971, pp. 40+.

1242. Davidoff, Paul and Linda Davidoff. "Opening the Suburbs: Toward Inclusionary Land Use Controls." *Syracuse Law Review,* Vol. 22, 1971, pp. 509+.

1243. Davidoff, Paul, Linda Davidoff and Neil Newton Gold. "Suburban Action: Advocate Planning for an Open Society." *Journal of the American Institute of Planners,* January 1970, pp. 12-22.

1244. Delafons, John. *Land-Use Controls in the United States.* Cambridge, Mass.: MIT Press, 2d Ed., 1969.

1245. Hirshon, Robert E. "The Interrelationship between Exclusionary Zoning and Exclusionary Subdivision Control." *Journal of Law Reform,* Winter 1972, pp. 351-360.

1246. Kristensen, Chris, John Levy and Tamar Savir. *The Suburban Lock-Out Effect.* White Plains, N.Y.: Suburban Action Institute, 1971 (Research Report no. 1).

1247. "Land-Use Controls: Zoning and Subdivision Regulations." In U.S. National Commission on Urban Problems. *Building the American City.* Washington, D.C.: Government Printing Office, 1969, pp. 199-234.

1248. Manvel, Allen D. *Local Land and Building Regulation: How Many Agencies? What Practices? How Much Personnel?* Prepared for the National Commission on Urban Problems. Washington, D.C.: Government Printing Office, 1968 (National Commission on Urban Problems Research Report no. 6).

1249. National Committe Against Discrimination in Housing. *NCDH Program of Litigation and Research to End Exclusionary Land-Use Controls and Other Regulatory Devices Which Block Housing for Low and Moderate Income Families in the Suburbs: Summary Report to the NCDH Board of Directors.* New York, April 1969.

1250. U.S. Advisory Commission on Intergovernmental Relations. "Guidance and Controls for Large-Scale Urban Development and New Communities." In *Urban and Rural America: Policeies for Future Growth.* Washington, D.C.: Government Printing Office, 1968, pp. 107-122.

1251. Williams, Norman, Jr. and Thomas Norman. "Exclusionary Land-Use Controls: The Case of North-Eastern New Jersey." *Land Use Controls Quaterly*, Fall 1970, pp. 1-26. Also in George Sternlieb and Lynne B. Sagalyn (eds.). *Housing: 1970–1971; An AMS Anthology.* New York: AMS Press, 1972, pp. 150-174.

See also: Local Regulation of Mobile Homes: 1669+.

## 2. SUBDIVISION REGULATIONS

1252. American Society of Planning Officials. *Mandatory Dedication of Land or Fees-in-Lieu of Land for Parks and Schools.* Chicago, Ill., February 1971. 44pp. (Planning Advisory Service Report no. 266).

1253. American Society of Planning Officials. *Street Standards in Subdivision Regulations.* Chicago, Ill., February 1964. 12pp. (Planning Advisory Service Report no. 183).

1254. American Society of Planning Officials. *Subdivision Fees Revisited.* Chicago, Ill., September 1965. 16pp. (Planning Advisory Service Report no. 202).

1255. American Society of Planning Officials. *Underground Wiring in New Residential Areas.* Chicago, Ill., October 1962. 24pp. (Planning Advisory Service Report no. 163).

1256. American Society of Planning Officials. *Varying Improvement Requirements in Subdivision Ordinances.* Chicago, Ill., July 1963. 16pp. (Planning Advisory Service Report no. 174).

1257. Cunningham, Roger A. "Public Control of Land Subdivision in Michigan: Description and Critique." *Michigan Law Review,* November 1967, pp. 1-80.

1258. Heyman, Ira Michael and Thomas K. Gilhool. "The Constitutionality of Imposing Increased Community Costs on New Suburban Residents through Subdivision Exactions." *Yale Law Journal,* June 1964, pp. 1119-1157.

1259. "The New Jersey Estoppel Statute in Subdivision Control Administration." In *Urban Law Annual 1968.* St. Louis, Mo.: School of Law, Washington University, 1968, pp. 167-173.

1260. Yearwood, Richard M. "Accepted Controls of Land Subdivision." *Journal of Urban Law,* Vol. 45, 1967, pp. 217+.

1261. Yearwood, R.M. "Land Subdivision and Development: American Attitudes." *American Journal of Economics and Sociology,* April 1970, pp. 113-126.

1262. Yearwood, Richard M. "Performance Bonding for Subdivision Improvements." *Journal of Urban Law,* Vol. 46, no. 1, 1968, pp. 67-85.

1263. Year wood, Richard M. "Subdivision Law: Timing and Location Control." *Journal of Urban Law,* Summer 1967, pp. 585-609.

See also: 37, 71-73, 75-78, 80-84, 86-89, 94, 95, 273, 1245.

## 3. ZONING

### a. General

1264. American Society of Planning Officials. *The Authority of the Zoning Administrator.* Chicago, Ill., September 1967. 17pp. (Planning Advisory Service Report no. 226).

1265. American Society of Planning Officials. *Characteristics of Zoning Appeal Boards.* Chicago, Ill., April 1965. 20pp. (Planning Advisory Service Report no. 197).

1266. American Society of Planning Officials. *Deep Lot Development.* Chicago, Ill., June 1963. 24pp. (Planning Advisory Service Report no. 172).

1267. American Society of Planning Officials. *A Glossary of Zoning Definitions.* Chicago, Ill., April 1968. 27pp. (Planning Advisory Service Report no. 233).

1268. American Society of Planning Officials. *Height Regulation in Residential Districts.* Chicago, Ill., August 1968. 12pp. (Planning Advisory Service Report no. 237).

1269. American Society of Planning Officials. *Illustrating the Zoning Ordinance.* Chicago, Ill., December 1962. 32pp. (Planning Advisory Service Report no. 165).

1270. American Society of Planning Officials. *Interim Zoning Ordinances.* Chicago, Ill., January 1969. 30pp. (Planning Advisory Service Report no. 242).

1271. American Society of Planning Officials. *Zoning Districts.* Chicago, Ill., July 1960. 36pp. (Planning Advisory Service Report no. 136).

1272. American Society of Planning Officials. *Zoning Ordinance Check-list.* Chicago, Ill., July 1969. 27pp. (Planning Advisory Service Report no. 248).

1273. Bair, Frederick H., Jr., and Ernest R. Bartley. *The Text of a Model Zoning Ordinance with Commentary.* Chicago, Ill.: American Society of Planning Officials, 1966. 3rd ed. 100pp.

1274. "The Constitutionality of Local Zoning." *Yale Law Journal,* April 1970, pp. 896-925.

1275. Fisher, Gerald A. "The General Public Interest vs. the Presumption of Zoning Ordinance Validity: A Debatable Question." *Journal of Urban Law,* August 1972, pp. 129-148.

1276. Klain, Ambrose. *Zoning in Suburbia: Keep It, Reject It or Replace It?* Monticello, Ill.: Council of Planning Librarians 1971. 17pp. (Exchange Bibliography no. 180).

1277. Krasnowiecki, Jan Z. "Zoning Litigation and the New Pennsylvania Procedures." *University of Pennsylvania Law Review,* June 1972, pp. 1027-1165.

1278. Lovelace, Eldridge and William L. Weismantel. *Density Zoning: Organic Zoning for Planned Residential Developments.* Washington, D.C.: Urban Land Institute, July 1961 (ULI Technical Bulletin no. 42).

1279. Mandelker, Daniel R. "The Role of Zoning in Housing and Metropolitan Development." In U.S. Congress. House. Committee on Banking and Currency. *Papers Submitted to Subcommittee on Housing Panels on Housing Production, Housing Demand, and Developing a Suitable Living Environment: Part 2.* Washington, D.C.: Government Printing Office, 1971, pp. 785-808.

1280. Pratter, J. and R.C. Ward. "New Concept in Residential Zoning." *Urban Law Annual 1971.* St. Louis, Mo.: School of Law, Washington University, 1971, pp. 133+.

1281. Raymond and May Associates. *Zoning Controversies in the Suburbs: Three Case Studies.* Prepared for the consideration of the National Commission on Urban Problems. Washington, D.C.: Government Printing Office, 1968. 82pp. (National Commission on Urban Problems Research Report no. 11)

1282. Spicer, Richard B. *Zoning for the Elderly.* Chicago, Ill.: American Society of Planning Officials, July 1970. 24pp. (ASPO Planning Advisory Service Report no. 259).

See also: 879, 2189, 3155, 3162; Apartments – Zoning: 1460+; Local Regulation of Mobile Homes: 1669+.

b. Exclusionary Zoning

1283. Aloi, Frank and Arthur Goldberg. "Racial and Economic Exclusionary Zoning: The Beginning of the End?" In *Urban Law Annual 1971.* St. Louis, Mo.: School of Law, Washington University, 1971, pp. 9+.

1284. "The Attack on Snob Zoning." *Savings and Loan News,* November 1970, pp. 30-36.

1285. Babcock, Richard F. "A Watershed in Suburban Zoning." *HUD Challenge,* November 1972, pp. 8-9.

1286. Bass, G. Allen. "The Equal Protection Clause: A Single-Edged Sword for the Gordian Knot of Exclusionary Zoning." *University of Missouri, Kansas City, Law Review,* Autumn 1971, pp. 24-50.

1287. Brooks, Mary. *Exclusionary Zoning.* Chicago, Ill.: American Society of Planning Officials, 1970 (Planning Advisory Service Report no. 254).

1288. Charkoudian, Leon. "Massachusetts' Anti-Snob Zoning Law." *State Government*, Spring 1972, pp. 106-109.

1289. "Constitutional Law–Equal Protection–Zoning–Snob Zoning: Must a Man's Home Be a Castle?" *Michigan Law Review*, December 1970, pp. 339-359.

1290. Cutler, Richard W. "Legality of Zoning to Exclude the Poor: A Preliminary Analysis of Evolving Law." *Brooklyn Law Review*, Spring 1971, pp. 483-500.

1291. Downs, Anthony. "Suburban Housing: A Program for Expanded Opportunities." *Real Estate Review*, Spring 1971, pp. 4-11. Also in George Sternlieb and Lynne B. Sagalyn (eds.). *Housing: 1970-1971; An AMS Anthology*. New York: AMS Press, 1972, pp. 28-34.

1292. Dupuy, Robert A. "Legitimate Use Exclusions through Zoning: Applying a Balancing Test." *Cornell Law Review*, Feb. 1972, pp. 461-475.

1293. "The Equal Protection Clause and Exclusionary Zoning after *Valtierra* and *Dandridge*." *Yale Law Journal*, November 1971, pp. 61-86.

1294. "Exclusionary Zoning and Equal Protection." *Harvard Law Review*, May 1971, pp. 1645-1669.

1295. Freilich, Robert H. and G. Allen Bass. "Exclusionary Zoning: Suggested Litigated Approaches." *Urban Lawyer*, Summer 1971, pp. 344-374.

1296. Jackson, Samuel C. "Attacking the Affluent Islands: A Legal Strategy for the 70's." In *Urban Law Annual 1971*. St. Louis, Mo.: School of Law, Washington University, 1971, pp. 3-8.

1297. Kirby, Ronald F. *et al Residential Zoning and Equal Housing Opportunities: A Case Study in Black Jack, Missouri*. Washington, D.C.: Urban Institute, 1972. 34 pp.

1298. Lazerow, Arthur S. "Discriminatory Zoning: Legal Battleground of the Seventies." *American University Law Review*, September 1971, pp. 157-183.

1299. Lyon, Edward L. "Exclusionary Zoning from a Regional Perspective." *Urban Law Annual 1972*. St. Louis, Mo.: School of Law, Washington University, 1972, pp. 239-244.

1300. Marcus, Norman. "Exclusionary Zoning: The Need for a Regional Planning Context." *New York Law Forum*, Vol. 16, no. 4, 1970, pp. 732-740.

1301. Mayne, Wiley E., Jr. "The Responsibility of Local Zoning Authorities to Nonresident Indigents." *Stanford Law Review*, April 1971, pp. 774-798.

1302. McMahan, Kent H. "Extending Standing to Nonresidents–A Response to the Exclusionary Effects of Zoning Fragmentation." *Vanderbilt Law Review*, March 1971, pp. 341-366.

1303. Monk, Carl C. "The Use of Zoning to Prevent Poor People from Moving into Suburbia." *Howard Law Journal*, Winter 1971, pp. 351-390.

1304. Mullin, Edward J. "Zoning and the House Jack Can't Build." *New Jersey Business*, July 1972, pp. 17-21.

1305. "The New Jersey Judiciary's Response to Exclusionary Zoning." *Rutgers Law Review*, Fall 1970, pp. 172-188.

1306. Nilon, John W., Jr. "The Pennsylvania Supreme Court and Exclusionary Suburban Zoning: From *Bilbar* to *Girsh*–A Decade of Change." *Villanova Law Review*, March 1971, pp. 507-532.

1307. Potvin, D. Joseph. "Suburban Zoning Ordinances and Building Codes: Their Effect on Low and Moderate Income Housing." *Notre Dame Lawyer*, Fall 1969, pp. 123-134.

1308. "Regional Impact of Zoning: A Suggested Approach," *University of Pennsylvania Law Review*, June 1966, pp. 1251-1259.

1309. Sager, Lawrence Gene. "Tight Little Islands: Exclusionary Zoning, Equal Protection, and the Indigent." *Stanford Law Review*, Vol. 21, 1969, pp. 767-800.

1310. Schoenbrod, David S. "Large Lot Zoning." *Yale Law Journal*, July 1969, pp. 1418-1441.

1311. "Segregation and the Suburbs: Low-Income Housing, Zoning, and the Fourteenth Amendment." *Iowa Law Review*, June 1971, pp. 1298+.

1312. Shields, Geoffrey and L. Sanford Spector. "Opening up the Suburbs: Notes on a Movement for Social Change." *Yale Review of Law and Social Action*, Summer 1972, pp. 300-333.

1313. Simmons, P. "Home Rule and Exclusionary Zoning: An Impediment to Low and Moderate Income Housing." *Ohio State Law Journal*, Vol. 33, 1972, pp. 621+.

1314. "Snob Zoning: Must a Man's Home Be a Castle?" *Real Estate Review*, Fall 1971, pp. 68-71.

1315. "State Police Power–Zoning–Validity of Local Ordinance Depends on Considerations of Regional, Not Merely Local, General Welfare." *Vanderbilt Law Review*, March 1972, pp. 466-473.

1316. "A Survey of the Judicial Responses to Exclusionary Zoning." *Syracuse Law Review*, Vol. 22, no. 2, 1971, pp. 537-581.

1317. "Toward Improved Housing Opportunities: A New Direction for Zoning Law." *University of Pennsylvania Law Review*, December 1972, pp. 330+.

1318. Walsh, Robert E. "Are Local Zoning Bodies Required by the Constitution to Consider Regional Needs?" *Connecticut Law Review*, Winter 1970-71, pp. 244-267.

1319. Weiner, Peter H. "The Constitutionality of Local Zoning." *Yale Law Journal*, April 1970, pp. 896-925.

1320. Williams, Norman, Jr. "The Three Systems of Land Use Control (or, Exclusionary Zoning and Revision of the Enabling Legislation)." *Rutgers Law Review*, Fall 1970, pp. 80-101.

See also: 1238, 1241-1243, 1245, 1246, 1249, 1251; Apartments–Zoning: 1460+; Local Regulation of Mobile Homes: 1669+; Planning for Low and Moderate Income Housing in the Suburbs: 3352+; The Impact of Housing Patterns on Employment Opportunities 3453+.

## E. LANDLORD-TENANT RELATIONS

### 1. GENERAL

1321. Burke, D.B. "Toward a Right to Control over the City Planning Process." *Journal of Urban Law*, 1969-1970, pp. 69-83.

1322. Conference on Tenants' Rights, Washington, D.C., 1966. *Tenants' Rights: Legal Tools for Better Housing; Report on a National Conference on Legal Rights of Tenants*. Washington, D.C.: Government Printing Office, 1967. 44 pp.

1323. Dooley, John A. and Joseph Goldberg. "A Model Tenants' Remedies Act." *Harvard Journal on Legislation*, March 1970, pp. 357-400.

1324. Garrity, Paul G. "Redesigning Landlord-Tenant Concepts for an Urban Society." *Journal of Urban Law*, Vol. 46, no. 4, 1969, pp. 695-721. 695-721.

1325. Halbutzel, Philip and Robert S. Cushman. "The Model Residential Landlord-Tenant Code: A Review and a Rebuttal." *Journal of Property Management*, September-October 1970, pp. 214-223.

1326. Halper, Emanuel B. "Sign It or Find Another Apartment: A View of Standard Form Leases." *Real Estate Review*, Summer 1972, pp. 67-73.

1327. Hamlar, Portia T. "Landlord and Tenant–Doctrine of Partial Constructive Eviction as Defense to Landlord's Suit for Back Rent Does Not Require Abandonment of Entire Premises." *Journal of Urban Law*, August 1971, pp. 201-217.

1328. Hecht, Neil S. "Variable Rental Provisions in Long Term Ground Leases." *Columbia Law Review*, April 1972, pp. 625-692.

1329. "Housing the Poor: A Study of the Landlord-Tenant Relationship." *University of Colorado Law Review*, December 1969, pp. 541+.

1330. Hubbard, F. Patrick. "Landlord Duties of the Local Public Agency: A Source of Protection for Residents in Urban Renewal Areas." *New York University Law Review*, November 1970, pp. 1015-1035. Also in George Sternlieb and Lynne B. Sagalyn (eds.). *Housing: 1970-1971; An AMS Anthology*. New York: AMS Press, 1972, pp. 411-432.

1331. "Landlord and Tenant–Lease-Eviction." *Journal of Urban Law*, November 1972, pp. 336-341.

1332. "Landlord-Tenant–FHA Aided Landlords Must Show Cause to Evict, *McQueen v. Drucker* Civil No. 70-1082W (D. Mass. Oct. 5, 1970)." *Boston University Law Review*, Fall 1970, pp. 628-630.

1333. "Landlord-Tenant Law: Plotting the Death of a Summary Proceeding Statute–A Test for Ripeness." *University of Florida Law Review*, Fall 1972, pp. 220+.

1334. Landlord's Duty to Protect Tenants from Criminal Acts of Third Parties: The View from 1500 Massachusetts Avenue." *Georgetown Law Journal*, May 1971, pp. 1153-1203.

1335. "The Landlord's Emerging Responsibility for Tenant Security." *Columbia Law Review*, February 1971, pp. 275-301.

1336. *Legal Problems of Landlord and Tenant*. Davis, Calif.: School of Law, University of California, 1971, 231pp.

1337. Lesar, Hiram H. "Landlord and Tenant Reform." *New York University Law Review*, November 1960, pp. 1279-1290.

1338. Levi, Julian. "New Landlord-Tenant Legal Relations–The Model Landlord-Tenant Code." *The Urban Lawyer*, Fall 1971, pp. 592-596.

1339. Lyman, William D. "A Response to ULTRA." *Journal of Property Management*, July/August 1972, pp. 149-172.

1340. Martin, Peter W. *The Ill-Housed; Cases and Materials on Tenants' Rights in Private and Public Housing*. Mineola, N.Y.: Foundation Press, 1971.

1341. McElhaney, J.W. "Retaliatory Evictions: Landlords, Tenants and Law Reform." *Maryland Law Review*, Summer 1969, pp. 193+.

1341. Moskovitz, Myron. "The Model Landlord-Tenant Code: An Unacceptable Compromise." *The Urban Lawyer*, Fall 1971, pp. 596-600.

1343. Mueller, Warren. "Residential Tenants and Their Leases: An Empirical Study." *Michigan Law Review*, December 1970, pp. 247-298.

1344. Murphy, J.G., Jr. "Proposal for Reshaping the Urban Rental Agreement." *Georgetown Law Journal*, February 1969, pp. 464+.

1345. National Association of Housing and Redevelopment Officials. Potomac Chapter. *Tenant/Landlor Relations; The Proceedings of a Workshop Sponsored by the Potomac Chapter, National Association of Housing and Redevelopment Officials, April 9, 1970*. Washington, D.C., 1970. 32pp.

1346. New Jersey Landlord-Tenant Relationship Study Commission. *Interim Report to the Governor and Legislature*. West New York, N.J., 1970, 41pp.

1347. "New Michigan Landlord-Tenant Law: Partial Answer to a Perplexing Problem." Spring 1969, pp. 836+.

1348. Nussbaum, Ronald J. "Tenants' Hearings and Rent Increases in FHA-Insured Projects." *Harvard Journal on Legislation*. May 1970, pp. 644-667.

1349. Obstfield, Harold B. "The Michigan Tenants' Rights Statute." *Harvard Journal on Legislation*, May 1969, pp. 563-569.

1350. "Plight of the Indigent Tenant: The Failure of the Law to Provide Relief." *Suffolk University Law Review*, Fall 1970, pp. 213+.

1351. Quinlan, Elsie M. "The Legal Corner–Developments in Landlord-Tenant Law." *Real Estate Review*, Fall 1972, pp. 96-100.

1352. Rasch, Joseph. *New York Landlord and Tenant, Including Summary Proceedings*. 2d edition. Rochester, N.Y.: Lawyers Co-operative Pub. Co., 1971. 3 vols.

1353. "Rent Administration–Computation of Proper Basis of Rental Property in Proceeding to Increase Rent." *New York Law Forum*, July 1960, pp. 363+.

1354. Rice, Henry Hart. "The Long-Term Net Lease as a Solution to the Urban Housing Problem." *Real Estate Review*, Spring 1971, pp. 99-103.

1355. Richey, Elinor. "Tenant Oppression: Our Smoldering Housing Scandal." *Antioch Review*, Fall 1964, pp. 337-350.

1356. Rose, Jerome G. "Here Comes the Quasi-Public Landlord." *Real Estate Review*, Summer 1971, pp. 31-34. Also in George Sternlieb and Lynne Sagalyn (eds.). *Housing: 1970-1971; An AMS Anthology*. New York: AMS Press, 1972, pp. 454-456.

1357. Sackman, J.L. "Apportionment of Award between Lessor and Lessee." *Appraisal Journal*, October 1970, pp. 539-553.

1358. Schier, Carl. "Protecting the Interests of the Indigent Tenant: Two Approaches." *California Law Review*, May 1966, pp. 670-693.

1359. Schoshinski, R.S. "Remedies of the Indigent Tenant: Proposal for Change." *Georgetown Law Journal*, Winter 1966, pp. 519+.

1360. Silverman, Abner D. "Policies Affecting Management-Tenant Relations in Subsidized Housing." *Journal of Property Management*, January/February 1972, pp. 19-21.

1361. "Tenant-Management Issues." *Journal of Housing*, November 1970, pp. 534-543.

1362. "Tenants' Remedies in the District of Columbia: New Hope for Reform." *Catholic University Law Review*, Fall 1968, pp. 80+.

1363. "Torts–Landlord-Tenant–Landlord Owes Duty to Provide Protection for Tenants against Criminal Acts by Third Parties." *Vanderbilt Law Review*, December 1970, pp. 195-200.

1364. "Torts–Negligence–Multi-Family Structures–Duty of Owner to Provide Police Protection." *Brooklyn Law Review*, April 1963, pp. 358+.

1365. Vaughan, Ted R. "The Landlord-Tenant Relation in a Low-Income Area." *Social Problems*, Fall 1968, pp. 208-218.

1366. Zenor, John L. "Judicial Expansion of Tenants' Private Law Rights: Implied Warranties of Habitability and Safety in Residential Urban Leases."

*Cornell Law Review*, February 1971, pp. 489-506.

See also: 1609; Public Housing—Landlord-Tenant Relations: 2774+.

## 2. BIBLIOGRAPHIES

1367. Jackson, Barbara (comp.). *Landlord and Tenant Relations: A Selective Bibliography*. Sacramento, Calif.: California State Law Library, 1970. 7pp.

1368. U.S. Department of Housing and Urban Development. Library. *The Landlord-Tenant Relationship; A Selected Bibliography.* Washington, D.C.: Government Printing Office, 1971. 53pp.

## 3. TENANT ORGANIZATIONS

1369. Brown, Shepard. "Trends in Tenant Movements." *Journal of Property Management*, August 1971, pp. 169-170.

1370. Flaum, Thea and Elizabeth Saltzman. *The Tenants' Rights Movement*. Chicago, Ill.: Urban Research Corporation, 1969. 57pp.

1371. Hanford, Lloyd D., Jr. "Tenant Movements: Retrospective and Perspective." *Journal of Property Management*, March-April 1971, pp. 69-75.

1372. Indritz, T. "Tenants' Rights Movement." *New Mexico Law Review*, January 1971, pp. 1+.

1373. Moskovitz, Myron and Peter J. Honigsberg. "The Tenant Union—Landlord Relations Act: A Proposal." *Georgetown Law Journal*, June 1970, pp. 1013-1062.

1374. Padnos, Michael. "The Tenant Movement." In U.S. Congress. House. Committee on Banking and Currency. *Papers Submitted to Subcommittee on Housing Panels on Housing Production, Housing Demand, and Developing a Suitable Living Environment: Part 2.* Washington, D.C.: Government Printing Office, 1971, pp. 651-700.

1375. "Tenant Unions: Their Law and Operation in the State and Nation." *University of Florida Law Review*, Fall 1970, pp. 79+.

## 4. RENT WITHHOLDING

1376. "Abatement of Rent in New York." *Syracuse Law Review*, Spring 1966, pp. 490+.

1377. "Article 7-A Revisited: New York City's Statutory Rent Strike Law." *Columbia Journal of Law & Social Problems*, Summer 1972, pp. 523+.

1378. Brill, Harry. *Why Organizers Fail; The Story of a Rent Strike.* Berkeley, Cal.: University of California Press, 1971. 192pp.

1379. Clough, J.H. "Pennsylvania's Rent Withholding Law." *Dickinson Law Review*, Summer 1969, pp. 583+.

1380. "Constitutional Law—Rent Abatement—Section 143-(b) of the New York Social Welfare Law Permitting Rent Abatement and Barring Eviction of Welfare Tenants Held Constitutional." *Villanova Law Review*, Fall 1967, pp. 205+.

1381. "DePaul v. Kauffman ([Pa.] 272 A 2d 500): The Pennsylvania Rent Withholding Act." *University of Pittsburgh Law Review*, Summer 1971, pp. 626+.

1382. Johnson, E.K. "Collective Tenant Action: Should the Rent Strike Be Institutionalized?" *Los Angeles Bar Bulletin*, February 1971, pp. 138+.

1383. Lipsky, Michael. *Protest in City Politics: Rent Strikes, Housing and the Power of the Poor.* New York: Rand McNally and Co., 1970.

1384. Lipsky, Michael. *Rent Strikes in New York City: Protest Politics and the Power of the Poor.* Ann Arbor, Mich.: University Microfilms, 1968 (Ph.D. dissertation, Princeton University, 1967). 134pp. (order no. 68-2496)

1385. Ominsky, H. and W. LaMar, Jr. "Pennsylvania Rent Withholding Act." *Pennsylvania Bar Association Quarterly*, October 1971, pp. 109+.

1386. "Rent Abatement Legislation: An Answer to Landlords." *Villanova Law Review*, Spring 1967, pp. 631+.

1387. "Rent Strike Legislation—New York's Solution to Landlord-Tenant Conflicts." *St. John's Law Review*, May 1966, pp. 253+.

1388. "Rent Withholding: A New Approach to Landlord-Tenant Problems." *Loyola University of Los Angeles Law Review*, April 1969, pp. 105+.

1389. "Rent Withholding—A Proposal for Legislation in Ohio." *Western Reserve Law Review*, July 1967, pp. 1705+.

1390. "Rent Withholding—Public and Private." *Chicago Bar Record*, January 1967, pp. 14+.

1391. "Rent Withholding for Minnesota: A Proposal." *Minnesota Law Review*, November 1970, pp. 82+.

1392. "Rent Withholding for Welfare Recipients: An Empirical Study of the Illinois Statute." *University of Chicago Law Review*, Summer 1970, pp. 798-848.

1393. "Rent Withholding in Pennsylvania." *University of Pittsburgh Law Review*, Fall 1968, pp. 148+.

1394. "Renters Turn Militant: Tenant Unions and Rent Strikes Pose New Problems for Mortgage Lenders, Underscore Need for Sound Apartment Financing Criteria." *Savings & Loan News*, March 1971, pp. 28-35.

1395. Simmons, P. "Passion and Prudence Rent Withholding under New York's Speigel Law." *Buffalo Law Review*, Spring 1966, pp. 572+.

1396. "Substandard Housing: The New Pennsylvania Rent Withholding Act as a Solution." *Duquesne University Law Review*, Spring 1967, pp. 413+.

1397. "Tenant Rent Strikes." *Columbia Journal of Law and Social Problems*, June 1967, pp. 1+.

See also: 1399-1401, 1409, 1411-1413, 1416, 1417.

5. HOUSING CODES WITHIN THE LANDLORD-TENANT RELATIONSHIP

1398. Daniels, Harley J. "Judicial and Legislative Remedies for Substandard Housing: Landlord-Tenant Reform in the District of Columbia." *Georgetown Law Journal*, March 1971, pp. 909-961.

1399. Fossum, John C. "Rent Withholding and the Improvement of Substandard Housing." *California Law Review*, March 1965, pp. 304-336.

1400. "Failure of a Landlord to Comply with Housing Regulations as a Defense to the Non-Payment of Rent." *Baylor Law Review*, Summer 1969, pp. 372+.

1401. "Housing Code Violations as a Defense for Nonpayment of Rent?" *San Diego Law Review*, Spring 1971, pp. 493+.

1402. Hux, Alan M. "Wisconsin Housing Codes Not an Implied Part of a Lease." *Urban Law Annual 1972*. St. Louis, Mo.: School of Law, Washington University, 1972, pp. 245-249.

1403. "*Javins v. First National Realty Corp.*—The Implied Warranty of Habitability and Rent Withholding in Urban Leases." *Northwestern University Law Review*, May-June 1971, pp. 227-247.

1404. Jefferson, William J. "New Power for Tenants: The Lessee's Right to a Livable Dwelling: *Javins v. First National Realty Corp." Harvard Civil Rights-Civil Liberties Law Review*, December 1970, pp. 193-204. Also in George Sternlieb and Lynne B. Sagalyn (eds.). *Housing: 1970-1971; An AMS Anthology*. New York: AMS Press, 1972, pp. 442-453.

1405. "Landlord and Tenant–Eviction–Public Policy and Congressional Purpose to Ensure Decent Housing Conditions Require Construction of Summary Eviction Statute to Prohibit Eviction in Retaliation for Tenant's Reports of Housing Code Violations to Authorities" (*Edwards v. Habib . . .*). *Harvard Law Review*, February 1969, pp. 932-938.

1406. "Landlord and Tenant: Lease Agreement Void as an Illegal Contract When Dwelling Is in Violation of Local Housing Code at Time of Letting: *Brown v. Southhall Realty Co.* ([DC] 237 A 2d 834)." *University of Pittsburgh Law Review*, Fall 1968, pp. 134+.

1407. "Landlord and Tenant–Leases–Lease Executed in Violation of District of Columbia Housing Regulations Is an Illegal Contract–*Brown vs. Southall Realty Co." Michigan Law Review*, June 1968, pp. 1753-1762.

1408. "Landlord and Tenant–Retaliatory Evictions and Housing Code Enforcement." *North Carolina Law Review*, April 1971, pp. 569+.

1409. "Landlord and Tenant–Right to Deposit Rent Payments in Escrow Fund in Protest of Housing Code Violations." *Wisconsin Law Review*, 1970, pp. 607+.

1410. "Landlord and Tenant Law–Warrant of Habitability Implied by Law in Leases of Urban Dwellings." *Vanderbilt Law Review*, March 1971, pp. 425-432.

1411. "Landlord-Tenant–Landlord's Violation of Housing Code during Lease Term Is Breach of Implied Warranty of Habitability Constituting Partial or Total Defense to an Eviction Action Based on Nonpayment of Rent–*Javins v. First National Realty Corp." Harvard Law Review*, January 1971, pp. 729-738.

1412. "Landlord-Tenant Law–A Tenant's Duty to Pay Rent Is Dependent upon a Landlord's Substantial Compliance with the Housing Regulations for the District of Columbia Which Imply a Warrant of Habitability in Urban Leases. *Javins v. First National Realty Corp.* no. 22405. . . ." *George Washington Law Review*, October 1970, pp. 152-165.

1413. "Landlord-Tenant–Violation of Housing Regulations Renders Lease Agreement Unenforceable in Action for Possession and Nonpayment of Rent." *Vanderbilt Law Review*, November 1968, pp. 1117+.

1414. "Leases and the Illegal Contract Theory–Judicial Reinforcement of the Housing Code." *Georgetown Law Journal*, May 1968, pp. 920+.

1415. Levine, J.R. "Warranty of Habitability." *Connecticut Law Review*, June 1969, pp. 61+.

1416. Mills, Joseph W. "Landloard and Tenant–Lease Eviction–A Lease Concerning Premises with Substantial Housing Code Violations Is Void as an Illegal Bargain Excusing the Payment of Rent with Landlord Precluded from Evicting out of Retaliation, *Robinson v. Diamond Housing Corp.* . . ." *Journal of Urban Law*, November 1972, pp. 336-341.

1417. "Rent Withholding and the Improvement of Substandard Housing." *California Law Review*, March 1965, pp. 304+.

1418. "Retaliatory Evictions and the Reporting of Housing Code Violations in the District of Columbia." *George Washington Law Review*, October 1967, pp. 190+.

1419. "Substandard Housing and the Law in the District of Columbia." *Howard Law Journal*, Winter 1966, pp. 137+.

1420. "Tenant Remedies–The Implied Warranty of Fitness and Habitability." *Villanova Law Review*, April 1971, pp. 710+.

1421. "Withholding Rent: New Weapon Added to Arsenal for War on Slumlords." *Journal of Housing*, March 16, 1964, pp. 67-72.

## F. ALTERNATIVE FORMS OF TENURE

### 1. APARTMENTS

#### a) General

1422. Aberle, John W. and Pe Sheng Wang. *The Characteristics, Preferences, and Home Buying Intentions of Apartment Residents in San Jose.* San Jose, Calif.: School of Business Administration, San Jose State College, 1965. 78l.

1423. Berman, Martin S. "Apartment Building Rehabilitation." *Journal of Property Management*, May/June 1964, pp. 235-237.

1424. "Density + Environment = Profits." *Professional Builder*, February 1972, pp. 72-81.

1425. "Four Special Projects for Special Multi-Family Markets." *House and Home*, January 1971, pp. 112-119.

1426. Grossman, Howard J. "Apartments in Community Planning: A Suburban Area Case Study." *Urban Land*, January 1966, pp. 3-6.

1427. Grossman, Howard J. *Survey and Analysis of New Apartment Construction in a Surburban County.* Norristown, Pa.: Montgomery County Planning Commission, 1965. 65pp.

1428. Guy, William B., Jr. "Some Aspects of Apartment Planning." *Journal of Property Management*, Spring 1962, pp. 146-151.

1429. "Homebuilding's Apartment Report." *NAHB Journal of Homebuilding*, March 1972, pp. 45-53.

1430. Liechenstein, M.I. *Reducing Crime in Apartment Dwellings: A Methodology for Comparing Security Alternatives.* Santa Monica, Calif.: The Rand Corporation, June 1971, 31pp.

1431. Loewenstein, Louis K. "High-Rise Hassle: How the 'Ups' Beat the 'Downs' in San Francisco." *Real Estate Review*, Spring 1972, pp. 24-29.

1432. Matherly, Michael Terry. *Distribution and Morphology of Apartments in the Santa Clara Valley, 1957-1969.* San Jose, Calif.: Institute for Business and Economic Research, San Jose State College, 1970. 70pp.

1433. Mohl, A. Frederick, Jr. "A Scientific Approach to Apartment Pricing: Formula for Pinpointing Rents of Apartment Units." *Journal of Property Management,* December 1960, pp. 77-84.

1434. Mowbray, John McC. "Apartments in Central Areas." *Urban Land*, January 1962, pp. 1+.

1435. "Much More Than Garden-Type Apartments: Bright Park-Like Projects Hold New Promise for High-Density Living." *Business Week*, March 14, 1970, pp. 146-147.

1436. National Housing Center. Library. *Apartment Houses; A Selected List of References in the National Housing Center Library, Washington, D.C.* 6th ed. rev. Washington, D.C., 1970. 101pp.

1437. Neutze, Graeme Max. *The Suburban Apartment Boom; Case Study of a Land Use Problem.* Washington, D.C.: Resources for Future, distributed by Johns Hopkins Press, Baltimore, Maryland, 1968. 170pp.

1438. Satterfield, Donald Wayne. *Segmented Demand as a Factor in Apartment Management.* Ann Arbor, Mich.: University Microfilms, 1971 (Ph.D. dissertation, University of Arkansas, 1971). 134pp. (order no. 71-19,581.)

1439. Shenkel, William M. "Apartment Income and Expenses: The Report of the Experience Exchange Board." *Journal of Property Management*, May/June 1969, pp. 102-112.

1440. Shenkel, William M. "Cash Flow and Multiple Regression Techniques: Comparative Analysis of Apartment Properties." *Journal of Property Management*, November-December 1969, pp. 264-276.

1441. Smith, Wallace F. *The Low-rise Speculative Apartment*. Berkeley, Calif.: Center for Real Estate and Urban Economics, Institute of Urban and Regional Development, University of California, 1964, 136pp.

1442. Stevens, O. Ellsworth. "Meeting the Onslaught of New Apartment Competition." *Journal of Property Management*, May/June 1964, pp. 236-257.

1443. Studdard, Kenneth E. "Tax Aspects of Apartment Ownership." *Residential Appraiser*, July 1962, pp. 13-16.

See also: Cost and Cost-Revenue Analysis by Housing Type—765+; 3337.

b) Appraisal and Finance

1444. "Apartment Loan Commitments." *Real Estate Analyst Mortgage Bulletin*, July 1971, pp. 299-306 (Entire Issue).

1445. Derbes, Max J., Jr. "Return Requirements of the Apartment Investment." *Real Estate Appraiser*, August 1963, pp. 16-35.

1446. Dunham, Howard W., Jr. "Gross Income Estimate of the Apartment." *Real Estate Appraiser*, August 1963, pp. 2-11.

1447. Eikmeyer, L.J. "Analyzing the High-Rise Apartment." *Appraisal Journal*, July 1966, pp. 444-448.

1448. Jones, James. "The Apartment Project: Development and Financing." *Appraisal Journal*, January 1972, pp. 96-102.

1449. Lewman, Harry and Jerome A. Martin. *Case Studies in Apartment House Valuation*. Chicago, Ill.: American Institute of Real Estate Appraisers, 1969, 2nd edition. 51pp.

1450. McConkey, Robert F. and John L. Schmidt. "Apartment Lending: Are You Gambling or Investing?" *Journal of Homebuilding*, October 1970, pp. 51-59.

1451. Neelley, Arthur E. "Apartment House Financing: Some Yardsticks for Judging a Good Residential Income Property Loan." *Savings & Loan News*, September 1960, pp. 20-22.

1452. "Professional Approach to Apartment Lending: Economic Analysis, Architectural Review Expose Bad Risks, Make Good Loans Better." *Savings and Loan News*, April 1964, pp. 46-49+.

1453. U.S. Congress. Senate. Committee on Banking and Currency. Subcommittee on Housing. *Apartment Loans by Savings and Loan Associations: Hearing, September 27, 1962....* Washington, D.C.: Government Printing Office, 1962. 27pp.

c. Market Analysis

1454. Harris, William W. "Our Changing Population and the Apartment Market." *Real Estate Appraiser*, November 1963, pp. 24-31.

1455. House and Home. *Characteristics of the 1962 Low-Rise Apartment House Market: Characteristics of Builders of Garden and Other Low-Rise Apartments; How They Are Diversified; Evidence of Their Concentration; Certain Products and Materials Used.* New York: Time, Inc., October 1962.

1456. Minskoff, Henry *et al.* "Apartment House Market." *National Real Estate Investor*, August 1966, pp. 63-66.

1457. Norcross, Carl and John Hysom. *Apartment Communities: The Next Big Market; A Survey of Who Rents and Why*. Washington, D.C.: The Urban Land Institute, 1968 (Technical Bulletin no. 61). 83pp.

1458. Sather, Kent N. "Analyzing Apartment Market Characteristics." *Journal of Property Management*, September/October 1970, pp. 231-233.

1459. Selgiman, Daniel. "The Real-Estate Markets: The Move to Apartments." *Fortune*, April 1963, pp. 98-101+.

d. Zoning

1460. American Society of Planning Officials. *Accessory Uses in Apartments and Hotels.* Chicago, Ill., February 1963. 4pp. (Planning Advisory Service Report no. 168).

1461. American Society of Planning Officials. *Apartment Densities for Medium-Sized Cities*. Chicago, Ill., January 1963. 4pp. (Planning Advisory Service Report no. 166).

1462. American Society of Planning Officials. *Apartments in the Suburbs.* Chicago, Ill., June 1964. 28pp. (Planning Advisory Service Report no. 187).

1463. "Apartments in Suburbia: Local Responsibility and Judicial Restraint." *Northwestern University Law Review*, July/August 1964, pp. 334-432.

1464. Babcock, Richard F. and Fred P. Bosselman. "Suburban Zoning and the Apartment Boom." *University of Pennsylvania Law Review*, June 1963, pp. 1040-1091.

1465. Parkins, John A., Jr. "Judicial Attitudes toward Multiple-Family Dwellings: A Reappraisal." *Washington and Lee Law Review*, Spring 1971, pp. 220-230.

1466. "Rezoning Suburbia." *Progressive Architecture*, May 1971, pp. 92-94.

1467. Sussna, Stephen. "What the Courts Say about Anti-Apartment Zoning." *Buildings*, March 1972, pp. 64-65.

1468. Westchester County, New York, Department of Planning. Planning Board. *Multi-Family Zoning in Westchester County, 1964*. White Plains, N.Y., December 1964.

## 2. CONDOMINIUMS

### a. General

1469. American Society of Planning Officials. *Condominium*. Chicago, Ill., June 1962. 24pp. (Planning Advisory Service Report no. 159).

1470. "Anatomy of a Master Plan." *House and Home*, June 1972,pp. 68-73.

1471. Anfuso, Frank A. "A Study of Condominiums." *Mortgage Bulletin*, March 1966, pp. 14-34.

1472. Associated Home Builders of the Greater Eastbay, Inc. *The Condominium Handbook. "Condominium Re-lives!" A Guide to the Economic Development and Sale of Condominiums in California*. Berkeley, Cal., 1970. 1 vol.

1473. Beaton, William R. *The Detached-House Condominium*. Gainesville, Fla.: Bureau of Economic and Business Research, College of Business Administration, University of Florida, 1967. 2 parts.

1474. Beaton, William R. "Single-family Units Sell in Condominium Cluster." *Journal of Property Management*, May/June 1968, pp. 135-140.

1475. Berman, Daniel S. *Condominiums: What They Are; Samples of Useful Forms; How to Start Them; Rules and Regulations; How to Finance One; Profit Possibilities*. New York: Benenson Publications, 1964. 200pp.

1476. Berman, Daniel S. *How to Organize and Sell a Profitable Real Estate Condominium*. Englewood Cliffs, N.J.: Prentice-Hall, 1966. 195pp.

1477. Buck, Gurdon H. "Condominiums That Grow—Another View." *Lawyers Title News*, March/April 1972, pp. 11-13+.

1478. Burke, Terence J. *et al. Condominium; Housing for Tomorrow. A Study Prepared by Graduate Students at the Harvard Graduate School of Business Administration*. Boston, Mass.: MR Management Reports, 1964. 94pp.

1479. Cagann, Robert A. "Maximizing the Profit Potential in Condominium Management." *Journal of Property Management*, January/February 1972, pp. 27-28.

1480. Clurman, David and Edna L. Hebard. *Condominiums and Cooperatives*. New York: Wiley-Interscience, 1970. 395pp.

1481. Condominium Symposium, National Housing Center, Washington, D.C., 1963. *Report*. 10pp.

1482. "Condominiums—A Symposium." *Appraisal Journal*, October 1962, pp. 453-469.

1483. "Condominiums Capture the Florida Market. They Make up 75% of New Starts: Selling Five or Six a Day, at $37,000 per." *Business Week*, November 4, 1972, pp. 82+.

1484. "Convert It to Condominium." *House and Home*, January 1971, pp. 106-111.

1485. "Converting a Small Apartment Building to a Condominium." *Journal of Property Management*, January/February 1971. Series of articles, pp. 29-44.

1486. "Converting to Condominium." *House & Home*, April 1972, pp. 100-105.

1487. Cribbet, John E. "Condominium—Home Ownership for Megalopolis." *Michigan Law Review*, May 1963, pp. 1207-1244.

1488. Evans, Donald D. "Condominiums." *Appraisal Journal*, July 1964, pp. 339-357.

1489. Everett, William S. "Condominium Advantages Create Booming Sales." *Journal of Property Management*, September/October 1968, pp. 234-235.

1490. Everett, William S. "Condominium and Co-operative Apartments—The New Frontier in Housing." *Journal of Property Management*, Fall 1961, pp. 4-16.

1491. Fitzpatrick, Barry M. *Condominium: the Basics for the Developer and the Mortgagee.* Presented to the Metropolitan Washington Savings and Loan League. Washington, D.C.: National Housing Center, 1972.

1492. Grezzo, Anthony D. *Condominiums; Their Development and Management.* Washington, D.C.: Office of International Affairs, Department of Housing and Urban Development, 1972. 71pp.

1493. Harrison, Gilbert Warner. "The FHA Condominium: Use as a Means of Meeting the Need for Moderate Income Housing." *New York Law Forum*, Fall 1965, pp. 458-502.

1494. Hippaka, William H. and Don C. Bridentstine. *Factors Contributing to the Success or Failure of Residential Condominium Developments.* San Diego, Calif.: School of Business Administration, San Diego State College, 1968. 200pp.

1495. King, T. Bertram. "Problems of Financing Condominiums." *Business Lawyer*, January 1969, pp. 445-457.

1496. Lanning, J. Clair. "Troubleshooting Condominiums with Management Know-How." *Journal of Property Management*, January/February 1972, pp. 31-33.

1497. "Latecomers to Homeownership Programs." *HUD Challenge*, July 1972, pp. 22-26.

1498. "Lender Guides Condominium Market Test: Western Federal (Savings of Denver) Uses Meticulous Care, Planning and Control to Successfully Guide Entry of Two Vastly Different Types of Condominiums into Denver's Residential Market." *Savings and Loan News*, June 1964, pp. 38-43.

1499. "Lessons Learned in Condominium Financing." *Building*, July 1972, pp. 50-51.

1500. Lum, Tan Tek. "Feasibility Analysis of Condominiums." *Appraisal Journal*, April 1972, pp. 246-252.

1501. Lum, T.T. *Some Counseling Aspects in Condominium Development.* Chicago, Ill.: American Society of Real Estate Counselors, 1972. 16pp.

1502. Moyer, J.L. "Condominiums: Building Profits with Better Management." *Journal of Property Management*, September/October 1965, pp. 237-244.

1503. National Association of Home Builders. *FHA Financing for Condominiums, Section 234, a Hypothetical Case.* Prepared by Norman J. Farquhar and Peter Balitsaris. Washington, D.C.: National Association of Home Builders, Builders Services Division, 1971. 125pp.

1504. Opelka, F. Gregory. "Condominium Conversions: The Move to Existing Housing Is No Surprise." *Savings & Loan News*, December 1971, pp. 70-71.

1505. Opelka, F. Gretory. "Condominium Value Does Not Equal Sales Price." *Savings and Loan News*, November 1970, pp. 78-79.

1506. Otsuji, H.H. "Solving the 'People Problem' in Condominiums." *Real Estate Review*, Winter 1972, pp. 20-24.

1507. Plum, Matthias, Jr. "A Viable Method for Low-Income Housing—Condominiums." *Mortgage Banker*, October 1967, pp. 32-36.

1508. Ramsey, Charles E. "Condominium: Has Caught on All Right and Looks as Though It's Here to Stay But Some Questions Remain." *Mortgage Banker*, December 1962, pp. 22-25+.

1509. Ramsey, Charles E. "Condominiums: The New Look in Co-ops." *Urban Land*, May 1962, pp. 1+.

1510. Reskin, Melvin A. and Hiroshi Sakai. *Modern Condominium Forms*. Boston, Mass.: Warren, Gorham and Lamont, 1971.

1511. "Roundup Report on Condominium—Its Problems, Its Potential." *Savings & Loan News*, January 1964, pp. 44-45+.

1512. Szego, G.C. *Cost-Reducing Condominium Systems for Low Cost Homes*. Arlington, Virginia: Institute for Defense Analyses. 1968. 131pp.

1513. Temple, Douglas M. "Insuring a Condominium." *CPCU Annals*, Spring 1964, pp. 45-50.

1514. U.S. Department of Housing and Urban Development. *Mortgage Insurance Guide for Condominium Housing Insured under National Housing Act.* Washington, D.C., April 1971. 139pp.

1515. Welfeld, Irving H. "The Condominium and Median-Income Housing." *Fordham Law Review*, February 1963, pp. 457-480.

1516. "What Sells Condominiums?" *Professional Builder*, March 1972, pp. 94-105.

See also: 1589, 2091, 2248.

b. Bibliographies

1517. Breuer, Ernest Henry. *Condominium; A Selected Bibliography of the Historical, Common Law, Federal and State Legislation Aspects of Unit Ownership, Horizontal Property and Airspace Ownership in Real Property*. Albany, N.Y.: New York State Library, 1962. 17pp.

1518. National Housing Center. Library. *Condominium and Cooperative Apartments; A Selected List of References*. Washington, D.C., 1963. 8pp.

1519. U.S. Department of Housing and Urban Development. Library and Information Division. *Condominium and Cooperative Housing, 1960-71; a Bibliography of Economic, Financial and Legal Factors*. Washington, D.C.: Government Printing Office, 1972. 32pp.

c. Appraisal

1520. Bruckner, Clarence C. "Appraisal of a Condominium Converted from an Apartment Building." *Real Estate Appraiser*, March/April 1972, pp. 13-17.

1521. Hubin, Vincent. "Considerations in Condominium Appraisal." *Appraisal Journal*, January 1971, pp. 71-81.

1522. Opelka, F. Gregory. "Condominium Conversion—Appraisal Considerations." *Appraisal Journal*, October 1972, pp. 588-599.

1523. Wagner, Percy E. "Analyzing and Appraising Condominium Projects." *Appraisal Journal*, October 1971, pp. 576-582.

1524. Wagner, Percy E. "Condominiums." *Appraisal Journal*, January 1964, pp. 7-20.

d. Legal Aspects

1525. Ashby, Lawrence C. and John H. Bailey, III. "Condominiums: Incorporation of the Common Elements – a Proposal." *Vanderbilt Law Review*, March 1970, pp. 321-368.

1526. Berger, Curtis J. "Condominium: Shelter on a Statutory Foundation." *Columbia Law Review*, June 1963, pp. 987-1026.

1527. Borgwardt, John F. "The Condominium—Vertical Subdivision." *Journal of the State Bar of California*, 1962, pp. 603-612.

1528. Clark, James C. "Condominium: A Reconciliation of Competing Interest." *Vanderbilt Law Review*, October 1965, pp. 1773-1809.

1529. Clurman, David. "Are Condominium Units Securities?" *Real Estate Review*, Spring 1972, pp. 18-23.

1530. "The Condominium." *Hastings Law Journal*, February 1963, entire issue.

1531. "Condominium—A Comparative Analysis of Condominium Statutes." *De Paul Law Review*, Autumn/Winter 1963, pp. 111+.

1532. "Condominiums." *University of Illinois Law Forum*, no. 1, 1970, entire issue.

1533. "Condominiums and the 1968 Housing and Urban Development Act: Putting the Poor in Their Place." *Southern California Law Review*, Vol. 43, 1970, pp. 309+.

1534. Davis, Tom L. "Provisions of FHA Section 234." *Journal of Property Management*, Fall 1962, pp. 22-25.

1535. Ellman, Howard N. "Fundamentals of Condominium and Some Insurance Problems." *Insurance Law Journal*, December 1963, pp. 733+.

1536. Fokes, W. Robert. "Legal and Practical Aspects of Condominiums." *Business Lawyer*, November 1963, pp. 233-241.

1537. Gorrell, James A. "Ohio Condominium Law." *Title News*, March 1964, pp. 4-8.

1538. Joliet, L.J. "Expandable Condominium: A Technical Analysis." *Law Notes*, Fall 1972, pp. 19+.

1539. Kenin, David S. "Condominium: A Survey of Legal Problems and Proposed Legislation." *University of Miami Law Review*, Winter 1962, pp. 145-181.

1540. Kerr, William K. "Condominium: Statutory Implementation." *St. Johns Law Review*, December 1963, pp. 1+.

1541. Lippman, William J. "Legal Problems of Condominiums." *Appraisal Journal*, October 1962, pp. 458-464.

1542. Mardian, Robert C. "Condominiums and Cluster Housing; Convenants, Conditions and Restrictions." *Savings and Loan Journal*, November 1964, pp. 19-20+.

1543. Pohoryles, Louis. "The FHA Condominium; A Basic Comparison with the FHA Cooperative." *George Washington Law Review*, June 1963, pp. 1014-1037.

1544. "Property: Condominium—A New concept in Real Property Estates." *Oklahoma Law Review*, November 1963, pp. 440+.

1545. Quirk, William J. *et al.* "A Draft Program of Housing Reform—The Tenant Condominium." *Cornell Law Review*, February 1968, pp. 361-405.

1546. "Right of First Refusal—Homogeniety in the Condominium." *Vanderbilt Law Review*, October 1965, pp. 1810+.

1547. Rohan, Patrick J. "Condominium: A Precis for Attorneys." *Oklahoma Bar Association Journal*, March 25, 1968, pp. 939+.

1548. Rohan, Patrick J. "Condominium Housing: A Purchaser's Perspective." *Stanford Law Review*, May 1965, pp. 842+.

1549. Rohan, Patrick J. "Drafting Condominium Instruments: Provisions for Destruction, Obsolescence and Eminent Domain." *Columbia Law Review*, April 1965, pp. 593-624.

1550. Rohan, Patrick J. "Perfecting the Condominium as a Housing Tool: Innovations in Tort Liability and Insurance." *Law and Contemporary Problems*, Spring 1967, pp. 305-318.

1551. Rohan, Patrick J. "Second Generation Condominium Problems: Construction of Enabling Legislation and Project Documents." *Valparaiso University Law Review*, Fall 1966, pp. 77-92.

1552. Rohan, Patrick J. and Melvin A. Reskin. *Condominium Law & Practice*. Albany, N.Y.: Matthew Bender, 1967. 1 vol.

1553. Ross, E.M. "Condominium and Preemptive Options: The Right of First Refusal." *Hastings Law Journal*, March 1967, pp. 585+.

1554. Schreiber, Aaron M. "The Lateral Housing Development: Condominium or Home Owners Association?" *University of Pennsylvania Law Review*, June 1969, pp. 1104-1162.

1555. Schwartz, William. "Condominium: A Hybrid Castle in the Sky." *Boston University Law Review*, Spring 1964, pp. 137-155.

1556. "Symposium on Condominiums." *Connecticut Law Review*, June 1969, entire issue.

1557. "Symposium on the Practical Problems of Condominiums." Parts I and II. *Practical Lawyer*, January 1965, pp. 35-64; February 1965, pp. 51-76.

1558. Teaford, Stephen D. "Homeownership for Low-Income Families: The Condominium." *Hastings Law Journal*, 1970, pp. 243-286. Also in George Sternlieb and Lynne Sagalyn (eds.). *Housing: 1970-1971; An AMS Anthology*. New York: AMS Press, 1972, pp. 457-502.

1559. "Torts–Condominium–Condominium Unit Owner Has Standing to Sue Unincorporated Unit Owners' Association for Injuries Inflicted because of the Association's Negligence." *Vanderbilt Law Review*, January 1972, pp. 271-279.

1560. U.S. Congress. House. Committee on the District of Columbia. *Horizontal Property Act of the District of Columbia; Report. . . .* Washington, D.C.: Government Printing Office, 1963. 5pp.

1561. U.S. Congress. House. Committee on the District of Columbia. Subcommittee no. 5. *Horizontal Property Regimes (Condominiums): Hearing, May 6, 1963, on H.R. 4276, to Provide for the Creation of Horizontal Property Regimes in the District of Columbia.* Washington, D.C.: Government Printing Office, 1964. 55pp.

1562. U.S. Congress. Senate. Committee on the District of Columbia. Subcommittee on the Judiciary. *Creation of Horizontal Property Regimes (Condominiums) in the District of Columbia: Hearings. . . .* Washington, D.C.: Government Printing Office, 1964. 40pp.

1563. Waggoner, Larry W. "Property–Multiple Ownership of Apartment Buildings–Establishment of Horizontal Property Regimes." *Michigan Law Review*, February 1962, pp. 527-530.

1564. Walbran, J.W. "Condominium: Its Economic Functions." *Missouri Law Review*, Fall 1965, pp. 531-565.

e. Market Analysis

1565. "About the Condominium Market in Various Regions of the U.S." *Savings Bank Journal*, April 1972, pp. 38-42+.

1566. Becker, William E. "High Cost Area is Good Market for Condominiums." *Apartment Construction News*, August 1970, pp. 28-31.

1567. Becker, William E. "A Marketing Primer for Condominiums and Cooperatives." *Real Estate Review*, Spring 1971, pp. 61-64.

1568. Elliot (Bill) and Associates. *A Survey of Condominium Housing Activity in Selected United States Metropolitan Market Areas*. Hackensack, N.J., 1970. 25pp.

f. Taxation

1569. Andrews, James. "Assessment Problems of Condominium Ownership." *Urban Land*, November 1963, pp. 1+.

1570. Clark, Louis M. "The Real Estate Condominium; Its Tax Problems and Implications." *Appraisal Journal*, October 1967, pp. 475-495.

1571. "Condominium–Tax Aspects of Ownership." *Vanderbilt Law Review*, October 1965, pp. 1832+.

1572. "Condominium and Cooperative Housing: Taxation by State and Federal Governments." *University of Florida Law Review*, Spring 1969, pp. 529+.

1573. Curry, R.L., III. "Tax Consideration of Condominiums." *Tulane Tax Institute*, V. 19, 1970, pp. 347+.

1574. Hilton, Holland. "The Appraisal of Condominiums for Assessment Purposes." *Real Estate Appraiser*, July 1967, pp. 2-8.

1575. International Association of Assessing officers. *Guidelines for Appraising Condominiums.* Chicago, Ill., 1969. 38pp.

1576. "Separate Assessment of Condominium." *Hastings Law Journal*, February 1963, pp. 289+.

1577. "Tax Treatment of Condominiums: A Comparison with Cooperatives." *Journal of Taxation*, October 1964, pp. 200-201.

3. COOPERATIVES

a. General

1578. "Cooperative Housing." In U.S. National Commission on Urban Problems. *Building the American City.* Washington D.C.: Government Printing Office, 1969, pp. 134-142.

1579. Davidson, William George III. *Cooperative Housing, An Analysis of the Economic Benefits Peculiar to the Cooperative Approach.* Philadelphia, Pa.: Graduate Division of the Wharton School, University of Pennsylvania, 1969. 99pp.

1580. Foundation for Cooperative Housing. *Ingredients for a Successful Self-Sustaining Cooperative Housing Program.* Washington, D.C., 1965. 32pp.

1581. Fox, Eugene H. "Cooperatives and Condominiums." *Journal of Property Management*, July/August 1965, pp. 178-183.

1582. Gladstone, William L. "The Co-Operative Housing Corporation: Tax Advantages and Potential Tax Pitfalls for Purchasers of Co-Operative Apartments, and the Co-Operative Housing Corporations Themselves." *Journal of Accountancy*, May 1962, pp. 55-58.

1583. Goldstein, Charles A. "Negotiating for a Cooperative Apartment." *Real Estate Review*, Spring 1971, pp. 75-83.

1584. Institute of Real Estate Management. *Cooperative Apartments, Their Organization and Profitable Operation.* 2nd edition. Chicago, Ill., 1961. 96pp.

1585. Jacobson, D. "Tax Problems of Sponsor and Tenant-Stockholder of a Co-Operative Housing Corporation." *Journal of Taxation*, July 1960, pp. 28-30.

1586. Kolodny, Robert. *Study of Low-Income Cooperative Housing Conversion in New York City: Interim Report.* New York: United Neighborhood Houses of New York, 1972. 56pp.

1587. Krooth, David L. "Cooperative Housing Has Role to Play in the Urban Renewal Program." *Journal of Housing*, January 1960, pp. 258-264.

1588. Liblit, Jerome (ed.). *Housing, the Cooperative Way; Selected Readings.* New York: Twayne, 1964. 300pp.

1589. McCord, Jim (ed.). *Cooperatives and Condominiums.* New York: Practising Law Institute, 1969. 576pp.

1590. "New York, N.Y.: Design for a 1600-Unit East Harlem Project Has Emerged from Administrative Limbo in Completely Revised Form." *Architectural Forum*, May 1971, pp. 42-45.

1591. Reach, Barbara. *Social Aspects of Cooperative and Non-Profit Housing: New and Rehabilitated.* New York: Community Service Society of New York, 1968. 43pp.

1592. Sullivan, Donald G. *Cooperative Housing and Community Development; A Comparative Evaluation of Three Housing Projects in East Harlem.* New York: Praeger, 1969. 217pp.

1593. U.S. Department of Housing and Urban Development. Office of International Affairs. *Cooperative Housing.* A Revision of "Cooperative Housing in the United States" by J. Robert Dodge. Prepared for the Agency for International Development. Washington, D.C., 1971. 69pp. (Ideas and Methods Exchange no. 52).

1594. U.S. Department of Housing and Urban Development. Office of International Affairs. *Cooperative Housing in the U.S.A.* Washington, D.C., 1972. 11pp. (HUD International Brief no. 13).

1595. Van Mater, Elena C. and Charles E. Buhl. *Final Report on the Parkchester Cooperative Ownership and Rehabilitation Low-Income Housing Demonstration Project.* Washington, D.C.: Metropolitan Washington Planning and Housing Association, 1969. 82pp.

See also 1480, 1490, 1572, 2093, 2149, 2154, 2532.

b. Legal Aspects

1596. "Cooperative Apartments–A Legal Hybrid." *University of Florida Law Review*, Spring 1960, pp. 123+.

1597. "Cooperative Housing Corporations and the Federal Securities Law." *Columbia Law Review*, January 1971, pp. 118-139.

1598. Johnson, D. "Legal Problems of Cooperative Housing in Illinois." *Illinois Bar Journal*, June 1962, pp. 940+.

1599. Miller, Walter M., Jr. "Cooperative Apartment–Real Estate or Securities?" *Boston University Law Review*, Fall 1965, pp. 465-505.

1600. Rohan, Patrick J. "Cooperative Apartment Transfers: Evaluation of Project Offerings and Representation of Purchasers." *Stanford Law Review*, May 1967, pp. 978+.

1601. Rohan, Patrick J. "Cooperative Housing: An Appraisal of Residential Controls and Enforcement Procedures." *Stanford Law Review*, June 1966, pp. 1323+.

1602. Rohan, Patrick J. "Cooperative Housing: The Treatment of Casualty Losses, Insurance and Project Termination." *California Western Law Review*, Spring 1966, pp. 70+.

1603. Rohan, Patrick J. and Melvin A. Reskin. *Cooperative Housing Law & Practice*. Albany, N.Y.: Matthew Bender, 1967. 1 vol.

See also: 1543.

4. MOBILE HOMES

a. General

1604. Bair, Frederick H., Jr. "Mobile Homes–A New Challenge." *Law and Contemporary Problems*, Spring 1967, pp. 286-304.

1605. Bair, Frederick H., Jr. *Mobile Homes and the General Housing Supply—Past, Present, and Outlook.* Chicago, Ill.: American Society of Planning Officials, 1970. 12pp.

1606. Bell, J.E., Jr. "Mobiles—A Possible Segment for Retailer Cultivation." *Journal of Retailing*, Fall 1970, pp. 3-15.

1607. "Break Away from Tradition in Mobile Home Parks!" *Professional Builder*, September 1970, pp. 76-84.

1608. Cloos, George W. and Edward W. Birgells, Jr. "Mobile Homes and the Housing Supply." *Federal Reserve Chicago, Business Conditions: A Review*, November 1972, pp. 2-16.

1609. "Community and the Park Owner versus the Mobile Home Park Resident: Reforming the Landlord-Tenant Relationship." *Boston University Law Review*, Fall 1972, pp 810+.

1610. Drury, Margaret J. *Mobile Homes: The Unrecognized Revolution in American Housing.* Revised Edition. New York: Praeger, 1972. 180pp.

1611. Engstrom, Robert E. "Mobile Homes in Transition." *Urban Land*, May 1972, pp. 3-7.

1612. Farnsworth, Clyde H., Jr., and H. Suzanne Jones. "Mobile and Modular Housing." *Federal Reserve Richmond, Monthly Review*, June 1970, pp. 2-5.

1613. Frederick County, Md., Planning Commission. *The Environmental Impact of the Mobile Home on Frederick County.* Report prepared by Lawrence W. Johnson. Frederick, Md., 1970. 43pp.

1614. French, Robert Mills and Jeffrey K. Hadden. "An Analysis of the Distribution and Characteristics of Mobile Homes in America." *Land Economics*, May 1965, pp. 131-139.

1615. French, R.M. and J.K. Hadden. "Mobile Homes: Instant Suburbia or Transportable Slums?" *Social Problems*, Fall 1968, pp. 219-226.

1616. Gerloff, C.M. "Mobile Homes in the Inner City?" *Federal Home Loan Bank Board Journal*, November 1970, pp. 21-24.

1617. Gibson, Constance. *Policy Alternatives for Mobile Homes.* New Brunswick, N.J.: Center for Urban Policy Research, Rutgers University, 1972. 59pp.

1618. Goldblatt, Abraham and Charles B. Pitcher. "Mobile Homes—A Growing Force in the Housing Sector." *Construction Review*, September 1972, pp. 4-9.

1619. Greenwald, C.S. "Mobile Homes in New England." *New England Economic Review*, May-June 1970, pp. 2-22.

1620. Homes, Robert E. "Housing and the Mobile Home Industry." *Arkansas Business and Economic Review*, November 1970, pp. 2-9.

1621. "Homes With/Without Wheels." *Federal Reserve San Francisco, Monthly Review*, June 1969, pp. 129-132.

1622. Kendig, Frank. "Facelift for Mobile Homes?" *Design & Environment*, Spring 1972, pp. 42-51.

1623. Kneeland, Douglas E. "From the 'Tin Can on Wheels' to the 'Mobile Home.' " *New York Times Magazine*, May 9, 1971, pp. 18-19+.

1624. Knight, Robert Lee. *Mobile Home and Conventional Home Owners: A Comparative Examination of Socio-Economic Characteristics and Housing-Related Preferences of Young Families in Chicago.* Ann Arbor, Mich.: University Microfilms, 1972 (Ph.D. dissertation, Northwestern University, 1971). 256pp. (order no. 72-7802)

1625. Magid, J.I. "Mobile Home Industry." *Financial Analyst Journal*, September 1969, pp. 29-32+.

1626. Mittelbach, Frank G. "The Role of Mobile Housing in California." In California Governor's Advisory Commission on Housing Problems. *Appendix to the Report on Housing in California.* San Francisco, 1963, pp. 535-552.

1627. "The Mobile Home Owner and the House He Lives In." *Urban Land*, September 1970, pp. 3-7. Also in George Sternlieb and Lynne Sagalyn (eds.). *Housing: 1970-1971; An AMS Anthology.* New York: AMS Press, 1972, pp. 288-298.

1628. "Mobile Home Parks: 1972." *NAHB Journal of Home Building*, August 1972, pp. 31-36.

1629. "Mobile Homes and the Housing Supply." *Federal Reserve Bank of Chicago, Business Conditions.* November 1972. (Entire issue). 16pp.

1630. "Mobile Homes Capture the Low-Cost Market." *Business Week*, May 13, 1972, pp. 146-148.

1631. "Mobile Homes in the National Income and Product Accounts." *Survey of Current Business*, July 1972, p. 11.

1632. "Mobile Homes Issue." *Mortgage Banker*, November 1972, entire issue.

1633. Morris, Earl W. and Margaret E. Woods (eds.). *Housing Crisis and Response: The Place of Mobile Homes in American Life.* Ithaca, N.Y.: N.Y. State College of Human Ecology at Cornell University. 1971. 75pp.

1634. Oregon University. Bureau of Governmental Research and Service. *Relocatable Housing: Siting Options for Mobile HOmes.* Eugene, Oregon, 1970. 70pp.

1635. Satterfield, H.D. "Mobile Homes: The Current Marketplace." *Journal of Commercial Bank Lending,* May 1969, pp. 37-44.

1636. Shiefman, Werba and Associates. "The Mobile Home Market." *Appraisal Journal,* July 1972, pp. 391-411.

1637. Starr, John O. "Guidelines for Mobile Home Park Development." *Appraisal Journal,* January 1971, pp. 41-51.

1638. "Study of a Proposed Mobile Home Park." *Appraisal Journal,* January 1971, pp. 52-56.

1639. Toal, William D. "Mobile Home Manufacturing–Infant Industry Grows Up." *Federal Reserve Bank of Atlanta, Monthly Review,* July 1971, pp. 129-135.

1640. "Trailers and Mobile Homes in Use Have Doubled in the Past 10 Years." *Real Estate Analyst,* March 9, 1970, pp. 89-96.

1641. U.S. Congress. Senate. Committee on Banking and Currency. Subcommittee on Housing and Urban Affairs. *Mobile Homes: Hearings, September 12 and 15, 1969, on S. 2740, a Bill to Amend Section 2 of the National Housing Act Relative to Mobile Homes.* Washington, D.C., 1969. 67pp.

1642. U.S. Department of Housing and Urban Development. *Mobile Home Park Development Standards.* Washington, D.C.: Government Printing Office, 1970. 54pp.

1643. Urban Land Institute. *Mobile Home Parks: Part I, An Analysis of Characteristics.* Washington, D.C., 1971. 80pp. (ULI Technical Bulletin no. 66)

1644. Wehrly, Max S. *Mobile Home Parks: Part 2, An Analysis of Communities.* Washington, D.C.: The Urban Land Institute, 1972. 136pp.

1645. "Why All the Excitement over Mobiles?" *Professional Builder,* September 1970, pp. 85-88.

See also: 47, 863.

b. Bibliographies

1646. Clark, Major L. III. *The Illusion of Mobile Homes as Supplemental Housing for Low Income Families.* Monticello, Ill.: Council of Planning Librarians, 1972 (Exchange Bibliography no. 349).

1647. Mobile Homes Manufacturers Association. *Mobile Home Industry Bibliography; July, 1965 through February, 1972.* Chicago, 1972.

1648. National Housing Center Library. *Mobile Homes: A Selected List of References.* Washington, D.C., 1971.

1649. U.S. Small Business Administration. *Mobile Homes and Parks.* Compiled by John M. Martin. Washington, D.C. June 1969. (Small Business Bibliography no. 41). 11pp.

1650. Vance, Mary. *Mobile Home Parks.* Monticello, Ill.: Council of Planning Librarians, 1960 (Exchange Bibliography no. 14).

c. Finance

1651. Asbury, Norman G. *A Formula for Financing Mobile Home Developments: Mobile Home Subdivisions, Mobile Home Parks.* Chicago, Ill.: Mobile Homes Manufacturers Association, 1970. 103pp.

1652. Breeze, H.H. and W.T. Altman. "Mobile Home Financing." *Journal of Commercial Bank Lending*, February 1970, pp. 31-45.

1653. Dennis, R.P. "Growing Opportunity in Mobile Home Financing." *Borrough's Clearing House*, October 1969, pp. 29-39+.

1654. "FHA-Insured Mobile Home Loans." *Banking*, October 1970, p. 36.

1655. "Financing of Mobile Homes." *Bankers Monthly*, November 1969, pp. 39-41.

1656. Lubell, D.P. "Legal Aspects of Mobile Home Lending by Institutional Lenders." *Los Angeles Bar Bulletin*, August 1970, pp. 408+.

1657. Mobile Homes Manufacturers Association. *Mobile Homes Finance Forum Proceedings: Banking and Finance Forum, Jan. 15, 1969, Louisville, Kentucky.* Sponsored by Banking and Finance Committee, Mobile Homes Manufacturers Association. Chicago, Ill., 1969. 49pp.

1658. National Association of Home Builders. *FHA Financing for Mobile Home Parks: Section 207: A Hypothetical Case.* Washington, D.C., 1971.

1659. Reil, K.P. "Bank Financing of Mobile Homes." *Federal Reserve Bulletin*, March 1971, pp. 179-182.

1660. Reimensynder, Harold G. "Mortgage Financing of Mobile Homes." *Robert Morris Associates Bulletin*, April 1964, pp. 335-342.

1661. Tooker, Lewis D. "Investment Potential in Mobile Homes." *Journal of Property Management*, May-June 1971, pp. 108-116.

1662. Williams, Franklin S. *The Mobile Home as a Rental Income Investment.* Ann Arbor, Mich.: University Microfilms, 1971 (Ph.D. dissertation, University of Arkansas, 1971). 205pp. (Order no. 71-19,562)

d. Taxation

1663. Berney, Robert E. and Arlyn J. Larson. "Micro-Analysis of Mobile Home Characteristics with Implications for Tax Policy." *Land Economics*, November 1966, pp. 453-463. Reply (Robert F. Rooney) with rejoinder, August 1968, pp. 414-418.

1664. Colorado State Legislative Council. *Report to the Colorado General Assembly: Mobile Home Taxation.* Denver, Colorado, November 1972.

1665. Galligan, John H. *Taxation and Zoning of Mobile Homes in New York.* New York: New York Conference of Mayors and Municipal Officials, 1972. 42pp.

1666. Peterson, J.R. and Harvey Diamond. *Mobile Homes in Georgia: A Study of the Personal Property Taxes Levied on Mobile Homes in the Metropolitan Areas of Georgia and the Significance of the Mobile Home Industry to the State.* Atlanta, Ga.: Industrial Development Division, Engineering Experiment Station, Georgia Institute of Technology, 1965. 29pp.

1667. Ranlett, John G. *An Evaluation of the Taxation of Mobilehomes in California.* Sacramento, Cal.: Fact Finding Committee on Revenue and Taxation, California Senate, 1965. 14pp.

1668. "Search for an Equitable Approach to Mobile Home Taxation." *De Paul Law Review*, Summer 1972, pp. 1008+.

See also: 1673.

e. Local Regulation of Mobile Homes

1669. American Society of Planning Officials. *Regulation of Mobile Home Subdivisions.* Chicago, Ill., April 1961. 45pp. (Planning Advisory Service Report no. 145).

1670. Bair, Frederick H., Jr. *Local Regulation of Mobile Homes Parks, Travel Trailer Parks and Related Facilities.* Chicago, Ill.: American Society of Planning Officials, 1965. 94pp.

1671. Bair, Frederick H., Jr. *Modular Housing, Including Mobile Homes; A Survey of Regulatory Practices and Planners' Opinions.* Chicago, Ill.: American Society of Planning Officials, 1971 (ASPO Planning Advisory Service Report no. 265).

1672. Bair, Frederick H., Jr. *Regulation of Modular Housing with Special Emphasis on Mobile Homes.* Chicago, Ill.: American Society of Planning Officials, July1August 1971. 104pp. (Planning Advisory Service Report no. 271).

1673. Bartke, Richard W. and Hilda R. Gage. "Mobile Homes: Zoning and Taxation." *Cornell Law Review*, April 1970, pp. 491-526.

1674. Eshelman, W.R. "Municipal Regulation of House Trailers in Pennsylvania." *Dickinson Law Review*, Spring 1962, pp. 301+.

1675. Mays, Arnold H. "Zoning for Mobile Homes: A Legal Analysis." *Journal of the American Institute of Planners*, August 1961, pp. 204-211.

1676. "Regulation of Mobile Homes." *Syracuse Law Review*, Fall 1961, pp. 125+.

1677. Worden, Rolfe A. "Zoning–Townships–Complete Exclusion of Trailer Camps and Parks." *Michigan Law Review*, March 1963, pp. 1010-1014.

See also: 1665.

5. OWNER-BUILT AND SELF-HELP HOUSING

1678. Davis, Tom L. "Cooperative Self-Help Housing," *Law and Contemporary Problems*, Summer 1967, pp. 409-415.

1679. Illinois Institute of Technology. Research Institute. *Study of Self- and Mutual-Help Programs.* Annapolis, Md.: Systems Sciences Research Div., IIT Research Institute, 1969.

1680. Kirschner Associates. *Study of Self- and Mutual-Help Housing Programs.* Proposal to Office of Urban Technology and Research, Dept. of Housing and Urban Development. Albuquerque, N.M., 1968.

1681. Margolis, Richard J. *Self-Help Housing in Urban Areas.* A report on self-help housing in the United States to the Office of Economic Opportunity. Washington, D.C.: International Self-Help Housing Association.

1682. Margolis, Richard J. *Something to Build on; The Future of Slef-Help Housing in the Struggle Against Poverty.* Washington, D.C.: International Self-help Housing Associates and the American Friends Service Committee, 1967. 84pp.

1683. Oregon University. Bureau of Governmental Research and Service *Self-Help Housing in Oregon.* Eugene, 1970. 52pp.

1684. Organization for Social and Technical Innovation. *Self-Help Housing in the U.S.A.* Cambridge, Mass., 1969. 158pp.

1685. "The Owner-Builder: Analysis and Recommendation." *Harvard Journal on Legislation*, March 1972, pp. 424-468.

1686. Shenkel, William L. "Self-Help Housing in the United States." *Land Economics*, May 1967, pp. 190-201.

1687. Thiokol Chemical Corp. *Study of Self- and Mutual-Help Housing Programs.* Ogden, Utah, 1968.

6. HOME OWNERSHIP

1688. Bearchell, Charles A. *An Analysis of Factors Influencing Decisions to Purchase New versus Used Single Family Residences in the San Fernando Valley.* Northridge, Calif.: Bureau of Business Services and Research, San Fernando Valley State College, 1968.

1689. Birnbaum, Howard and Rafael Weston. *Home Ownership and the Wealth Position of Black and White Americans.* Cambridge, Mass.: Program on Regional and Urban Economics, Harvard University, 1972.

1690. Downs. Anthony. "Home Ownership and American Free Enterprise." In Anthony Downs (ed.). *Urban Problems and Prospects.* Chicago, Ill.: Markham, 1970, pp. 156-164.

1691. Glaze, Bert Theodore. *Changing Patterns of Urban Home Ownership: Some Theoretical and Policy Implications.* Ann Arbor, Mich.: University Microfilms, 1963 (Ph.D. dissertation, The Ohio State University, 1962). 420pp. (order no. 63-1214)

1692. Grannatt, Milton H. *Survey of New Homeowners in the Lehigh Valley, 1968.* Bethlehem, Penn.: Center for Business Economics and Urban Studies, Lehigh University, 1968.

1693. Hampel, Donald J. *A Comparative Study of the Home Buying Process in Two Connecticut Housing Markets.* Storrs, Conn.: Center for Real Estate and Urban Economic Studies, University of Connecticut, 1970. 218pp.

1694. Hempel, Donald J. *The Role of the Real Estate Broker in the Home Buying Process.* Storrs, Conn.: Center for Real Estate and Urban Economic Studies, School of Business Administration, University of Connecticut, 1969. 81pp.

1695. Hoffman, Bernard Benjamin, Jr. *Forced Home Ownership: A Study of a Hypothesis Which Claims That Involuntary Ownership, Blighted Neighborhoods and Inordinate Property Taxation Are Associated with Elderly and Single Owners in Older Suburbia and the Rural-Urban Fringe.* Ann Arbor, Mich.: University Microfilms, 1968 (D.S.S. dissertation, Syracuse University, 1968). 154pp. (order no. 68-13,832)

1696. "Homing in on the Homing Instinct: Ambitious New Survey Seeks to Pinpoint the Motivations That Prompt People to Buy Homes." *Business Week*, October 14, 1967, pp. 104-106+.

1697. Juster, F. Thomas and Robert E. Lipsey. "A Note on Consumer Asset Formation in the United States." *Economic Journal*, December 1967, pp. 834-855.

1698. Kain, John F. and John M. Quigley. "Housing Market Discrimination, Homeownership, and Savings Behavior." *American Economic Review*, June 1972, pp. 263-277.

1699. Linden, F. "Home Ownership: 1980." *Conference Board Record*, October 1969, pp. 57-60.

1700. Linden, F. "Tomorrow's Home Buyer." *Conference Board Record*, November 1969, pp. 51-53.

1701. Malone, John R. "A Statistical Comparison of Recent New and Used House Buyers." Unpublished Ph.D. dissertation, University of Chicago, 1963.

1702. Marcuse, Peter. *To Buy Or Not to Buy.* Washington, D.C.: The Urban Institute, March, 1971 (Urban Institute Working Paper 112-126).

1703. McQuade, Walter. "Why People Don't Buy Houses." *Fortune*, December 1967, pp. 153-154.

1704. Payne, John C. "101 Home Buyers: the Consumer, the Conveyancing Process, and Some Questions of Professional Conduct." *Alabama Law Review*, Spring 1964, pp. 275-350.

1705. Sengstock, Frank S. and Mary C. Sengstock. "Homeownership: A Goal for All Americans." *Journal of Urban Law*, vol. 46, no. 3, 1969, pp. 313-602.

See also: 237-242, 247, 249, 252, 258-260, 295-309, 673, 699, 705, 708-710, 714, 716, 760, 979, 1070, 1714, 1729, 1757, 1796, 2333, 2334, 3498; Low Income Housing–Home Ownership: 2127+.

# III. SOCIAL/POLITICAL FRAMEWORK

## A. HOUSING SPECIFIC SEGMENTS OF SOCIETY

### 1. THE ELDERLY

#### a. General

1706. American Society of Planning Officials. *Planning and an Aging Population.* Chicago, Ill., July 1961. 40pp. (Planning Advisory Service Report no. 148).

1707. Ashley, E.E., III. "Types of Housing for the Elderly." *Construction Review*, May 1961, pp. 6-11.

1708. Beyer, Glenn H. *Economic Aspects of Housing for the Aged.* Ithaca, N.Y.: Center for Housing and Environmental Studies, Cornell University, 1961. 50pp.

1709. Beyer, Glenn H. and Margaret E. Woods. *Living & Activity Patterns of the Aged.* Ithaca, N.Y.: Center for Housing and Environmental Studies, Cornell University, 1963. 29pp.

1710. Beyer, Glenn H. and Sylvia G. Wahl. *The Elderly and Their Housing.* Ithaca, N.Y.: Agricultural Experiment Station, Cornell University, 1963. 63pp.

1711. Bronson, Edith P. "An Experiment in Intermediate Housing Facilities for the Elderly." *Gerontologist*, Pt. 1, Spring 1972, pp. 22-26.

1712. Caravety, Raymond D. and David S. Haviland. *Life Safety from Fire: A Guide for Housing the Elderly.* Prepared for the Federal Housing Administration. Washington, D.C.: Government Printing Office, 1968. 90pp.

1713. Buttrick, Shirley M. *Interaction Patterns, Housing and Morale of the Aged.* Ann Arbor, Mich.: University Microfilms, 1969 (D.S.W. dissertation, Catholic University of America, 1969). 237pp. (order no. 69-19,707)

1714. Chen, Yung-Ping. "Home Ownership: the Case of the Elderly." *California Real Estate Magazine*, July 1972, pp. 26-28.

1715. Conference on Housing for an Aging Population, New Brunswick, N.J., 1961. *Housing for an Aging Population. A Report of the Conference, October 10, 1961. . . .* Trenton, N.J.: New Jersey Division of Aging, 1962. 60pp.

1716. Dick, H.R. *et al.* "Residential Patterns of Aged Persons prior to Institutionalization." *Journal of Marriage and the Family*, February 1964, pp. 96-98.

1717. Eckersberg, Alfred K. "Housing for the Elderly." *Urban Land*, November 1961, pp. 1, 3-7.

1718. Erlich, Ira F. "Life-styles among Persons 70 Years and Older in Age-Segregated Housing." *Gerontologist*, Pt. 1, Spring 1972, pp. 27-31.

1719. Frieden, Elaine. "Social Differences and Their Consequences for Housing the Aged." *Journal of the American Institute of Planners*, May 1960, pp. 119-124.

1720. Grier, George W. and Joan Heifitz, with the assistance of Sheila Morgenstein. *Housing Older People: Their Needs, The Federal Programs.* Washington, D.C.: The President's Council on Aging, 1964. 166pp.

1721. Heslin, Philip Joseph. *A Study of Four Housing Modalities for the Elderly Which Provide Ascending Levels of Elderly Population Density as Related to Intra-Generational Social Interaction, Anomia, Isolation, and Life Satisfaction.* Ann Arbor, Mich.: University Microfilms, 1972 (Ph.D. dissertation, University of Minnesota, 1972). 173pp. (order no. 72-27,758).

1722. "Housing." *Gerontologist*, Part 2, Summer 1972, pp. 3-10.

1723. Interfaith Conference on Housing for Senior Citizens, Washington, D.C., 1964. *Major Statements and Workshop Reports.* Washington, D.C. Housing and Home Finance Agency, Office of the Administrator, 1964. 75pp.

1724. Jackson, Mercer L., Jr. "Housing for Older Americans." *HUD Challenge*, July 1972, pp. 4-7.

1725. Kipfer, Joseph D. *Age Has Many Faces; A Report on Church-Sponsored—Government-Related Housing for the Aged.* Philadelphia, Pa.: Research and Survey, National Division of the Board of Missions of the Methodist Church, 1965. 76pp.

1726. Langford, Marilyn. *Community Aspects of Housing for the Aged.* Ithaca, N.Y.: Center for Housing and Environmental Studies, Cornell University, 1962. 49pp.

1727. Michigan State Task Force on Senior Citizen Housing. *A Ten Year Plan for Housing Older People in Michigan; A Report.* Grand Rapids, 1966. 43pp.

1728. Mittelbach, Frank G. "Housing for California's Senior Citizens." In California Governor's Advisory Commission on Housing Problems. *Appendix to the Report on Housing in California.* San Francisco, 1963, pp. 621-648.

1729. Murray, J. "Homeownership and Financial Assets: Findings from the 1968 Survey of the Aged." *Social Security Bulletin*, August 1972, pp. 3-23.

1730. Murray, J. "Living Arrangements of People Aged 65 and Older: Findings from 1968 Survey of the Aged." *Social Security Bulletin*, September 1971, pp. 3-14.

1731. Musson, Noverre and Helen Heusinkveld. *Housing for the Elderly.* New York: Reinhold Publishing Corp., 1963. 216pp.

1732. National Council on the Aging. *Building for Older People; Financing, Construction, Administration. . . .* New York, 1961.

1733. Nelson, Edith Lavina. *The Evolution of Federal and State Legislation Aiding Housing for the Elderly in New York State.* Ann Arbor, Mich.: University Microfilms, 1963 (Ph.D. dissertation, Syracuse University, 1962). 245pp. (order no. 63,3183)

1734. New York (State) Executive Department. Division of Housing and Community Renewal. *Characteristics of Housing and Family Groupings of the Aging Population in New York State, 1957.* New York, 1960.

1735. New York (State) Executive Department. Division of Housing and Community Renewal. *How to Provide Housing Which the Elderly Can Afford; A Guide to Its Development by Builders, Organization Sponsors Such as Unions and Denominational Groups, and Other Private and Public Interests.* New York, 1960. 36pp.

1736. New York (State) Division of Housing and Community Renewal. *New York State's Housing Program for Senior Citizens.* New York, 1965. 21pp.

1737. Pennsylvania Workshop on Housing the Elderly, Harrisburg, 1963. *Proceedings.* Harrisburg, Pa., 1963. 28pp.

1738. "Proposals on Housing for the Elderly," *American Institute of Architects Journal*, January 1972, p. 46.

1739. Research Conference on Patterns of Living and Housing of the Middle-Aged and Older People, Washington, D.C., 1965. *Patterns of Living and Housing of Middle-Aged and Older People; Proceedings.* Washington, D.C.: Government Printing Office, 1966. 181pp. (Public Health Service publication 1496)

1740. Rosow, Irving. *Housing and Social Integration of the Aged.* Cleveland, Ohio: Western Reserve University, 1964. 213pp.

1741. Smith, Wallace F. *Housing for the Elderly in California.* Berkeley, Calif.: Center for Real Estate and Urban Economics, University of California, 1961.

1742. Smith, Wallace F. "Housing for the Elderly, An Evaluation of Existing and Proposed Programs." *Appraisal Journal*, April 1961, pp. 177-185.

1743. Smith, Wallace F. "The Housing Preferences of Elderly People." *Appraisal Journal*, October 1962, pp. 515-522.

1744. Spector, Sidney. "Housing for Senior Citizens." *New York Law Forum*, Spring 1965, pp. 30-50.

1745. U.S. Congress. Senate. Committee on Banking and Currency. *Housing for the Elderly. Hearings. . . .* Washington, D.C.: Government Printing Office, 1963. 187pp.

1746. U.S. Congress. Senate. Committee on Banking and Currency. *Senior Citizens Housing Act of 1962; Report. . . .* Washington, D.C.: Government Printing Office, 1962. 25pp.

1747. U.S. Congress. Senate. Special Committee on Aging. *Housing for the Elderly. A Report of the Subcommittee on Housing for the Elderly to the Special Committee on Aging, United States Senate.* Washington, D.C.: Government Printing Office, 1962. 57pp.

1748. U.S. Congress. Senate. Special Committee on Aging. *Housing Problems of the Elderly. Hearings. . . .* Washington, D.C. Government Printing Office, 1961.

1749. U.S. Congress. Senate. Special Committee on Aging. *Housing Problems of the Elderly. Hearings. . . .* Washington, D.C.: Government Printing Office, 1964.

1750. U.S. Congress. Senate. Special Committee on Aging. *Usefulness of the Model Cities Program to the Elderly. Hearings. . . .* Washington, D.C.: Government Printing Office, 1968.

1751. U.S. Congress. Senate. Special Committee on Aging. Subcommittee on Housing for the Elderly. *Adequacy of Federal Response to Housing Needs of Older Americans. Hearings. . . .* Washington, D.C.: Government Printing Office, 1971.

1752. U.S. Department of Housing and Urban Development. Federal Housing Administration. *Minimum Property Standards Housing for the Elderly, with Special Consideration for the Handicapped.* Washington, D.C., 1966. 117pp.

1753. U.S. Housing and Home Finance Agency. Office of the Assistant Commissioner for Programs. *Some Facts about FHA Housing for the Elderly; Projects and People.* Washington, D.C.: Government Printing Office, 1964. 13pp.

1754. U.S. Housing and Home Finance Agency. *What's New in Housing the Elderly?* Washington, D.C., 1961. 34pp.

1755. U.S. Housing and Home Finance Agency. Office of Program Policy. *Senior Citizens and How They Live: An Analysis of 1960 Census Data.* Washington, D.C., 1962.

1756. Vogelsang, Frederic. *Training Needs in Managing Housing for the Elderly.* Washington, D.C.: National Association of Housing and Redevelopment Officials, 1968. 157pp.

1757. Wallin, Peter L. "Homeownership Problems of the Elderly." *Clearinghouse Review*, August-September 1972, pp. 227-232.

1758. *White House Conference on Aging, Nov. 28 - Dec. 2, 1971: Population, Housing and Income and Federal Housing Programs.* Washington, D.C.: U.S. Department of Housing and Urban Development, 1971. 122pp.

1759. White House Conference on Aging, Washington, D.C., 1971. *Housing the Elderly.* Washington, D.C.: Government Printing Office, March 1971. 120pp.

1760. Williams, Constance and Deborah S. Peterson. *Housing Costs and Choices of the Older Consumer; An Exploratory Study.* Boston, Mass.: Special Services Department, Women's Educational and Industrial Union, 1960.

See also 723, 727, 1282, 2641, 3104; Relocation–The Elderly and Relocation: 3078+; Public Housing–The Elderly in Public Housing: 2862+.

b. Bibliographies

1761. National Housing Center. Library. *Housing for Our Senior Citizens; A List of Selected References*. Washington, D.C., 1962. 9pp.

1762. New York University. Graduage School of Public Administration. *Bibliography: Management of Housing for the Elderly*. New York, 1962. 28pp.

1763. U.S. Department of Health, Education, and Welfare. Special Staff on Aging. *Selected References on Aging: No. 4, Housing Senior Citizens*. Washington, D.C., 1962. 22pp.

1764. U.S. Housing and Home Finance Agency. Library. *Housing for the Aged; A Reading List for Architects*. Washington, D.C. 1963. 25pp.

1765. U.S. Housing and Home Finance Agency. Library. *Housing for the Elderly: Annotated References*. Washington, D.C.: Government Printing Office, 1965. 36pp.

1766. Vance, Mary. *Housing for the Elderly*. Monticello, Ill.: Council of Planning Librarians, 1963 (Exchange Bibliogrpahy no. 27).

2. THE HANDICAPPED

1767. Baker, Madeline *et al. State and Local Efforts to Eliminate Architectural Barriers to the Handicapped*. Washington, D.C.: National League of Cities, 1967. 162pp.

1768. California Department of Public Health. *Handicapped Persons Pilot Project; Residential Care Needs*. Berkeley, Calif., 1969. 57pp.

1769. Dwoskin, Stephen. "The Disabled's Encounter with the Environment." *Design and Environment*, Summer 1970, pp. 60-63.

1770. Massachusetts Association of Paraplegics. *Housing Needs of the Handicapped*. Bedford, Mass., 1970. 65pp.

1771. Pastalan, Leon A. *Vistula Manor Demonstration Housing for the Physically Disabled*. Final report prepared for the Toledo Metropolitan Housing Authority. Toledo, Ohio: Toledo Research Foundation, University of Toledo, 1969. 84pp.

1772. U.S. Congress. House. Committee on Banking and Currency. *Housing for Physically Handicapped Families and Persons. Hearing before the Subcommittee on Housing . . . on H.R. 7394, a Bill to Amend Title II of the Housing Act of 1959 to Extend the Program of Loans for Housing for the Elderly so as to Include Housing for Handicapped Families and Persons, October 21, 1963.* Washington, D.C.: Government Printing Office, 1963. 40pp.

1773. U.S. Congress. Senate. Committee on Banking and Currency. *Paraplegic Housing Program. Report....* Washington, D.C.: Government Printing Office, 1970. 5pp.

1774. U.S. Department of Housing and Urban Development. Housing Assistance Administration. *Housing for the Physically Impaired: A Guide for Planning and Design*. Washington, D.C.: Government Printing Office. 1968. 49pp.

1775. U.S. Department of Housing and Urban Development. Housing Assistance Administration. *Housing for the Physically Impaired: A Guide for Planning and Design*. Washington, D.C.: Government Printing Office, 1968. 49pp.

1776. U.S. Department of Housing and Urban Development. Library and Information Division. *The Built Environment for the Elderly and the Handicapped*. Washington, D.C.: Government Printing Office, June 1971. 46pp.

3. SINGLE PERSONS

1777. Fielding, Byron. "Low-Income, Single-Person Housing: What's Happening as a Result of the 'Congregate Housing' Provisions of the 1970 Act?" *Journal of Housing*, March 1972, pp. 131-136.

1778. New School for Social Research. Center for New York City Affairs. *A Program for Tenants in Single Room Occupancy (SRO) and for Their New York City Neighbors*. A report prepared for the Borough President of Manhattan, the Community Planning Board no. 7 and its Council of Advisors. New York, 1969.

1779. "No Room for Singles: A Gap in the Housing Law." *Yale Law Journal*, December 1970, pp. 395-432.

4. MINORITIES

a. General

1780. Abrams, C. "Housing Problems and the Negro." *Daedalus*, Winter 1966, pp. 64-76.

1781. Arlington Community Action Committee, Arlington County, Va. *A Study, Report, and Recommendations on the Housing Needs of Economic and Racial Minority Groups in Arlington County, Virginia ...* Arlington, Va., April 1966, 33pp.

1782. Canaday, Ben. *Mortgage Availability for Nonwhites in the Chicago Area: A Report.* Chicago, Ill.: Chicago Commission on Human Relations, 1965.

1783. Case, Fred E. *Minority Families in the Metropolis.* Los Angeles, Calif.: Real Estate Research Program, Division of Research, Graduate School of Business Administration, University of California, 1966. 47pp.

1784. Center for the Study of Democratic Institutions. *Race and Housing: An Interview with Edward P. Eichler, President, Eichler Homes, Inc.* Santa Barbara, Calif., 1964. 23pp.

1785. "The First American Indian Mortgage Company." *HUD Challenge*, July 1971, pp. 10-11.

1786. Glazer, Nathan and Davis McEntire. *Studies in Housing and Minority Groups.* Berkeley, Calif.: University of California, 1960. 288pp.

1787. Grier, Eunice S. "Research Needs in the Field of Housing and Race." *Journal of Intergroup Relations*, Summer 1960, pp. 21-31.

1788. Grier, Eunice and George Grier. *The Impact of Race on Neighborhoods in the Metropolitan Setting.* Washington, D.C.: Washington Center for Metropolitan Studies, 1961. 13pp.

1789. Herman, Judith Magidson. *Housing for the Other America; A Fifty-State Stragegy.* New York: American Jewish Committee, 1969. 45pp.

1790. Ladd, Florence C. "Black Youths View Their Environments: Some Views of Housing." *Journal of the American Institute of Planners*, March 1972, pp. 108-116.

1791. Laessig, Robert Ernest. *Racial Disparities in Urban Housing Quality.* Ann Arbor, Mich.: University Microfilms, 1972 (Ph.D. dissertation, Cornell University, 1971). 321pp. (order no. 72-8871)

1792. Leaman, Samuel Hardy. *A Study of Housing Decisions by Negro Home Owners and Negro Renters.* Chapel Hill, N.C.: Center for Urban and Regional Studies, University of North Carolina, 1967 (Environmental Policies and Urban Development Thesis Series no. 8). 136pp.

1793. Philadelphia Community Renewal Agency. *The Negro Housing Problem: A Program for Philadelphia.* Philadelphia, 1966. 117pp.

1794. Schermer, George. "Housing Conditions and Housing Needs of Low and Moderate Income Minority Groups." Unpublished report prepared for the U.S. Commission on Civil Rights, June 1966.

1795. Spiegel, Allen David. *Housing and Related Patterns of Middle Income Negroes*. Ann Arbor, Mich.: University Microfilms, 1970 (Ph.D. dissertation, The Florence Heller Graduate School for Advanced Studies in Social Welfare, Brandeis University, 1969). 285pp. (order no. 70-19,983)

1796. Stacey, William A. *Black Home Ownership: A Sociological Case Study of Metropolitan Jacksonville*. New York: Praeger, 1972. 132pp.

1797. Tilly, Charles *et al. Race and Residence in Wilmington, Delaware*. New York: Bureau of Publications, Teachers College, Columbia University, 1965.

1798. Tucker, Sterling. *Beyond the Burning; Life and Death of the Ghetto*. New York: Association Press, 1968. 160pp.

1799. Tucker, Sterling. *Why the Ghetto Must Go*. New York: Public Affairs Committee, 1968. 28pp.

1800. U.S. Department of Housing and Urban Development. *The House on W. 114th Street*. Washington, D.C.: Government Printing Office, 1968. 60pp.

1801. U.S. Housing and Home Finance Agency. Office of Program Policy. *Our Nonwhite Population and Its Housing: The Changes between 1950 and 1960*. Washington, D.C.: Government Printing Office, 1963. 104pp.

1802. Wolman, H.I. and N.C. Thomas. "Black Interests, Black Groups, and Black Influence in the Federal Policy Process: The Cases of Housing and Education." *The Journal of Politics*, November 1970, pp. 875-897.

See also: 325-328, 1689, 1698, 2535, 3484, 3500; The Effect of Race on Property Values: 796+; Minorities and Housing Markets: 1023+.

b. Bibliographies

1803. Bolan, Lewis. *The Role of Urban Planning in the Residential Integration of Middle Class Negroes and Whites*. Monticello, Ill.: Council of Planning Librarians, 1968 (Exchange Bibliography no. 41).

1804. Boyce, Byrl N. and Sidney Turoff. *Minority Groups and Housing; a Bibliography, 1950-1970*. Morristown, N.J.: General Learning Press, 1972. 202pp.

1805. Messner, Stephen D. *Minority Groups and Housing; A Selected Bibliography, 1950-67*. Storrs, Conn.: Center for Real Estate and Urban Economic Studies, University of Connecticut, 1968. 60pp.

1806. The Negro Bibliographic and Research Center. *Bibliographic Survey: The Negro in Print; Focus on Housing.* Washington, D.C., 1966.

1807. U.S. Department of Housing and Urban Development. Intergroup Relations Service. *Basic References on Housing Minorities and Equal Housing Opportunity.* Washington, D.C., 1965, 9pp.

1808. U.S. Department of Housing and Urban Development. Library. *Equal Opportunity: A Bibliography of Research on Equal Opportunity in Housing.* Washington, D.C.: Government Printing Office, 1969. 24pp.

1809. U.S. President's Committee on Equal Opportunity in Housing. *Equal Opportunity in Housing: A Selected Bibliography of Materials for Study and Use.* Compiled by the Committee. Washington, D.C., 1965. 16pp.

1810. von Furstenberg, George M. *Discrimination in Housing: A Selected Bibliography.* Monticello, Ill.: Council of Planning Librarians, 1972 (Exchange Bibliography no. 298).

c. Discrimination and Housing

*1) General*

1811. Abrams, C. "Discrimination and the Struggle for Shelter." *New York Law Forum*, January 1960, pp. 3+.

1812. Berg, Irving. *Racial Discrimination in Housing: A Study in Quest for Governmental Access by Minority Interest Groups, 1945-1962.* Ann Arbor, Mich.: University Microfilms, 1968 (Ph.D. dissertation, University of Florida, 1967). 377pp. (order no. 68-9511)

1813. Berger, Stephen D. *The Social Consequences of Residential Segregation of the Urban American Negro.* New York: Metropolitan Applied Research Center, 1970. 68pp.

1814. Black, Algernon David. *Fair Play in Housing: Who's My Neighbor?* New York: Public Affairs Committee, 1968. 28pp.

1815. Blumberg, L. and M. Lalli. "Little Ghettoes: A Study of Negroes in the Suburbs." *Phylon*, Summer 1966, pp. 117-131.

1816. Blumberg, L. "Segregated Housing: Marginal Location and the Crisis of Confidence." *Phylon*, Winter 1964, pp. 321-330.

1817. "Damages—Mental Illness—Damages Recoverable for Mental Distress Resulting from Racial Discrimination in Housing Rental—*Gray v. Serruto Builders, Inc. Harvard Law Review,* January 1971, pp. 746-748.

1818. Ginger, Ann Fagan. "A Little Democracy–Housing for America's Minorities in 1960." *Lawyers Guild Review*, Spring 1960, pp. 6-17.

1819. Grier, Eunice and George Grier. *Discrimination in Housing: A Handbook of Fact*. New York: Anti-defamation League of B'nai B'rith, 1960. 67pp.

1820. Grier, Eunice and George Grier. "Equality and Beyond: Housing Segregation in the Great Society." *Daedalus*, Winter 1966, pp. 77-106.

1821. Grier, George W. *Bias in Newspaper Real Estate Advertising*. Washington, D.C.: Washington Center for Metropolitan Studies, 1970. 35pp.

1822. Grier, George and Eunice Grier. *Equality and Beyond: Housing Segregation and the Goals of the Great Society*. Chicago, Ill.: Quadrangle Books, 1966. 115pp.

1823. Kistin, Helen. *Housing Discrimination in Massachusetts*. Boston, Mass.: Housing Advisory Research Committee, Massachusetts Committee on Discrimination, 1964.

1824. Langendorf, Richard, "Residential Desegregation Potential." *Journal of the American Institute of Planners*, March 1969, pp. 90-95.

1825. Lieberson, Stanley. "The Impact of Residential Segregation on Ethnic Assimilation." *Social Forces*, October 1961, pp. 52-57.

1826. McEntire, Davis. *Residence and Race: Final and Comprehensive Report to the Commission on Race and Housing*. Berkeley, Calif.: University of California Press, 1960. 409pp.

1827. Marston, W.G. "Social Class as a Factor in Ethnic and Racial Segregation." *International Journal of Comparative Sociology*, June 1968, pp. 145-153.

1828. McGhee, Milton L. and Ann Fagan Ginger. "The House I Live in: A Study of Housing for Minorities." *Cornell Law Quarterly*, Winter 1961, pp. 194-257.

1829. Mercer, Norman A. "Discrimination in Rental Housing: A Study of Resistance of Landlords to Non-White Tenants." *Phylon*, Spring 1962, pp. 47-54.

1830. Moore, Joan W. and Frank G. Mittelbach. *Residential Segregation in the Urban Southwest: A Comparative Study*. Los Angeles, Calif.: Graduate School of Business Administration, University of California, June 1966.

1831. National Committee Against Discrimination in Housing. *At the Core of Urban Chaos: The Broken Promise: Will It Be Redeemed?* New York, 1971. 24pp.

1832. National Committee Against Discrimination in Housing. *How the Federal Government Builds Ghettoes.* New York, October 1968.

1833. National Committee Against Discrimination in Housing. *Patterns and Practices of Housing Discrimination in San Leadro, California.* New York, 1971. 30pp.

1834. National Conference on Equal Opportunity in Housing. *Challenge to American Communities. Report. . . .* Washington, D.C.: National Committee Against Discrimination in Housing, 1963. 50pp.

1835. Pascal, Anthony H. *The Economics of Housing Segregation.* Santa Monica, Calif.: Rand Corp., 1967. 220pp.

1836. Pascal, Anthony Henry. *The Economics of Housing Segregation.* Ann Arbor, Mich.: University Microfilms, 1968 (Ph.D. dissertation, Columbia University, 1967). 234 pp. (order no. 68-5621).

1837. Rafferty, Maureen. *Bias in Newspaper Real Estate Advertising: A*

1838. Rice, C.E. "Bias in Housing: Toward a New Approach." *Santa Clara Lawyer*, Spring 1966, pp. 162+.

1839. Roof, W. Clark. "Residential Segregation of Blacks and Racial Inequality in Southern Cities: Toward a Causal Model." *Social Problems*, Winter 1972, pp. 393-407.

1840. Rosen, Harry M. and David H. Rosen. *But Not Next Door.* New York: I. Obolensky, 1962. 175pp.

1841. Smith, Clarence G. and George Hopkins III. *Containment of Minority Groups through Housing.* Toledo, Ohio: Toledo Chapter, National Association for Advancement of Colored People, 1968.

1842. Taeuber, Karl E. "The Effect of Income Redistribution on Racial Residential Segregation." *Urban Affairs Quarterly,* September 1968, pp. 5-14.

1843. Taeuber, K. E. "Problem of Residential Segregation." *Academy of Political Science Proceedings,* July 1968, pp. 101-110.

1844. Taeuber, K. E. and A. F. Taeuber. "Negro as an Immigrant Group: Recent Trends in Racial and Ethnic Segregation in Chicago." *American Journal of Sociology*, January 1964, pp. 374-382.

1845. United Planning Organization of the National Capital Area. *Study of Discrimination and Equal Opportunity in Housing, Community Facilities, and Services*. Washington, D.C.: District of Columbia Community Renewal Program, 1965. 148pp.

1846. U.S. Commission on Civil Rights. *Civil Rights U.S.A.; Housing in Washington, D.C.* Washington, D.C., 1962. 45pp.

1847. U.S. Commission on Civil Rights. *Discrimination in Housing in the Boston Metropolitan Area; Report*. Washington, D.C., 1963. 83pp.

1848. U.S. Commission on Civil Rights. *Family Housing and the Negro Serviceman; 1963 Staff Report*. Washington, D.C., 1964. 48pp.

1849. U.S. Commission on Civil Rights. *Hearings, Baltimore, Maryland, August 17-19, 1970*. Washington, D.C.: Government Printing Office, 1971. 1043pp.

1850. U.S. Commission on Civil Rights. *Hearings, St. Louis, Missouri, January 14-17, 1970*. Washington, D.C.: Government Printing Office, 1971. 755pp.

1851. U.S. Commission on Civil Rights. *Housing in Saint Louis: Staff Report*. Washington, D.C., 1970. 51pp.

1852. U.S. Commission on Civil Rights. *Housing in Washington. Hearings. . . .* Washington, D.C., 1962. 478pp.

1853. U.S. Commission on Civil Rights. Massachusetts State Advisory Committee. *Report on Massachusetts: Housing Discrimination in the Springfield-Holyoke-Chicopee Metropolitan Area*. Washington, D.C., December 1966. 74pp.

1854. U.S. Commission on Civil Rights. *Report, 1961: Book 4, Housing*. Washington, D.C.: Government Printing Office, 1961. 206pp.

1855. Vaughan, Garrett A. "The Role of Residential Race Segregation in Causing and Perpetuating Inferior Housing for Lower-Income Nonwhites." *Journal of Economics and Business*, Fall 1972, pp. 53-60.

1856. Warner, A. E. and Milton S. Goldberg. "Governments and Housing: Accessibility of Minority Groups to Living Space." *Land Economics*, November 1961, pp. 369-373.

1857. Weaver, Robert C. "The Changing Status of Racial Groups." *Journal of Intergroup Relations*, Winter 1960/1961, pp. 6-17.

1858. White House Conference "To Fulfill These Rights," June 1-2, 1966. *Report*. Washington, D.C.: Government Printing Office, 1966. 177pp.

1859. Wolfinger, Raymond E. and Fred I. Greenstein. "The Repeal of Fair Housing in California: An Analysis of Referendum Voting." *American Political Science Review*, September 1968, pp. 753-769.

See also: 324, 329-331, 735, 1689, 1698, 1810; Site Selection in Federally Assisted Housing: 2560+; The Effect of Race on Property Values: 796+; Minorities and Housing Markets: 1023+; Exclusionary Zoning: 1283+.

*2) Legal Aspects and Anti-Discrimination Legislation*

1860. Abrams, Charles. "The Housing Order and Its Limits." *Commentary*, January 1963, pp. 10-14.

1861. Abrams, S. D. and E. B. Baldwin. "Local Fair Housing Legislation: Adoption, Enforcement, and Related Problems." *Urban Lawyer*, Summer 1970, pp. 277-314.

1862. Aldrich, R. D. "Rumford Act—Protection or Deprivation?" *Los Angeles Bar Bulletin*, September 1964, pp. 439+.

1863. "Application of the Fourteenth Amendment to Builders of Private Housing." *University of Kansas Law Review*, March 1964, pp. 426+.

1864. Aurbach, Herbert A. *et al.* "Restrictive and Protective Viewpoints of Fair Housing Legislation: A Comparative Study of Attitudes." *Social Problems*, Fall 1960, pp. 118-125.

1865. Avins, A. "Anti-discrimination Legislation as an Infringement on Freedom of Choice." *New York Law Forum*, January 1960, pp. 13+.

1866. Avins, A. "Civil Rights Act of 1966, the Civil Rights Bill of 1966, and the Right to Buy Property." *Southern California Law Review*, Winter 1967, pp. 274+.

1867. Avins, Alfred (ed.). *Open Occupancy vs. Forced Housing under the Fourteenth Amendment: A Symposium on Anti-discrimination Legislation, Freedom of Choice, and Property Rights in Housing*. New York: Bookmailers, 1963. 316pp.

1868. Bartell, Jeffrey B. *et al.* "The Mediation of Civil Rights Disputes: Open Housing in 'Milwaukee." *Wisconsin Law Review*, No. 4 (1968), pp. 1127-1191.

1869. Branscomb, A. W. "Analysis of Attempts to Prohibit Racial Discrimination in the Sale and Rental of Publicly Assisted Private Housing." *George Washington Law Review*, April 1960, pp. 758-778.

1870. Butler, Patrick H. "Voluntary Plans to Prevent De Facto Segregation in Housing Receive Statutory Protection in Indiana." In *Urban Law Annual 1968*. St. Louis, Mo.: School of Law, Washington University, 1968, pp. 154-156.

1871. Caldwell, Wallace F. "Fair Housing Laws and Fundamental Liberties." *Journal of Human Relations*, 2nd Quarter 1966, pp. 230-241.

1872. Casstevens, Thomas W. *Politics, Housing and Race Relations: California's Rumford Act and Proposition 14*. Berkeley, California: Institute of Governmental Studies, University of California, June 1967. 97pp.

1873. Casstevens, Thomas W. *Politics, Housing, and Race Relations: The Defeat of Berkeley's Fair Housing Ordinance*. Berkeley, Calif.: Institute of Governmental Studies, University of California, 1965. 117pp.

1874. C-E-I-R, Inc. *Survey of Home Builders' Opinion on Impact of a Possible Executive Anti-Discrimination Order*. An Analysis Prepared for the National Association of Home Builders. Arlington, Va., 1962. 17pp.

1875. "Civil Rights–Discrimination in Public Accommodations and Housing–State and Federal Remedies Available in Oregon." *Oregon Law Review*, February 1965, pp. 123+.

1876. "Civil Rights–Fair Housing–Publication of 'Mrs. Murphy' Racial Preference Advertisement Violates Fair Housing Act of 1968 But Injunctive Relief Denied." *Wayne Law Review*, May/June 1972, pp. 1101-1110.

1877. Clancy, J. G., and H. N. Nemerovski. "Some Legal Aspects of Proposition Fourteen." *Hastings Law Journal*, August 1964, pp. 3+.

1878. Colvin, G. L. "Discriminatory Housing Markets, Racial Unconscionability, and Section 1988: The Contract Buyers League Case." *Yale Law Journal*, January 1971, pp. 516-566.

1879. Commerce Clearing House. *Fair Housing Act of 1968 with Explanation*. Chicago, Ill., 1968. 32pp.

1880. "Constitutional Law: Civil Rights: Discrimination in Housing." *UCLA Law Review*, January 1963, pp. 401+.

1881. "Constitutional Law–Equal Protection and the 'Right' To Housing." *North Carolina Law Review*, February 1972, pp. 369+.

1882. "Constitutional Law–Equal Protection–Fair Housing Legislation." *Western Reserve Law Review*, November 1966, pp. 328+.

1883. "Constitutional Law—Equal Protection of the Laws—State Statute Prohibiting Discrimination in Private Sale of Publicly Assisted Housing Denies Equal Protection of the Laws." *Harvard Law Review*, June 1962, pp. 1647+.

1884. "Constitutional Law—Racial Discrimination in Public Housing—Standing to Sue—Proof of Denial of Admission to a Public Housing Project on Account of Race or Color Necessary to Maintain Action to Enjoin Such Discrimination." *New York Law Forum*, January 1960, pp. 96+.

1885. "Constitutional Law—State Action: Significant Involvement in Ostensibly Private Discriminations." *Michigan Law Review*, February 1967, pp. 777+.

1886. "Constitutional Law: The End of Private Racial Discrimination in Housing through Revival of the Civil Rights Act of 1866." *Tulsa Law Journal*, March 1970, pp. 146+.

1887. "Controversy in Congress over 'Open Housing': Pro & Con." *Congressional Digest*, November 1966, pp. 257-288.

1888. Denno, T. F. "New Fair Housing Law: 1866." *American University Law Review*, June 1969, pp. 491+.

1889. "Development of Open Occupancy Laws: A Survey of Legislation Against Discrimination in Housing." *Gavel*, September 1963, pp. 13+.

1890. "Discrimination—Housing—Controlled Occupancy Pattern Is Illegal Per Se—Party Adopting Controlled Occupancy Pattern Cannot Enjoin Interference with the Pattern Due to Equitable 'Unclean Hands' Doctrine." *Notre Dame Lawyer*, August 1960, pp. 563+.

1891. "Discrimination in Employment and in Housing: Private Enforcement Provisions of the Civil Rights Acts of 1964 and 1968." *Harvard Law Review*, February 1969, pp. 834+.

1892. District of Columbia Commissioners. *A Proposed Anti-Discrimination Housing Ordinance for the District of Columbia. Summary of Hearing before the Board of Commissioners, November 30 and December 3, 1962*. Washington, D.C.: Government of the District of Columbia, 1963.

1893. Donnici, P. J. "State Responsibility for Residential Racial Discrimination: The Decline and Fall of California's Proposition 14." *University of San Francisco Law Review*, October 1966, pp. 12+.

1894. Dubofsky, J. E. "Fair Housing: A Legislative History and a Perspective." *Washburn Law Journal*, Winter 1969, pp. 149+.

1895. "Due Process of Law–In General–Fair Housing Act is Constitutional but Commission's Power to Issue 'Appropriate' Orders is Too Broad–*Colorado Anti-Discrimination Comm'n. v. Case.*" *Harvard Law Review*, January 1964, pp. 553-556.

1896. Duncan, John B., and Albert Mindlin. "Municipal Fair Housing Legislation: Community Beliefs and Facts." *Phylon*, Fall 1964, pp. 217-237.

1897. Eley, Lynn W. and Thomas W. Casstevens. *The Politics of Fair-Housing Legislation: State and Local Case Studies*. San Francisco, Calif.: Chandler Publishing Co., 1968. 415pp.

1898. "Enforcement Procedure of Oberlin, Ohio, Fair Housing Ordinance Held Unconstitutional." *Michigan Law Review*, February 1966, pp. 710-721.

1899. *Enforcing Fair Housing Laws: Apartments in White Suburbia*. A report of the work in 1969-70 of the Administrative Process Project in cooperation with the New Jersey Division on Civil Rights to improve the administration of the State law against discrimination in Housing, July, 1970. Newark, N.J.: Administrative Process Project, Rutgers Law School, 1971. 459pp.

1900. "Equal Protection Juggernaut and Exemptions from Open-Housing Laws." *Washington University Law Quarterly*, Winter 1972, pp. 145+.

1901. "Fair Housing Act of 1968–Racial Discrimination in Housing–Affirmative Relief–United States May Obtain Affirmative Relief Where There Has Been Pre-Act and Some Post-Act Pattern or Practice of Racial Discrimination in the Rental of Private Housing." *Georgia Law Review*, Spring 1971, pp. 603+.

1902. "Federal Fair Housing Requirements: Title VIII of the 1968 Civil Rights Act." *Duke Law Journal*, August 1969, pp. 733+.

1903. "The Federal Order of Nondiscrimination." *Real Estate Analyst*, December 19, 1962, pp. 511-515.

1904. "Foreword: 'State Action,' Equal Protection, and California's Proposition 14." *Harvard Law Review*, November 1967, pp. 69+.

1905. Forster, A. and S. Rabkin. "Constitutionality of Laws against Discrimination of Publicly Assisted Housing." *New York Law Forum*, January 1960, pp. 38+.

1906. "Fourteenth Amendment and the State Action Doctrine." *Washington & Lee Law Review*, Spring 1967, pp. 133+.

1907. Goldblatt, Harold. *Evaluations of the Fair Housing Practices Law by Landlords and Brokers Three Years after Passage*. New York: New York City Commission on Human Relations, 1961.

1908. Goldblatt, Harold and Florence Cromien. "The Effective Social Reach of the Fair Housing Practices Law of the City of New York." *Social Problems*, Spring 1962, pp. 365-370.

1909. Hager, Don J. "Housing Discrimination, Social Conflict, and the Law." *Social Problems*, Summer 1960, pp. 80-87.

1910. Horowitz, H. W. "Fourteenth Amendment Aspects of Racial Discrimination in 'Private' Housing." *California Law Review*, March 1964, pp. 1+. Critique (F. A. Allen), pp. 46+.

1911. "Housing–State Legislative Prohibition of Discrimination in Private Housing–Demise of Legislation Dependent upon Government Loan Insurance." *Notre Dame Lawyer*, March 1962, pp. 394+.

1912. "Integration Ordinance: *Honi Soit Qui Mal Y Pense*." *Stanford Law Review*, January 1965, pp. 280+.

1913. "*Jones v. Mayer*: The Thirteenth Amendment and the Federal Anti-Discrimination Laws." *Columbia Law Review*, June 1969, pp. 1019-1056.

1914. Kaplan, Marshall. "Discrimination in California Housing: The Need for Additional Legislation." *California Law Review*, October 1962, pp. 635-649.

1915. Kozol, L. H. "Massachusetts Fair Housing Practices Law." *Massachusetts Law Quarterly*, September 1962, pp. 295+.

1916. Levine, B. "Evaluation of an Appropriate Legislative and Judicial Response to Discrimination in Housing." *South Texas Law Journal*, Vol. 11, 1970, pp. 295+.

1917. Lilley, William III. "Courts Lead Revolutionary Trend toward Desegregation of Residential Areas; Administration and Congress Follow Courts in Promoting Residential Intergration." *National Journal*, December 1, 1971, pp. 2336-2348.

1918. "*Massachusetts Commission against Discrimination v. Franzaroli* ([Mass.] 256 N E 2d 311): A Problem in Administrative Enforcement of Fair Housing Laws." *University of Pennsylvania Law Review*, July 1970, pp. 1263-1274.

1919. Mayhew, Leon H. *Law and Equal Opportunity; A Study of the Massachusetts Commission Against Discrimination.* Cambridge, Mass.: Harvard University Press, 1968. 313pp.

1920. Michelman, Frank I. "The Advent of a Right to Housing: A Current Appraisal." *Harvard Civil Rights–Civil Liberties Law Review*, April 1970, pp. 207-226.

1921. Miller, B.A. "Anti-Open Occupancy Legislation: An Historical Anomaly." *University of Detroit Law Journal*, December 1965, pp. 165+.

1922. Miller, Loren. "The Law and Discrimination in Housing." *Lawyers Guild Review*, Winter 1960, pp. 123-136.

1923. National Committee Against Discrimination in Housing. *Citizens' Guide to the Federal Fair Housing Law of 1968.* New York, 1968. 23pp.

1924. New Jersey Legislature. Senate. Committee on Revision and Amendment of Laws. *Public Hearing on Senate Bill No. 1, Concerning Discrimination in Sale and Rental of All Real Property, Held, Trenton, New Jersey, April 10, 1961.* Trenton, N.J., 1961. 65pp.

1925. Nixon, Richard. "Federal Policies Relative to Equal Housing Opportunity." Statement by the President, June 11, 1971. *Weekly Compilation of Presidential Documents*, June 14, 1971, pp. 892-905.

1926. "Nondiscrimination Implications of Federal Involvement in Housing." *Vanderbilt Law Review*, June 1966, pp. 865+.

1927. "Non-Discrimination in the Sale or Rental of Real Property: Comments on *Jones v. Alfred H. Mayer Co.* (88 Sup Ct 2186) and Title VIII of the Civil Rights Act of 1968: A Symposium." *Vanderbilt Law Review*, April 1969, pp. 455+.

1928. "Open Housing–1866 Civil Rights Act–1968 Civil Rights Act–Thirteenth Amendment." *Louisiana Law Review*, December 1968, pp. 158+.

1929. "Open Housing Law to Cover 80% of Dwellings by 1970." *Congressional Quarterly Weekly Report*, April 12, 1968, pp. 791-795.

1930. "Open Housing: Title VIII of the 1968 Civil Rights Act." *Boston College Industrial & Commercial Law Review*, Spring 1969, pp. 688+.

1931. Pearl, Laurence D. and Benjamin B. Terner. "Fair Housing Laws: Halfway Mark." *Georgetown Law Journal*, Fall 1965, pp. 156-172.

1932. Pearl, L. D. and B. B. Terner. "Survey: Fair Housing Laws–Design for Equal Opportunity." *Stanford Law Review*, July 1964, pp. 849+.

1933. The Potomac Institute. *Metropolitan Housing Desegregation: The Case for an Affirmative Program under Title VI of the Civil Rights Act of 1964*. Washington, D.C., 1965. 35pp.

1934. Prentice-Hall Inc. *Equal Opportunity in Housing*. Prepared and published by Prentice-Hall in cooperation with U.S. Department of Housing and Urban Development. Englewood Cliffs, N.J., 1971.

1935. "Prohibition of Private Discrimination in the Rental or Sale of Real Property." *Wake Forest Law Review*, December 1970, pp. 88+.

1936. Rice, L. "Residential Segregation by Law, 1910-1917." *Journal of Southern History*, May 1968, pp. 179-199.

1937. Roberts, Robert Joseph, S.J. *The Emergence of a Civil Right: Anti-Discrimination Legislation in Private Housing in the United States*. Ann Arbor, Mich.: University Microfilms, 1961 (Ph.D. dissertation, St. Louis University, 1961). 441pp. (Order No. 61-6488)

1938. Robison, J. B. "Housing—the Northern Civil Rights Frontier." *Western Reserve Law Review*, December 1961, pp. 101+.

1939. "Rumford Fair Housing Act Reviewed." *Southern California Law Review*, Vol. 37, 1964, pp. 427+.

1940. Saks, J. Harold and Sol Rabkin. "Racial and Religious Discrimination in Housing: A Report of Legal Process." *Iowa Law Review*, Spring 1960, pp. 488-524.

1941. Seeley, James J. "The Public Referendum and Minority Group Legislation: Postscript to *Reitman v. Mulkey*." *Cornell Law Review*, July 1970, pp. 881-910.

1942. Semer, M. P. and M. E. Sloane. "Equal Housing Opportunity and Individual Property Rights." *Federal Bar Journal*, Winter 1964, pp. 47+.

1943. Sloane, M. E. "Housing Discrimination—The Response of Law." *North Carolina Law Review*, December 1963, pp. 106+.

1944. Sloane, Martin E. "One Year's Experience, Current and Potential Impact of the Housing Order." *George Washington Law Review*, March 1964, pp. 457-488.

1945. Sloane, M. E. and M. H. Freedman. "Executive Order on Housing: The Constitutional Basis for What It Fails to Do." *Howard Law Journal*, Winter 1963, pp. 1+.

1946. "Surveys the Scope and Results of Fair Housing Laws." *Public Management*, September 1963, pp. 205-206.

1947. "Text of Executive Order on Housing Discrimination." *Congressional Quarterly Weekly Report*, November 30, 1962, pp. 2219-2220.

1948. Thagard, T. W., Jr. "Making of a Civil Rights Case: *Jones v. Alfred H. Mayer Company* (88 Sup. Ct. 2186)." *Alabama Lawyer*, October 1969, pp. 438+.

1949. Thomas, Norman C. *Rule 9: Politics, Administration, and Civil Rights*. New York: Random House, 1966. 121pp.

1950. "Unconstitutionality of Proposition 14: An Extension of Prohibited 'State Action.'" *Stanford Law Review*, November 1966, pp. 232+.

1951. U.S. Congress. House. Committee on the District of Columbia. *Antidiscrimination Regulations re Sale or Rental of Private Property. Hearing before Subcommittee 6* . . . March 28, 1963. Washington, D.C.: Government Printing Office, 1963. 46pp.

1952. U.S. Congress. Senate. Committee on Banking and Currency. Subcommittee on Housing. *Fair Housing Act of 1967. Hearings. . . .* Washington, D.C.: Government Printing Office, 1967. 508pp.

1953. U.S. Housing and Home Finance Agency. Office of the Administrator. *State Statutes and Local Ordinances and Resolutions Prohibiting Discrimination in Housing and Urban Renewal Operations*. Washington, D.C.: Government Printing Office, December 1961. 115pp.

1954. Van Alstyne, W. W. "O'Meara Case and Constitutional Requirements of State Anti-Discrimination Housing Laws." *Howard Law Journal*, Spring 1962, pp. 158+.

See also: 2050, 2160; Exclusionary Zoning: 1283+; Site Selection in Federally-Assisted Housing: 2560+.

*3) Patterns of Residential Segregation*

1955. Adams, Sanuel L. "Blueprint for Segregation: A Survey of Atlanta (Ga.) Housing." *New South*, Spring 1967, pp. 73-84.

1956. Clemence, Theodore G. "Residential Segregation in the Mid-Sixties." *Demography*, Vol. 4, no. 2 (1967), pp. 562-568.

1957. Edwards, Ozzie L. "Patterns of Residential Segregation within a Metropolitan Ghetto." *Demography*, May 1970, pp. 185-193.

1958. Lee, Douglas Boardman. *Analysis and Description of Residential Segregation, an Application of Centrographic Techniques to the Study of Spatial Distribution of Ethnic Groups in Cities*. Ithaca, N.Y.: Center for

Housing and Environmental Studies, Division of Urban Studies, Cornell University, 1965. 151pp.

1959. McClure, Edward Ellis. "Patterns of Racial Segregation in Southern Cities: Implications for Planning Policy." Unpublished Ph.D. dissertation, Harvard University, 1971.

1960. Meade, Anthony Carl. *The Residential Segregation of Population Characteristics in the Atlanta Standard Metropolitan Statistical Area: 1960*. Ann Arbor, Mich.: University Microfilms, 1971 (Ph.D. dissertation, University of Texas, 1971). 132pp. (order no. 71-29,478)

1961. Poston, Dudley L. and Jeffrey Passel. "Texas Population in 1970: Racial Residential Segregation in Cities." *Texas Business Review*, July 1972, pp. 142-147.

1962. Raiser, William Leigh. *Metropolitan Growth and Socioeconomic Residential Segregation*. Ann Arbor, Mich.: University Microfilms, 1970 (Ph.D. dissertation, Michigan State University, 1969). 74pp. (order no. 70-15,116)

1963. Roof, W. C. and T. L. Van Valey. "Residential Segregation and Social Differentiation in American Urban Areas." *Social Forces*, September 1972, pp. 87-91.

1964. Schelling, Thomas C. *Models of Segregation*, Santa Monica, Calif.: Rand Corporation, 1969. 82pp.

1965. Schnore, Leo F. "Social Class Segregation Among Nonwhites in Metropolitan Centers." *Demography*, 1967, pp. 126-133.

1966. Taeuber, Karl. "Negro Residential Segregation: Trends and Measurement." *Social Problems*, Summer 1964, pp. 42-50.

1967. Taeuber, Karl E. and Alma F. Taeuber. "The Pattern of Negro Residential Segregation." In *Negroes in Cities: Residential Segregation and Neighborhood Change*. Chicago, Ill.: Aldine, 1965, pp. 11-95.

See also: 2993.

d. Integration

1968. Amdur, Reuel Seeman. "An Exploratory Study of Nineteen Negro Families in the Seattle Area Who Were First Negro Residents in White Neighborhoods, of Their White Neighbors, and of the Integration Process Together with a Proposed Program to Promote Integration in Seattle." Unpublished M.S.W. thesis, University of Washington, 1962.

1969. Arter, Rhetta Marie. *WINS Pilot Preview; Report of an Action-Research, Demonstration Project on the Process of Achieving Equal Housing Opportunities, Women's Integrating Neighborhood Services.* Sponsored by the Educational Foundation of National Council of Negro Women, Inc. 1st ed. New York: Research And Action Associates, 1961. 202pp.

1970. Barth, Ernest A. T. *Case Studies of the Process of Integration in Neighborhoods of Seattle, Washington.* Seattle, Washington: Greater Seattle Housing Council, 1960.

1971. Baum, Daniel Jay. *Toward a Free Housing Market.* Coral Gables, Fla.: University of Miami Press, 1971. 241pp.

1972. Baum, D. J. and J. W. Mohr. "Toward a Free Housing Market." *Rutgers Law Review*, Summer 1970, pp. 712+.

1973. "Benign Quotas: A Plan for Integrated Private Housing." *Yale Law Journal*, November 1960, pp. 126-134.

1974. Berry, John M. "Opening Housing." *Editorial Research Reports*, August 16, 1967, pp. 599-616.

1975. Beshear, Steven L. *et al.* "Open Housing Meets My Old Kentucky Home: A Study of Open Housing, with Special Attention to Implications for Kentucky." *Kentucky Law Journal*, No. 1 1967/1968, pp. 140-235.

1976. Blume, N. "Open Housing Referenda." *Public Opinion Quarterly*, Winter 1971-1972, pp. 563-570.

1977. Bradburn, Norman M. *et al. Racial Integration in American Neighborhoods: A Comparative Survey.* Chicago, Ill.: National Opinion Research Center, 1970. 599pp.

1978. Bradburn, Norman M. *et al. Side by Side: Integrated Neighborhoods in America.* Chicago, Ill.: Quadrangle Books, 1971. 209pp.

1979. Bullough, Bonnie Louise. *Alienation Among Middle Class Negroes: Social-Psychological Factors Influencing Housing Desegregation.* Ann Arbor, Mich.: University Microfilms, 1968 (Ph.D. dissertation, University of California at Los Angeles, 1968). 250pp. (order no. 68-16,517)

1980. Bullough, Bonnie. *Social-Psychological Barriers to Housing Desegregation.* Los Angeles, Calif.: Housing, Real Estate and Urban Land Studies, Graduate School of Business Administration, University of California, July 1969. 134pp.

1981. "The Challenge of Open Occupancy." *House & Home*, November 1962, pp. 91-95.

1982. Clark, Henry. *The Church and Residential Segregation; A Case Study of an Open Housing Covenant Campaign*. New Haven, Conn.: College & University Press, 1965. 254pp.

1983. Cohen, Oscar. "The Case for Benign Quotas in Housing." *Phylon*, Spring 1960, pp. 20-29.

1984. "Constitutionality of the 'Benign' Quota." *Tennessee Law Review*, Fall 1972, pp. 55+.

1985. "Fair Housing: Next Steps." *Social Action*, May 1967, pp. 2-36.

1986. Freeman, Hal M. "Desegregation of Chicago Suburbs." *Journal of Intergroup Relations*, Autumn 1965, pp. 259-268.

1987. Freeman, Linton C. and Morris Sunshine. *Patterns of Residential Segregation*. Cambridge, Mass.: Schenkman, 1970. 159pp.

1988. Gitelman, M. "Fair Housing in Colorado." *Denver Law Journal*, Winter 1965, pp. 1+.

1989. Greene, Kenneth Roger. *Black Demands for Open Housing: The Responses of Three City Governments*. Ann Arbor, Mich.: University Microfilms, 1972 (Ph.D. dissertation, Michigan State University, 1971). 234pp. (order no. 72-8657)

1990. Grier, Eunice S. "Factors Hindering Integration in American Urban Areas." *Journal of Intergroup Relations*, Fall 1961, pp. 293-301.

1991. Grier, Eunice and George Grier. *Case Studies in Racially Mixed Housing*. Washington, D.C.: The Washington Center for Metropolitan Studies, 1962. 3 volumes.

1992. Grier, Eunice and George Grier. *Privately Developed Interracial Housing: An Analysis of Experience*. Berkeley, Calif.: University of California Press, 1960. 264pp.

1993. Haggstrom, Warren Conrad. *Self Esteem and Other Characteristics of Residentially Desegregated Negroes*. Ann Arbor, Mich.: University Microfilms, 1963 (Ph.D. dissertation, University of Michigan, 1962). 253pp. (order no. 63-359)

1994. Hamilton, H. D. "Direct Legislation: Some Implications of Open Housing Referenda." *American Political Science Review*, March 1970, pp. 124-137.

1995. Hecht, James L. *Because It Is Right; Integration in Housing*. Boston, Mass.: Little, Brown, 1970. 290pp.

1996. Hunt, Chester L. "Integrated Housing in Kalamazoo." In Alfred N. Page and Warren R. Seyfried (eds.). *Urban Analysis: Readings in Housing and Urban Development*. Glenview, Ill.: Scott, Foresman, 1970, pp. 296-310. (Reprinted from *Research Report on Integrated Housing in Kalamazoo*. Kalamazoo, Mich.: Upjohn Institute for Community Research, 1959, pp. 3-25.)

1997. Jayne, Dorothy S. *First Families: A Study of Twenty Pioneer Negro Families Who Moved into White Neighborhoods in Metropolitan Philadelphia*. Philadelphia, Pa.: Commission on Human Relations, 1960.

1998. Leacock, Eleanor. *Toward Integration in Suburban Housing: The Bridgeview Study*. New York: Anti-Defamation League of B'nai B'rith, 1965. 47pp.

1999. McGraw, B. T. "Equal Opportunity in Housing–Trends and Implications." *Phylon*, Spring 1964, pp. 5-17.

2000. National Academy of Sciences. Advisory Committee to the Department of Housing and Urban Development. *Freedom of Choice in Housing; Opportunities and Constraints*. Report of the Social Science Panel, Division of Behavioral Sciences and the Recommendations of the Advisory Committee. Washington, D.C., 1972. 62pp.

2001. Navasky, V. S. "Benevolent Housing Quota." *Howard Law Journal*, January 1960, pp. 30+.

2002. NCDH Brotherhood-in-Action Housing Conference. *Affirmative Action to Achieve Integration; A Report Based on the NCDH Brotherhood-in-Action Housing Conference, New York, 1965*. New York: National Committee Against Discrimination in Housing, 1966. 40pp.

2003. Nesbitt, George B. "Misconceptions in the Movement for Civil Rights in Housing." *Journal of Intergroup Relations*, Winter 1960/1961, pp. 61-67.

2004. Nesbitt, George and Elfriede Hoeber. "The Fair Housing Committee: It's Needs for a New Perspective." *Land Economics*, May 1965, pp. 97-110.

2005. "New Way to Integrate the Suburbs." *Business Week*, March 28, 1970, pp. 168+.

2006. New York (City) Housing and Redevelopment Administration. *Equal Opportunity Policy of the Housing and Redevelopment Administration*. New York, 1969. 23pp.

2007. Northwood, Lawrence K. and Ernest A. T. Barth. *Urban Desegregation: Negro Pioneers and Their White Neighbors*. Seattle, Washington: University of Washington Press, 1965. 131pp.

2008. Northwood, L.K. and L.H. Klein. "Benign Quota, an Unresolved Issue: Attitudes of Agency Personnel." *Phylon*, Summer 1964, pp. 109-122.

2009. "Open Housing–a Reality in 1968?" *Suffolk University Law Review*, Fall 1968, pp. 149+.

2010. Piven, Frances Fox and Richard A. Cloward. "The Case Against Urban Desegregation: Although Efforts at Integration Have Produced Significant Gains in Some Areas, They Have Worked Against the Interests of Urban Negro Poor in Housing and Education." *Social Work*, January 1967, pp. 12-21.

2011. Planners for Equal Opportunity. New York Chapter. *Planning for Open City: Research Findings and Recommendations for New York's Operation Open City: A Report to Operation Open City of the New York Urban League*. New York, 1967. 26pp.

2012. Potomac Institute. *The Federal Role in Equal Housing Opportunity; An Affirmative Program to Implement Executive Order 11063*. Prepared by Arthur J. Levin. Washington, D.C. 1964. 28pp.

2013. Potomac Institute. *A Guide to Equal Opportunity in Housing*. Washington, D.C., 1967.

2014. Price, Margaret. *Neighborhoods: Where Human Relations Begin. A Study of Residential Patterns in Philadelphia, Washington, D.C., & Baltimore*. Atlanta, Ga.: Southern Regional Council, February 1967. 44pp.

2015. "The Role of Housing in Promoting Social Integration." *Human Settlements*, July 1972, pp. 1-13.

2016. Rubin, Morton. "The Function of Social Research for a Fair Housing Practice Committee." *Journal of Intergroup Relations*, Fall 1961, pp. 325-331.

2017. Saltman, Juliet Z. *Open Housing as a Social Movement; Challenge, Conflict, and Change*. Lexington, Mass.: Heath Lexington Books, 1971. 213pp.

2018. Saltman, Juliet Zion. *Open Housing as a Social Movement: A Sociological Study of Challenge, Conflict, and Change*. Ann Arbor, Mich.: University Microfilms, 1971 (Ph.D. dissertation, Case Western Reserve University, 1971). 442pp. (order no. 71-22,846)

2019. Sauer, Robert A. "Free Choice in Housing." *New York Law Forum*, December 1964, pp. 525-554.

2020. Schermer, George and Arthur J. Levin. *Housing Guide to Equal Opportunity: Affirmative Practices for Integrated Housing*. Washington, D.C.: Potomac Institute, June 1968. 92pp.

2021. Shaffer, Helen B. "Interracial Housing." *Editorial Research Reports*, February 6, 1963, pp. 87-104.

2022. Smith, G. Nelson. "The Toledo Way: City Fights for Fair Housing." *Public Management*, August 1967, pp. 212-216.

2023. Sudman, Seymour and Norman Bradburn. *Social Psychological Factors in Intergroup Housing: Results of Pilot Test*. Chicago, Ill.: National Opinion Research Center, May 1966. 159pp.

2024. Sudman, S., N. M. Bradburn and G. Gockel. "The Extent and Characteristics of Racially Integrated Housing in the United States." *Journal of Business*, January 1969, pp. 50-92.

2025. Tillman, James A., Jr. "Fair Housing: A Conceptual and Analytic Frame of Reference." *Journal of Intergroup Relations*, Fall 1960, pp. 18-29.

2026. Tillman, James A., Jr. *Not by Prayer Alone; A Report on the Greater Minneapolis Interfaith Fair Housing Program*. Philadelphia, Pa.: United Church Press, 1964. 223pp.

2027. Tillman, James A., Jr. "The Quest for Identity and Status: Facets of the Desegregation Process in the Upper Midwest." *Phylon*, Winter 1961, pp. 329-339.

2028. U.S. Housing and Home Finance Agency. Office of Program Policy. *Equal Opportunity in Housing; A Series of Case Studies*. Washington, D.C.: Government Printing Office, 1964. 89pp.

2029. Wilner, Daniel M., Rosabelle Price Walkley and Stuart W. Cook. *Human Relations in Interracial Housing; A Study of the Contact Hypothesis*. New York: Russell & Russell, 1969. 167pp.

2030. Works, E. "Residence in Integrated and Segregated Housing and Improvement in Self-Concepts of Negroes." *Sociology and Social Research; An International Journal*, April 1962, pp. 294-301.

2031. Zelder, Raymond E. "Residential Desegregation: Can Nothing Be Accomplished?" *Urban Affairs Quarterly*, March 1970, pp. 265-277.

See also: 807-809; The Effect of Race on Property Values: 796+; Minorities and Housing Markets: 1023+.

e. Attitudes toward Minorities and Housing

2032. Brunn, S. D. and W. L. Hoffman. "Spatial Response of Negroes and Whites Toward Open Housing: The Flint Referendum." *Association of American Geographers, Annals*, March 1970, pp. 18-36.

2033. Engel, J. F. and R. D. Blackwell. "Attitudes of Affluent Suburbia toward the Negro Neighbor." *Michigan State University Business Topics*, Autumn 1969, pp. 42-49.

2034. Erskine, H. "Polls: Negro Housing." *Public Opinion Quarterly*. Fall 1967, pp. 482-498.

2035. Gamberg, Herbert Victor. *White Perceptions of Negro Race and Class as Factors in the Racial Residential Process*. Ann Arbor, Mich.: University Microfilms, 1964 (Ph.D. dissertation, Princeton University, 1964). 232pp. (order no. 64-12,123)

2036. Greenfield, Robert W. "Factors Associated with Attitudes toward Desegregation in a Florida Residential Suburb." *Social Forces*, October 1961, pp. 31-42.

2037. Grossman, Joel Stephen. *Psychological Determinants of Reaction to Neighborhood Racial Change*. Ann Arbor, Mich.: University Microfilms, 1967. (Ph.D. dissertation, Western Reserve University, 1966). 199pp. (order no. 67-4640)

2038. Hahn, Harlan. "Northern Referenda on Fair Housing: The Response of White Voters." *Western Political Quarterly*, September 1968, pp. 483-495.

2039. Hamilton, Howard D. "Voting Behavior in Open Housing Referenda." *Social Science Quarterly*, December 1970, pp. 715-729.

2040. Meer, Bernard and Edward Freedman. "The Impact of Negro Neighbors on White Home Owners." *Social Forces*, September 1966, 11-19.

2041. Rose, Arnold and Leon Warshay. "Inconsistencies in Attitudes Toward Negro Housing." *Social Problems*, Spring 1961, pp. 286-292.

2042. Royer, Donald M. *Attitudes of White and Negro Residents Towards Living in Integrated Neighborhoods in Thirteen Indiana Communities* Indianapolis, Indiana: Indiana Civil Rights Commission, 1964.

2043. Works, E. "Prejudice-Interaction Hypothesis from the Point of View of the Negro Minority Group." *American Journal of Sociology*, July 1961, pp. 47-52.

See also: 2046, 2049.

f. Realtors and Minorities

2044. "Anti-Blockbusting Ordinance." *Harvard Journal on Legislation*, March 1970, pp. 402+.

2045. Brown, W. H., Jr. "Access to Housing: The Role of the Real Estate Industry." *Economic Geography*, January 1972, pp. 66-78.

2046. Biochel, Margery R. *et al.* "Exposure, Experience and Attitudes: Realtors and Open Occupancy." *Phylon*, Winter 1969, pp. 325-337.

2047. "Blockbusting." *Georgetown Law Journal*, October 1970, pp. 170+.

2048. "Blockbusting: A Novel Statutory Approach to an Increasingly Serious Problem." *Columbia Journal of Law and Social Problems*, Summer 1971, pp. 538-578.

2049. Bradshaw, Barbara. *A Survey of Attitudes of Realtors Toward Open Occupancy*. Towson, Md.: Center for Sociological Studies, Goucher College, 1964.

2050. Chapman, R. M. "The Real Estate Broker and the Unruh Civil Rights Act." *Los Angeles Bar Bulletin*, September 1970, pp. 475+.

2051. Chicago, Illinois, Commission on Human Relations. *Selling and Buying Real Estate in a Racially Changing Neighborhood: A Survey*. Chicago, Ill., 1962. 57pp.

2052. "Fair Housing Laws and Brokers' Defamation Suits: The New York Experience." *Michigan Law Review*, March 1966, pp. 919-930.

2053. Glassberg, Susan Spiegel. "Legal Control of Blockbusting." *Urban Law Annual 1972*. St. Louis, Mo.: School of Law, Washington University, 1972, pp. 145-170.

2054. Helper, Rose. *Racial Policies and Practices of Real Estate Brokers*. Minneapolis, Minn.: University of Minnesota Press, 1969. 387pp.

2055. "Housing—Virginia Attacks Blockbusting." *University of Richmond Law Review*, Winter 1972, pp. 416+.

2056. Schechter, Alan H. "The Impact of Open Housing Laws on Suburban Realtors." Paper presented at the 1971 Annual Meeting of the American Political Science Association, Conrad Hilton Hotel, Chicago, Illinois, September 7-11, 1971.

g. Dynamics of Racial Residential Change

2057. Barresi, C. M. "Racial Transition in an Urban Neighborhood." *Growth and Change*, July 1972, pp. 16-22.

2058. Caplan, Eleanor K. and Eleanor P. Wolf. "Factors Affecting Racial Change in Two Middle Income Housing Areas." *Phylon*, Fall 1960, pp. 225-233.

2059. De Graaf, L.B. "City of Black Angels: Emergence of the Los Angeles Ghetto: 1890-1930." *Pacific Historical Review*, August 1970, pp. 323-352.

2060. Edwards, Ozzie. "Family Composition as a Variable in Residential Succession." *American Journal of Sociology*, Jan. 1972, pp. 731-741.

2061. Fishman, J. A. "Some Social and Psychological Determinants of Intergroup Relations in Changing Neighborhoods; An Introduction to the Bridgeview Study." *Social Forces*, October 1961, pp. 42-51.

2062. Henderson, George. "Twelfth Street: An Analysis of a Changed Neighborhood." *Phylon*, Spring 1964, pp. 91-96.

2063. McKee, J.B. "Changing Patterns of Race and Housing: A Toledo Study." *Social Forces*, March 1963, pp. 253-260.

2064. Meyer, Douglas K. "The Changing Negro Residential Patterns in Lansing, Michigan, 1850-1969." Unpublished Ph.D. dissertation, Department of Geography, Michigan State University, 1970.

2065. Meyer, Douglas K. "Spatiotemporal Trends of Racial Residential Change." *Land Economics*, Feb. 1972, pp. 62-65.

2066. Molotch, Harvey. "Racial Change in a Stable Community." *American Journal of Sociology*, September 1969, pp. 226-238. Reply (Avery M. Guest and James J. Zuiches) with rejoinder, November 1971, pp. 457-471.

2067. Morrill, Richard L. "The Negro Ghetto—Problems and Alternatives." *Geographical Review*, July 1965, pp. 339-361.

2068. Northwood, Lawrence K. and Louise H. Klein. "The 'Tipping Point'—A Questionable Quality of Neighborhoods." *Journal of Intergroup Relations*, Autumn 1965, pp. 226-239.

2069. Pryor, F. L. "Empirical Note on the Tipping Point." *Land Economics*, November 1971, pp. 413-417.

2070. Rose, H. M. "Development of an Urban Subsystem: The Case of the Negro Ghetto." *Association of American Geographers, Annals*, March 1970, pp. 1-17.

2071. Rose, H. M. "Spatial Development of Black Residential Subsystems." *Economic Geography*, January 1972, pp. 43-65.

2072. Sanoff, Henry *et al.* "Changing Residential Racial Patterns." *The Urban and Social Change Review*, Spring 1971, pp. 68-71.

2073. Sanoff, Henry *et al. Residential Patterns of Racial Change: A Study of a Southern City*. Raleigh, N.C.: Urban Affairs and Community Services Center, North Carolina State University, 1967. 35pp.

2074. Taeuber, Alma F. "A Comparative Analysis of Negro Residential Succession." Unpublished Ph.D. dissertation, University of Chicago, 1962.

2075. Taeuber, Karl E. and Alma F. Taeuber. "The Process of Neighborhood Change." In *Negroes in Cities: Residential Segregation and Neighborhood Change*. Chicago, Ill.: Aldine, 1965, pp. 99-194.

2076. Wolf, Eleanor Paperno. *Changing Neighborhood: A Study of Racial Transition*. Ann Arbor, Mich.: University Microfilms, 1960 (Ph.D. dissertation, Wayne State University, 1959). 306pp. (order no. 60-2334)

2077. Wolf, Eleanor P. "Racial Transition in a Middle-Class Area." *Journal of Intergroup Relations*, Summer 1960, pp. 75-81.

2078. Wolf, Eleanor P. "The Tipping-Point in Racially Changing Neighborhoods." *Journal of the American Institute of Planners*, August 1963, pp. 217-222.

See also: 1968, 1996, 1997, 2007, 2037, 2040, 2042, 2043, 3482; The Effects of Race on Property Values: 796+; Minorities and Housing Markets: 1023+.

## 5. LOW INCOME HOUSING

### a. General

2079. Aronov, Edward. "Management Practices and Consumer Protection in Low-Income Rental Housing." In U.S. Congress. House. Committee on Banking and Currency. *Papers Submitted to Subcommittee on Housing Panels on Housing Production, Housing Demand, and Developing a Suitable Living Environment: Part 1*. Washington, D.C.: Government Printing Office, 1971, pp. 397-412.

2080. Askwig, William James. *A Rent Stamp Program to Increase Standard Rental Housing for Low-Income Households in Metropolitan Areas in the United States*. Ann Arbor, Mich.: University Microfilms, 1970 (Ph.D. dissertation, Texas Tech University, 1969). 196pp. (order no. 70-12,296)

2081. Bailey, John M. and Henry Schubort. "One Billion Subsidy for Slums: 1/3 of All Welfare Payments Are Spent on Housing–Most of It Substandard; Here Is a Proposal to Use These Funds More Constructively." *Architectural Forum*, July/August 1969, pp. 56-57.

2082. Biderman, C. "Shelter for Whom? Rich as Well as Poor Are Getting into Low Income Housing." *Barrons*, December 27, 1971, pp. 5+.

2083. Boykin, J. H. "Changing Roles of Government and Private Enterprise in Low-Income Housing." *Appraisal Journal*, January 1970, pp. 8-23.

2084. Brooks, Mary E. *Lower Income Housing: The Planners' Response*. Sponsored by the Taconic Foundation and the Rockefeller Brothers Fund. Chicago, Ill.: American Society of Planning Officials, 1972. 69pp. (Planning Advisory Report no. 282)

2085. Burstein, Joseph. "Housing Our Low-Income Population: Federal and Local Powers and Potentials." *New York Law Forum*, December 1964, pp. 464-491.

2086. California University. Department of Architecture. *Low Income Housing Demonstration Project Report*. Henry Sanoff, Principal Investigator. Berkeley, Calif., 1965. 251pp.

2087. Cogswell, Arthur R. "Housing, the Computer, and the Architectural Process." *Law and Contemporary Problems*, Spring 1967, pp. 274-285.

2088. Colorado State Legislative Council. *Report to the Colorado General Assembly: Low and Moderate Income Housing*. Denver, Colorado, December 1972.

2089. Conrad, Joseph, Jr. "Getting Involved in Low-Income Housing." *Journal of Property Management*, September-October 1970, pp. 234-239.

2090. Furstenthal, Joseph, John L. Lineweaver and Richard H. Reel, Jr. *Federally Assisted Low Income Housing Programs–Three Case Studies*. Berkeley, Calif.: The Center for Real Estate and Urban Economics, Institute of Urban and Regional Development, University of California, 1972.

2091. Garrity, P. G. "Community Economic Development and Low-Income Housing Development." *Law & Contemporary Problems*, Spring 1971, pp. 191-204.

2092. George, Ellen S. "Low-Income Housing and the Equal Protection Clause." *Cornell Law Review*, January 1971, pp. 343-364.

2093. Hick, R.K. "Lower Income Housing: Condominium vs. Cooperative." *Illinois Bar Journal*, September 1970, pp. 62+.

2094. Hood, Nicholas. "Low-Income Housing Projects Can Be Made Manageable with People Participation." *Mortgage Banker*, November 1970, pp. 96-100.

2095. Hoskins, W. Lee. "Housing the Poor: A Frontal Attack." *Federal Reserve Philadelphia, Business Review*, November 1970, pp. 6-16.

2096. "Housing in Salt Lake County—A Place to Live for the Poor?" *Utah Law Review*, Summer 1972, pp. 193+.

2097. Hudson, James H., Patricia Mathews and the Urban Institute Housing Group. *Variations in Operations; Housing for Lower-Income Households*. Washington, D.C.: Urban Institute, 1969, 74pp. (Urban Institute Working Paper 112-7)

2098. Huttman, E. D. and J. P. Huttman. "The Effect of Public Expenditure in Providing Adequate Housing for Low Income Families: A Comparative Socio-Economic Analysis of Programs in Five Countries." *Annals of Regional Science*, June 1970, pp. 123-126.

2099. Johnson, Donald N. *Housing for Low and Moderate Income Families: Needs, Programs, and Developments*. La Grande, Oregon: Bureau of Governmental Research and Service, University of Oregon, 1972. 131pp.

2100. Lagus, Margaret. "An Aggressive Approach to Low-Income Housing." *California Savings and Loan Journal*, September 1970, pp. 10-11.

2101. *Land Bank Handbook; Advance Acquisition of Sites for Low-and Moderate-Income Housing*. Edited by Carol Van Alstyne. Greensboro, N.C.: Piedmont Triad Council of Governments, 1972.

2102. Loeb, D. N. "Low-Income Tenant in California: A Study in Frustration." *Hastings Law Journal*, January 1970, pp. 287+.

2103. "Low-Income Housing Development Decision-Making in Oregon." *Willamette Law Journal*, December 1972, pp. 396+.

2104. Lowry, Ira S. "Housing Assistance for Low-Income Urban Families: A Fresh Approach." In U.S. Congress. House. Committee on Banking and Currency. *Papers Submitted to Subcommittee on Housing Panels on Housing Production, Housing Demand, and Developing a Suitable Living Environment: Part 2.* Washington, D.C.: Government Printing Office, 1971, pp. 489-524.

2105. Lowry, Ira S., Judith M. Gueron and Karen M. Eisenstadt. *Welfare Housing in New York City.* New York: The New York City Rand Institute, November 1972. 265pp.

2106. Massachusetts Special Commission on Low-Income Housing. *Final Report.* Boston, Mass.: Wright & Potter, 1965. 151pp.

2107. Nordstrom, Jane. "ADC Housing: Costs, Conditions, Consequences." *Smith College Studies in Social Work*, February 1965, pp. 125-154.

2108. Olsen, E. O. *An Efficient Method of Improving the Housing of Low-Income Families.* New York: The New York City Rand Institute, December 1969.

2109. Philadelphia Housing Association. *Housing Grants for the Very Poor: Report of the Committee on Low-Income Housing.* Philadelphia, May 1966.

2110. "Private Business and Low-Income Housing." *Journal of Housing*, January 1970, pp. 22-39.

2111. Rafsky, William L. *Publicly Assisted Housing.* New York, N.Y.: Institute for Public Administration, September 1966. 12pp.

2112. Rein, Martin. *Welfare and Housing.* Cambridge, Mass.: Joint Center for Urban Studies of the Massachusetts Institute of Technology and Harvard University, Spring 1971, revised February 1972. (Joint Center Working Paper no. 4).

2113. Schorr, Alvin L. "Housing the Poor." In Warner Bloomberg, Jr., and Henry J. Schmandt. *Power, Poverty, and Urban Policy.* Beverly Hills, Calif.: Sage Publications, 1968, pp. 115-150.

2114. Schwarz, Ted. "Low-Income Housing Headaches Can Be Overcome." *Nation's Cities*, October 1970, pp. 19-23.

2115. "Six Goals for a Program of Low-Income Housing; 25 Recommendations for Reaching NAHRO's Six Goals for a National Program of Low-income Housing." *Journal of Housing*, July 8, 1963, pp. 253-265 and July 31, 1963, pp. 307-316.

2116. Smart, Walter *et al. The Large Poor Family–A Housing Gap*. Prepared for the Consideration of the National Commission on Urban Problems. Washington, D.C.: Government Printing Office, 1968. 28pp. (U.S. National Commission on Urban Problems Research Report no. 4).

2117. Taylor, H. Ralph and George A. Williams. "Housing in Model Cities." *Law and Contemporary Problems*, Summer 1967, pp. 397-408.

2118. U.S. Department of Health, Education, and Welfare. *The Role of Public Welfare in Housing: A Report to the House Committee on Ways and Means and the Senate Committee on Finance*. Washington, D.C.: Government Printing Office, 1969. 80pp.

2119. U.S. Department of Housing and Urban Development. *Report on Experimental Project Philadelphia Housing Information Service*. Washington, D.C., 1969. 41pp.

2120. U.S. Housing and Home Finance Agency. Office of Program Policy. *Low-Income Housing Demonstration; A Search for Solutions*. Washington, D.C.: Government Printing Office, 1964. 23pp.

2121. U.S. President's Task Force on Low Income Housing. *Toward Better Housing for Low-Income Families*. Washington, D.C.: Government Printing Office, 1970. 20pp.

2122. Urban America. Nonprofit Housing Center. *Greater Indianapolis Housing Development Corporation; Prospectus and Final Report*. Submitted to the Indianapolis Housing and Relocation Task Force. Washington, D.C., 1968. 81pp.

2123. Ward, Amelia G. *et al. Analysis of Some Lower Income Housing Market Problems for Metropolitan Baltimore*. Baltimore, Md.: Baltimore Regional Planning Council, 1968. 50pp.

2124. Westchester County, New York, Planning Board. *Welfare: Households and Housing: Residential Analysis for Westchester County*. White Plains, N.Y., 1970.

2125. Whitehead, Ralph, Jr. "After Two Years, Chicago's Seesaw Battle over Low-Income Housing Is (Almost) Settled." *City*, Summer 1971, pp. 8-12.

2126. Worsnop, Richard L. "Low-Income Housing." *Editorial Research Reports*, October 28, 1970, pp. 795-812.

See also: 191, 205, 243, 319, 332, 337, 341, 346, 349, 350, 374, 380, 677, 690, 692, 694, 696, 746, 992, 998, 1586, 1595, 1794, 3318, 3319, 3320a, 3320b, 3322, 3327, 3328, 3329, 3331, 3334, 3335; Exclusionary Zoning: 1283+; Owner Built and Self-Help Housing: 1678+; Low Income

Housing–Home Ownership: 2127+; Housing the Migrant Worker: 2166+; Inner City Housing: 2170+; Governmental Goals and Programs: 2280+; Planning for Low and Moderate Income Housing in the Suburbs: 3352+; The Concept of "Filtering": 3507a+.

b. Home Ownership

2127. Abrams, Charles. *Home Ownership for the Poor; A Program for Philadlephia*. New York: Praeger, 1970.

2128. Berger, C.J. "Homeownerhsip for Lower Income Families: the 1968 Housing Act's 'Cruel Hoax.'" *Connecticut Law Review*, June 1969, pp. 30+.

2129. Butler, W.H. "Approach to Low and Moderate Income Home Ownership." *Rutgers Law Review*, Fall 1967, pp. 67+.

2130. Edson, Charles L. *Home Ownership for Low-Income Families*. Chicago, Ill.: National Legal Aid and Defender Association, 1969. 90pp.

2131. Frieden, Bernard and JoAnn Newman. "Home Ownership for the Poor?" *Trans-action*, October 1970, pp. 47-53.

2132. Marcuse, Peter. Homeownership for Low Income Families: Financial Implications." *Land Economics*, May 1972, pp. 134-143.

2133. National Association of Housing and Redevelopment Officials. *Home Ownership for Low-Income Families*. Washington, D.C., 1969.

2134. Quirk, William J. and Leon E. Wein. "Home-Ownership for the Poor: Tenant Condominiums, the Housing and Urban Development Act of 1968, and the Rockefeller Program." *Cornell Law Review*, July 1969, pp. 811-870.

2135. Schaffer, Lawrence D. "Urban Experiment in Lower-Income Home Ownership Opportunities." *Journal of Property Management*, May/June 1970, pp. 108-113.

2136. Teaford, Stephn D. "Homeownership for Low-Income Families: The Condominium." *Hastings Law Journal*, Vol. 21, 1970, pp. 323-329.

2137. Thiokol Chemical Corp. *Forest Heights Low Income Home Ownership Program: Research and Final Report*. Submitted to Office of Research and Technology, U.S. Dept. of Housing and Urban Development. Ogden, Utah, 1970. 1 vol.

2138. "Urban Housing–Homeownership for Low and Moderate Income Families–Title I of the Housing and Urban Development Act of 1968." *Case Western Reserve Law Review*, February 1969, pp. 494+.

2139. von Furstenberg, George M. "Improving the Feasibility of Homeownership for Lower-income Families through Subsidized Mortgage Financing." In U.S. President's Committee on Urban Housing. *Report: Technical Studies, Volume I.* Washington, D.C.: Government Printing Office, 1967, pp. 113-146.

See also: 754, 1507, 1558, 2696, 2737, 2969, 3281a; 235/236: 2607+.

## 6. MODERATE INCOME HOUSING

2140. Gelfand, Jack E. "The Credit Elasticity of Lower-Middle Income Housing Demand." *Land Economics*, November 1966, pp. 464-472.

2141. Gelfand, J. E. *Financing Lower-Middle Income Housing.* Philadelphia, Penn.: Bureau of Economic and Business Research, Temple University, 1964.

2142. Gelfand, Jack E. "Mortgage Credit and Lower-Middle Income Housing Demand." *Land Economics*, May 1970, pp. 163-170.

2143. Lewis, Doris K. "Union-Sponsored Middle-Income Housing: 1927-1965." *Monthly Labor Review*, June 1965, pp. 629-636.

2144. Morris, Eugene J. "The Development of New Middle Income Housing in New York." *New York Law Forum*, December 1964, pp. 492-524.

2145. New York (State) Study Committee for Urban Middle-Income Housing. *Space for Urban Living: A Plan for Action to Provide Urban Homes for Middle-Income Families Utilizing Air Rights over Public Facilities.* Albany, N.Y., 1961. 16pp.

2146. "Opportunities Still Exist in HOAP Subsidies." *Mortgage and Real Estate Executives Report*, January 14, 1972, pp. 4-5.

2147. Ricks, R. Bruce. "The Housing Opportunity Allowance Program (HOAP)." *Federal Home Loan Bank Board Journal*, February 1971, pp. 1-2.

2148. Rodwin, Lloyd. *Housing and Economic Progress; A Study of the Housing Experiences of Boston's Middle-Income Families.* Cambridge, Mass.: Harvard University Press & Technology Press, 1961. 228pp.

2149. Scott, Edward P. "The Cooperative Apartment in Government Assisted Low-Middle Income Housing." *University of Pennsylvania Law Review*, March 1963, pp. 638-663.

2150. Sternlieb, George. *The Blue Collar Worker and Housing.* New Brunswick, N.J.: Center for Urban Policy Research, Rutgers University, 1971. 15pp.

2151. Sternlieb, George. "Death of the American Dream House." *Society (formerly Trans-action)*, Feb. 1972, pp. 39-42.

See also: 310, 690, 992, 1036, 1493, 1794, 1795, 2180, 3320a, 3320b, 3322, 3329, 3330, 3331; Exclusionary Zoning: 1283+; Inner City Housing: 2170+; Governmental Goals and Programs: 2280+; Planning for Low and Moderate Income Housing in the Suburbs: 3352+; The Concept of "Filtering": 3507a+.

## 7. RURAL HOUSING

### a. General

2152. Bird, Ronald, Lucia Beverly, and Anne Simmons. *Status of Rural Housing in the United States.* Washington, D.C.: Government Printing Office, 1968. 31pp.

2153. Cochran, Clay L. "Rural Housing: Need and Nonresponse." *Poverty and Human Resources*, November-December 1970. pp. 5-15.

2154. Foundation for Cooperative Housing. *Cooperative Housing for Rural America. A Report prepared for the U.S. Department of Agriculture.* Washington, D.C., 1968. 21+pp.

2155. Jones, Lawrence Arthur. *Rural Home Financing through the Voluntary Home Mortgage Credit Program.* Washington, D.C.: Government Printing Office, 1966. 22pp.

2156. Neville, James F. "The Other FHA Is Changing Rural America." *Real Estate Review*, Spring 1972, pp. 41-43.

2157. Parker, W. Russell. *Multi-Unit Retirement Housing for Rural Areas; A Guide to Design Considerations for Architects, Engineers, and Builders.* Washington, D.C.: Agricultural Research Service, U.S. Department of Agriculture, 1965. 23pp.

2158. Reno, Lee P. *Pieces and Scraps; Farm Labor Housing in the United States.* Washington, D.C.: Rural Housing Alliance, 1970. 160pp.

2159. Rural Housing Alliance. *Low-Income Housing Programs for Rural America.* Washington, D.C., 1971. 32pp.

2160. U.S. Congress. House. Committee on the Judiciary. Subcommittee No. 4. *The Role of the Farmers Home Administration in the Achievement of Equal Opportunity in Housing; A Report of the Civil Rights Oversight Subcommittee. . . .* Washington, D.C.: Government Printing Office, 1972. 5pp.

2161. U.S. Congress. Senate. Select Committee on Nutrition and Human Needs. *Promises to Keep: Housing Need and Federal Failure in Rural America.* Rev. ed. Washington, D.C.: Government Printing Office, 1972. 42pp.

2162. U.S. Department of Agriculture. Economic Research Service. *Financing of Rural Non-farm Housing in the United States.* By Edmund T. Hamlin. Washington, D.C.: Government Printing Office, 1970. 54pp.

2163. U.S. Department of Agriculture. Economic Research Service. *Rural Housing; Trends and Prospects.* By Robert E. Freeman. Washington, D.C.: Government Printing Office, 1970. 38pp.

2164. U.S. Department of Agriculture. Economic Research Service. *Status of Rural Housing in the United States.* Washington, D.C.: Government Printing Office, 1968.

2165. U.S. Department of Agriculture. Farmers Home Administration. *Rental and Co-op Housing in Rural Areas, Loans for Rental and Cooperative Housing for Senior Citizens and Other Residents in Rural Areas.* Rev. 1970. 7pp.

See also: 240, 2180.

b. Housing The Migrant Worker

2166. "Housing of Migrant Agricultural Workers." *Texas Law Review,* July 1968, pp. 933+.

2167. "Laws and Legislation Providing for the Housing of Migrant Agricultural Workers." *Williamette Law Journal,* March 1970, pp. 111+.

2168. U.S. Department of Agriculture. Agricultural Research Service. *Housing for Migrant Agricultural Workers.* By J.W. Simons. Washington, D.C.: Government Printing Office, 1970. 43pp.

2169. Winger, Alan R. and Gary Mammel. "Housing the Low-Income Migrant: An Issue in Regional Development." Unpublished paper, June 1970.

## 8. INNER-CITY HOUSING

### a. General

2170. Ackerman, B. "Regulating Slum Housing Markets on Behalf of the Poor: Of Housing Codes, Housing Subsidies and Income Redistribution Policy." *Yale Law Journal*, May 1971, pp. 1093+.

2171. Babcock, Richard F. and Fred P. Bosselman. "Citizen Participation: A Suburban Suggestion for the Central City." *Law and Contemporary Problems*, Spring 1967, pp. 220-231.

2172. Burchell, Robert W., James W. Hughes and George Sternlieb. *Housing Costs and Housing Restraints.* New Brunswick, N.J.: Center for Urban Policy Research, Rutgers University, 1970.

2173. Case, Fred E. "Housing Demand Characteristics of Underhoused Families in the Inner City." *Annals of Regional Science*, December 1969, pp. 15-26.

2174. Case, Fred E. "Housing the Underhoused in the Inner City." *Journal of Finance*, February 1971, pp. 427-444.

2175. Case, Fred E. (ed.). *Inner-City Housing and Private Enterprise.* New York: Praeger, 1972. 237pp.

2176. Case, Fred E. "Prediction of the Incidence of Urban Residential Blight." *Regional Science Association Papers and Proceedings, Volume Eleven, 1963.* Philadelphia, Pa.: Regional Science Association, 1963, pp. 211-214.

2177. Clark, William Arthur Valentine. *The Dynamics of Rental Housing Areas in U.S. Central Cities.* Ann Arbor, Mich.: University Microfilms, 1965 (Ph.D. dissertation, University of Illinois, 1964). 147pp. (order no. 65-796)

2178. Cordasco. F. and R.G. Galatioto. "Ethnic Displacement in the Interstitial Community: The East Harlem Experience." *Phylon*, Fall 1970, pp. 302-312.

2179. Culver, David M. *Tenement House Reform in Boston, 1846-1898.* Ann Arbor, Mich.: University Microfilms, 1972 (Ph.D. dissertation, Boston University Graduate School, 1972). 318pp. (order no. 72-25,258)

2180. Davis, J.T. "Middle Class Housing in the Central City." *Economic Geography*, July 1965, pp. 238-251.

2181. Droettboom, Theodore, Jr., *et al.* "Urban Violence and Residential Mobility." *Journal of the American Institute of Planners*, September 1971, pp. 319-325.

2182. Falick, P. "Tort Remedy for the Slum Tenant." *Illinois Bar Journal*, November 1969, pp. 204+

2183. "Finding a Profit in Slum Streets; Pittsburgh Group Called Action-Housing." *Business Week*, February 4, 1967, pp. 52-54+.

2184. Forman, Robert E. *Black Ghettos, White Ghettos, and Slums.* Englewood Cliffs, N.J.: Prentice-Hall, 1971. 184pp.

2185. Fried, Marc and Peggy Gleicher. "Some Sources of Residential Satisfaction in an Urban Slum: Meanings That the Slum Areas Have for Their Residents and the Consequent Effects That Relocation Would Have for Them." *Journal of the American Institute of Planners*, November 1961, pp. 305-315.

2186. Frieden, Bernard J. *The Future of Old Neighborhoods: Rebuilding for a Changing Population.* Cambridge, Mass.: MIT Press, 1964. 209pp.

2187. Friedman, L.M. and M.J. Spector. "Tenement House Legislation in Wisconsin: Reform and Reaction." *American Journal of Legal History*, January 1965, pp. 41+.

2188. Goering, J.M. *et al. Population and Housing in East Harlem 1950-1970.* New York: New York City Rand Institute, June 1972. 34pp.

2189. Goldschmidt, Leopold A. *Zoning for City Housing Markets.* Chicago, Ill.: American Society of Planning Officials, April 1972. 16pp. (Planning Advisory Service Report no. 279).

2190. Halstead, Roland W., Jr., "Boston Infill." *Federal Home Loan Bank Board Journal*, August 1971, pp. 12-16.

2191. Hartshorn, T.A. "Inner City Residential Structure and Decline." *Association of American Geographers, Annals*, March 1971, pp. 72-96. Reply (B.S. Weller) with rejoinder, March 1972, pp. 134-142.

2192. Hartshorn, Truman Asa. *Urban Blight: The Structure and Change of Substandard Housing in Cedar Rapids, Iowa, 1940-1960.* Ann Arbor, Mich.: University Microfilms, 1968 (Ph.D. dissertation, University of Iowa, 1968). 153pp. (order no. 68-16,811)

2193. Hoffman, Morton. "The Outlook for Downtown Housing." *Journal of the American Institute of Planners*, February 1961, pp. 43-55.

2194. Hunter, David R. *The Slums: Challenge and Response.* New York: Free Press of Glencoe, 1964. 294pp.

2195. Illinois General Assembly. House of Representatives. Committee on Slum Housing and Rent Gouging. *Report.* Springfield, Ill., 1965.

2196. Illinois University. Department of Urban Planning and Landscape Architecture. *The Aging City, Factors Related to the Gray Area Problem in Chicago.* Urbana, Ill., 1965.

2197. Illinois University. Department of Urban Planning and Landscape Architecture. *East Humboldt Park: A Study of a Gray Area Neighborhood, Chicago, Illinois.* Urbana, Ill., 1965. 40pp.

2198. Jensen, Robert. "Urban Housing." *Architectural Record,* April 1971, pp. 115-138.

2199. Kral, Franklin I. "The Real Estate Crisis in the Inner City." *Chicago Bar Record,* May 1972, pp. 367-371.

2200. "Law and the Demise of the Urban Ghetto." *Catholic University Law Review,* Winter-Spring 1969, pp. 39 and 143+.

2201. Little (Arthur D.), Inc. *Project Infill: An Experiment in Housing Technology.* New York, 1971. 92pp.

2202. Lubitz, Edward. *The Tenement Problem in New York City and the Movement for Its Reform, 1856-1867.* Ann Arbor, Mich.: University Microfilms, 1971 (Ph.D. dissertation, New York University, 1970). 601pp. (order no. 71-15,410)

2203. Lubove, Roy. *The Progressives and the Slums: Tenement House Reform in New York City, 1890-1917.* Pittsburgh: The University of Pittsburgh Press, 1962.

2204. Mandelker, Daniel R. and David G. Heeter. "Investment Activities of Relocated Tenement Landlords—A Pilot Study." In *Urban Law Annual 1968.* St. Louis, Mo.: School of Law, Washington University, 1968, pp. 33-56.

2205. Manuel, Allen D. *Housing Conditions in Urban Poverty Areas.* Prepared for the consideration of the National Commission on Urban Problems. Washington, D.C.: Government Printing Office, 1968. (National Commission on Urban Problems Research Report no. 9).

2206. Marsh, Robert J. *The Residential Enclave: An Examination of Some Systematic Interrelationships as to Their Potential to Effect Control of the Deterioration of an Inner City Neighborhood.* Ann Arbor, Mich.: University

Microfilms, 1968 (Ph.D. dissertation, Michigan State University, 1967). 134pp. (order no. 68-4180)

2207. Melamed, Anshel. "The Gray Areas: Unutilized Pòtentials and Unmet Needs." *Land Economics*, May 1965, pp. 151-158.

2208. Mixon, J. "Installment Land Contracts: A Study of Low Income Transactions, with Proposals for Reform and a New Program to Provide Home Ownership in the Inner City." *Houston Law Review*, May 1970, pp. 523+

2209. Muth, Richard S. "The Economics of Slum Housing." In W.D. Gardner (ed.). *America's Cities*. Ann Arbor, Mich.: Bureau of Business Research, University of Michigan, 1970.

2210. New York (State) Executive Department. Division of Housing and Community Renewal. *Responding to Urban Needs*. New York, 1965. 48pp.

2211. New York (State) Division of Housing and Community Renewal. *Slum Removal Study: New York City*. New York, 1968. 36pp.

2212. Northam, R.M. "Vacant Urban Land in the American City." *Land Economics*, November 1971, pp. 345-355.

2213. Nowicki, Joseph A. "Appraising in the Ghetto." *Real Estate Appraiser*, September/October 1969, pp. 5-9.

2214. Peattie, Lisa R. *Slums*. Monticello, Ill.: Council of Planning Librarians, 1970 (Exchange Bibliography no. 113).

2215. Riis, Jacob August. *Jacob Riis Revisited; Poverty and the Slum in Another Era*. Edited with an introduction by Francesco Cordasco. Garden City, N.Y.: Doubleday, 1968. 418pp.

2216. Rockford, Illinois, City-County Planning Commission. *An Evaluation of Housing Problems in Deteriorating Areas*. Rockford, Ill., 1972. 97pp.

2217. Rydell, C.P. *The Landlord Reinvestment Model: A Computer Based Method of Evaluating the Financial Feasibility of Alternative Treatments for Problem Buildings*. New York: The New York City Rand Institute, October 1970. 16pp.

2218. Sax, Joseph L. and Fred J. Hiestand. "Slumlordism as a Tort." *Michigan Law Review*, March 1967, pp. 869-922. "Slumlordism as a Tort—A Dissenting View" (Walter J. Blum and Allison Dunham), January 1968, pp. 451-464. "Slumlordism and Tort—A Brief Response" (Joseph L. Sax), pp. 465-468.

2219. Silberman, Charles E. "Up From Apathy–The Woodlawn Experience." *Commentary*, May 1964, pp. 57-58.

2220. Sporn, Arthur D. "Empirical Studies in the Economics of Slum Ownership." *Land Economics*, November 1960, pp. 333-340. Also in Alfred N. Page and Warren R. Seyfried (eds.). *Urban Analysis: Readings in Housing and Urban Development.* Glenview, Ill.: Scott, Foresman, 1970, pp. 328-334.

2221. Stegman, M.A. "Economics of Slums." *Appraisal Journal,* April 1971, pp. 293-296.

2222. Stegman, Michael. "The Myth of the Slumlord." *American Institute of Architects Journal*, March 1970, pp. 45-49.

2223. Stegman, Michael A. "Slumlords and Public Policy." *Journal of the American Institute of Planners*, November 1967, pp. 419-424. (Review article).

2224. Steiner, Oscar H. *Our Housing Jungle–And Your Pocketbook; How to Turn Our Growing Slums into Assets.* New York: University Publishers, 1960. 180pp.

2225. Sternlieb, George. "Hawthornism and Housing." *Urban Affairs Quarterly*, September 1970, pp. 94-103.

2226. Sternlieb, George. "Slum Housing: A Functional Analysis." *Law and Contemporary Problems*, Spring 1967, pp. 349-356. Also in Alfred N. Page and Warren R. Seyfried (eds.). *Urban Analysis: Readings in Housing and Urban Development.* Glenview, Ill.: Scott, Foresman, 1970, pp. 334-339.

2227. Sternlieb, George. *The Tenement Landlord.* New Brunswick, N.J.: Rutgers University Press, 1969. 269pp.

2228. Sternlieb, George, Robert W. Bruchell and James W. Hughes. "Ticking Time Bomb: The Realities of Inner-City Housing Costs." *Real Estate Review*, Spring 1972, pp. 34-40.

2229. Stewart, Henry Hadley, Jr. *A Natural Experiment Concerning the Effects of Housing Improvement on Selected Attitudes of Slum Dwellers.* Ann Arbor, Mich.: University Microfilms, 1969 (Ph.D. dissertation, Florida State University, 1968). 141pp. (order no. 69-11,332)

2230. Van Cleef, Eugene. "Downtown: Demolition or Renovation." *Journal of Property Management,* July/August 1967, pp. 156-160.

2231. Walsh, R.E. "Slum Housing: The Legal Remedies of Connecticut Towns and Tenants." *Connecticut Bar Journal*, December 1966, pp. 539+.

2232. Ward, D. "Emergence of Central Immigrant Ghettoes in American Cities: 1840-1920." *Association of American Geographers' Annals,* June 1968, pp. 348-359.

2233. "What's a Nice PUD Doing in a Former Slum?" *House and Home*, July 1970, pp. 48-55.

2234. Wolf, Eleanor P. and Mel J. Ravitz. "Lafayette Park: New Residents in the Core City." *Journal of the American Institute of Planners*, August 1964, pp. 234-239.

2235. Yandle, Thomas Bruce, Jr. *Externalities in Housing: The Prevention of Urban Blight.* Ann Arbor, Mich.: University Microfilms, 1970 (Ph.D. dissertation, Georgia State University, 1970). 132pp. (order no. 70-20,641)

See also: 675, 739, 741, 758, 862, 1034, 1616; Housing Codes: 1126+; Housing Codes within the Landlord-Tenant Relationship: 1398+.

b. Abandonment

2236. "Abandonment: The Sputnik of the Seventies." *HUD Challenge*, April 1972, pp. 26-30.

2237. Center for Community Change and the National Urban League. "Housing Abandonment." *Architecutral Forum*, April 1971, pp. 42-45.

2238. Citizens' Budget Commission, Inc. *Abandoned Buildings: A Time for Action*. New York, 1970.

2239. Cranker, Glenn. "Abandoned and Vacant Housing Units: Can They Be Used during Housing Crisis? *New York University Review of Law and Social Change,* Spring 1971, pp. 3-68.

2240. "Housing: The Shell Game." *Newsweek*, February 28, 1972, pp. 60-61.

2241. "Housing Abandonment." *Real Estate Appraiser*, March-April 1972, pp. 37-42.

2242. "Housing Abandonment–The Problem and a Proposed Solution." *Real Property, Probate & Trust Journal*, Summer 1972, pp. 382+

2243a. "In the Inner Cities: Acres of Abandoned Buildings; Landlords Are Now Fleeing the Inner City, Along with Many of Their Tenants; When They Go, They Often Abandon Houses and Apartment Buildings; The Result Is a New Kind of Crisis for Many Large American Cities." *U.S. News and World Report*, January 26, 1970, pp. 54-56.

2243b. International City Management Association. *Abandoned Residential Buildings.* Washington, D.C., May 1972 (Management Information Service Report Vol. 4, no. LS-5).

2244a. Lilley, William III and Timothy B. Clark. "Urban Report/Federal Programs Spur Abandonment of Housing in Major Cities." *National Journal*, January 1, 1972, pp. 26-33.

2244b. Linton, Mields, and Coston. *A Study of the Problems of Abandoned Housing and Recommendations for Action by the Federal Government and Localities.* A research report prepared under contract to the U.S. Department of Housing and Urban Development, Office of Research and Technology. Washington, D.C., 1971.

2245. Nachbaur, William T. "Empty Houses: Abandoned Residential Buildings in the Inner City." *Howard Law Journal*, Vol. 17, no. 1, 1971, pp. 3-68.

2246. National Urban Coalition. "Statement on Abandonment and the Need to Revitalize Our Cities." *City*, March-April 1972, pp. 60-64.

2247a. National Urban League and Center for Community Change. *The National Survey of Housing Abandonment.* New York, 1971. 118pp.

2247b. Real Estate Research Corporation. *Possible Program for Counteracting Housing Abandonment.* Preliminary report prepared for the Office of Research and Technology, Department of Housing and Urban Development. Chicago, Ill., 1971. 99pp.

2248. Schreiberg, Sheldon. "Abandoned Buildings: Tenant Condominiums and Community Redevelopment–New York City's Experience." *Urban Lawyer*, Spring 1970, pp. 186-218.

2249. Scudder, Samuel. "HUD Seeks to Reduce Its Ownership of Inner-City Abandoned Properties." *National Journal*, February 26, 1972, pp. 371+.

2250. Sternlieb, George. "Abandoned Housing: What Is to Be Done?" *Urban Land*, March 1972, entire issue (17pp.).

2251. Sternlieb, George. "Abandonment: Urban Housing Phenomenon." *HUD Challenge*, May 1972, pp. 12-14.

2252. Sternlieb, George. "Abandonment and Rehabilitation: What Is to Be Done?" In U.S. Congress. House. Committee on Banking and Currency. *Papers Submitted to Subcommittee on Housing Panels on Housing Production, Housing Demand, and Developing a Suitable Living Environment: Part 1.* Washington, D.C.: Government Printing Office,

1971, pp. 315-372. Also in George Sternlieb and Lynne B. Sagalyn (eds.). *Housing: 1970-1971; An AMS Anthology*. New York: AMS Press, 1972, pp. 62-119.

2253. Sternlieb, George. "Some Aspects of the Abandoned House Problem." New Brunswick, N.J.: Center for Urban Policy Research, Rutgers University, 1970.

2254a. Sternlieb, George, Robert W. Burchell and Virginia Paulus. *Residential Abandonment: The Environment of Decay*. Monticello, Ill.: Council of Planning Librarians, 1972 (Exchange Bibliography no. 342).

2254b. Washington University. Institute for Urban and Regional Studies. *Urban Decay in St. Louis*. St. Louis, Missouri, 1972.

2255. "The Wildfire of Abandonment: Entire Blocks Are Rotting as Landlords Claim: 'We Can't Make a Buck.'" *Business Week*, April 4, 1970, pp. 57+.

See also: 2227.

c. Finance

2256. "Associations Learn How to Finance Urban Housing Needs." *Savings and Loan News*, October 1968, pp. 26-30.

2257. "Bankrolling the Slum Clearance Job: Insurance Companies, Traditionally Shy of High-Risk Financing, Are Allocating $1 Billion for Housing and Job-Creating Enterprises." *Business Week*, October 14, 1967, pp. 58+

2258. "Can Associations Save the Inner City?" *Savings and Loan News*, March 1970, pp. 34-40.

2259. Fitzhugh, Gilbert, Robert C. Weaver, and Joseph A. Califano, Jr. "The Life Insurance Companies and the Problems of the Central Cities: News Briefing." *Weekly Compilation of Presidential Documents*, September 18, 1967, pp. 1284-1288.

2260. Gehrke, H., Jr. "United Thrift Industry and the Inner City Crisis." *Commercial and Financial Chronicle*, May 30, 1968, pp. 2154-2155.

2261. "Inner City Innovation: Philadelphia S & L's Fund Lancaster Housing Project." *Federal Home Loan Bank Board Journal*, April 1971, pp. 19-21.

2262. Joint Savings Bank—Savings and Loan Committee on Urban Problems. *Urban Financing Guide*. New York: National Association of Mutual Savings Banks, 1968. 48pp.

2263. "Life Insurers Push to Rebuild Slums: Insurance Industry's $1-billion Program for Financing Slum Rehabilitation Passes the Halfway Mark Despite Its Own Conservatism and a Slew of Other Problems." *Business Week*, July 20, 1968, pp. 52+.

2264. "Miami's Inner City Housing Story." *Federal Home Loan Bank Board Journal*, November 1970, pp. 14-17+.

2265. Murray, Thomas F. "Problems and Techniques in Financing Ghetto Housing." *Bankers Monthly* (Boston), Spring 1969, pp. 34-40.

2266. Stegman, Michael A. *Housing Investment in the Inner City: The Dynamics of Decline. A Study of Baltimore, Maryland, 1968-1970.* Cambridge, Mass.: MIT Press, 1972. 289pp.

2267. Thiemann, Charles Lee. "District Banks and the Inner City." *Federal Home Loan Bank Board Journal*, November 1970, pp. 10-11+.

2268. U.S. Congress. House. Committee on Banking and Currency. Ad Hoc Subcommittee on Home Financing Practices and Procedures. *Financing of Inner-City Housing. Hearings. . . .* Washington, D.C.: Government Printing Office, 1968.

2269. U.S. Congress. Senate. Committee on Banking and Currency. Subcommittee on Financial Institutions. *Financial Institutions and the Urban Crisis. Hearings . . . on Private Investment in the Inner City.* Washington, D.C.: Government Printing Office, 1968. 470pp.

d. Insurance Problems

2270. Bernstein, George K. "Critical Evaluation of FAIR Plans." *Journal of Risk and Insurance*, June 1971, pp. 273+.

2271. DuBois, Frederick M. "Where Do We Go from Here with F.A.I.R. Plans?" *CPCU* (Chartered Property & Casualty Underwriters) *Annals*, December 1971, pp. 355-369.

2272. Friedman, Gilbert B. "Uninsurables in the Ghetto." *New Republic*, September 14, 1968, pp. 10-14.

2273. Shapiro, Harvey D. *Fire Insurance and the Inner City*. New York: New York City Rand Institute, 1971. 32pp.

2274. Syron, Richard F. *An Analysis of the Collapse of the Normal Market for Fire Insurance in Substandard Urban Core Areas*. Boston, Mass.: Federal Reserve Bank of Boston, January 1972. 188pp. (Federal Reserve Bank of Boston Research Report no. 49).

2275. Syron, Richard F. "The Hard Economics of Ghetto Fire Insurance." *New England Economic Review*, March/April 1972, pp. 2-11.

2276. U.S. Congress. House. Committee on Banking and Currency. Subcommittee on Housing. *Operation of the Urban Property Protection and Reinsurance Program: Hearings. . . .* Washington, D.C.: Government Printing Office, 1969. 378pp.

2277. U.S. Department of Housing and Urban Development. Federal Insurance Administration. Office of Compliance and Review. *Report on FAIR Plan Operations 1971: California, Connecticut, District of Columbia, Illinois, Massachusetts, New Jersey, New York, Ohio, Pennsylvania, Rhode Island.* Washington, D.C., January 1972.

2278. U.S. President's National Advisory Panel on Insurance in Riot-Affected Areas. *Meeting the Insurance Crisis in Our Cities.* Washington, D.C.: Government Printing Office, 1968.

2279. Whitman, Andrew F. and C. Arthur Williams, Jr. "Environmental Hazards and Rating Urban Core Properties." *Journal of Risk and Insurance*, September 1970, pp. 419-436.

## B. GOVERNMENTAL GOALS AND PROGRAMS–ANALYSIS, CRITIQUE, ALTERNATIVES

### 1. NATIONAL HOUSING GOALS

2280. Clay, Philip L. *National Housing Goals and Measures of Progress.* Cambridge, Mass.: Joint Center for Urban Studies of the Massachusetts Institute of Technology and Harvard University, September 1972. (Joint Center Working Paper no. 14).

2281. Cooper, J.R. *Can the 1968-78 National Housing Goals Be Achieved?* Urbana, Ill.: University of Illinois, 1971. 57pp.

2282. Downs, Anthony. "Moving toward Realistic Housing Goals." In Kermit Gordon (ed.). *Agenda for the Nation.* Washington, D.C.: The Brookings Institution, 1968, pp. 141-178. Also in Anthony Downs. *Urban Problems and Prospects.* Chicago, Ill.: Markham, 1970, pp. 115-155.

2283. Fleishman, Joel L. "Goals and Strategies of a National Housing and Urban Growth Policy." In U.S. Congress. House. Committee on Banking and Currency. *Papers Submitted to Subcommittee on Housing Panels on Housing Production, Housing Demand, and Developing a Suitable Living Environment: Part 2.* Washington, D.C.: Government Printing Office, 1971, pp. 703-736.

2284. Frank, Edward. "The Prospects for Meeting National Housing Goals." *Journal of Environmental Systems*, December 1971, pp. 329-340.

2285. "Housing Goals: Housing Study to Show Drop in Earlier Goals for 1970." *Congressional Quarterly Weekly Report*, March 13, 1970, pp. 751-754.

2286. "Industry's Contribution to Meeting the National Housing Goals." *HUD Challenge*, October 1972, pp. 4-13.

2287. Janis, Jay. "Meeting the National Housing Goals." *Urban Land*, April 1971, pp. 9-15.

2288. Kelly, Robert Andrew. *Housing Goals and the Housing Mix.* Ann Arbor, Mich.: University Microfilms, 1972 (Ph.D. dissertation, Georgetown University, 1971). 244pp. (order no. 72-10,412)

2289. Kristof, Frank S. "Housing Policy Goals and the Turnover of Housing." *Journal of the American Institute of Planners*, August 1965, pp. 232-245.

2290. Kristof, Frank S. *Pursuit of Housing Policy Goals in New York City.* New York: New York City Housing and Redevelopment Board, 1965. 30pp. (Report no. 12).

2291. Schussheim, Morton J. "National Goals and Local Practices: Joining Ends and Means in Housing." In U.S. Congress. House. Committee on Banking and Currency. *Papers Submitted to Subcommittee on Housing Panels on Housing Production, Housing Demand, and Developing a Suitable Living Environment: Part 1.* Washington, D.C.: Government Printing Office, 1971, pp. 141-158.

2292. Thurow, Lester C. "Goals of a Housing Program." In U.S. Congress. House. Committee on Banking and Currency. *Papers Submitted to Subcommittee on Housing Panels on Housing Production, Housing Demand, and Developing a Suitable Living Environment: Part 2.* Washington, D.C.: Government Printing Office, 1971, pp. 437-450.

2293. U.S. Congress. House. Committee on Banking and Currency. *First Annual Report on National Housing Goals, Message from the President of the United States. . . .* Washington, D.C., 1969. 101pp.

2294. U.S. Congress. House. Committee on Banking and Currency. *Second Annual Report on National Housing Goals. Message from the President of the United States. . . .* Washington, D.C., 1970. 148pp.

2295. U.S. Congress. House. Committee on Banking and Currency. *Third Annual Report on National Housing Goals: Message from the President of the United States.* Washington, D.C., 1971.

2296. U.S. Congress. House. Committee on Banking and Currency. *Fourth Annual Report on National Housing Goals: Message from the President of the United States....* Washington, D.C., 1972. 106pp.

2297. U.S. Congress. House. Committee on Banking and Currency. Subcommittee on Housing. *National Housing Goals. Hearings....* Washington, D.C.: Government Printing Office, 1969. 607pp.

2298. U.S. Department of Housing and Urban Development. *Progress toward Meeting the National Housing Goals.* Washington, D.C., 1970. 92pp.

2299. U.S. General Accounting Office. *Opportunity to Improve Allocation of Program Funds to Better Meet the National Housing Goal.* Washington, D.C., 1970. 61pp.

See also: 489, 971.

## 2. HOUSING LEGISLATION

2300. American Enterprise Institute for Public Policy Research. *Housing and Urban Development Bills.* Washington, D.C., 1968. 37pp.

2301. Ashley, Thomas L. "The Urban Growth and New Community Development Act." *Mortgage Banker*, February 1971, pp. 20-23.

2302. Coan, C.A.S., Jr. "Housing and Urban Development Act of 1968: Landmark Legislation for the Urban Crisis." *Urban Lawyer*, Spring 1969, pp. 1+.

2303. Commerce Clearing House. *Explanation of Housing and Urban Development Act of 1968. P.L. 90-448, as Signed by the President on August 1, 1968.* New York, 1968. 48pp.

2304. "Detailed Provisions of Proposed 1970 Legislation on Housing Assistance Programs for Lower-Income Families." *Journal of Housing*, March 1970, pp. 122-123.

2305. "Economic Opportunity Act Puts Housing, Renewal in Front Lines of Anti-Poverty War; Anti-Poverty Bill Passes: Contents Summarized in Relationship to Housing Renewal." *Journal of Housing*, August 1964, pp. 352-363.

2306. Edson, C.L. "From Capitol Hill: The Housing and Urban Development Act of 1970." *Urban Lawyer*, Winter 1971, pp. 142+.

2307. Foard, A. "Provisions of the 1968 Housing and Development Act." *Record of the Association of the Bar of the City of New York*, November 1968, pp. 567+.

2308. Freilich, R.H. and L.B. Seidel. "Recent Trends in Housing Law: Prologue to the 70's." *The Urban Lawyer*, Winter 1970, pp. 1-13. Also in *Municipal Attorney*, May 1970, pp. 71-77 and 98-104.

2309. Hershman, M. "Housing and Urban Development Act of 1968." *Real Property, Probate & Trust Journal*, Winter 1968, pp. 537+.

2310. Holmes, Lee B. "A Legislative Outlook for 1971." *Mortgage Banker*, January 1971, pp. 22-30.

2311. "The Housing Act of 1961: A Summary of Provisions Which Affect Municipalities." *New Jersey Municipalities*, May 1962, pp. 19-21+.

2312. "Housing and Urban Development Act of 1965." *Boston College Industrial & Commercial Law Review*, Winter 1966, pp. 314+.

2313. "Housing and Urban Development Act of 1965." *Construction Review*, October 1965, pp. 9-16.

2314. "Housing and Urban Development Act of 1968: Private Enterprise and Low-Income Housing," *William & Mary Law Review*, Summer 1969, pp. 936+.

2315. "Housing Program to Stress Renewed Cities; 1965 Proposals: Controversy in Housing Programs–Centered on Public Housing, Urban Renewal." *Congressional Quarterly Weekly Report*, February 19, 1965, pp. 275-280+.

2316. Ingram, Helen Meyer. *Congress and Housing Policy.* Ann Arbor, Mich.: University Microfilms, 1970 (Ph.D. dissertation, Columbia University, 1967). 368pp. (order no. 70-23,442)

2317. Ingram, Helen. "A Question of Representation: The Impact of Urban Congressmen upon Housing Legislation." *Journal of Urban Law*, Vol. 47, no. 1, 1969-70, pp. 85-111.

2318. Levi, Julian H. *Municipal and Institutional Relations within Boston; The Benefits of Section 112 of the Federal Housing Act of 1961.* Chicago, Ill.: University of Chicago Press, 1964. 157pp.

2319. "Major Housing Bill to Help Poor Purchase Homes: Riot and Flood Insurance, New Towns Aid Included." *Congressional Quarterly Weekly Report*, August 2, 1968, pp. 2031-2036.

2320. Nenno, Mary K. "Housing and Urban Development Legislation of 1970." *Journal of Housing*, January 1971, pp. 17-22.

2321. "The New Frontier for Housing Proposed by the President's Task Force on Housing Legislation." *House & Home*, February 1961, pp. 82-87.

2322. Newman, William A. "The Proposed Housing Consolidation and Simplication Act of 1971." *Journal of Law Reform*, Winter 1972, pp. 361-384.

2323. Northrup, Graham. "The Housing Act of 1968." *Urban Land*, October 1968, pp. 3-9.

2324. O'Block, Robert P. with Robert H. Kuehn, Jr. *An Economic Analysis of the Housing and Urban Development Act of 1968.* Boston, Mass: Division of Research, Graduate School of Business Administration, Harvard University, 1970. 82pp.

2325. "Poverty Law and Legislative Change." *Howard Law Journal*, Winter 1969, pp. 284+.

2326. "Proposed Housing Consolidation and Simplification Act of 1971." *University of Michigan Law Journal of Law Reform*, Winter 1972, pp. 361+.

2327. Sparkman, John. "Outlook for Housing Legislation in 1971." *Mortgage Banker*, July 1971, pp. 12-24.

2328. Spiezio, Nicholas J. "The Housing and Urban Development Act of 1970." *Mortgage Banker*, February 1971, pp. 12-19.

2329. U.S. Congress. House. Committee on Banking and Currency. Subcommittee on Housing. *Compilation of the Housing and Urban Development Act of 1965: Public Law 89-117, with Related Documents.* Washington, D.C.: Government Printing Office, 1965. 318pp.

2330. U.S. Congress. House. Committee on Banking and Currency. Subcommittee on Housing. *Compilation of the Housing and Urban Development Act of 1968: Public Law 90-448 with Related Documents.* Washington, D.C.: Government Printing Office, 1968.

2331. U.S. Congress. House. Committee on Banking and Currency. Subcommittee on Housing. *Demonstration Cities, Housing and Urban Development, and Urban Mass Transit: Hearings. . . .* Washington, D.C., 1966. 2 Vols. 1123pp.

2332. U.S. Congress. House. Committee on Banking and Curency. *Emergency Home Finance Act of 1970 and Housing and Urban Development Act of 1970: Public Laws 91-351 and 91-609 and Section-by-Section Summaries.* Washington, D.C., 1971. 108pp.

2333. U.S. Congress. House. Committee on Banking and Currency. *Emergency Home Ownership Act. Hearings. . . .* Washington, D.C.: Government Printing Office, 1960. 375pp.

2334. U.S. Congress. House. Committee on Banking and Currency. *Emergency Home Ownership Act; Report. . . .* Washington, D.C.: U.S. Government Printing Office, 1960. 50pp.

2335. U.S. Congress. House. Committee on Banking and Currency. Subcommittee on Housing. *General Housing Legislation: Hearings. . . .* Washington, D.C., 1960. 557pp.

2336. U.S. Congress. House. Committee on Banking and Currency. Subcommittee on Housing. *Highlights of the Housing and Urban Development Act of 1965: Public Law 89-117, Together with a Section-by-Section Analysis and Legislative History.* Washington, D.C.: Government Printing Office, 1965. 43pp.

2337. U.S. Congress. House. Committee on Banking and Currency. *Housing Act of 1960; Report. . . .* Washington, D.C.: Government Printing Office, 1960. 140pp.

2338. U.S. Congress. House. Committee on Banking and Currency. *Housing Act of 1961. Hearings. . . .* Washington, D.C.: Government Printing Office, 1961. 885pp.

2339. U.S. Congress. House. Committee on Banking and Currency. *Housing Act of 1961; Report, Together with Minority Views. . . .* Washington, D.C.: Government Printing Office, 1961. 171pp.

2340. U.S. Congress. House. Committee on Banking and Currency. *Housing Act of 1964: Report, August 5, 1964 (to Accompany H.R. 12175).* Washington, D.C.: Government Printing Office, 1964. 125pp.

2341. U.S. Congress. House. Committee on Banking and Currency. *Housing and Community Development Legislation. Hearings. . . .* Washington, D.C.: Government Printing Office, 1964. 929pp.

2342. U.S. Congress. House. Committee on Banking and Currency. Subcommittee on Housing. *Housing and Urban Development Act of 1965: Hearings. . . .* Washington, D.C.: Government Printing Office, 1965, 2 vols., 1215pp.

2343. U.S. Congress. House. Committee on Banking and Currency. *Housing and Urban Development Act of 1965; Report to Accompany H.R. 7984.* Washington, D.C.: Government Printing Office, 1965. 191pp.

2344. U.S. Congress. House. Committee on Banking and Currency. Subcommittee on Housing. *Housing and Urban Development Act of 1966. Report. . . .* Washington, D.C.: Government Printing Office, 1966. 432pp.

2345. U.S. Congress. House. Committee on Banking and Currency. Subcommittee on Housing. *Housing and Urban Development Act of 1968. Report.* . . . Washington, D.C.: Government Printing Office, 1968. 359pp.

2346. U.S. Congress. House. Committee on Banking and Currency. *Housing and Urban Development Act of 1969. Public Law 91-152 and Section-by-Section Summary.* . . . Washington, D.C.: Government Printing Office, 1969. 41pp.

2347. U.S. Congress. House. Committee on Banking and Currency. *Housing and Urban Development Act of 1972: Hearings.* . . . Washington, D.C.: Government Printing Office, 1972. 797pp.

2348. U.S. Congress. House. Committee on Banking and Currency. Subcommittee on Housing. *Housing and Urban Development Legislation, 1969: Hearings.* . . . Washington, D.C.: Government Printing Office, 1969. 623pp.

2349. U.S. Congress. House. Committee on Banking and Currency. Subcommittee on Housing. *Housing and Urban Development Legislation, 1970: Hearings, June 2-11, 1970.* Washington, D.C., 1970.

2350. U.S. Congress. House. Committee on Banking and Currency. Subcommittee on Housing. *Housing and Urban Development Legislation–1971. Hearings.* . . . Washington, D.C.: Government Printing Office, 1971. 3 vols.

2351. U.S. Congress. House. Committee on Banking and Currency. Subcommittee on Housing. *Housing and Urban Development Legislation and Urban Insurance. Hearings.* . . . Washington, D.C.: Government Printing Office, 1968. 2 vols.

2352. U.S. Congress. House. Committee on Banking and Currency. Subcommittee on Housing. *National Housing Act Amendment: Hearing, August 30, 1962, on H.R. 11262.* Washington, D.C.: Government Printing Office, 1962. 22pp.

2353. U.S. Congress. House. Committee on Banking and Currency. *The Senior Citizens Housing Act of 1962. Hearings.* . . . Washington, D.C.: Government Printing Office, 1962. 420pp.

2354. U.S. Congress. House. Committee on Banking and Currency. *Senior Citizens Housing Act of 1962. Report.* Washington, D.C.: Government Printing Office, 1962. 24pp.

2355. U.S. Congress. House. Committee on Banking and Currency. Subcommittee on Housing. *To Amend and Extend Laws Relating to Housing and Urban Development. Hearings.* . . . Washington, D.C.: Government Printing Office, 1967. 803pp.

2356. U.S. Congress. Senate. Committee on Banking and Currency. Subcommittee on Housing. *Congress and American Housing.* Washington, D.C.: Government Printing Office, September 1963.

2357. U.S. Congress. Senate. Committee on Banking and Currency. Subcommittee on Housing and Urban Affairs. *Congress and American Housing, 1892-1967.* Washington, D.C.: Government Printing Office, 1968. 50pp.

2358. U.S. Congress. Senate. Committee on Banking and Currency. *HHFA and VA Housing Legislation. Hearing.* . . . Washington, D.C.: Government Printing Office, 1964. 37pp.

2359. U.S. Congress. Senate. Committee on Banking and Currency. *Housing Act of 1960. Report.* . . . Washington, D.C.: Government Printing Office, 1960. 49pp.

2360. U.S. Congress. Senate. Committee on Banking and Currency. *Housing Act of 1961; Report.* . . . Washington, D.C.: Government Printing Office, 1961. 110pp.

2361. U.S. Congress. Senate. Committee on Banking and Currency. *Housing Act of 1964: Report, July 29, 1964 (to Accompany S. 3049), Together with Individual Views.* Washington, D.C.: Government Printing Office, 1964. 73pp.

2362. U.S. Congress. Senate. Committee on Banking and Currency. Subcommittee on Housing. *The Housing and Community Development Act of 1964; Questions and Answers on Provisions of S.2468.* Washington, D.C.: Government Printing Office, 1964. 37pp.

2363. U.S. Congress. Senate. Committee on Banking and Currency. Housing and Urban Development Act of 1965; Report. . . . Washington, D.C.: Government Printing Office, 1965. 104pp.

2364. U.S. Congress. Senate. Committee on Banking and Currency. *Housing and Urban Development Act of 1967; Report.* . . . Washington, D.C.: Government Printing Office, 1967. 71pp.

2365. U.S. Congress. Senate. Committee on Banking and Currency. *Housing and Urban Development Act of 1970. Report of the Committee on Banking and Currency.* Washington, D.C.: Government Printing Office, 1970. 69pp.

2366. U.S. Congress. Senate. Committee on Banking and Currency. Subcommittee on Housing and Urban Affairs. *Housing and Urban Development Legislation of 1968, Hearings.* . . . Washington, D.C.: Government Printing Office, 1968. 2 vols. 1433pp.

2367. U.S. Congress. Senate. Committee on Banking and Currency. Subcommittee on Housing and Urban Affairs. *Housing and Urban Development Legislation of 1969. Hearings....* Washington, D.C.: Government Printing Office, 1969. 596pp.

2368. U.S. Congress. Senate. Committee on Banking and Currency. *Housing and Urban Development Legislation of 1970. Hearings before the Subcommittee on Housing and Urban Affairs.* Washington, D.C.: Government Printing Office, 1970.

2369. U.S. Congress. Senate. Committee on Banking and Currency. Subcommittee on Housing. *Housing Legislation of 1960: Hearings. ...* Washington, D.C., 1960. 1041pp.

2370. U.S. Congress. Senate. Committee on Banking and Currency. *Housing Legislation of 1961. Hearings. ...* Washington, D.C.: Government Printing Office, 1961. 153pp.

2371. U.S. Congress. Senate. Committee on Banking and Currency. Subcommittee on Housing. *Housing Legislation of 1964: Hearings, February 19–March 3, 1964, on S.2468, and Other Pending Bills to Amend the Federal Housing Laws.* Washington, D.C.: Government Printing Office, 1964. 1189pp.

2372. U.S. Congress. Senate. Committee on Banking and Currency. Subcommittee on Housing. *Housing Legislation of 1965: Hearings, March 29-April 9, 1965, on S. 1354 and Other Pending Bills to Amend the Federal Housing Laws.* Washington, D.C.: Government Printing Office, 1965. 1078pp.

2373. U.S. Congress. Senate. Committee on Banking and Currency. Subcommittee on Housing. *Housing Legislation of 1966. Hearings. ...* Washington, D.C.: Government Printing Office, 1966. 2 vols. 1246pp.

2374. U.S. Congress. Senate. Committee on Banking and Currency. Subcommittee on Housing and Urban Affairs. *Housing Legislation of 1967. Hearings. ...* Washington, D.C.: Government Printing Office, 1967. 2 vols. 1637pp.

2375. U.S. Congress. Senate. Committee on Banking, Housing and Urban Affairs. Subcommittee on Housing and Urban Affairs. *1971 Housing and Urban Development Legislation. Hearings. ...* Washington, D.C.: Government Pringtin Office, 1971. 2 vols.

2376. U.S. Congress. Senate. Committee on Banking and Currency. *Section-by-Section Analysis of the Housing Act of 1964 as Recommended by the Subcommittee on Housing.* Washington, D.C.: Government Printing Office, 1964. 7pp.

2377. U.S. Congress. Senate. Committee on Banking and Currency. *Section-by-Section Analysis of the Provisions of S. 3049, the Housing Act of 1964 (Public Law 88-560).* Washington, D.C.: Government Printing Office, 1964. 24pp.

2378. U.S. Congress. Senate. Committee on Banking and Currency. *To Amend Title VI of the Housing and Urban Development Act of 1965. Hearings. . . .* Washington, D.C.: Government Printing Office, 1970. 1 vol.

2379. U.S. Congress. Senate. Committee on Banking and Currency. *To Amend Title VII of the Housing and Urban Development Act of 1965. Hearings.* Washington, D.C.: Government Printing Office, 1970.

2380. U.S. Congress. Senate. Committee on Banking, Housing and Urban Affairs. *Housing and Urban Development Act of 1972: Report of the Committee on Banking, Housing and Urban Affairs. . . .* Washington, D.C.: Government Printing Office, 1972.

2381. U.S. Congress. Senate. Committee on Banking, Housing and Urban Affairs. *Housing Legislation of 1967. Hearings. . . .* Washington, D.C.: Government Printing Office, 1967. 2 vols.

2382. U.S. Department of Housing and Urban Development. *Emergency Home Finance Act of 1970, Public Law 91-351 and Housing and Urban Development Act of 1970, Public Law 91-609, Section-by-Section Summaries.* Washington, D.C., 1971. 39pp.

2383. U.S. Department of Housing and Urban Development. *Housing and Urban Development Act of 1968, Public Law 90-448, Approved August 1, 1968; Summaries. . . .* Washington, D.C., 1968. 103pp.

2384. U.S. Housing and Home Finance Agency, Office of General Counsel. *Summary of the Housing Act of 1961. . . .* Washington, D.C.: Government Printing Office, 1961. 35pp.

2385. Weaver, R.C. "Housing and Community Development Act of 1964." *Title News*, July 1964, pp. 2+.

See also: 663-669, 680, 689, 1081, 1533, 1534, 1746, 2711, 3095, 3185, 3191.

## 3. THE DEPARTMENT OF HOUSING AND URBAN DEVELOPMENT—ORIGINS, STRUCTURE, FUNDING

2387. Barbrook, Alec T. "The Making of a Department." *Urban Affairs Quarterly*, March 1971, pp. 277-296.

2388. Ink, D.A. "Establishing the New Department of Housing and Urban Development." *Public Administration Review*, September 1967, pp. 224-228.

2389. Ink, Dwight A. "The Department of Housing and Urban Development—Building a New Federal Department." *Law and Contemporary Problems*, Summer 1967, pp. 375-383.

2390. "Origin of HUD-FHA." *HUD Challenge*, June 1971, pp. 4-7.

2391. U.S. Congress. Senate. Committee on Appropriations. *Department of Housing and Urban Development; Space, Science, Veterans, and Certain Other Independent Agencies Appropriations Bill, 1972: Report.* Washington, D.C.: Government Printing Office, 1971.

2392. U.S. Congress. Senate. Committee on Banking, Housing and Urban Affairs. Subcommittee on Housing and Urban Affairs. *Withholding of Funds for Housing and Urban Development Programs, Fiscal Year 1971. Hearings. . . .* Washington, D.C.: Government Printing Office, 1971. 228pp.

2393. U.S. Dept. of Housing and Urban Development. *Summary of the HUD Budget, 1972/73.* Washington, D.C., 1972.

2394. Willmann, John B. *The Department of Housing and Urban Development.* New York: Praeger, 1967. 207pp.

2395. Zentner, Joseph Lyle. *The 1968-69 U.S. Presidential Transition with Special Reference to the Housing and Urban Development Department.* Ann Arbor, Mich.: University Microfilms, 1971 (Ph.D. dissertation, University of Missouri—Columbia, 1970). 364pp. (order no. 71-3398)

## 4. FEDERAL HOUSING PROGRAMS—GENERAL

### a. Guides to Programs and Policies

2396. Adams, Richard V. "The Role of Federal Housing Agencies." *Federal Home Loan Bank Board Journal*, September 1971, pp. 25-26.

2397. Arbanas, J.A. "Housing and Home Finance Activities of the United States Government." *Chicago Bar Record*, March 1960, pp. 296+.

2398. Davies, Richard O. *Housing Reform During the Truman Administration.* Columbia, Mo.: University of Missouri Press, 1966. 197pp.

2399. Davies, Richard Oakley. *The Truman Housing Program.* Ann Arbor, Mich.: University Microfilms, 1964 (Ph.D. dissertation, University of Missouri, 1963). 329pp. (order no. 64-4796)

2400. Deihl, Richard H. "HUD: Bridge to Low-Cost Housing." *Federal Home Loan Bank Board Journal*, November 1970, pp. 1-5.

2401. Dickerman, John M. *Guide to Federal Programs in Low and Moderate Income Family Housing.* Washington, D.C.: Retail Lumber Dealers Foundation, 1970. 56pp.

2402. Edson, Charles L. "Everyman's HUD." *Real Estate Review*, Winter 1972, pp. 79-87.

2403. Edson, Charles L. and Bruce S. Lane. *A Practical Guide to Low- and Moderate-Income Housing.* Washington, D.C.: Bureau of National Affairs, 1972.

2404. Ellickson, Robert. "Government Housing Assistance to the Poor." *Yale Law Journal*, January 1967, pp. 508-544.

2405. Fitzpatrick, B.T. "FHA and FNMA Assistance for Multifamily Housing." *Law and Contemporary Problems*, Summer 1967, pp. 439-464.

2406. "Formula for Using HUD Programs." *HUD Challenge*, April 1972, pp. 4-7.

2407. Franklin, Herbert M. "Federal Power and Subsidized Housing." *Urban Lawyer*, Winter 1971, pp. 61-77.

2408. "Government Financial Aid Plays Big Role in Private Housing." *Federal Reserve Chicago. Business Conditions: A Review*, December 1959, pp. 11-16.

2409. "Government Programs to Encourage Private Investment in Low-Income Housing." *Harvard Law Review*, April 1968, pp. 1295-1324.

2410. "Government-Sponsored Credit Agencies." *Federal Reserve New York. Monthly Review*, April 1970, pp. 87-91.

2411. Jones, Richard E. "Sponsorship of Subsidized Housing for Low and Moderate Income Families under the National Housing Act." *George Washington Law Review*, July 1970, pp. 1073-1090.

2412. Kaplan, Peter E. "Everything You Always Wanted to Know about HUD Affirmative Marketing." *NAHB Journal of Homebuilding*, May 1972, pp. 26-27.

2413. Korb, K.A. "Primer for FHA Multi-Family Rental Housing." *Massachusetts Law Quarterly*, December 1963, pp. 461+.

2414. Marcuse, Peter. "Comparative Analysis of Federally-Aided Low- and Moderate-Income Housing Programs." *Journal of Housing*, October 1969, pp. 536-539.

2415. National Association of Real Estate Boards. *Realtor's Guide to Housing Programs.* 2d Ed. Washington, D.C., 1969.

2416. National Urban Coalition. *Guide to Federal Low- and Moderate-Income Housing and Community Development Programs.* Washington, D.C., 1968. 24pp.

2417. "The New Look in Government-Subsidy Housing." *House and Home*, December 1970, pp. 66-78,

2418. *Packaging Subsidized Housing Deals.* Lewis R. Kaster and Stanley Berman, co-chairmen. New York: Practising Law Institute, 1971. 502pp.

2419. Robins, Philip K. "FHA Mortgage Insurance and Subsidies." *Federal Reserve Chicago*, March 1972, pp. 8-15.

2420. Romney, George. "Accomplishments of HUD/1969-1972." *HUD Challenge*, February 1972, pp. 4-10.

2421. Sachs, Daniel Y. *Handbook for Housing and Urban Renewal Commissioners.* Washington, D.C.: National Association of Housing and Redevelopment Officials, 1972. 130pp.

2422. Schecter, Henry B. "Federal Housing Subsidy Programs." In U.S. Congress. Joint Economic Committee. *The Economics of Federal Subsidy Programs: A Compendium of Papers Submitted to the Joint Economic Committee: Part 5–Housing Subsidies.* Washington, D.C.: Government Printing Office, 1972, pp. 597-630.

2423. Thaler, David. "Government Subsidized Housing: Sleeper Market of The Seventies." *House and Home*, December 1970, pp. 53-61. Also in George Sternlieb and Lynne B. Sagalyn (eds.). *Housing: 1970-1971; An AMS Anthology.* New York: AMS Press, 1972, pp. 520-534.

2424. U.S. Dept. of Housing and Urban Development. *Accomplishments of HUD, 1969-1972.* Washington, D.C., 1972.

2425. U.S. Department of Housing and Urban Development. *Annual Report of the Department of Housing and Urban Development.* Washington, D.C.: Government Printing Office. First, 1965, published in 1967, through the seventh, 1971, published in 1972.

2426. U.S. Department of Housing and Urban Development. *Digest of Insurable Loans and Summaries of Other Federal Housing Administration Programs. A HUD Guide.* Washington, D.C.: Government Printing Office, 1970.

2427. U.S. Department of Housing and Urban Development. *Home Mortgage Insurance.* Washington, D.C., 1972. 14pp.

2428. U.S. Department of Housing and Urban Development. *How HUD Supports Advanced Housing Technology.* Washington, D.C.: Government Printing Office, 1971. 8pp.

2429. U.S. Department of Housing and Urban Development. *HUD Programs.* Washington, D.C., issued periodically.

2430. U.S. Department of Housing and Urban Development. Office of Economic Analysis. *The Role of the Federal Government in Residential Mortgage Credit Insurance.* Washington, D.C., October 1972. 107pp.

2431. U.S. Housing and Home Finance Agency. Office of General Counsel. *Chronology of Major Federal Actions Affecting Housing and Community Development, July 1892 through 1963.* Washington, D.C.: Government Printing Office, 1964. 69pp.

2432. U.S. Housing and Home Finance Agency. *Urban Affairs and Housing; The Coordinated Programs of the Housing and Home Finance Agency.* Washington, D.C., 1962. 32pp.

2433. Weaver, Robert C. "HUD at Two: Sec. (Robert C.) Weaver Reviews Program Innovations and Looks at Future." *Nation's Cities*, November 1967, pp. 7-9.

2434. Welfeld, Irving H. "A New Framework for Federal Housing Aids." *Columbia Law Review*, December 1969, pp. 1355-1391.

2435. Widnall, W.B. "Federal Housing Programs." *Title News*, March 1969, pp. 7+.

See also: 697, 1360, 1752-1754, 2146, 2147, 2156, 3041, 3053, 3062, 3064, 3066-3068; Secondary Mortgage Markets: 603+.

b. Analyses of Programs and Policies

*1.) General*

2436. Aaron, Henry. "Federal Housing Subsidies." In U.S. Congress. Joint Economic Committee. *The Economics of Federal Subsidy Programs: A Compendium of Papers Submitted to the Joint Economic Committee: Part 5–Housing Subsidies.* Washington, D.C.: Government Printing Office, 1972, pp. 571-596.

2437. Aaron, Henry J. *Shelter and Subsidies: Who Benefits from Federal Housing Policies?* Washington, D.C.: The Brookings Institution, 1972. 238pp.

2438. Aaron, Henry J. and George M. von Furstenberg. "The Inefficiency of Transfers in Kind: The Case of Housing Assistance." *Western Economic Journal*, June 1971, pp. 184-191.

2439. Abrams, Charles. "The Ethics of Power in Government Housing Programs." *Journal of the American Institute of Planners*, August 1963, pp. 223-224.

2440. Atlanta Region Metropolitan Planning Commission. *Housing All Atlantans: Subsidy Programs*. Atlanta, Ga., May 1970.

2441. "The Bankruptcy of Subsidized Housing." *Business Week*, May 27, 1972, pp. 42-45+.

2442. Baskin, Seymour. "FHA Processing and Fees and Social Purposes." In U.S. Congress. House. Committee on Banking and Currency. *Papers Submitted to Subcommittee on Housing Panels on Housing Production, Housing Demand, and Developing a Suitable Living Environment: Part 1.* Washington, D.C.: Government Printing Office, 1971, pp. 373-382.

2442. Bish, Robert Lee. *The Distribution of Housing Taxes and Subsidies and Effects on Housing Consumption of Low-Income Families*. Ann Arbor, Mich.: University Microfilms, 1968 (Ph.D. dissertation, Indiana University, 1968). 130pp. (order no. 68-15,435)

2444. Blackburn, Benjamin B. "Subsidized Housing: It's Not Working Out." *Mortgage Banker*, June 1972, pp. 24-30.

2445. Break, George F. *The Economic Impact of Federal Loan Insurance*. Washington, D.C.: National Planning Association, 1961.

2446. Breckenfeld, Gurney. "Housing Subsidies Are a Grand Delusion." *Fortune*, February 1972, pp. 136-139+.

2447. Brueggeman, William B. *et al.* "Multiple Housing Programs and Urban Housing Policy." *Journal of the American Institute of Planners*, May 1972, pp. 160-167.

2448. Chamber of Commerce of the U.S. Construction and Community Development Department. *The Impact of Federal Urban Renewal and Public Housing Subsidies*. Washington, D.C., 1964. 87pp.

2449. Cochran, Clay and George Rucker. "Every American Family Housing Need and Non-Response." In U.S. Congress. House. Committee on Banking and Currency. *Papers Submitted to Subcommittee on Housing Panels on Housing Production, Housing Demand, and Developing a Suitable Living Environment: Part 2.* Washington, D.C.: Government Printing Office, 1971, pp. 525-540.

2450. Colean, Miles L. "Snare and Delusion: Federal Housing Policies Are an Inflationary Fraud." *Barron's*, November 30, 1970, pp. 1+.

2451. "Coming: Federal Aid in Housing for 24 Million; Now It's Housing Subsidies for Families with Moderate Income Not Just the Poor; Rising Costs and Shortages Could Make Such Government Aid Commonplace in the Years to Come." *U.S. News and World Report*, June 15, 1970, pp. 74-76.

2452. de Leeuw, Frank. *The Distribution of Housing Services: Exploring Policy Effects*. Washington, D.C.: The Urban Institute, June 5, 1972. 40pp. (Urban Institute Working Paper no. 208-5).

2453. Downs, Anthony. "Are Subsidies the Best Answer for Housing Low and Moderate Income Households?" *The Urban Lawyer*, Summer 1972, pp. 405-416.

2454. Downs, Anthony. *Federal Housing Subsidies: Their Nature and Effectiveness, and What We Should Do About Them; Summary Report.* Chicago, Ill.: Real Estate Research Corp., 1972. 48pp.

2455. Downs, Anthony. "Housing the Urban Poor: The Economics of Various Strategies." *American Economic Review*, September 1969, pp. 646-651. Also in Anthony Downs. *Urban Problems and Prospects.* Chicago, Ill.: Markham, 1970, pp. 165-175.

2456. Eastman, Charles M. "Hypotheses Concerning Market Effects on Neighborhood Development Programs." *Urban Affairs Quarterly*, March 1972, pp. 287-300.

2457. "8 Projects That Set a Standard for Government-Subsidy Housing." *House & Home*, December 1970, pp. 66-78.

2458. "Fact vs. *Fortune* re Housing Subsidy Programs." *NAHB Journal of Homebuilding*, June 1972, pp. 29-30.

2459. "Five Projects Show that the Best of Today's Subsidized Housing is Very Good Indeed," *House and Home*, February 1972, pp. 76-87.

2460. Franklin, Herbert M. "The Federal Government As 'Houser of Last Resort': A Policy for Democratic Urban Growth." *Urban Law Annual 1972.* St. Louis, Mo.: School of Law, Washington University, 1972, pp. 23-44.

2461. Franklin, Herbert M. "Federal Power and Subsidized Housing." *The Urban Lawyer*, Winter 1971, pp. 61-77.

2462. Frieden, Bernard J. "Improving Federal Housing Subsidies: Summary Report." In U.S. Congress. House. Committee on Banking and Currency. *Papers Submitted to Subcommittee on Housing Panels on Housing Production, Housing Demand, and Developing a Suitable Living Environment: Part 2.* Washington, D.C.: Government Printing Office, 1971, pp. 473-488.

2463. Friedman, Lawrence Meir. *Government and Slum Housing; A Century of Frustration.* Chicago, Ill.: Rand McNally, 1968. 206pp.

2464. Friedman, Lawrence M. "Government and Slum Housing: Some General Considerations." *Law and Contemporary Problems*, Spring 1967, pp. 357-370.

2465. Glazer, Nathan. "Housing Problems and Housing Policies." *Public Interest*, Spring 1967, pp. 21-56.

2466. Grier, George C. "The Negro Ghettos and Federal Housing Policy." *Law and Contemporary Problems*, Summer 1967, pp. 550-560.

2467. Gruen, Nina and Claude Gruen. "Housing Policy and Class Integration." *Annals of Regional Science*, December 1971, pp. 102-111.

2468. Heinberg, John D. *Housing Policy and Economic Stabilization, A Review and Analysis of the Evidence.* Washington, D.C.: Urban Institute, 1969. 8pp.

2469. "Housing Programs." Part II in U.S. National Commission on Urban Problems. *Building the American City.* Washington, D.C.: Government Printing Office, 1969, pp. 56-197.

2470. "HUD Interest Subsidy Housing Programs: Some Economic Realities Affecting Project Feasibility and Investor Participation." *University of Missouri at Kansas City Law Review*, Fall 1972, pp. 37+.

2471. "HUD's Chief Tells Why He Thinks Subsidy Housing Is a Good Long-Term Bet for Builders." *House & Home*, December 1970, pp. 62-65.

2472. Isler, Morton L. "The Goals of Housing Subsidy Programs." In U.S. Congress. House. Committee on Banking and Currency. *Papers Submitted to Subcommittee on Housing Panels on Housing Production, Housing Demand, and Developing a Suitable Living Environment: Part 2.* Washington, D.C.: Government Printing Office, 1971, pp. 415-436.

2473. Isler, Morton L. *Thinking about Housing: A Policy Research Agenda.* Washington, D.C.: The Urban Institute, 1970. 47pp.

2474. Jackson, Philip C., Jr. "From MBA's President: Unsubsidized Housing Programs Should Be Spun Off from HUD." *Mortgage Banker*, August 1972, pp. 11-14.

2475. Jones, Oliver H. "An MBA Editorial: Can FHA Be Replaced?" *Mortgage Banker*, August 1972, pp. 6-10.

2476. Jones, Oliver H. "On the Survival of FHA." *Mortgage Banker*, March 1972, pp. 6+.

2477. Keith, Nathaniel Schnieder. *Housing America's Low- and Moderate-Income Families; Progress and Problems under Past Programs, Prospects under Federal Act of 1968.* Prepared for the consideration of the National Commission on Urban Problems. Washington, D.C.: Government Printing Office, 1968. 30pp. (National Commission on Urban Problems Research Report no. 7)

2478. Kristof, Frank S. "Federal Housing Policies: Subsidized Production, Filtration and Objectives: Part I." *Land Economics*, November 1972, pp. 309-320.

2479. Kummerfeld, Donald D. "The Housing Subsidy System." In U.S. Congress. House. Committee on Banking and Currency. *Papers Submitted to Subcommittee on Housing Panels on Housing Production, Housing Demand, and Developing a Suitable Living Environment: Part 2.* Washington, D.C.: Government Printing Office, 1971, pp. 451-473.

2480. Lane, Sylvia. "Housing the Underhoused." *Annals of Regional Science*, December 1970, pp. 68-79. Also in George Sternlieb and Lynne Sagalyn (eds.). *Housing: 1970-1971; An AMS Anthology*. New York: AMS Press, 1972, pp. 201-213.

2481. Lewis, Cynthia D. "Tenant Selection in Federally-Subsidized Housing." *Journal of Property Management*, May/June 1972, pp. 102-105.

2482. Lilley, William III. "Urban Report/Policy Makers Condemn Housing Program; Seek Alternative to Builder-subsidy Approach." *National Journal*, July 24, 1971, pp. 1535-1543.

2483. Lipsky, Michael *et al.* "Citizen Participation in Federal Housing Policies." In U.S. Congress. House. Committee on Banking and Currency. *Papers Submitted to Subcommittee on Housing Panels on Housing Production, Housing Demand, and Developing a Suitable Living Environment: Part 2.* Washington, D.C.: Government Printing Office, 1971, pp. 895-925.

2484. Lubove, R. "Houses and a Few Well Placed Fruit Trees: An Object Lesson in Federal Housing." *Social Research; An International Quarterly of Political and Social Science*, Winter 1960, pp. 469-486.

2485. Macey, John. *Publicly Provided and Assisted Housing in the U.S.A.; Report on HUD's Housing Management Policies and Programs.* Washington, D.C.: The Urban Institute, 1972. 80pp.

2486. McFarland, M. Carter. "Unlearned Lessons in the History of Federal Housing Aid." *City*, Winter 1972, pp. 30-34.

2487. O'Toole, William J. "A Prototype of Public Housing Policy: The USHC." *Journal of the American Institute of Planners*, May 1968, pp. 140-152.

2488. Olsen, E.O. and J.R. Prescott. *An Analysis of Alternative Measures of Tenant Benefits of Government Housing Programs with Illustrative Calculations from Public Housing.* New York: The New York City Rand Institute, November 1969.

2489. Penner, Rudolph G. and William L. Silber. "Federal Housing Credit Programs: Costs, Benefits, and Interactions." In U.S. Congress. Joint Economic Committee. *The Economics of Federal Subsidy Programs: A Compendium of Papers Submitted to the Joint Economic Committee: Part 5–Housing Subsidies.* Washington, D.C.: Government Printing Office, 1972, pp. 660-675.

2490. Pinner, Elizabeth Lucia. *Housing: Commodity and/or Community.* Ann Arbor, Mich.: University Microfilms, 1967 (Ph.D. dissertation, Bryn Mawr College, 1966). 236pp. (order no. 67-3812)

2491. Rabinovitz, Francine F. "The Role of the Department of Housing and Urban Development in Suburban and Metropolitan Development." In U.S. Congress. House. Committee on Banking and Currency. *Papers Submitted to Subcommittee on Housing Panels on Housing Production, Housing Demand, and Developing a Suitable Living Environment: Part 2.* Washington, D.C.: Government Printing Office, 1971, pp. 737-762.

2492. Ricks, R. Bruce. "Housing Policy as a Component of Urban Policy." *Urban Land*, November 1972, pp. 10-19.

2493. Romney, George. "A Picture of Success." *Mortgage Banker*, July 1972, pp. 12+.

2494. Schomer, Morton W. "Consumer Protection–The Role of HUD in Protecting the Homeowner." In U.S. Congress. House. Committee on Banking and Currency. *Papers Submitted to Subcommittee on Housing*

*Panels on Housing Production, Housing Demand, and Developing a Suitable Living Environment: Part 2.* Washington, D.C.: Government Printing Office, 1971, pp. 383-396.

2495. Schorr, A.L. "National Community and Housing Policy." *Social Service Review*, December 1965, pp. 433-443.

2496. Schorr, Alvin Louis. *Slums and Social Insecurity, an Appraisal of the Effectiveness of Housing Policies in Helping to Eliminate Poverty in the United States.* Washington, D.C.: Government Printing Office, 1963. (U.S. Social Security Administration. Division of Research and Statistics. Research report no. 1).

2497. Schussheim, Morton J. "Housing in Perspective." *Public Interest*, Spring 1970, pp. 18-30.

2498. Schussheim, Morton J. *Toward a New Housing Policy: The Legacy of the Sixties.* New York: Committee for Economic Development, 1969. 64pp. (CED Supplementary Paper no. 29).

2499. Silzer, Vykki J. *Housing Problems, Government Housing Policies and Housing Market Responses: An Annotated Bibliography.* Monticello, Ill.: Council of Planning Librarians, 1972 (Exchange Bibliography no. 344).

2500. Solomon, Arthur P. *The Cost Effectiveness of Subsidized Housing.* Cambridge, Mass.: Joint Center for Urban Studies of the Massachusetts Institute of Technology and Harvard University, Spring 1971, revised February 1972. (Joint Center Working Paper no. 5).

2501. Solomon, Arthur P. "Housing and Public Policy Analysis." *Public Policy*, Summer, 1972, pp. 443-471.

2502. Stanton, H.R. "Social Determinants of Housing Policy in Puerto Rico: A Case Study of Rapid Urbanization." *American Behavioral Scientist*, March 1972, pp. 563-580.

2503. Stegman, Michael A. "Kaiser, Douglas, and Kerner on Low-Income Housing Policy." *Journal of the American Institute of Planners*, November 1969, pp. 422-427.

2504. Stegman, Michael A. "National Housing and Land-Use Policy." *Journal of Urban Law*, May 1972, pp. 629-666.

2505. Stockfisch, Jacob A. *An Investigation of the Opportunities for Reducing the Cost of Federally Subsidized Housing for Lower-Income Families.* Arlington, Va.: Institute for Defense Analyses, 1968.

2506. "Subsidized Housing: Homes for People." *NAHB Journal of Homebuilding*, June 1972, pp. 26-29.

2507. Taggart, Robert. *Low Income Housing: A Critique of Federal Aid.* Baltimore, Md.: The Johns Hopkins Press, 1970. 146pp.

2508. Thornton, Allan Fitzhugh. *The Economic Impact of Federal Housing Administration Insurance Programs.* Ann Arbor, Mich.: University Microfilms, 1965 (Ph.D. dissertation, The American University, 1965). 189pp. (order no. 65-11,380)

2509. "221(d)4: A Winning or Losing Number?" *Professional Builder,* April 1971, pp. 88-91.

2510. U.S. Congress. House. Committee on Banking and Currency. *Current Discounts on FHA and VA Home Loans. Staff Report.* Washington, D.C.: Government Printing Office, 1960. 253pp.

2511. U.S. Congress. House. Committee on Banking and Currency. Subcommittee on Housing. *FHA and FNMA in the Current Money Market: Hearing. . . .* Washington, D.C., 1966. 82pp.

2512. U.S. Congress. House. Committee on Government Operations. Legal and Monetary Affairs Subcommittee. *Operations of the Federal Housing Administration of the Department of Housing and Urban Development. Hearings . . . October 13 and 14, 1971.* Washington, D.C.: Government Printing Office, 1971. 135pp.

2513. U.S. Congress. Joint Economic Committee. *The Economics of Federal Subsidy Programs: A Compendium of Papers: Part 5, Housing Subsidies.* Washington, D.C.: Government Printing Office, 1972.

2514. U.S. Congress. Senate. Committee on Banking and Currency. *Housing Legislation of 1961. Hearings. Appendix: Review of Federal Housing Programs.* Washington, D.C.: Government Printing Office, 1961. 153pp.

2515. U.S. Congress. Senate. Committee on Banking and Currency. Subcommittee on Housing. *Progress Report on Federal Housing Programs: Hearing. . . .* Washington, D.C.: Government Printing Office, 1962. 132pp.

2516. U.S. Congress. Senate. Committee on Banking and Currency. Subcommittee on Housing and Urban Affairs. *Progress Report on Federal Housing Programs; Description of Each of the Federal Programs on Housing and Urban Development and the Progress of These Programs.* Washington, D.C.: Government Printing Office, 1967. 157pp.

2517. U.S. Congress. Senate. Committee on Banking and Currency. Subcommittee on Housing and Urban Affairs. *Progress Report on Federal Housing and Urban Development Programs: Description of Each of the Federal Programs on Housing and Urban Development (Including Mass Transportation) and the Progress of These Programs.* Washington, D.C.: Government Printing Office, 1969. 183pp.

2518. U.S. Congress. Senate. Committee on Banking and Currency. Subcommittee on Housing and Urban Affairs. *Progress Report on Federal Housing and Urban Development Programs; Description of Each of the Federal Programs on Housing and Urban Development (Including Mass Transportation) and the Progress of These Programs*. Washington, D.C.: Government Printing Office, 1970. 185pp.

2519. U.S. Congress. Senate. Committee on Banking and Currency. *Status of HHFA Programs. Hearings....* Washington, D.C.: Government Printing Office, 1960. 143pp.

2520. U.S. Congress. Senate. Committee on Banking, Housing and Urban Affairs. Subcommittee on Housing and Urban Affairs. *Improved Technology, and Removal of Prevailing Wage Requirements in Federally Assisted Housing. Hearings ... June 20-23, 1972*. Washington, D.C.: Government Printing Office, 1972. 559pp.

2521. U.S. Congress. Senate. Committee on Government Operations. Permanent Subcommittee on Investigations. *Investigation into FHA Multiple Dwelling Projects: Report; Together with Individual Views*. Washington, D.C.: Government Printing Office, 1967. 60pp.

2522. U.S. Congress. Senate. Committee on Government Operations. Subcommittee on Investigations. *Investigation into FHA Multiple Dwelling Projects: Hearings, August 24-30, 1966, Pursuant to Senate Resolution 183. 89th Congress; Including Index*. Washington, D.C., 1966. 390pp.

2523. U.S. Department of Housing and Urban Development. Office of International Affairs. *Estimating Housing Assistance Requirements and Subsidy Costs*, By Richard Metcalf. Prepared for the Use of the Agency for International Development. Washington, D.C., 1972. 52pp.

2524. U.S. Department of Housing and Urban Development. *Report on Improving Program Management, 1972*. Washington, D.C., 1972. 1 vol. annual.

2525. U.S. General Accounting Office. *Construction Costs for Certain Federally Financed Housing Projects Increased Due to Inappropriate Minimum Wage Rate Determinations; Department of Labor. Report....* Washington, D.C., 1970. 61pp.

2526. U.S. General Accounting Office. *Examination of Financial Statements Pertaining to Insurance Operations of the Federal Housing Administration, fiscal year 1969*; Dept. of Housing and Urban Development. Report to the Congress by the Comptroller General of the United States. Washington, D.C., 1969. 41pp.

2527. U.S. General Accounting Office. *Increased Risk of Loss Because of Inadequate Mortgage Servicing Activities*. Washington, D.C., 1964.

2528. U.S. General Accounting Office. *Lack of Information on Construction Costs Incurred by Sponsor-Controlled Subcontractors May Unduly Increase Insured Mortgages on Multifamily Housing Projects, Federal Housing Administration, Housing and Home Finance Agency: Report....* Washington, D.C., 1965.

2529. U.S. General Accounting Office. *Need for Increased Efforts to Minimize Rental Delinquencies on Acquired Properties, Federal Housing Administration, Department of Housing and Urban Development; Report....* Washington, D.C., 1966. 24pp.

2530. U.S. General Accounting Office. *Opportunities to Improve Effectiveness and Reduce Costs of Homeownership Assistance Programs.* Washington, D.C., 1972.

2531. U.S. General Accounting Office. *Opportunities to Reduce Costs in Acquiring Properties Resulting from Defaults on Home Loans.* Washington, D.C., 1972.

2532. U.S. General Accounting Office. *Questions Regarding Mortgage Loan Insurance Ceilings and Land Appraisals for Large Cooperative Housing Communities; Report to the Congress....* Washington, D.C., 1970. 48pp.

2533. U.S. General Accounting Office. *Review of Selected Phases of Workable Programs for Community Improvement under the Administration of the Fort Worth Regional Office, Housing and Home Finance Agency; Report....* Washington, D.C., 1962.

2534. U.S. General Accounting Office. *Selection of Purchasers of Residential Properties Sold by the Federal Housing Administration; Report....* Washington, D.C., 1969. 18pp.

2535. U.S. General Accounting Office. *Slow Progress in Eliminating Sub-Standard Indian Housing; Department of the Interior; Department of Housing and Urban Development.* Washington, D.C., 1971. 68pp.

2536. U.S. General Accounting Office. *Tighter Control Needed on Occupancy of Federally Subsidized Housing; Dept. of Housing and Urban Development.* Report to the Congress by the Comptroller General of the United States. Washington, D.C., 1971. 43pp.

2537. U.S. General Accounting Office. *Wage Rates for Federally Financed Building Construction Improperly Determined in Excess of the Prevailing Rates for Similar Work in New England Areas, Department of Labor....* Washington, D.C., 1965. 25pp.

2538. U.S. General Accounting Office. *Wage Rates for Federally Financed Housing Construction Improperly Determined in Excess of the Prevailing Rates for Similar Work in Southeastern Areas of the United States. . . .* Washington, D.C., 1964. 47pp.

2539. U.S. General Accounting Office. *Weaknesses in Administration of Requirement for the Workable Program for Community Improvement for the City of Cincinnati, Ohio. . . .* Washington, D.C., 1964. 17pp.

2540. Urban America, Inc. *The Ill-Housed; A Compendium of Recent Writings and Reports on National Housing Policy*. Edited by Donald Canty. Washington, D.C., 1969. 62pp.

2541. von Furstenberg, George M. "Distribution of Federally Assisted Rental Housing." *Journal of the American Institute of Planners*, September 1971, pp. 326-330.

2542. von Furstenberg, George M. "The Distribution of Federally Assisted Rental Housing Services by Regions and States." In U.S. Congress. Joint Economic Committee. *The Economics of Federal Subsidy Programs: A Compendium of Papers Submitted to the Joint Economic Committee: Part 5—Housing Subsidies*. Washington, D.C.: Government Printing Office, 1972, pp. 631-641.

2543. von Furstenberg, George M. "The Impact of Rent Formulas and Eligibility Standards in Federally Assisted Housing." In U.S. President's Committee on Urban Housing. *Report: Technical Studies, Volume I*. Washington, D.C.: Government Printing Office, 1967, pp. 103-112.

2544. von Furstenberg, George M. and Howard R. Moskof. "Federally Assisted Rental Housing Programs: Which Income Groups Have They Served or Whom Can They Be Expected to Serve?" In U.S. President's Committee on Urban Housing. *Report: Technical Studies, Volume I*. Washington, D.C.: Government Printing Office, 1967, pp. 147-165.

2545. Wallace, James E. *Federal Subsidies in Rental Housing*. Cambridge, Mass.: Joint Center for Urban Studies of the Massachusetts Institute of Technology and Harvard University, February 1971, revised February 1972. (Joint Center Working Paper no. 7).

2546. Weaver, Robert C. "The Evolving Goals of the Department of Housing and Urban Development." In Schnore, Leo F. and Henry Fagin (eds.). *Urban Research and Policy Planning*. Beverly Hills, Calif.: Sage Publications, 1967, pp. 583-601.

2547. Wehbring, Kurt J. "Block Grants: A Means for Achieving a National Housing and Urban Development Policy." In U.S. Congress. House. Committee on Banking and Currency. *Papers Submitted to Subcommittee on Housing Panels on Housing Production, Housing*

*Demand, and Developing a Suitable Living Environment: Part 2*. Washington, D.C.: Government Printing Office, 1971, pp. 825-838.

2548. Welfeld, Irving. "That 'Housing Problem'—American vs. the European Experience." *Public Interest*, Spring 1972, pp. 78-95.

2549. Wendt, Paul F. "The Determination of National Housing Policies." *Land Economics*, August 1969, pp. 322-332.

2550. Wendt, Paul Francis. *Housing Policy—the Search for Solutions; A Comparison of the United Kingdom, Sweden, West Germany, and the United States Since World War II*. Berkeley, Calif.: University of California Press, 1962.

2551. Wenzlick, Roy. "As I See It: The HUD Subsidy Program is an Expensive Failure." *Real Estate Analyst*, April 1972, pp. 173-176.

2552. Wheaton, William L.C. *et al.* "Housing Needs and Urban Development." In U.S. Congress. House. Committee on Banking and Currency. *Papers Submitted to Subcommittee on Housing Panels on Housing Production, Housing Demand, and Developing a Suitable Living Environment: Part 2*. Washington, D.C.: Government Printing Office, 1971, pp. 607-626.

2553. Winthrop, Henry. "Yield Insurance and Low-cost Housing: A Contribution to the Anti-Poverty Program." *Land Economics*, May 1968, pp. 141-152.

2554. Wolman, Harold Lewis. *Politics and Public Policy: A Study of the Housing Political System*. Ann Arbor, Mich.: University Microfilms, 1969 (Ph.D. dissertation, University of Michigan, 1968). 347pp. (order no. 69-12,275)

2555. Wolman, Harold. *Politics of Federal Housing*. New York: Dodd, Mead, 1971. 227pp.

2556. Wood, Robert. "Housing and Environmental Escapism." *Journal of the American Institute of Planners*, November 1970, pp. 422-425.

See also: 102, 251, 343, 380, 412, 428, 441, 442, 453, 584, 655-660, 695, 696, 836, 896, 897, 908, 911, 938, 998, 1751, 2160, 2170, 2276; Secondary Mortgages Markets: 603+.

*2) Methods for Evaluating Housing Programs*

2557. DeSalvo, Joseph S. "A Methodology for Evaluating Housing Programs." *Journal of Regional Science*, August 1971, pp. 173-185.

2558. Grebler, Leo. "Criteria for Appraising Gvoernmental Housing Programs." *American Economic Review, Papers and Proceedings*, May 1960, pp. 321-332. Also in Alfred N. Page and Warren R. Seyfried (eds.). *Urban Analysis: Readings in Housing and Urban Development*. Glenview, Ill.: Scott, Foresman, 1970, pp. 413-420.

2559. Ross, William B. "A Proposed Methodology for Comparing Federally Assisted Housing Programs." *The American Economic Review, Papers and Proceedings*, May 1968, pp. 91-100.

c. Site Selection in Federally-Assisted Housing

2560. "Administrative Law—Urban Renewal—HUD Has Affirmative Duty to Consider Low Income's Impact Upon Racial Concentration.—Shannon v. HUD, 436F. 2d. 809. (4d Cir 1970)." *Harvard Law Review*, Feb. 1972, pp. 870-880.

2561. "California's Low-Income Housing Referendum: Equal Protection and the Problem of Economic Discrimination." *Columbia Journal of Law and Social Problems*, Winter 1972, pp. 135-155.

2562. "Civil Rights—Housing—Federal Programs for Low- and Moderate-income Families—Approval of a Project Site without Evaluating the Effect of the Project on Racial Concentration Violates the Civil Rights Acts." *George Washington Law Review*, July 1971, pp. 1229+.

2563. "Civil Rights—Housing Law—Effects of Racial Concentration in Renewal Area." *Duquesne Law Review*, Winter 1971, pp. 289+.

2564. "Civil Rights—Urban Housing—HUD Must Institutionalize Procedures for Determining Racial and Socioeconomic Effects of Site Location for Federally Assisted Housing Projects." *New York University Law Review*, May 1971, pp. 560+.

2565. "Constitutional Law—Equal Protection—City Housing Authority Intentionally Discriminating in Selection of Public Housing Sites Directed to Select Future Sites in Accordance with Specific Plan for Integration." *New York University Law Review*, December 1969, pp. 1172-1183.

2566. "Constitutional Law—Equal Protection—Mandatory Referendum Approval of Low-Rent Housing Projects." *Tulane Law Review*, April 1972, pp. 806+.

2567. "Constitutional Law—Public Housing for Low Income Families—Mandatory Referendum Requirement." *Wisconsin Law Review*, 1972, pp. 268+.

2568. "Constitutional Law—Requirement That no Low Rent Housing Project Should Be Developed, Constructed or Acquired in Any Manner by State Public Body until Project has been Approved by Majority of Those Voting at Community Election is Constitutional." *Texas Southern University Law Review*, Fall 1971, pp. 167+.

2569. "Discriminatory Site Selection in Public Housing and Federal Judicial Response." *Northwestern University Law Review*, November-December 1969, pp. 720-735.

2570. Duiker, Gerard and Theodore Shouldberg. "A Locational Analysis of Low Income Housing in Seattle and King County." In *Urban Law Annual 1970*. St. Louis, Mo.: School of Law, Washington University, 1970, pp. 85-102.

2571. Fielding, B. "HUD's New Project Selection System." *Journal of Housing*, November 1971, pp. 537-540.

2572. "*Gautreaux v. Public Housing Authority* (296 F Supp 907): Equal Protection and Public Housing." *University of Pennsylvania Law Review*, January 1970, pp. 437+.

2573. Gilson, R.J. "Public Housing and Urban Policy: *Gautreaux v. Chicago Housing Authority*." *Yale Law Journal*, March 1970, pp. 712-729.

2574. Goodman, Walter. "The Battle of Forest Hills—Who's Ahead?" *New York Times Magazine*, Feb. 20, 1972, pp. 8+.

2575. Grinstead, Darrel J. "Overcoming Barriers to Scattered-Site Low-Cost Housing." *Prospectus*, April 1969, pp. 327-346.

2576. "Growing Issue: Communities vs. Low-Income Housing." *Congressional Quarterly*, Jan. 8, 1972, pp. 51-55.

2577. Gruen, Nina Jaffe. *Low and Moderate Income Housing in the Suburbs: An Analysis for the Dayton, Ohio, Region*. New York: Praeger, 1972. 234pp.

2578. Hecht, James L. "Mixed Housing in the Suburbs." *Nation*, March 6, 1972, pp. 305-308.

2579. "Housing—Public Housing—District Court Orders Housing Authority Not to Build in Black Ghetto and to Institute New Tenant Assignment Plan in Order to Remedy Past Discriminatory Practices—*Gautreaux v. Chicago Housing Authority. . . .*" *Harvard Law Review*, April 1970, pp. 1441-1449.

2580. "Housing Law—Discriminatory Site Location and Tenant Allocation Procedures—Equitable Relief." *Wisconsin Law Review*, 1970, pp. 559+.

2581. "HUD and Regional Planning Agency Clash over the Issue of Low-Cost Housing." *ASPO* (American Society of Planning Officials) *Planning*, July 1971, pp. 95+.

2582. "Is—or Isn't—HUD Forcing Low-Cost Housing into Suburbs? A Look at Some Cases." *House and Home*, Feb. 1972, pp. 12+.

2583. Lefcoe, George. "From Capitol Hill: The Impact of Civil Rights Litigation on HUD Policy." *The Urban Lawyer*, Winter 1972, pp. 112-128.

2584. Lefcoe, G. "Public Housing Referendum Case (*James v. Valtierra*, 91 Sup Ct 1331), Zoning and the Supreme Court." *California Law Review*, November 1971, pp. 1384+.

2585. Lilley, William III. "Chicago Case Shows Courts Hold Key to Mandatory Housing Desegregation." *National Journal*, Jan. 22, 1972, pp. 162-163.

2586. Maxwell, D.O. "HUD's Project Selection Criteria—A Cure for 'Impermissible Color Blindness'?" *Notre Dame Lawyer*, October 1972, pp. 92+.

2587. Murasky, Donna M. "*James v. Valtierra*: Housing Discrimination by Referendum!" *University of Chicago Law Review*, Fall 1971, pp. 115-142.

2588. Novara, Gary W. "Urban Renewal—HUD Must Look beyond Short Range Land Use Factors to Eventual Social Implications of Its Plans." *Journal of Urban Law*, February 1972, pp. 621-627.

2589. Peel, Norman D., Garth E. Pickett, and Stephen T. Buehl. "Racial Discrimination in Public Housing Site Selection." *Stanford Law Review*, November 1970, pp. 63-147. Also in George Sternlieb and Lynne Sagalyn (eds.). *Housing: 1970-1971; An AMS Anthology*. New York: AMS Press, 1972. pp. 322-410.

2590. "Poor, Equal Protection, and Public Housing: *James v. Valtierra.*" *University of Kansas Law Review*, Winter 1972, pp. 253+.

2591. Pratter, J. "Gateway to Frustration—Housing in St. Louis." *Urban Lawyer*, Fall 1972, pp. 746-756.

2592. Pratter, Jerome. "Dispersed Subsidized Housing and Suburbia: Confrontation in Black Jack." *Land-Use Controls Annual 1971*. Chicago, Ill.: American Society of Planning Officials, 1972, pp. 147-155.

2593. "Public Housing: Affluent Suburb–Montgomery County, Maryland." *Journal of Housing*, September 1971, pp. 403-406.

2594. "Public Housing and Discrimination in Site Selection." *Chicago-Kent Law Review*, Fall-Winter 1970, pp. 253+.

2595. "Public Housing and Urban Policy: *Gautreaux vs. Chicago Housing Authority.*" *Yale Law Journal*, March 1970, pp. 712-729.

2596. Silverman, Jane A. "Chicago's 'Gautreaux' Cases: Do They Portend a New Role for the Courts in Public Housing–Or a New Form of Public Housing?" *Journal of Housing*, June 1972, pp. 336-340.

2597. Starr, Roger. "The Lesson of Forest Hills." *Commentary*, June 1972, pp. 45-49.

2598. Travis, Dempsey J. and Samuel C. Jackson. "Opportunity or Detour?–Two Views of New HUD Site Selection Criteria." *Savings Bank Journal*, May 1972, pp. 34-35+.

2599. "Valtierra." *ASPO Planning*, July 1970, pp. 94-95.

See also: 302; Planning for Low and Moderate Income Housing in Suburbs: 3352+.

5. 221(d)(3)

2600. Berkeley, Ellen Perry. "Chicago, Ill.: The Nation's Largest 221d3 Project Adds 504 Housing Units to the Mid-South Side." *Architectural Forum*, May 1971, pp. 38-41.

2601. Murray, Robert. "Controversial 221d3 Financing Catches On." *House & Home*, August 1962, pp. 98-101.

2602. Prothro, A. M. and Morton W. Schomer. "The Section 221 (d)(3) Below Market Interest Rate Program for Low and Moderate Income Families." *New York Law Forum*, Spring 1965, pp. 16-29.

2603. "The Two Faces of 221 (d) 3." *Savings and Loan News*, March 1968, pp. 30-31+.

2604. U.S. Housing and Home Finance Agency. Urban Renewal Administration. *Urban Renewal Service, Utilizing FHA Section 221 (d)(3) Below Market Interest Rate*. Washington, D.C.: Government Printing Office, 1964. 24pp.

2605. "Where D(3) Helped Wipe Out a Slum: Housing Law that Offers Low-Cost Financing to Private Builders Putting Up Moderate Income Housing Has Produced a Show Case in La Clede Town, until Recently a St. Louis Slum." *Business Week*, December 17, 1966, pp. 162-164+.

2606. "Woodland Gardens—A 221(d)(3) Project in Which the Participants Have Been Concerned as Much with Process as with Product." *Architectural Forum*, July-August 1969, pp. 72-77.

See also: 3094.

6. 235/236

2607. "Abuses in the Low Income Homeownership Programs—the Need for a Consumer Protection Response by the FHA." *Temple Law Quarterly*, Spring 1972, pp. 461+.

2608. American Society of Planning Officials. *Section 235 and Modulars Marry . . . Long Marriage or Early Breakup?* Chicago, Ill., June 1971. 7pp. (Planning Advisory Service Memo no. M-4).

2609. Bach, Victor. *Subsidizing Home Ownership through the 235 Program: The Wrong Instrument for the Right Purpose*. Cambridge, Mass.: Joint Center for Urban Studies of the Massachusetts Institute of Technology and Harvard University, January 1971, revised February 1972. (Joint Center Working Paper no. 2).

2610. Carnegie, Christa Lew. "Homeownership for the Poor: Running the Washington Gauntlet." *Journal of The American Institute of Planners*, May 1970, pp. 160-167.

2611. Dockser, William B. *Low and Moderate Income Housing—Section 235 and 236 Developments*. By William B. Dockser, President, Kaufman and Broad Asset Management, Inc., Washington, D.C. Stamford, Conn.: Condyne, Inc., 1971. 96pp.

2612. Edson, Charles L. "Sections 235 and 236: The First Year." *The Urban Lawyer*, Winter 1970, pp. 14-28.

2613. Farquhar, Norman. *FHA Financing for Rental Housing: Section 236, A Hypothetical Case*. Washington, D.C.: National Association of Home Builders, 1969. 85pp.

2614. Fielding, Byron. "Home Ownership for Low Income Families." *Journal of Housing*, June 1969, pp. 278-293.

2615. Gray, R. L. "Good Counseling the Answer in Successful 235 Housing." *Mortgage Banker*, August 1971, pp. 6-14.

2616. Jackson, Philip C., Jr. "MBA, FHA, HUD, 235/236: 'The Commitment Is Massive, But So Is the Problem'." *Mortgage Banker*, June 1972, pp. 4-14.

2617. Lambarth, Douglas D. "The '235' Hassle: Counseling and Preventive Law." *Clearinghouse Review*, May 1971, pp. 1-2+.

2618. Levy, Leonard, Michael Meyer and Joseph King. "The Section 236 Story: Federal Housing Subsidies in Action." *Real Estate Review*, Summer 1971, pp. 78-83.

2619. Lilley, William III and Timothy B. Clark. "Immense Costs, Scandals, Social Ills Plague Low-Income Housing Programs." *National Journal*, July 12, 1972, pp. 1075-1083.

2620. Los Angeles County, California, Department of Urban Affairs. *Survey of HUD 236 Housing Program in Los Angeles County*. Los Angeles, Calif., 1972.

2621. "Low Income Housing: Section 236 of the National Housing Act and the Tax Reform Act of 1969." *University of Pittsburgh Law Review*, Spring 1970, pp. 443+.

2622. Monogan, John S. "A Picture of Failure." *Mortgage Banker*, July 1972, pp. 13-26.

2623. Nonprofit Housing Center. *Private Capital and Low-Income Housing: A Case Study of Private Investment in Federally Assisted Limited Dividend Housing under Sections 235 and 236*. Washington, D.C., 1972. 94pp.

2624. Oppenheim, Stephen G. "235 as a Tool for a Better Environment." *HUD Challenge*, July 1971, pp. 18-21.

2625. Schafer, Robert and Charles G. Field. "Section 235 of the National Housing Act; Homeownership for Low Income Families?" *Journal of Urban Law*, Vol. 46, no. 3, 1968, pp. 667-685.

2626. "Section 235 Existing Homeownership Program Suspended." *Journal of Housing*, January 1971, pp. 15-16.

2627. "Section 235 New Homes—As Seen by Their Owners." *HUD Challenge*, July 1971, pp. 13-17.

2628. Stegman, Michael A. "Home Ownership Opportunities for the Poor." In *Housing and Economics: The American Dilemma*. Cambridge, Mass.: MIT Press, 1970, pp. 317-326.

2629. Stegman, Michael A. "Private Investment and Public Housing." *Urban Affairs Quarterly*, December 1972, pp. 161-179.

2630. Supplee, Andrew R. *FHA Financing for Sales Housing, Section 235; a Hypothetical Case*. Washington, D.C.: Builders Services Division, National Association of Home Builders, 1970. 46pp.

2631. Tatar, E. S. "The Investor and the Section 236 Housing Program." *Houston Law Review*, May 1971, pp. 876+.

2632. "Tax Advantages under Section 236 of the National Act." *Houston Law Review*, May 1971, pp. 911+.

2633. "The Two Sides of Subsidized Housing: Associations Debate FHA 235-236 Loan Availability and Costs, Procedures and Performance." *Savings and Loan News*, December 1971, pp. 30-37.

2634. U.S. Commission on Civil Rights. *Home Ownership for Lower Income Families: A Report on the Racial and Ethnic Impact of the Section 235 Program*. Washington, D.C.: Government Printing Office, 1971. 121pp.

2635. U.S. Congress. House. Committee on Banking and Currency. *Interim Report on HUD Investigation of Low- and Moderate-Income Housing Programs. Hearing. . . .* Washington, D.C.: Government Printing Office, 1971. 278pp.

2636. U.S. Congress. House. Committee on Banking and Currency. *Investigation and Hearing of Abuses in Federal Low- and Moderate-Income Housing Programs; Staff Report and Recommendations*. Washington, D.C.: Government Printing Office, 1970. 180pp.

2637. U.S. Department of Housing and Urban Development. *Rental and Cooperative Housing for Lower Income Families: Section 236 of the National Housing Act: HUD Program Guide for Sponsors, Builders, Lenders*. Washington, D.C., September 1971.

2638. U.S. Department of Housing and Urban Development. *Section 235(i) Homeownership for Lower Income Families HUD Program Guide for Builders, Sponsors, Lenders, Sellers*. Washington, D.C., April 1972.

2639. U.S. Department of Housing and Urban Development. Office of Audit. *Audit Review of Section 235, Single Family Housing*. Washington, D.C., 1971. 73pp.

2640. U.S. Department of Housing and Urban Development. Office of Audit. *Report on Audit of Section 236 Multifamily Housing Program*. Washington, D.C., January 29, 1972.

2641. U.S. General Accounting Office. *Department of Housing and Urban Development's Comparison of Costs under Sections 202 and 236 for Housing Projects for the Elderly*. Washington, D.C., 1972.

2642. U.S. General Accounting Office. *Opportunity for Reducing Interest Costs under Section 235 and 236 Housing Programs*. Washington, D.C., 1972.

2643. Watson, Norman V. "A Multifaceted Program to Curb 235 Foreclosures." *Mortgage Banker*, August 1972, pp. 36-38+.

See also: 658, 659, 681, 682; Low Income Housing–Home Ownership: 2127+.

7. NONPROFIT HOUSING

2644. Baumann, Ruth. *Fundamentals of Nonprofit Housing in Wisconsin*. Madison, Wisc.: Institute of Governmental Affairs, University of Wisconsin, 1971. 19pp.

2645. Higginbottom, Elzie. "Fulfilling Nonprofit Housing Goals with Limited Dividend Partnerships." *Mortgage Banker*, November 1970, pp. 76-80.

2646. Interfaith Housing Corporation. *The Suburban Noose: A Study of Non-Profit Housing Development for the Modest-Income Family in Metropolitan Boston*. Boston, 1969.

2647. Keyes, Langley C., Jr. "The Role of Nonprofit Sponsors in the Production of Housing." In U.S. Congress. House. Committee on Banking and Currency. *Papers Submitted to Subcommittee on Housing Panels on Housing Production, Housing Demand, and Developing a Suitable Living Environment: Part 1*. Washington, D.C.: Government Printing Office, 1971, pp. 159-181.

2648. "Nonprofit Sponsors." *HUD Challenge*, September 1972, pp. 4-13.

2649. Philadelphia Housing Association. Financial Committee. *The Philadelphia Housing Development Corporation: Prospects and Possibilities for a Non-Profit Housing Corporation: Report*. Philadelphia, Pa., December 1966. 37pp.

2650. "Sponsoring of Low- and Moderate-Income Housing through Local Limited Partnerships Having Nonprofit Corporate General Partners." *Boston College Industrial & Commercial Law Review*, March 1972, pp. 910+.

2651. U.S. Congress. Senate. Committee on the Judiciary. *Federal Charters for Nonprofit Corporations. Hearings before the Subcommittee on Federal Charters, Holidays and Celebrations. . . .* Washington, D.C.: Government Printing Office, 1972.

2652. U.S. Department of Housing and Urban Development. *New Opportunities for Open Occupancy through Nonprofit Sponsorship.* Washington, D.C.: Government Printing Office, 1968. 26pp.

2653. U.S. Department of Housing and Urban Development. *Nonprofit-Sponsored Housing for Open Occupancy.* Washington, D.C.: Government Printing Office, 1967. 28 pp.

See also: 1591, 3094.

8. OPERATION BREAKTHROUGH

2654. Alderfer, Evan B. "Operation Breakthrough." *Federal Reserve Bank of Philadelphia. Business Review*, November 1970, pp. 19-23.

2655. "Breakthrough Builder Breaks Through." *Mortgage Banker*, November 1970, pp. 32-35.

2656. "Breakthrough Update." *Professional Builder*, June 1971, pp. 13-16+.

2657. Bryan, Jack. " 'Breakthrough' Begins: Housing Enters the Industrial Age." *Journal of Housing*, March 1970, pp. 127-139.

2658. Burstein, Joseph. "A Lawyer's View of Operation Breakthrough." *Urban Lawyer*, Spring, 1970, pp. 137-145.

2659. Colean, Miles. "Operation Breakthrough: 'It Might Just Work'." *Mortgage Banker*, November 1970, pp. 15-16+.

2660. Delaware State Planning Office. *Operation Breakthrough for the State of Delaware*. Dover, 1970.

2661. Dixon, J.M. and M. Villeco. "Breakthrough?" *Architectural Forum*, April 1970, pp. 50-61.

2662. Farmer, M. "Toward a Decent Home for Every American Family." *Architectural Record*, October 1969, pp. 131-134.

2663. Finger, Harold B. "Operation Breakthrough: A Nationwide Effort to Produce Millions of Homes." *HUD Challenge*, November/December 1969, pp. 6-9.

2664. Finger, Harold B. *Operation Breakthrough: A New Approach Is Being Taken in the United States to Improve the Process of Producing and Providing Housing*. Washington, D.C.: U.S. Department of Housing and Urban Development, 1970. 9pp.

2665. Finger, Harold B. "Operation Breakthrough: The Scientific Approach." *HUD Challenge*, March 1971, pp. 12-14.

2666. "HUD Tests New Strategies for Mass Housing Systems: Operation Breakthrough, Model Cities and 'New Towns' Programs Lead Efforts to Cut Building Costs, Upgrade Home Financing and Create Well-Planned Environments for Burgeoning Markets." *Savings and Loan News*, January 1971, pp. 41-47.

2667. Hudson, J. W. "Breakthrough Two Years Later." *Systems Building News*, October 1971, pp. 32-39.

2668. "Is a Breakthrough Near in Housing? Broad Spectrum of Companies Will Bid to Participate in HUD's Plan to Mass-Produce Low-Cost Homes; The Real Hurdle Now Is Not Technology, Labor, Land or Even Mortgage Money–But Public Acceptance." *Business Week*, September 13, 1969, pp. 80-82+.

2669. Jensen, Robert. "Operation Breakthrough: The Systems, the Sites and the Designers Are Chosen. The Question Now: On What Standards Should the Program Be Judged?" *Architectural Record*, April 1970, pp. 137-152.

2670. "Labor Looks at Breakthrough and Speaks Its Mind." *HUD Challenge*, March 1971, pp. 4-10.

2671. "Local Projects Adopt 'Breakthrough' Techniques." *Journal of Housing*, January 1971, pp. 37-39.

2672. National Academy of Sciences–National Research Council. Building Research Advisory Board. *Housing Systems Proposals for Operation Breakthrough*. Prepared for the U.S. Department of Housing and Urban Development. Washington, D.C.: Government Printing Office, 1971. 590pp.

2673. "Operation Breakthrough." *HUD Challenge*, June 1972, pp. 4-23. pp. 42-47.

2674. "Operation Breakthrough." *HUD Challenge*, June 1972, pp. 4-23.

2675. " 'Operation Breakthrough'." *Real Estate Analyst*, February 24, 1970, pp. 59-64.

2676. "Operation Breakthrough Begins." *Journal of Housing*, March 1970, pp. 136-137.

2677. Operation Breakthrough: Can It Do the Job?" *Mortgage Banker*, November 1970, pp. 14-16+.

2678. "Operation Breakthrough, Recipient of Kudos, Criticism, Moves Ahead on Projects." *Government Executive*, May 1971, pp. 44-53.

2679. "Operation Breakthrough: The Housing Industry Will Never Be the Same." *California Savings and Loan Journal*, January 1971, pp. 10-12.

2680. Pearl, Augusta. "First Operation Breakthrough Project Completed: Horizon Village, Kalamazoo, Michigan." *Journal of Housing*, May 1972, pp. 166-169.

2681. Pellish, David. "A New Government-Industry Partnership for Building More Housing," *Architectural Forum*, July-August 1970, pp. 58-61.

2682. Pfrang, E. O. *References from Guide Criteria for Operation Breakthrough Housing Systems*. Sponsored by Dept. of Housing and Urban Development. Washington, D.C.: National Bureau of Standards, 1970. 22pp.

2683. Raney, Dan and Suzanne Stephens. "Operation Breakthrough: Operation P/R." *Progressive Architecture*, April 1970, pp. 120-133.

2684. "Technology: Operation Breakthrough." *Architectural Forum*, May 1971, pp. 58-62.

2685. U.S. Department of Housing and Urban Development. *Operation Breakthrough: Questions and Answers*. Washington, D.C., March 1971, 23pp.

2686. U.S. Department of Housing and Urban Development. Library. *Operation Breakthrough: Mass Produced and Industrialized Housing: A Bibilography*. Washington, D.C., 1970. 72pp.

2687. U.S. National Bureau of Standards. *Climatological Data at the Eleven Prototype Sites in the United States for the Evaluation of HUD Operation Breakthrough Housing Systems*, by T. Kusada. Sponsored by Dept. of Housing and Urban Development. Washington, D.C., 1970. 136pp.

2688. Ward, Robertson, Jr. "Breakthrough." *American Institute of Architects Journal*, March 1971, pp. 17-22.

2689. "Winners Assembled for Breakthrough." *Business Week*, February 28, 1970, p. 35.

9. PUBLIC HOUSING

a. General

2690. Bailey, James. "The Case History of a Failure: Ten Years Ago, This St. Louis (Mo., Pruitt-Igoe) Project Was Expected to Set a New Standard in Housing Design; Now $7 Million Will Be Spent in an Attempt to Save It." *Architectural Forum*, December 1965, pp. 22-25.

2691. Brincefield, James C., Jr. "The Low Rent Public Housing Program: Some Observations, Suggestions and Predictions." *Urban Lawyer*, Winter 1971, pp. 31-60.

2692. Brown, Robert Kevin. *The Development of the Public Housing Program in the United States*. Atlanta, Ga.: Bureau of Business and Economic Research, School of Business Administration, Georgia State College of Business Administration, 1960. 92pp.

2693. Burstein, Joseph. "New Techniques in Public Housing." *Law and Contemporary Problems*, Summer 1967, pp. 528-549.

2694. "Constitutionality of the Use of Middle Income Public Housing Rentals to Subsidize Low Income Public Housing." *Tulsa Law Journal*, January 1967, pp. 69+.

6295. Fairley, W., M. I. Liechenstein and A. F. Westin. *Improving Public Safety in Urban Apartment Dwellings: Security Concepts and Experimental Design for New York City Housing Authority Buildings*. Santa Monica, Calif.: Rand Corporation, June 1971. 155pp.

2696. Fisher, Martha. "Pueblo Indians of New Mexico Are Becoming Homeowners via Public Housing." *Journal of Housing*, January 1971, pp. 30-34.

2697. Freedman, Leonard. *Public Housing: The Politics of Poverty*. New York: Holt, Rinehart and Winston, Inc., 1969. 217pp.

2698. Fried, Joseph P. "Simeon Golar's City-within-a-City." *New York Times Magazine Section*, April 30, 1972, pp. 16-17+.

2699. Friedman, L. M. "Public Housing and the Poor: An Overview." *California Law Review*, May 1966, pp. 642+.

2700. Green, Ronald C. *Determining Legislative Intent: A Methodology Study of Public Housing Legislation*. Ann Arbor, Mich.: University Microfilms, 1971 (Ph.D. dissertation, State University of New York at Albany, 1971). 363pp. (order no. 71-26,768)

2701. Greiveldinger, Geoffrey. "Turnkey Public Housing in Wisconsin." *Wisconsin Law Review*, No. 1, 1969, pp. 231-252.

2702. Hamilton, Raymond Warren. *The Public Housing Program in the United States: An Analysis and Evaluation*. Ann Arbor, Mich.: University Microfilms, 1971 (Ph.D. dissertation, University of Maryland, 1971). 181pp. (order no. 71-25,270)

2703. "HOAP, Turnkey Program Offering New Opportunities." *Journal of Homebuilding*, August 1971, pp. 14-15.

2704. "Home Ownership through Public Housing." *Journal of Housing*, August-September 1969, pp. 402-408.

2705. "HUD's Turnkey III Handbook." *Low Income Housing Bulletin, March 1972, pp. 1-4.*

2706. Illinois University. Committee on Housing Research and Development. *Families in Public Housing: An Evaluation of Three Residential Environments in Rockford, Illinois*. Urbana, Ill., 1972.

2707. Illinois University. Committee on Housing Research and Development. *A Response to Need: Designs for Family Housing*. Urbana, Ill., 1970. 36pp.

2708. Keppel, David H. "Public Welfare and Public Housing: Clarifies Relationships between These Two Allied Fields." *Public Welfare*, April 1960, pp. 99-102+.

2709. Latimer, Margaret Webb. *Tenants of the City: The Present, Potential and Former Occupants of Public Housing in New York City*. Ann Arbor, Mich.: University Microfilms, 1971 (Ph.D. dissertation, Columbia University, 1970). 163pp. (order no. 71-5461).

2710. Ledbetter, William H., Jr. "Public Housing–A Social Experiment Seeks Acceptance." *Law and Contemporary Problems*, Summer 1967, pp. 490-527.

2711. "Legislative History of Public Housing Traced through 25 Years." *Journal of Housing*, October 15, 1962, pp. 431-445.

2712. Mayer, Albert. "Public Housing Architecture Evaluated from PWA (Public Works Administration) Days up to 1962." *Journal of Housing*, October 15, 1962, pp. 446-468.

2713. "New Image for Public Housing." *Professional Builder*, Aug. 1972, pp. 156-161.

2714. New Jersey State Advisory Committee to the United States Commission on Civil Rights. *Public Housing in Newark's Central Ward.* A report by the N.J. State Advisory Committee to the U.S. Commission on Civil Rights. Trenton, N.J., 1968.

2715. New York Metropolitan Regional Council. *Low-Income Public Housing in the Region: An Assessment of Low-Income Public Housing Units and Local Housing Authorities in the 22-County Metropolitan New York Region.* New York, February 1970.

2716. Peattie, Lisa. *Conventional Public Housing.* Cambridge, Mass.: Joint Center for Urban Studies of the Massachusetts Institute of Technology and Harvard University, Spring 1971, revised February 1972. (Joint Center Working Paper no. 3).

2717. "Public Housing." In U.S. National Commission on Urban Problems. *Building the American City.* Washington, D.C.: Government Printing Office, 1969, pp. 108-133.

2718. "Public Housing." *Vanderbilt Law Review,* May 1969, pp. 875+.

2719. "Public Housing: The Still Troubled Scene." *Low-Income Housing Bulletin,* June 1972, pp. 1-3.

2720. Putter, Harmon and Meyer Kailo. "Urban Renewal and Public Housing: A Model for Interagency Cooperation." *Pratt Planning Papers,* September 1966, pp. 11-13.

2721. Rainwater, Lee. "The Lessons of Pruitt-Igoe." *Public Interest,* Summer 1967, pp. 116-126.

2722. Ribicoff, Abraham A. "Raze or Lower? A Huge Public Housing Project Isn't Fit to Live In." *Barron's,* Jan. 10, 1972, p. 9+.

2723. Rural Housing Alliance. *Public Housing.* Washington, D.C., 1972.

2724. Ruttger, Max J. III. "Public Housing in Itself Justifies Use Variance." *Urban Law Annual 1972.* St. Louis, Mo.: School of Law, Washington University, 1972, pp. 251-256.

2725. Scheibla, Shirley. "St. Louis Blues; Over $200 Million in U.S. Housing Subsidy Is Down the Drain." *Barron's,* January 24, 1972, pp. 9+.

2726. Schermer (George) Associates. *Report on Five Cities.* A report to the National Commission on Urban Problems. Washington, D.C., 1968. 23pp.

2727. "Single-Family Houses–Are They 'In' in Public Housing, Renewal Programs?" *Journal of Housing,* November 1961, pp. 449-453.

2728. Smith, F. "Public Housing in Oklahoma." *Tulsa Law Journal*, January 1967. pp. 1+.

2729. Stanley, Patrick A. and Roger Y. Dewa. *Public Housing in Hawaii; The Evolution of Housing Policy*. Honolulu, Ha.: Legislative Reference Bureau, University of Hawaii, 1967.

2730. U.S. General Accounting Office. *Benefits Could Be Realized through Reuse of Designs for Public Housing Projects*. Washington, D.C., 1971.

2731. U.S. General Accounting Office. *Need to Strengthen Concrete Inspections and Testing Requirements in the Construction of Low-rent Public Housing Projects; Report. . . .* Washington, D.C., 1970. 31pp.

2732. U.S. General Accounting Office. *Reviews at Selected Local Housing Authorities to Ascertain Status of Prior Findings and Recommendations. . . .* Washington, D.C., 1961.

2733. U.S. General Accounting Office. *Review of Local Housing Authorities. . .* Washington, D.C., 1961.

2734. U.S. General Accounting Office. *Review of the Housing Authority of the City and County of Denver, Colorado, 1959. . . .* Washington, D.C., 1960.

2735. U.S. Housing and Home Finance Agency. *Views on Public Housing; Symposium of Letters*. Washington, D.C., 1960. 159pp.

2736. U.S. National Capital Housing Authority. *A Quarter-Century of Slum Fighting: Report for the Fiscal Year Ended June 30, 1959; and a Review of the Authority's Work from 1934 through June 30, 1968*. Washington, D.C., 1960. 19pp.

2737. Vogelsang, Frederic. "Low-Income Families in Miami Get Chance at Ownership of Modular Town-Houses in New Scattered Site Public Housing Project." *Journal of Housing*. June 1972, pp. 223-228.

2738. Woodyatt, Lyle John. *The Origins and Evolution of the New Deal Public Housing Program*. Ann Arbor, Mich.: University Microfilms, 1968 (Ph.D. dissertation, Washington University, 1968) 269pp. (order no. 68-17,213)

2739. "Worse Than Slums; Public Housing Is a Monument to the Welfare State." *Barrons*, July 27, 1970, pp. 1+.

2740. Worsnop, Richard L. "Public Housing in War on Poverty." *Editorial Research Reports*, July 22, 1964, pp. 523-540.

See also: 172, 179, 184, 3099; Site Selection in Federally-Assisted Housing: 2560+.

b. Tenant Selection

2741. Dale, M. J. "Gaining Admission to Low-Rent Public Housing." *Boston College Industrial & Commercial Law Review*, November 1971, pp. 35+.

2742. Ellis, Joseph M. "*Shapiro, Dandridge*, and Residence Requirements in Public Housing." *Urban Law Annual 1972*. St. Louis, Mo.: School of Law, Washington University, 1972, pp. 131-143.

2743. "Judicial Review of Public Housing Admissions." *Urban Law Annual 1971*. St. Louis, Mo.: School of Law, Washington University, 1971, pp. 228+.

2744. Starr, Roger. "Which of the Poor Shall Live in Public Housing? The Urban Condition (1)." *Public Interest*, Spring 1971, pp. 116-124.

2745. U.S. General Accounting Office. *Review of Eligibility Requirements, Rents, and Occupancy of Selected Low-Rent Housing Projects....* Washington, D.C., 1963.

2746. Walsh, Robert E. "The Constitutionality of a Length-of-Residency Test for Admission to Public Housing." *Journal of Urban Law*, August 1971, pp. 121-129.

See also: 1884.

c. Economic Analyses

2747. Bish, Robert L. "Public Housing: The Magnitude and Distribution of Direct Benefits and Effects on Housing Consumption." *Journal of Regional Science*, December 1969, pp. 27-39.

2748. Lym, Glenn Robert. "Effect of a Public Housing Project on a Neighborhood: Case Study of Oakland, California." *Land Economics*, November 1967, pp. 461-466.

2749. Nourse, Hugh O. "Redistribution of Income from Public Housing." *National Tax Journal*, March 1966, pp. 27-37.

2750. Olsen, Edgar Oliver. *A Welfare Economic Evaluation of Public Housing*. Ann Arbor, Mich.: University Microfilms, 1968 (Ph.D. dissertation, Rice University, 1968). 131pp. (Order no. 68-15,646)

2751. Prescott, J. R. "The Economics of Public Housing: A Normative Analysis." Unpublished Ph.D. dissertation, Harvard University, 1964.

2752. Smolensky, Engene, "Public Housing or Income Supplements—The Economics of Housing for the Poor." *Journal of the American Institute of Planners*, March 1968, pp. 94-101. Comment (Michael A. Stegman), May 1968, pp. 195-198. Also in Michael A. Stegman. *Housing and Economics: The American Dilemma*. Cambridge, Mass.: MIT Press, 1970, pp. 252-278.

2753. Smolensky, Eugene and J. Douglas Gomery. *Efficiency and Equity Effects in the Benefits from Federal Public Housing Programs in 1965*. Madison, Wisconsin: Institute of Poverty, University of Wisconsin, 1971 (Working Paper no. 2).

See also: 831, 832, 834, 910, 2488.

d. Housing Costs in Public Housing

2754. de Leeuw, Frank. *The Cost of Leased Public Housing*. Washington, D.C.: The Urban Institute, 1971 (Urban Institute Working Paper S8-112-5).

2755. de Leeuw, Frank and Eleanor Lippman Tarutis. *Operating Costs in Public Housing: A Financial Crisis*. Washington, D.C.: The Urban Institute, 1969. 63pp.

2756. Pratt Institute, Brooklyn. School of Architecture. *Methods of Reducing the Cost of Public Housing; Research Report*. Brooklyn, N.Y., 1960. 139pp.

2757. Rydell, C. Peter. *Factors Affecting Maintenance and Operating Costs in Federal Public Housing Projects*. New York, N.Y.: The New York City Rand Institute, 1970.

2758. Rydell, C. Peter. "Review of Factors Affecting Maintenance and Operating Costs in Public Housing." *Regional Science Association Papers, Volume Twenty-seven, 1971*. Philadelphia, Pa.: Regional Science Association, 1971, pp. 229-2245. (Summarizes the author's *Factors Affecting Maintenance and Operating Costs in Federal Public Housing Projects*. New York: The New York City Rand Institute, 1970.)

2759. U.S. General Accounting Office. *Audit of the Financial Statements of the Low-Rent Public Housing Program Fund, Fiscal Year 1968; Report to the Congress*. . . Washington, D.C., 1969. 25pp.

2760. U.S. General Accounting Office. *Benefits Could Be Realized by Revising Policies and Practices for Acquiring Existing Structures for Low-Rent Public Housing*. Washington, D.C.: Government Printing Office, 1972.

2761. U.S. General Accounting Office. *Examination of Financial Statements, Low-Rent Public Housing Program Fund, Fiscal Year 1967; Report....* Washington, D.C., 1968. 23pp.

2762. U.S. General Accounting Office. *High Costs Pertaining to Sites for Selected Low-Rent Housing Projects in the Area Administered by the San Francisco Regional Office, Public Housing Administration, Housing and Home Finance Agency; Report to the Congress of the United States by the Comptroller General of the United States.* Washington, D.C., 1963. 35pp.

2763. U.S. General Accounting Office. *Inadequate Criteria for Identifying and Eliminating Elaborate or Extravagant Designs or Materials in Constructing and Equipping Low-Rent Housing Projects, Public Housing Administration, Housing and Home Finance Agency; Report....* Washington, D.C., 1964. 68pp.

2764. U.S. General Accounting Office. *Inclusion of Balconies and Use of High-Cost Brick in Constructing Low-Rent Public Housing Projects, Public Housing Administration, Department of Housing and Urban Development; Report...* Washington, D.C., 1966. 55pp.

2765. U.S. General Accounting Office. *Omission of Facilities for Metering Electricity in Individual Dwelling Units Proposed to Reduce Construction Costs of Low-Rent Public Housing Projects; Report....* Washington, D.C., 1968. 23pp.

2766. U.S. General Accounting Office. *Opportunities for Reducing Federal Contributions by Maximizing Investment of Excess Funds Held by Local Housing Authorities, Department of Housing and Urban Development; Report....* Washington, D.C., 1967. 34pp.

2767. U.S. General Accounting Office. *Opportunity for Accelerating Construction and Reducing Cost of Low-Rent Housing; Report...* Washington, D.C., 1970. 40pp.

2768. U.S. General Accounting Office. *Proposed Acquisition of Unnecessary and Expensive Property for Developing a Low-Rent Housing Project by the St. Louis Housing Authority, Public Housing Administration, Housing and Home Finance Agency; Report....* Washington, D.C., 1964. 13pp.

2769. U.S. General Accounting Office. *Review of Financing of Community Facilities by the Department of Housing and Urban Development; Report....* Washington, D.C., 1969. 28pp.

2770. U.S. General Accounting Office. *Review of Maintenance Employment Classifications and Wage Rates at Selected Local Housing Authorities in Region VI; Report to the Congress. . . .* Washington, D.C., 1966. 39pp.

2771. U.S. General Accounting Office. *Undue Increases in Maximum Federal Contributions Resulting from Method of Financing Off-site Community Facilities for Low-rent Housing Projects: Public Housing Administration, Housing and Home Finance Agency; Report. . .* Washington, D.C., 1963. 31pp.

2772. U.S. General Accounting Office. *Unnecessary Payments to Local Housing Authorities Owning Former Federal Land to Be Used for Low-rent Housing Project Sites, Public Housing Administration, Housing and Home Finance Agency; Report. . . .* Washington, D.C., 1964.

2773. Walsh, Albert A. "Is Public Housing Headed for a Fiscal Crisis?" *Journal of Housing*, February 1969, pp. 65-71. Also in Michael A. Stegman. *Housing and Economics: The American Dilemma.* Cambridge, Mass.: MIT Press, 1970, pp. 279-289.

e. Landlord-Tenant Relations

2774. Abel, Michael R. "Municipal Corporations–Constitutional Law–Eviction from Public Housing Projects." *North Carolina Law Review*, June 1969, pp. 953-963.

2775. Barron, R. D. and P. F. Fishman. "St. Louis Public Housing Rent Strike: A Model for Inducing Community Action." *NLADA Brief Case*, February 1970, pp. 111+.

2776. "Constitutional Law–Eviction of State's Tenants Necessitates a Limited Hearing According to the State Action Doctrine of the Fourteenth Amendment." *Buffalo Law Review*, Winter 1972, pp. 524+.

2777. "Eviction Procedures in Public Housing." *Dickinson Law Review*, Winter 1969, pp. 307+.

2778. "Fines in Public Housing." *Columbia Law Review*, December 1968, pp. 1538-1553.

2779. Genung, G. R., Jr. "HUD's New Public Housing Lease and Grievance Procedures Cause of Controversy." *Journal of Housing*, March 1971, pp. 119-121.

2780. Lefcoe, George. "HUD's Authority to Mandate Tenants' Rights in Public Housing." *Yale Law Journal*, January 1971, pp. 463-514.

2781. Lempert, Richard and Kiyoshi Ikeda. "Evictions from Public Housing: Effects of Independent Review." *American Sociological Review*, October 1970, pp. 852-860. Also in George Sternlieb and Lynne Sagalyn (eds.). *Housing: 1970-1971; An AMS Anthology*. New York: AMS Press, 1972, pp. 433-441.

2782. Louis, Al and Vivian Brown. "Public Housing's Neglected Resources: The Tenants; A Review of the Positive Payoffs of Their Involvement in Policy Making in St. Louis, Philadelphia, and Other Cities." *City*, Fall 1972, pp. 15-21.

2783. "Nonfinancial Eligibility and Eviction Standards in Public Housing–The Problem Family in the Great Society." *Cornell Law Review*, July 1968, pp. 1122+.

2784. Pennsylvania Economy League (Eastern Division). *Retaining Tenant Leaders in Philadelphia Public Housing: A Study of the Impact of Income Limits for Continued Occupancy on the Retention of Leaders within the Public Housing Population*. Philadelphia, Pa., 1966.

2785. "Public Housing: Due Process and Termination of Tenancy." *Howard Law Journal*, Spring 1971, pp. 610+.

2786. "Public Housing: Model Lease and Grievance Procedure." *Low-Income Housing Bulletin*, March 1971, pp. 6-8.

2787. "Public Housing–Tenant's Rights in Eviction Actions–Real or Illusory?" *Syracuse Law Review*, Spring 1969, pp. 694+.

2788. "Public Landlords and Private Tenants: The Eviction of 'Undesirables' from Public Housing Projects." *Yale Law Journal*, April 1968, pp. 988-1006.

2789. "Remedies for Tenants in Substandard Public Housing." *Columbia Law Review*, March 1968, pp. 561-587.

2790. Scheshinski, R. S. "Public Landlords and Tenants: A Survey of the Developing Law." *Duke Law Journal*, June 1969, pp. 399+.

2791. Smith, J. C., Jr. "Due Process and the Poor in Public Housing." *Howard Law Journal*, Spring 1969, pp. 422+.

2792. Torts–New York City Housing Authority Held Liable for Failure to Provide Adequate Police Protection." *Dickinson Law Review*, Spring 1970, pp. 543+.

2793. "What Is the Responsibility of Local Housing Authorities for the Safety and Security of Their Residents?" *Journal of Housing*, Feb/Mar. 1972, pp. 72-81.

f. Management and Administration

2794. Broberg, Merle. *A Study of a Performance Control System as an Indicator of Organizational Goals: The Housekeeping Inspection System of the Philadelphia Housing Authority, 1962-1967.* Ann Arbor, Mich.: University Microfilms, 1970 (Ph.D. dissertation, The American University, 1969). 271pp. (order no. 70-23,268)

2795. Bryan, Jack. "Public Housing Modernization Is Bringing Not only Modernized Buildings but Modernized Tenant/Management Relationships." *Journal of Housing*, April 1971, pp. 167-178.

2796. Cox, Lawrence. "The Challenge in Public Housing Management." *HUD Challenge*, July-August 1970, pp. 4-10.

2797. Hamlar, Portia T. "HUD's Authority to Mandate Effective Management of Public Housing." *Journal of Urban Law*, August 1972, pp. 79-128.

2798. Hartman, Chester W. and Gregg Carr. "Housing Authorities Reconsidered." *Journal of the American Institute of Planners*, January 1969, pp. 10-21. Comment (Beatrice L. Cohen) with rejoinder, November 1969, pp. 432-436. Comment (Dorothy Gazzolo) with rejoinder, November 1969, pp. 436-438.

2799. Hartman, Chester W. and Gregg Carr. *Local Public Housing Administration: An Appraisal.* Berkeley, Calif.: Institute of Urban and Regional Development, University of California, December 1970.

2800. Hipshman, May B. *Public Housing at the Crossroads: The Boston Housing Authority.* Boston, Mass.: Citizens' Housing and Planning Association of Metropolitan Boston, 1967.

2801. Hirshen, Al. *The HUD Modernization Program.* Chicago, Ill.: American Bar Center, National Legal Aid and Defender Association, 1970. 48pp.

2802. Lebergott, Stanley. "Slum Housing: A Proposal." *Journal of Political Economy*, November/December 1970, pp. 1362-1366. Reply (Benton F. Massell, "Maintenance of Slum Housing: Optimal Policy Subject to a Political Constraint.") with rejoinder, September/October 1972, pp. 1060-1066.

2803. Mulvihill, R. "Problems in the Management of Public Housing." *Temple Law Quarterly*, Winter 1962, pp. 163+.

2804. Schwartz, Sidney. *Control of Local Housing Authorities.* Ann Arbor, Mich.: University Microfilms, 1970 (Ph.D. dissertation, New York University, 1969). 407pp. (order no. 70-16,007)

2805. Stoots, Cynthia F. *Local Housing Authorities.* Monticello, Ill.: Council of Planning Librarians, 1970 (Exchange Bibliography no. 135).

2806. Temple University. Center for Social Policy and Community Development. *Model Curricula and Training Techniques for Use in Training Para-Professional Employees of Public Housing Authorities.* Washington, D.C.: U.S. Department of Housing and Urban Development, 1972. 227pp.

2807. Weisman, Celia B. *The Study of a Conditional Benefit: Subsidized Public Housing.* Ann Arbor, Mich.: University Microfilms, 1971 (Ph.D. dissertation, Cornell University, 1970). 317pp. (order no. 71-6274)

2808. "Why are Public Housing Directors Retiring or Being Fired." *Journal of Housing*, February 1971, pp. 86-87.

2809. White, Edward, Jr. "Tenant Participation in Public Housing Management." *Journal of Housing*, August/September 1969, pp. 416-421.

See also: 2872, 2873.

g. Racial Aspects

2810. Baron, Harold M. "Building Babylon (Chicago, Ill.): A Case of Racial Controls in Public Housing." *Focus/Midwest*, no. 56, 1972, pp. 4-27.

2811. "De Facto Segregation in Low-rent Public Housing." *In Urban Law Annual 1968.* St. Louis, Mo.: School of Law, Washington University, 1968, pp. 174-195.

2812. Kelley, Joseph Benedict. *Racial Integration Policies of the New York City Housing Authority, 1958-1961.* Ann Arbor, Mich.: University Microfilms, 1964 (Ph.D. dissertation, Columbia University, 1963). 309pp. (order no. 64-2763)

2813. Kelley, Joseph B. "Racial Integration Policies of the New York City Housing Authority." *Social Service Review*, June 1964, pp. 153-162.

2814. Killingsworth, Mark R. "Desegregating Public Housing." *New Leader*, October 7, 1968, pp. 13-14.

2815. Luttrell, Jordan D. "Public Housing Administration and Discrimination in Federally Assisted Low-Rent Housing." *Michigan Law Review*, March 1966, pp. 871-889.

2816. Nagel, S.S. "Discrimination Issues in Public Housing." *NLADA Brief Case*, January 1970, pp. 89+.

2817. "Public Housing and Integration: A Neglected Opportunity." *Columbia Journal of Law and Social Problems*, May 1970, pp. 253+.

2818. "Segregation in Public Housing–an Old Problem with New Solutions." *Syracuse Law Review*, Vol. 22, 1971, pp. 1139+.

See also: 1884, 2821, 2831, 2846; Site Selection in Federally-Assisted Housing: 2560+.

h. Rents in Public Housing

2819. Abeles, Schwartz and Associates. *The Impact of the Brooke Amendment on Public Housing Tenants and Local Housing Authorities: A Report to the Joint HEW-HUD Task Force on Welfare Rents in Public Housing*. New York, 1971. 2 vols.

2820. Community Service Society of New York. Department of Public Affairs. Committee on Housing and Urban Development. *Rent and Income Policies in Public Housing: Views and Recommendations*. New York, 1968.

2821. Delaware Valley Housing Association. *Racism and Exploitation in Public Housing: HUD and the Brooke Amendment*. Philadelphia, Pa., 1970. 11pp.

2822. Genung, George R., Jr. "Where We Have Come with the 'Brooke Amendment'–the 1969 Legislative Effort to Ease Public Housing Problems." *Journal of Housing*, May-June 1970, pp. 232-235.

2823. "Higher Rents for Welfare Recipients in Public Housing: An Analysis under the Equal Protection Clause." *Southern California Law Review*, Winter 1972, pp. 263+.

2824. Prescott, James Russell. "Rental Formation in Federally Supported Public Housing." *Land Economics*, August 1967, pp. 341-345.

i. Social Aspects

2825. Aiken, M. and R. R. Alford. "Community Structure and Innovation: The Case of Public Housing." *American Political Science Review*, September 1970, pp. 843-864. Reply (S.V. Stephens) with rejoinder, June 1971, pp. 499-501.

2826. Allen, Van Sizar. *An Approach to Low Rent Public Housing Tenant Education in Greensboro, North Carolina*. Ann Arbor, Mich.: University Microfilms, 1970 (Ph.D. dissertation, University of North Carolina at Chapel Hill, 1969). 514pp. (order no. 70-3189)

2827. Bellin, S. S. and L. Kriesberg. "Relationship Among Attitudes, Circumstances, and Behavior: The Case of Applying for Public Housing." *Sociology and Social Research: An International Journal*, July 1967, pp. 453-469.

2828. Browning, Grainger. *Social Prestige in a Low Income Housing Community*. Ann Arbor, Mich.: University Microfilms, 1962 (Ph.D. dissertation, Boston University Graduate School, 1962). 176pp. (order no. 62-3787)

2829. Coit, Elizabeth. *Report on Family Living in High Apartment Buildings*. Prepared for Public Housing Administration. Washington, D.C.: Government Printing Office, 1965. 28pp.

2830. Connors, John Francis III. *The Adequacy of Federal Low-Rent Public Housing for Large Families: A Study of Value Conflict within a Social Reform Agency*. Ann Arbor, Mich.: University Microfilms, 1965. (Ph.D. dissertation, Catholic University of America, 1964). 345pp. (order no. 65-5550)

2831. Ford, Winfield Scott, Jr. *Racial Attitudes, Behavior, and Perception of Public Housing Residents in a Border State City*. Ann Arbor, Mich.: University Microfilms, 1970 (Ph.D. dissertation, University of Kentucky, 1969). 208pp. (order no. 70-2573)

2832. Hirshen, Al and Vivian Brown. "Public Housing's Neglected Resource: The Tenants." *City*, Fall 1972, pp. 15-21,

2833. Huttman, E. D. "The Pathology of Public Housing." *City*, Fall 1971, pp. 32-34.

2834. Huttman, Elizabeth Dickerson. *Stigma and Public Housing: A Comparison of British and American Policies and Experience*. Ann Arbor, Mich.: University Microfilms, 1970 (Ph.D. dissertation, University of California at Berkeley, 1969). 964pp. (order no. 70-6124)

2835. Illinois University. Committee on Housing Research and Development. *Activities and Attitudes of Public Housing Residents*. Champaign, Ill., 1971. 92pp.

2836. Joint Committee on Housing and Welfare. *Community Services and Public Housing; Seven Recommendations for Local Housing Authority Action*. Prepared by Subcommittee on Community Services and Public Housing of the Joint Committee on Housing and Welfare. Chicago, Ill.: National Association of Housing and Redevelopment Officials, 1961. 15pp.

2837. Kriesberg, Louis, "Neighborhood Setting and the Isolation of Public Housing Tenants." *Journal of the American Institute of Planners*, January 1968, pp. 43-49.

2838. Levin, J. and G. Taube. "Bureaucracy and the Socially Handicapped: A Study of Lower-status Tenants in Public Housing." *Sociology and Social Research; An International Journal*, January 1970, pp. 209-219.

2839. McLain, O. "Social Work in a Public Housing Project." *Social Casework*, October, 1960, pp. 408-412.

2840. Preston, David. "The Human Dimension in Public Housing." *Social Work*, January 1964, pp. 29-37.

2841. "Reducing Tenant Anxiety in Public Housing Projects." *Design and Environment*, Summer 1971, pp. 36-37.

2842. Reynolds, H. W., Jr. "Public Housing and Social Values in an American City." *Social Service Review*, June1965, pp. 157-164.

2843. Scobie, Richard Spencer. *Family Interaction as a Factor in Problem-tenant Identification in Public Housing*. Ann Arbor, Mich.: University Microfilms, 1972 (Ph.D. dissertation, The Florence Heller Graduate School for Advanced Studies in Social Welfare, Brandeis University, 1972). 269pp.

2844. Silverman, Abner D. "User Needs and Social Services." In U.S. Congress. House. Committee on Banking and Currency, *Papers Submitted to Subcommittee on Housing Panels on Housing Production, Housing Demand, and Developing a Suitable Living Environment: Part 2.* Washington, D.C.: Government Printing Office, 1971, pp. 579-606.

2845. Spencer, Gary. *The Structure and Dynamics of Social Intervention: A Comparative Study of the Reduction of Dependency in Three Low-income Public Housing Projects*. Ann Arbor, Mich.: University Microfilms, 1969 (Ph.D. dissertation, Boston University Graduate School, 1969). 353pp. (order no. 69-18, 762).

2846. Spiegel, H.B.C. "Tenants' Intergroup Attitudes in a Public Housing Project With Declining White Population." *Phylon*, Spring 1960, pp. 30-39.

2847. Taube, Gerald. *The Social Structural Sources of Residential Satisfaction-Dissatisfaction in Public Housing*. Ann Arbor, Mich.: University Microfilms, 1972 (Ph.D. dissertation, The Florence Heller Graduate School for Advanced Studies in Social Welfare, Brandeis University, 1972). 263pp. (order no. 72-20, 811).

2848. Taube, G. and J. Levin. "Public Housing as Neighborhood: The Effect of Local and Non-local Participation." *Social Science Quarterly*, December 1971, pp. 534-542.

2849. U.S. Joint Task Force on Health, Education, and Welfare Services and Housing. *Two-year Progress Report*, by I. Jack Fasteau and Abner D. Silverman. Washington, D.C.: U.S. Department of Health, Education, and Welfare, 1964. 79pp.

2850. U.S. Joint Task Force on Health, Education, and Welfare Services and Housing. Ad Hoc Committee on New Programs in Health, Education and Welfare. *New Programs in Health, Education and Welfare for Persons and Families of Low Income; Services for Families Living in Public Housing*. Washington, D.C.: U.S. Department of Health, Education, and Welfare, 1965. 14pp.

2851. U.S. Joint Task Force on Health, Education, and Welfare Services and Housing. Committee on Use of Program Resources. *Services for Families Living in Public Housing: Planning for Health, Education, and Welfare Services in the Public Housing Community*. Washington, D.C.: U.S. Department of Health, Education, and Welfare, 1963-65. 2 vols.

2852. Weinandy, Janet E. *et al. Working with the Poor; The Report of a Three-year Family Consultation Service in Public Housing*. Syracuse, N.Y.: Youth Development Center, Syracuse University, 1965. 51pp.

2853. Welfare Council of Metropolitan Chicago. *Human Needs in Public Housing*. Chicago, Ill., 1971. 253pp.

2854. Yancey, W.L. "Architecture, Interaction, and Social Control: The Case of a Large-scale Public Housing Project." *Environment and Behavior*, March 1971, pp. 3-22.

j. Leased Public Housing

2855. Christensen, Edward A. "The Public Housing Leasing Program: A Workable Rent Subsidy?" In *Urban Law Annual 1968*. St. Louis, Mo.: School of Law, Washington University, 1968, pp. 57-74.

2856. Citizens Budget Commission, Inc. *Report on New York: Leasing Low-Rent Housing*. New York, 1970. 9pp.

2857. de Leeuw, Frank and Sam H. Leaman. "The Section 23 Leasing Program." In U.S. Congress, Joint Economic Committee. *The Economics of Federal Subsidy Programs: A Compendium of Papers Submitted to the Joint Economic Committee: Part 5—Housing Subsidies*. Washington, D.C.: Government Printing Office, 1972, pp. 642-659.

2858. Friedman, L.M. and J.E. Krier. "New Lease on Life: Section 23 Housing and the Poor." *University of Pennsylvania Law Review*, February 1968, pp. 611+.

2859. "Oakland Leased Housing Program." *Stanford Law Review*, February 1968, pp. 538+.

2860. Palmer, R.G. "Section 23 Housing: Low-rent Housing in Private Accommodations." *Journal of Urban Law*, Vol. 48, no. 1, 1970-71, pp. 255-278.

2861. U.S. General Accounting Office. *Administration of the Leased-Housing Program.* Washington, D.C., 1970. 60pp.

See also: 2754.

k. The Elderly in Public Housing

2862. Carp, Frances Merchant. *A Future for the Aged: Victoria Plaza and Its Residents.* San Antonio, Texas: University of Texas Press, 1966. 287pp.

2863. Community Service Society of New York. *Senior Advisory Service for Public Housing Tenants.* New York, 1969. 217pp.

2864. Garrison, Alexander S. *Client Analysis of the Federally-Aided Low-Rent Housing Program for the Elderly in Syracuse, New York: A Further Development of an Applied Method.* Ann Arbor, Mich.: University Microfilms, 1972 (Ph.D. dissertation, Cornell University, 1971). 223pp. (order no. 72-8853).

2865. Howard, Mildren Stenswick and W. Russell Parker. *Housing for the Elderly: A Report of Recommendations Made to the National Capital Housing Authority for Proposed Apartment Units for Low-Income Elderly Occupants.* Washington, D.C.: Agricultural Research Service, U.S. Department of Agriculture, 1963. 20pp.

2866. Kaplan, Bernard and William Hammond. "Public Housing of Elderly in Chicago." *Geriatrics*, December 1961, pp. 655-663.

2867. New York (State) Executive Department. Division of Housing and Community Renewal. Bureau of Project Development. *Recommended Standards for State-Aided Low Rent Public Housing Projects for Senior Citizens.* New York, 1961. 20pp.

2868. New York (State) Executive Department. Division of Housing and Community Renewal. Bureau of Research and Statistics. *Study of Experience with Specially Designed Apartments for the Aging in New York State-aided Low Rent Public Housing Projects.* New York, 1962. 74pp.

2869. "Public Housing for the Elderly." *Journal of Housing*, March 1963, pp. 77-92.

2870. "Public Housing for the Elderly." *Progressive Architecture*, March 1961, pp. 144-159.

2871. U.S. Housing and Home Finance Agency. Public Housing Administration. *115,000 Senior Citizens; The Story of What Public Housing Has Done and Is Doing for Them*. Washington, D.C.: Government Printing Office, 1961. 24pp.

2872. Westmeyer, Troy R. *Management of Public Housing for the Elderly*. New York, Graduate School of Public Administration, New York University, 1963.

2873. Zuckerman, Isadore. *An Investigation of the Needs of the Elderly in Public Housing and Their Relationship to Administrative Practice*. Ann Arbor, Mich.: University Microfilms, 1972, (D.P.A. dissertation, New York University, 1970). 317 pp. (order no. 72-3162).

## 10. REHABILITATION

### a. General

2874. Abeles, Peter Lee. "The Cost of Rehabilitation." *Building Research*, January-March 1968, pp. 60-63.

2875. Ables, James Quentin and William W. Mathews. *The Processing Compendium of Housing Rehabilitation*. St. Louis, Mo.: Gemini Publications, 1970. 104pp.

2876. Actenberg, Emily J. "Rehabilitation Loans and Grants in Boston." Unpublished M.C.P. thesis, Massachusetts Institute of Technology, 1970.

2877. Alexander, James Jr. "Rapid Rehabilitation." *Current Municipal Problems*, November 1970, pp. 207-214.

2878. Alstyne, Carroll Van. "Network Analysis Technique." *Journal of Housing*, May 1970, pp. 244-248.

2879. Architects' Renewal Committee in Harlem, Inc. *Housing in Central Harlem: Part 1: The Potential for Rehabilitation and Vest Pocket Reconstruction*. New York, 1967. 120pp.

2880. Ash, Joan. "Residential Rehabilitation in the USA." *Urban Studies*, February 1967, pp. 22-40.

2881. Babgy, Dale Gordon. "Housing Rehabilitation Costs." Unpublished Ph.D. dissertation, Harvard University, 1970.

2882. Baltimore Urban Renewal and Housing Agency. *Baltimore, Maryland: A Demonstration of Rehabilitation/Harlem Park.* Baltimore, Md., 1965. 95pp.

2883. "Baltimore's War on Blight: Can a City Rehabilitate Its Run-down Neighborhoods without Displacing the People Living There?" *Savings & Loan News,* November 1962, pp. 29-36.

2884. Berger, Curtis, Eli Goldston and Guido Rothrauff, Jr. "Slum Area Rehabilitation by Private Enterprise." *Columbia Law Review,* May 1969, pp. 739-769.

2885. Brown, Daniel H. "Association Sponsorship of Housing Rehabilitation." *Building Research,* January-March 1968, pp. 54-58.

2886. Bryan, Jack. "Baltimore Is Rehabilitating Vacant Buildings to Increase Its Public Housing Supply." *Journal of Housing,* September 1971, pp. 428-429.

2887. Bryan, Jack. "The Rocky Road to Low Income Rehabilitation for the Private Investor." *Journal of Housing,* February 1970, pp. 76-89.

2888. "Can Production-Line Methods Put Profits in Rehabilitation Jobs Like These?" *House and Home,* August 1966, pp. 88-93.

2889. "Can Slum Labor Be Used to Rehabilitate the Slums." *House and Home,* June 1968, pp. 76-82.

2890. Carlson, David B. "Rehabilitation: Stepchild of Urban Renewal." *Architectural Forum,* August 1962, pp. 131-134.

2891. "Casebook of Inner City Renovations." *House & Home,* November 1972, pp. 73-87.

2892. Chamber of Commerce of the United States. Urban Action Clearinghouse. *Camden Group Rehabilitates Dilapidated Row Houses into "New Again" Units for Sale to Low Income Families.* Washington, D.C., 1969 (Case Study no. 15).

2893. "Cities and Suburbs/Project Rehab Is Upgrading Rental Housing in Effort to Rehabilitate Neighborhoods." *National Journal,* January 8, 1972, pp. 78-79.

2894. Citizens' Housing and Planning Association of Metropolitan Boston. *Conference on Rehabilitation.* Boston, 1968. 26pp.

2895. Community Service Society of New York. Committee on Housing and Urban Development. *The Role of Government Aided Rehabilitation in New York City's Housing Program: Views and Recommendations.* New York, 1968.

2896. "Conservation and Rehabilitation of Housing: An Idea Approaches Adolescence." *Michigan Law Review*, March 1965, pp. 892+.

2897. "The Corporations Try Rehab." *Journal of Housing*, February 1970, pp. 77-82.

2898. Davis, Lloyd. "With Citizen Participation, New Haven Has Neighborhood Rehab Success Story." *Journal of Housing*, March 1965, pp. 132-135.

2899. DeGrazia, Victor. "Rehabilitation is Not Working as a Resource for Community Development." *Journal of Housing*, December 1967, pp. 622-625.

2900. Dyment, Robert G. "Do-It-Yourself Rehabilitation: Schenectady (N.Y.). Frustrated by Federal Red Tape, Uses Local Financing for Housing Program." *Nation's Cities*, December 1970, pp. 13-14.

2901. Edgerton, William H. "Cost Guidelines of Urban Housing Rehabilitation." *Architectural Record*, August 1969, pp. 71-72.

2902. "Fighting Urban Decay." *Federal Home Loan Bank Board Journal*, May 1972, pp. 6-9.

2903. "First Test of Instant Rehabilitation." *Practical Builder*, February 1967, pp. 82-83.

2904. Gabel, Hortense. "The Need for Massive Rehabilitation." *Building Research*, January-March 1968, pp. 14-16.

2905. Gabel, Hortense. *The New York City Rehabilitation Experiment.* Prepared for the City of New York Housing and Development Administration, March 1970. 213pp.

2908. Gergen, David R. "Renewal in the Ghetto: A Study of Residential Rehabilitation in Boston's Washington Park." *Harvard Civil Rights–Civil Liberties Law Review*, Spring 1968, pp. 243-310.

2907. "Getting at the Inner City Rehabilitation Problem." *American Builder*, January 1968, pp. 46-49.

2908. Goldston, Eli. "BURP and Make Money." *Harvard Business Review*, September-October 1969, pp. 84-99.

2909. Haakenson, Robert. "A Privately Supported Route to Rehabilitation." *American Institute of Architects Journal*, March 1967, pp. 69-70.

2910. Haas, John H. *3 R's of Housing–A Guide to Housing Rehabilitation, Relocation Housing, Refinancing*. Washington, D.C.: General Improvement Contractors Association, 1962.

2911. Harrison, D.C. "Housing Rehabilitation and the Pittsburgh Graded Property Tax." *Duquesne University Law Review*, Summer 1964, pp. 213-243.

2912. Heinberg, John Dorsey. *Public Policy toward Residential Rehabilitation: An Economic Analysis*. Ann Arbor, Mich.: University Microfilms, 1968. (Ph.D. dissertation, University of Wisconsin, 1967). 299pp. (order no. 68-1467).

2913. Hershman, Arlene. "Those High-Rolling Rehabs." *Dun's*, February 1972, pp. 46-48.

2914. Hirschmann, Ruth. *A Demonstration of Rehabilitation, Harlem Park, Baltimore, Maryland.* Baltimore, Maryland: Baltimore Urban Renewal and Housing Agency, 1965. 95pp.

2915. "HUD Expands Scope of Rehab Program." *NAHB Journal of Homebuilding*, April 1972, pp. 36-41.

2916. "Industry Builds a Showcase in the Slums: U.S. Gypsum's Experiment in Harlem Shows a Faster, Cheaper Way to Rehabilitate Old Buildings–and Demonstrates Its Wares." *Business Week*, February 26, 1966, pp. 40-41.

2917. "Instant Rehabilitation for Low-Income Families." *Journal of Property Management*, September/October 1967, pp. 204-205.

2918. "Instant Rehabilitation Not So Instant." *Architectural Record*, January 1967, pp. 175-176.

2919. Institute of Public Administration. *Rapid Rehabilitation of Old Law Tenements: An Evaluation.* New York, 1968. 88pp.

2920. Javits, Jacob K. "The Banker's Role in Slum Housing and Rehabilitation." *Mortgage Banker*, June 1967, pp. 6-8+.

2921. Johnson, Philip M. "Rehabilitation Feasibility Studies in Federally-Assisted Areas." *Appraisal Journal*, April 1966, pp. 183-195.

2922. Kelley, Edward N. "Big Business in Urban Rehabilitation." *Journal of Property Management*, March-April 1968, pp. 68-74.

2923. Kenower, J. *MICAH: A Case Study in Housing Rehabilitation through Non-Profit Sponsorship*. Providence, R.I.: Rhode Island Department of Community Affairs, 1969. 93pp.

2924. Keyes, Langley C., Jr. *The Boston Rehabilitation Program: An Independent Analysis.* Cambridge, Mass.: Joint Center for Urban Studies of M.I.T. and Harvard University, 1970. 173pp.

2925. Keyes, Langley C., Jr. *The Rehabilitation Planning Game: A Study in the Diversity of Neighborhoods.* Cambridge, Mass.: M.I.T. Press, 1969.

2926. Kristof, Frank. *A Large Scale Residential Rehabilitation Program for New York City.* New York: New York City Housing and Development Administration, 1967 (Report no. 14).

2927. Levin, Melvin (ed.) *Innovations in Housing Rehabilitation.* Boston: Boston University Urban Institute, 1969 (Monograph no. 2).

2928. Loshbough, Bernard L. "Pittsburgh Renovates 22 Houses in Aging Neighborhoods to Demonstrate Effectiveness of Combined Private Enterprise and Government as a Rehabilitation Team." *Journal of Housing*, no. 4, 1967, pp. 204-210.

2929. Loshbough, Bernard E. "Rehabilitation of Housing: Federal Programs and Private Enterprise." *Law and Contemporary Problems*, Summer 1967, pp. 416-438.

2930. McFarland, M. Carter. "Residential Rehabilitation." In *Essays in Urban Land Economics.* Los Angeles, Calif.: Real Estate Research Program, University of California, 1966, pp. 108-142.

2931. McFarland, Carter M. and Walter K. Vinrett (ed.). *Residential Rehabilitation.* Minneapolis, Minn.: School of Architecture, University of Minnesota, 1966. 331pp.

2932. Martin, I. Maxmilian. "Rowhouse Rejuvenation." *Journal of Property Management*, September/October 1967, pp. 204-205.

2933. Montero, Frank C. "Social Aspects of Rehabilitation." *Building Research*, January-March 1968, pp. 17-21.

2834. Nash, William Wray, Jr. *A Survey of Housing Rehabilitation Practices and Their Implications for Urban Renewal.* Ann Arbor, Mich.: University Microfilms, 1961 (Ph.D. dissertation, University of Pennsylvania, 1961) 317pp. (order no. 61-2051)

2935. Nellum, A. L. and Associates. *Manpower and Rebuilding: A Study of Six Manpower Development and Training Programs Operating in Conjunction with Rehabilitation and Construction of Housing.* Washington, D.C., 1969. 245pp.

2936. "New Experiment in Low Cost Rehab: Can This Be Done to Slums for $12 a Square Foot?" *House and Home*, June 1967, pp. 62-63.

2937. "A New Kind of Team—Three Trade Associations, a Non Profit Citizen's Group, and HUD—Combine to Rehabilitate Slums." *Architectural Record*, January 1967, pp. 142-149.

2938. New York (City) Community Renewal Program. *Between Promise and Performance, A Proposed Ten-Year Program of Community Renewal in New York City*. New York, 1968. 162pp.

2939. New York (City) Housing and Redevelopment Board. *The Neighborhood Conservation Program*. New York, 1966. 183pp.

2940. New York (State) Temporary State Housing Rent Commission. *Prospects for Rehabilitation; A Demonstration Study of Housing in Morningside Heights, New York City*. New York, 1960. 114pp.

2941. "New York's Housing: Ring in the Old." *First National City Bank of NY Monthly Economic Letter*, August 1971, pp. 13-15.

2942. Niebanck, Paul L. and John B. Pope. *Residential Rehabilitation: The Pitfalls of Non-profit Sponsorship*. Philadelphia, Pa.: Institute for Environmental Studies, University of Pennsylvania, 1968. 128pp.

2943. Osgood, H. N. and A. H. Zwerner. "Rehabilitation and Conservation." *Law and Contemporary Problems*, Fall 1960, pp. 705-731.

2944. "The Problem: Slum Housing Breeds Men Without Skills. A Solution: Slum Rehab Gives Jobless Men a Trade." *House and Home*, June 1968, pp. 76-81.

2945. Rams, Edwin M. *Rehabilitation in Urban Renewal Areas: A Real Estate Viewpoint*. Washington, D.C.: Urban Research Associates, 1965.

2946. Rams, Edwin M. "Residential Rehabilitation-Value Concepts and Valuations." *Residential Appraiser*, June 1962, pp. 7-14.

2947. "A Realistic Look at Rehab." *Practical Builder*, February 1967, pp. 70-81.

2948. "Rehab Housing: The Role of S & L's." *Federal Home Loan Bank Board Journal*, August 1971, pp. 26-31.

2949. "Rehabilitation Projects and Middle and Low Income Housing: A Panel Discussion (Aronsohn, Silbert, Berman, Dukess, Paschow)." *New York University Institute of Federal Taxation*, 1971, pp. 1159+.

2950. "Renewal without the Bulldozer: Novel Experiment May Pave the Way for Rehabilitating Slum Dwellings without Tearing Them Down—by Renovating the Core and Dropping in Prefab Kitchens and Baths." *Business Week*, December 19, 1966, pp. 173-174.

2951. Robinson, M. J. "Urban Rehab: Are the Profits Worth the Risk?" *House and Home*, November 1972, pp. 68-72.

2952. "St. Louis Cooperates on Rehab Program." *Engineering News Record*, January 16, 1969. pp. 57-58.

2953. Schaaf, A. H. "Economic Feasibility Analysis for Urban Renewal Housing Rehabilitation." *Journal of the American Institute of Planners*, November 1969, pp. 399-404.

2954. Schaaf, A. H. "The Government Isn't Doing Enough for Rehabilitated Housing." *Real Estate Review*, Fall 1971, pp. 28-31.

2955. Schaaf, A. H. "The Potential of Subsidized Housing Rehabilitation." In *American Real Estate and Urban Economics Association, Proceedings, Vol. V, 1970*, pp. 105-116.

2956. Slayton, William L. "Rehabilitation Potential Probe for Urban Renewal Public Housing." *Journal of Housing*, December 1965, pp. 594-599.

2957. "Small Remodeler Can Make Urban Rehab Work." *House and Home*, September 1968, pp. 114-115.

2958. The South End Urban Renewal Committee. *Prospects for Rehabilitation*. Boston, Mass.: Boston Redevelopment Authority. 9pp.

2959. Stanford Research Institute. *A Capital Improvement Program for Rehabilitation of Three Public Multifamily Housing Projects and an Analysis of Alternative Future Prospects for the Housing Authority*. Prepared for the Housing Authority of the City of Oakland. Menlo Park, Calif., 1969. 228pp.

2960. Starr, Roger. "Old Building and Low-Income Rents and Profit-seeking Rehabilitation." *Journal of Housing*, January 1967, pp. 28-32.

2961. Starr, Roger. "A Private Venture into Slum Building Rehabilitation." *Appraisal Journal*, July 1967, pp. 341-347.

2962. U.S. Department of Housing and Urban Development. *Cost and Time Associated with Tenement Rehabilitation in Manhattan, New York City*. Washington, D.C., 1968. 79pp.

2963. U.S. Department of Housing and Urban Development. *Multi-family Rehabilitation Processing Guide, A HUD Handbook*. Washington, D.C., January 1969. 35+pp.

2964. U.S. Department of Housing and Urban Development. *Neighborhood Conservation and Property Rehabilitation . . . . Bibliography*. Washington, D.C., 1969. 78pp.

2965. U.S. Department of Housing and Urban Development. *Rehabilitation Guide for Residential Properties*. Washington, D.C., January 1968. 58pp.

2966. U.S. Department of Housing and Urban Development. *Rehabilitation Programs. A Report to the Subcommittee on Housing and Urban Affairs of the Committee on Banking and Currency, United States Senate*. Washington, D.C.: Government Printing Office, 1967. 52pp.

2967. U.S. General Accounting Office. *Improvements Needed in the Management of the Urban Renewal Rehabilitation Program. . . .* Washington, D.C., 1969. 46pp.

2968. U.S. General Accounting Office. *Problems in the Program for Rehabilitating Housing to Provide Homes for Low-income Families in Philadelphia, Pa.* Washington, D.C., 1971. 64pp.

2969. United States Gypsum Company. *Lower Income Home Ownerships Through Urban Rehabilitation, A New Venture for Private Business*. Buffalo, N.Y., 1969. 22pp.

2970. "Urban Fix-up: A Neglected Market Beckons the Builder." *House & Home*, August 1965, pp. 78-87.

2971. Urban League of Rhode Island. *A Study of the Resource Capabilities for Rehabilitation and Preferences of the Families in the Lippett Hill Rehabilitation Area in Providence, Rhode Island, 1960-61*. Providence, R.I., 1962. 124pp.

2972. Urban Planning Aid, Inc. *Evaluation of the Boston Rehabilitation Program*. Cambridge, Mass., 1969, 72pp.

2973. Warren, J. Michael. "Conservation and Rehabilitation of Housing: An Idea Approaches Adolescence." *Michigan Law Review*, March 1965, pp. 892-912.

2974. Weinstein, Jerome I. "Rehabilitation Success Depends on Solving Problems of Property Acquisition." *Journal of Housing*, May 1970, pp. 241-243.

2975. Weinstein, Jerome I. "Rehabilitation up to 'New Again' Standards." *Journal of Housing*, September 1968, pp. 471-473.

2976. Whittlesey, Robert. *The South End Row House and Its Rehabilitation for Low-income Residents*. Boston, Mass.: South End Community Development, Inc., 1969.

See also: 1104, 1595, 2135, 2252.

b. Tax Incentives

2977. Belin, D. W. "Real Estate Rehabilitation: A New Tax Incentive: The Tax Rules." *New York University Institute on Federal Taxation*, 1971, pp. 1055+.

2978. Frosh, Lane and Edson. *Utilization of Tax Incentives by Non-Profit Organizations to Foster Rehabilitation of Low and Moderate Income Housing. Report to U.S. Department of Housing and Urban Development*. Prepared by Frosh, Lane and Edson as consultants to Arthur D. Little, Inc. Washington, D.C., 1972. 122pp.

2797. Heinberg, John D. and Emil M. Sunley, Jr. "Tax Incentives for Rehabilitating Rental Housing." Paper presented at the American Real Estate and Urban Economics Association Conference, 1972.

2980. Meir, D. Tax Shelters and Real Estate: The Rehabilitation of Low Income Housing. *Suffolk University Law Review*, Fall 1972, pp. 1+.

2981. Sunley, Emil, Jr. "Tax Incentive for the Rehabilitation of Housing." *Appraisal Journal*, July 1971, pp. 381-394. Also in George Sternlieb and Lynne B. Sagalyn (eds.). *Housing: 1970-1971; An AMS Anthology*. New York: AMS Press, pp. 555-569.

2982. "Value of Tax Incentives as a Means of Encouraging the Rehabilitation of Low-Income Housing." *University of Cincinnati Law Review*, Vol. 41, 1972, pp. 151+.

2983. Vanderzell, John H. *The Role of Local Governments in Encouraging Housing Rehabilitation and Conservation through Economic Incentives*. Harrisburg, Pa.: Department of Internal Affairs, 1960. 43pp.

2984. Venning, Robert S. "Accelerated Depreciation for Housing Rehabilitation." *Yale Law Journal*, April 1970, pp. 961-972.

## 11. RELOCATION

### a. General

2985. Adkins, William G. and Frank F. Eichman, Jr. *Consequences of Displacement by Right of Way to 100 Home Owners, Dallas, Texas; A Report to the Texas Highway Dept. and to the Bureau of Public Roads, U.S. Dept. of Commerce*. College Station, Texas: Texas Transportation Institute, A. & M. College of Texas, 1961. 24pp.

2986. Baltimore Urban Renewal and Housing Agency. Research Division. *Ten Years of Relocation Experience in Baltimore, Maryland*. Baltimore, June 1961.

2987. Baltimore, Maryland, Urban Renewal and Housing Agency. *Displacement and Relocation—Past and Future*. Baltimore, March 1965.

2988. Bates, Stephen E. "Mobile Homes: East Chicago, Indiana Uses Them Successfully for Temporary Relocation." *Journal of Housing*, March 1971, pp. 131-133.

2989. Bourne, L. S. "Location Factors in the Redevelopment Process: A Model of Residential Change." *Land Economics*, May 1969, pp. 183-193.

2990. Cagle, T. and I. Deutscher. "Housing Aspirations and Housing Achievement: The Relocation of Poor Families." *Social Problems*, Fall 1970, pp. 243-256.

2991. Collins, John B. "Relocation of Negroes Displaced by Urban Renewal, with Emphasis on the Philadelphia Experience." Unpublished Master's thesis, Wharton School, University of Pennsylvania, 1961.

2992. Community Service Society of New York. Department of Public Affairs. *A Demonstration Project in Relocation: Report of the Committee on Family and Child Welfare and the Committee on Housing and Urban Development*. New York, April 1962. 59pp.

2993. Davis, F. James. "The Effects of a Freeway Displacement on Racial Housing Segregation in a Northern City." *Phylon*, Fall 1965, pp. 209-215.

2994. Doherty, Richard M. "The Growing Problem of Relocation." *Real Estate Appraiser*, February 1963, pp. 20-25.

2995. Downs, Anthony. "Losses Imposed on Urban Households by Uncompensated Highway and Renewal Costs." In Anthony Downs. *Urban Problems and Prospects*. Chicago, Ill.: Markham, 1970, pp. 192-227.

2996. Ellithorpe, Vera May. *The Process of Relocation: Factors Affecting Housing Choice*. Ann Arbor, Mich.: University Microfilms, 1964 (Ph.D. dissertation, The Ohio State University, 1963). 225 pp. (order no. 64-7007)

2997. Fried, Marc. "Function of the Working-Class Community in Modern Urban Society: Implications for Forced Relocation." *Journal of the American Institute of Planners*, March 1967, pp. 90-103.

2998. Gorland, Emanuel. "Relocation Adjustment Payments." *Journal of Housing*, no. 10, 1967, pp. 564-567.

2999. Groberg, Robert P. *Centralized Relocation: A New Municipal Service*. Washington, D.C.: National Association of Housing and Redevelopment Officials, 1969. 208pp.

3000. Groberg, Robert P. *The Moving Picture: A Survey of Centralized Municipal Relocation Services*. Washington, D.C.: National Association of Housing and Redevelopment Officials, 1968.

3001. Harrington, Michael. "Housing and the Public Sector." *Architectural Forum*, May 1971, pp. 32-33.

3002. Harrison, Joseph Wellman. *Relocation Costs and Resource Allocation*. Ann Arbor, Mich.: University Microfilms, 1964 (Ph.D. dissertation, University of Virginia, 1964). 134pp. (order no. 64-12,387)

3003. Hartman, Chester. "The Housing of Relocated Families." *Journal of the American Institute of Planners*, November 1964, pp. 266-286. Comment (Edward J. Logue), with rejoinder, November 1965, pp. 338-344.

3004. Hartman, Chester. "The Limitations of Public Housing: Relocation Choices in a Working-Class Community." *Journal of the American Institute of Planners*, February 1963, pp. 40-47.

3005. Hartman, Chester. "The Politics of Housing: Displaced Persons." *Society*, July/August 1972, pp. 53-65.

3006. House, Patricia A. "Relocation of Families Displaced by Expressway Development: Milwaukee Case Study." *Land Economics*, February 1970, pp. 75-78.

3007. Kaluzny, Richard L. *Patterns of Residential Relocation: Implications for Public Policy*. Chapel Hill, N.C.: Center for Urban and Regional Studies, University of North Carolina, 1968 (Environment Policies and Urban Development Thesis Series no. 11). 75pp.

3008. Levin, J. A. "Social Status Ambiguity and Residential Relocation." Unpublished dissertation, Harvard University, 1966.

3009. Lichfield, Nathaniel. "Relocation: The Impact on Welfare Housing." *Journal of the American Institute of Planners*, August 1961, pp. 199-203.

3010. Management Services Associates, Inc., New York. *A Report Concerning Certain Aspects of Relocation.* Prepared for the Office of Development Coordinator and the Redevelopment Authority of the City of Philadelphia. New York, 1961. 62pp.

3011. Mao, James C. T. "Relocation and Housing Welfare: A Case Study." *Land Economics*, November 1965, pp. 365-370.

3012. Massachusetts Legislative Research Bureau. *Report Relative to Relocation Assistance for Persons and Firms Displaced by Public Action, January 8, 1962.* Boston, Mass., 1962. 42pp.

3013. Meltzer (Jack) Associates and Chicago Community Renewal Program. *Relocation in Chicago.* Chicago, Ill.: Community Renewal Program, 1964. 85pp.

3014. Mermin, Alvin A. *Relocating Families; the New Haven Experience, 1956 to 1966.* Washington, D.C.: National Association of Housing and Redevelopment Officials, 1970. 138pp.

3015. Millspaugh, M. "Problems and Opportunities of Relocation." *Law and Contemporary Problems*, Winter 1961, pp. 6-36.

3016. Monson, Astrid. "Urban Renewal Relocation: A Plea for Constructive Criticism." *Pratt Planning Papers*, October 1965, pp. 5-12.

3017. Nann, Richard Chun. *Urban Renewal and Relocation of Chinese Community Families.* Ann Arbor, Mich.: University Microfilms, 1971 (D.S.W. dissertation, University of California at Berkeley, 1970). 132pp. (order no. 71-20,757)

3018. Niebanck, Paul L. with Mark R. Yessian. *Relocation in Urban Planning; From Obstacle to Opportunity.* Philadelphia, Pa.: University of Pennsylvania Press, 1968. 123pp.

3019. Parish, Nathaniel J. "Policy and Operational Improvements in the Residential Relocation Process." *Pratt Planning Papers*, October 1965, pp. 13-20.

3020. Philadelphia Housing Association. *Meeting the Needs of Displaced Households: Recommendations Based on Analysis of the Community Renewal Program's Studies of Relocation in Philadelphia.* Philadelphia, Penn., April 1966. 11pp.

3021. Reynolds, Harry W., Jr. "Population Displacement in Urban Renewal." *American Journal of Economics and Sociology*, January 1963, pp. 113-128.

3022. Rudolph, Jacquiline Simone. *Residential Relocation: a Case Study of the Consequences of Urban Planned Change.* Ann Arbor, Mich.: University Microfilms, 1967. (Ph.D. dissertation, Purdue University, 1966). 242pp. (order no. 67-5493)

3023. Seferi, Mania Louise. *Resident Participation in Relocation Planning: The Case of the Denver Neighborhood of Auroria.* Ann Arbor, Mich.: University Microfilms, 1971 (Ph.D. dissertation, University of Colorado, 1970). 329pp. (order no. 71-5298)

3024. Short, James L. "Relocation: A Myth or Reality?" *Urban Affairs Quarterly*, September 1967, pp. 62-74.

3025. "Six Problems of Relocation Point to Need for Fresh Look, Recasting of Role." *Journal of Housing*, July 1964, pp. 308-310.

3026. "Skid Row: Gives Renewalists Rough, Tough Relocation Problems." *Journal of Housing*, August/September 1961, pp. 327-336.

3027. Smith, Wallace F. "The Relocation Dilemma." *Appraisal Journal*, July 1969, pp. 424-432.

3028. Southern Illinois University, Edwardsville. Public Administration and Metropolitan Affairs Program. *Problems of Relocation in East St. Louis; The Lessons of Franklin Park and the Impending Highway 460 Relocation Issues.* Prepared for the city of East St. Louis. Edwardsville, 1966. 31pp.

3029. Thursz, Daniel. *Where Are They Now? A Study of the Impact of Relocation on Former Residents of Southwest Washington Who Were Served in an HWC Demonstration Project.* Washington, D.C.: Health and Welfare Council of the National Capital Area, November 1966. 148pp.

3030. United South End Settlements, Boston. *Castle Square Residential Relocation Program, Final Report.* Boston, Mass.: Boston Redevelopment Authority, 1964. 57pp.

3031. U.S. Advisory Commission on Intergovernmental Relations. *Relocation: Unequal Treatment of People and Businesses Displaced by Governments; A Commission Report.* Washington, D.C., 1965. 141pp.

3032. U.S. Commission on Civil Rights. Connecticut Advisory Committee. *Family Relocation under Urban Renewal in Connecticut; Problems and Proposals in a Typical Federal Government Program Involving Relocation; Report. . . .* Washington, D.C., 1963. 74pp.

3033. U.S. General Accounting Office. *Inadequate Policies and Practices Relating to the Relocation of Families from Urban Renewal Areas. . . .* Washington, D.C., 1964. 20pp.

3034. U.S. General Accounting Office. *Inadequate Relocation Assistance to Families Displaced from Certain Urban Renewal Projects in Kansas and Missouri. . . .* Washington, D.C., 1964. 17pp.

3035. U.S. General Accounting Office. *Review of Relocation Housing Programs for Small Homes as Administered by the Office of the Administrator and the Federal Housing Administration, Housing and Home Finance Agency, April 1960. . . .* Washington, D.C., 1961.

3036. U.S. Housing and Home Finance Agency. *The Housing of Relocated Families: Summary of a Bureau of the Census Survey of Families Recently Displaced from Urban Renewal Sites.* Washington, D.C., 1965. 15pp.

3037. U.S. Housing and Home Finance Agency. "The Housing of Relocated Families: Summary of a Census Bureau Survey." In James Q. Wilson (ed.). *Urban Renewal: The Record and the Controversy.* Cambridge, Mass.: MIT Press, 1966.

3038. U.S. Housing and Home Finance Agency. Office of the Administrator. Library. *Relocation in Urban Areas: A Selected List of Books and Articles, 1951-1961.* Washington, D.C., July 1961, 29pp.

3039. Watts, Lewis Gould. *Attitudes toward Moving of Middle-Income Negro Families Facing Urban Renewal.* Ann Arbor, Mich.: University Microfilms, 1964 (Ph.D. dissertation, Brandeis University, 1964). 231pp. (order no. 64-12,876)

3040. Watts, Lewis G. *et al. The Middle-income Negro Family Faces Urban Renewal.* Waltham, Mass.: Florence Heller Graduate School for Advanced Studies in Social Welfare, Brandeis University, 1964. 112pp.

b. Legislation and Legal Aspects

3041. *American Bar Association National Institute: Uniform Relocation Assistance and Land Acquisition Policies; Proceedings.* Chicago, Ill.: American Bar Association, 1972.

3042. Cahn, Edgar S. *et al. The Legal Lawbreakers: A Study of the Nonadministration of Federal Relocation Requirements*. Washington, D.C.: Citizens Advocate Center, 1970. 92pp.

3043. Christy, Lawrence C. and Peter W. Coogan. "Family Relocation in Urban Renewal." *Harvard Law Review*, February 1969, pp. 864-907.

3044. "Civil Rights—Urban Renewal—Displacees Have Standing to Object to Relocation Program's Failure to Meet Federal Standards, and Allegations of Unequal Satisfaction of the Standards State a Justiciable Equal Protection Claim—*Norwalk CORE v. Norwalk Redevelopment Agency. . . .*" *Harvard Law Review*, January 1969, pp. 691-697.

3045. Franklin, Herbert M. "Expanding Relocation Responsibilities of Local Renewal Agencies." *New York Law Forum*, Spring 1965, pp. 51-79.

3046. Gorland, Emanuel. "Relocation Inequities and Problems are Emerging as Result of 1970 Uniform Relocation Act." *Journal of Housing*, March 1972, pp. 137-138.

3047. Hartman, C. W. "Relocation: Illusory Promises and No Relief." *Virginia Law Review*, June 1971, pp. 745+.

3048. "Highway Relocation Planning and Early Judicial Review." *Harvard Journal on Legislation*, January 1970, pp. 179+.

3049. "Housing Act—Injunctive Relief for Persons Displaced by Urban Renewal Projects." *Ohio State Law Journal*, Summer 1969, pp. 616+.

3050. "Housing and Urban Renewal—Standing—Negro and Puerto Rican Citizens Displaced by Urban Renewal Program Have Standing to Enforce the Relocation Requirements of Section 105 (c) of the Housing Act and to Claim a Denial of Equal Protection of the Law in the Implementation of the Relocation Program." *Villanova Law Review*, Fall 1968, pp. 149+.

3051. "In the Path of Progress: Federal Highway Relocation Assurances." *Yale Law Journal*, December 1972, pp. 373-401.

3052. "Judicial Review of Displacee Relocation in Federal Urban Renewal Projects: A New Approach?" *Valparaiso University Law Review*, Spring 1969, pp. 258+.

3053. Levin, D. R. "Dramatic New Uniform Relocation Assistance and Land Acquisition Policies." *Planning, Zoning & Eminent Domain Institute, (Southwestern Legal Foundation)*, 1972, pp. 95+.

3054. Mandelker, D. R. "Model State Relocation Law." *Urban Law Annual 1971*. St. Louis, Mo.: School of Law, Washington University, 1971, pp. 117+.

3055. "Note and Comments: Judicial Review of Displacee Relocation in Urban Renewal." *Yale Law Journal*, April 1968. pp. 966-987.

3056. Pinsky, David E. "Relocation Payments in Urban Renewal: More Just Compensation." *New York Law Forum*, Spring 1965, pp. 80-102.

3057. "Protecting the Standing of Renewal Site Families to Seek Review of Community Relocation Planning." *Yale Law Journal*, May 1964, pp. 1080-1097.

3058. "Relocation, Accidental Inequalities, and the Equal Protection Doctrine." *University of Pennsylvania Law Review*, February 1969, pp. 579+.

3059. "Relocation: An Investigation into Relocation under the Federal-Aid Highway Program." *Columbia Journal of Law and Social Problems*, Summer 1971, pp. 466-501.

3060. "Relocation Assistance: An Open Door Policy to Equal Housing Opportunity." *Catholic University Law Review*, Spring 1972, pp. 639+.

3061. Roberts, N. A. "Homes, Roadbuilders and the Courts: Highway Relocation and Judicial Review of Administrative Action." *Southern California Law Review*, December 1972, pp. 51+.

3062. Snitzer, E. L. "Uniform Relocation Assistance and Real Property Acquisition Policies Act of 1970—A New Era." *Pennsylvania Bar Association Quarterly*, October 1971, pp. 114+.

3063. Tondro, T. J. "Urban Renewal Relocation: Problems of Enforcement of Conditions on Federal Grants to Local Agencies." *University of Pennsylvania Law Review*, December 1968, pp. 183-227.

3064. U.S. Congress. House. Committee on Public Works. *Proposed Amendments to the Uniform Relocation Assistance and Real Property Acquisitions Policies Act of 1970. Hearings before the Subcommittee on Roads. . . .* Washington, D.C.: Government Printing Office. 1972.

3065. U.S. Congress. House. Committee on Public Works. *Uniform Relocation Assistance and Land Acquisition Policy. Hearings. . . .* Washington, D.C.: Government Printing Office, 1968. 615pp.

3066. U.S. Congress. House. Committee on Public Works. *Uniform Relocations Assistance and Land Acquisition Policies—1970. Hearings. . . .* Washington, D.C.: Government Printing Office, 1970. 1118pp.

3067. U.S. Congress. Senate. Committee on Government Operations. Subcommittee on Intergovernmental Relations. *Amending the Uniform Relocation Act. Hearing, Ninety-second Congress, Second Session, on S. 1819 . . . February 24, 1972*. Washington, D.C.: Government Printing Office, 1972. 2 vols.

3068. U.S. Congress. Senate. Committee on Government Operations. *Uniform Relocation Assistance and Land Acquisition Policies Act of 1969. Hearings. . . .* Washington, D.C.: Government Printing Office, 1969. 306pp.

3069. "Urban Law–Judicial Review–Urban Renewal Displaces Have Standing to Contest Relocation Standards." *New York University Law Review*, December 1968, pp. 1257+.

3070. "Urban Law–Urban Renewal–Relocation and Demolition May Be Enjoined until Public Agency Demonstrates It Is Ready, Willing and Able to Proceed with the Urban Renewal Project–Talbot vs. Romney." *New York University Law Review*, March 1971, pp. 199-208.

3071. "Urban Renewal–Relocation of Displacees–Removing Procedural Barriers to Obtaining 'A Decent Home and Suitable Living Environment.' " *De Paul Law Review*, Summer 1969, pp. 885+.

See also: 1330.

c. Social/Psychological Consequences

3072. Back, Kurt W. *Slums, Projects, and People; Social Psychological Problems of Relocation in Puerto Rico*. Durham, N.C.: Duke University Press, 1962. 123pp.

3073. Fried, Marc. "Grieving for a Lost Home: Psychological Costs of Relocation." In James Q. Wilson (ed.). *Urban Renewal: The Record and the Controversy*. Cambridge, Mass.: MIT Press, 1966, pp. 359-379.

3074. Harrington, M. "Resettlement and Self-Image." *Human Relations*, May 1965, pp. 115-137.

3075. Miller, Paul Eldor. *Forced Relocation in Urban Renewal: A Sociological Analysis*. Ann Arbor, Mich.: University Microfilms, 1971 (Ph.D. dissertation, State University of New York at Buffalo, 1970). 291pp. (order no. 71-7196)

3076. Montgomery, D. S. "Relocation and Its Impact on Families." *Social Casework*, October 1960, pp. 402-407.

3077. Moore, J. E. "Relocation of People: A Challenging Aspect of Urban Renewal and Redevelopment." *Social Casework*, December 1966, pp. 657-662.

See also: 3079, 3080, 3082-3084.

d. The Elderly and Relocation

3078. Brudney, Juliet F. *The Janus Project; Advocacy and Service for the Elderly Relocatee.* Philadelphia: Institute for Environmental Studies, University of Pennsylvania, 1969. 126pp.

3079. Goldstein, Sidney. *Residential Displacement and Resettlement of the Aged; A Study of Problems of Rehousing Aged Residents Displaced by Freeway Construction in Downtown Providence*. Providence, R.I.: Rhode Island Division on Aging, 1960. 73pp.

3080. Jackson, Jacquelyn Johnson. "Social Impacts of Housing Relocation upon Urban Low-income Black Aged." *Gerontologist*, Pt. 1 Spring 1972, pp. 32-37.

3081. Niebanck, Paul Lowance. *The Relocation of Elderly Persons: Planning for the Residents of Older Urban Areas*. Ann Arbor, Mich.: University Microfilms, 1967. (Ph.D. dissertation, University of Pennsylvania, 1966). 458pp. (order no. 67-7867)

3082. Niebanck, Paul L. with John B. Pope. *The Elderly in Older Urban Areas; Problems of Adaptation and the Effects of Relocation*. Philadelphia, Pa.: Institute for Environmental Studies, University of Pennsylvania, 1965. 174pp.

3083. Pennsylvania University. Institute for Urban Studies. *Essays on the Problems Faced in the Relocation of Elderly Persons*. Philadelphia, Pa., 1964. 137pp. (Prepared in cooperation with the National Association of Housing and Redevelopment Officials.)

3084. U.S. Congress. Senate. Special Committee on Aging. Subcommittee on Involuntary Relocation of the Elderly. *Relocation of Elderly People: Hearings: Pts. 1-6, October 22-December 7, 1962*. Washington, D.C.: Government Printing Office, 1963. 546pp.

12. RENT SUPPLEMENTS

3085. Aronov, Edward and Hamilton Smith. "Large Families, Low Incomes, Leasing." *Journal of Housing*, October 1965, pp. 482-487.

3086. Cogen, Joel, and Kathryn Feidelson. "Rental Assistance for Large Families: an Interim Report; New Haven's Low-income Housing Demonstration." *Pratt Planning Papers*, June 1964, pp. 9-20.

3087. Community Service Society of New York. Department of Public Affairs. Committee on Housing and Urban Development. *Rent Subsidies: Recommended Guidelines*. New York, November 1964. 11pp.

3088. "Controversial Urban Programs Starting Slowly: On Model Cities (Program), Rent Supplements." *Congressional Quarterly Weekly Report*, May 31, 1968, pp. 1271-1275.

3089. "Controversy over the Administration's Rent Subsidy Program." *Congressional Digest*, January 1966, pp. 1-32.

3090. Dasso, Jerome. "An Evaluation of Rent Supplements." *Land Economics*, November 1968, pp. 441-449.

3091. Donahue, Wilma. "Rent Supplement Experiment Tests Mingling Low-income, Moderate-income, Elderly." *Journal of Housing*, October 1965, pp. 477-481.

3092. Edgley, Charles, W.G. Steglich and Walter J. Cartwright. "Rent Subsidy and Housing Satisfaction: The Case of Urban Renewal in Lubbock, Texas." *American Journal of Economics and Sociology*, April 1968, pp. 113-123.

3093. Fielding, Byron. "How Useful Are Rent Supplements in Meeting Low-income Housing Needs? A Progress Report on a Program That May Be Facing Its Biggest Crisis Since It Was Created Four Years Ago." *Journal of Housing*, January 1969, pp. 12-26.

3094. Gallagher, J.R. and J.J. O'Donnell. *Non-Profit Housing Rent Supplement Program under Section 221(d)(3)*. Washington, D.C.: Urban America, Inc., 1969. 327pp.

3095. "Housing Bill Passed with Modified Rent Subsidy Plan." *Congressional Quarterly Weekly Report*. July 2, 1965, pp. 1269-1272.

3096. Kinney, E. "The Rent Supplement Program: Its Operations and the Alternatives." *Case Western Reserve Law Review*, August 1969, pp. 776+.

3097. Krier, J.E. "Rent Supplement Program of 1965: Out of the Ghetto, into the . . . ?" *Stanford Law Review*, February 1967, pp. 555+.

3098. Lawson, Simpson. "Housing: Its 'Experimental' Phase Nearly Over, the Rent Supplement Program Starts to Show the Effects of Its Arduous Birth." *City*, January 1968, pp. 21-31.

3099. National Capital Housing Authority. *Report on Large Family-Rent Subsidy Demonstration Program*. Washington, D.C., 1966, 79pp.

3100. Reeves, Marilyn Langford. *Philadelphia's Rent Subsidy Program: a Local Approach Using Private Market Housing.* Ithaca, N.Y.: Division of Urban Studies, Center for Housing and Environmental Studies, Cornell University, 1969. 102pp.

3101. Smith, Walter L. "The Implementation of the Rent Supplement Program—a Staff View." *Law and Contemporary Problems*, Summer 1967, pp. 482-489.

3102. Tilly, Charles and Joe Feagin. "Boston's Experiment with Rent Subsidies." *Journal of the American Institute of Planners*, September 1970, pp. 323-329. Also in George Sternlieb and Lynne B. Sagalyn (eds.). *Housing: 1970-1971; An AMS Anthology.* New York: AMS Press, 1971, pp. 570-576.

3103. U.S. Congress. House. Committee on Banking and Currency. *Correction of Misleading and False Statements Concerning Rent Supplement Program Made in Minority Report on the Housing and Urban Development Act of 1965, H.R. 7984. . . .* Washington, D.C.: Government Printing Office, 1965. 15pp.

3104. U.S. Congress. Senate. Special Committee on Aging. Subcommittee on Housing for the Elderly. *Rent Supplement Assistance to the Elderly: Hearing, July 11, 1967.* Washington, D.C.: Government Printing Office, 1967. 59pp.

3105. U.S. Department of Housing and Urban Development. Federal Housing Administration. *Rent Supplement Program: Public Information Guide and Instruction Handbook.* Washington, D.C., May 1966.

3106. Welfeld, Irving. "Rent Supplements and the Subsidy Dilemma." *Law and Contemporary Problems*, Summer 1967, pp. 465-481. Also in Michael A. Stegman (ed.). *Housing and Economics: The American Dilemma.* Cambridge, Mass.: MIT Press, 1970, pp. 232-251.

## 13. URBAN RENEWAL

### a. General

Alonso, William. "The Historic and Structural Theories of Urban Form: Their Implications for Urban Renewal." *Land Economics*, May 1964, pp. 227-231.

3108. Atkins, R.S. and E.M. Krokosky. "Optimum Housing Allocation Models for Urban Areas." *ASCE Journal of the Urban Planning and Development Division*, April 1971, pp. 41-53.

3109. Bellush, Jewel and Murray Hausknecht. "Entrepreneurs and Urban Renewal." *Journal of the American Institute of Planners*, September 1966, pp. 289-297.

3110. Bellush, Jewel and Murray Hausknecht (eds.). *Urban Renewal: People, Politics, and Planning.* 1967. 542pp.

3111. Bloom, Max R. "Fiscal Productivity and the Pure Theory of Urban Renewal." *Land Economics*, February 1962, pp. 134-144.

3112. Brownfield, Lyman. "The Disposition Problem in Urban Renewal." *Law and Contemporary Problems*, Autumn 1960, pp. 732-776.

3113. Brownfield, Lyman and Marian S. Rosen. "Leasing in the Disposition of Urban Renewal Land." *Law and Contemporary Problems*, Winter 1961, pp. 37-48.

3114. Clawson, Marion, "Urban Renewal in 2000." *Journal of the American Institute of Planners*, May 1968, pp. 173-179.

3115. Cox, Lawrence M. *Urban Renewal Experience in the United States.* Washington, D.C.: U.S. Department of Housing and Urban Development, February 1971. 16pp.

3116. Davis, Otto A. "A Pure Theory of Urban Renewal." *Land Economics*, May 1960, pp. 220-226. Comment (Morton J. Schussheim), November 1960, pp. 395-396; Comment (Nathaniel Lichfield), February 1963, pp. 99-103; "Urban Renewal—A Reply to Two Critics" (Davis), February 1963, pp. 103-108.

3117. Doxiadis, C.A. *Urban Renewal and the Future of the American City*. Chicago: Public Administration Service, 1966.

3118. Duggar, George C. "The Relation of Local Government Structure to Urban Renewal." *Law and Contemporary Problems.* Winter 1961, pp. 49-69.

3119. Fisher, H. Benjamin. *The Renewal of Urban Land: Process, Decisions, and Simulation.* Chapel Hill, N.C.: Center for Urban and Regional Studies, University of North Carolina, 1967 (Environment Policies and Urban Development Thesis Series no. 7). 162pp.

3120. Fox, Clara. *A Vertical Neighborhood in an Urban Renewal Community; Report of the Goddard Tower Cooperative.* New York: Goddard-Riverside Community Center, 1969. 84pp.

3121. Friedly, Philip H. "Welfare Indicators for Public Facility Investments in Urban Renewal Areas." *Socio-Economic Planning Sciences*, December 1969, pp. 291-314.

3122. Galanis, John. "Urban Blight Turns to Beauty under Milwaukee Housing Plan." *Federal Home Loan Bank Board Journal*, March 1970, pp. 6-10.

3123. Gans, Herbert J. *The Urban Villagers: Group and Class in the Life of Italian-Americans.* New York: Free Press, 1963, Chapters 13 and 14.

3124. Gershen, Alvin E. "Urban Renewal and Moderate Income Housing: A New Dimension." *Jersey Plans*, Winter 1966, pp. 56-62.

3125. Goodfriend, Stanley L. "Carl Sandburg Village: The Study of an Urban Renewal Project." *Journal of Property Management.* Winter 1963, pp. 68-77.

3126. Greer, Scott. *Urban Renewal and American Cities.* Indianapolis, Ind.: Bobbs-Merrill, 1965. 201pp.

3127. Harris, William W. "Feasibility Studies in Urban Renewal Projects." *Real Estate Appraiser*, October 1967, pp. 21-29.

3128. Hommann, Mary. *Wooster Square Design: A Report on the Background, Experience, and Design Procedures in Redevelopment and Rehabilitation in an Urban Renewal Project.* New Haven, Conn.: New Haven Redevelopment Agency, 1965. 191pp.

3129. Kingsley, G. Thomas. "The Design Process in Urban Renewal: An Analysis of the San Francisco Experience." Unpublished M.C.P. thesis, University of California, 1963.

3130. Kovak, Richard M. "Urban Renewal Controversies." *Public Administration Review*, July/Aug. 1972, pp. 359-372.

3131. Landauer Associates, Inc. *Market and Land Use Study: The Farm Urban Renewal Project, Brookline, Massachusetts.* Brookline, Mass., 1964. 49pp.

3132. Lash, James. "Renewal: Area Problem: Housing Must Be Part of Metropolitan Planning with Private-Public Center for Market Analysis." *National Civic Review*, April 1962, pp. 200-205.

3133. Montgomery, Rober. "Improving the Design Process in Urban Renewal." *Journal of the American Institute of Planners*, February 1965, pp. 7-20.

3134. National Housing Center Library. *Urban Renewal: A Selected Annotated Bibliography*. Washington, D.C., 1965. 131pp. (Bibliography Series no. 8).

3135. New York (City) Planning Commission. Community Renewal Program. *New York City's Renewal Strategy, 1965.* New York, December 1965.

3136. New York (State) Executive Department. Division of Housing and Community Renewal. *Housing and Community Renewal in New York State, 1939-1964.* New York, 1965. 49pp.

3137. Philadelphia Housing Association. *Ends and Means of Urban Renewal, Papers from the Philadelphia Housing Association's Fiftieth Anniversary Forum.* Philadelphia, 1961. 102pp.

3138. Reynolds, H.W., Jr. "Local Government Structure in Urban Planning, Renewal, and Relocation." *Public Administration Review,* March 1964, pp. 14-20.

3139. Rothenberg, Jerome. "Urban Renewal Programs." In Robert Dorfman (ed.). *Measuring Benefits of Government Investments.* Washington, D.C.: The Brookings Institution, 1965, pp. 292-341. Also in Alfred N. Page and Warren R. Seyfried (eds.). *Urban Analysis: Readings in Housing and Urban Development.* Glenview, Ill.: Scott, Foresman, 1970, pp. 361-386.

3140. Rutledge, Edward and William R. Valentine. "Urban Renewal Planning for Balanced Communities." *Journal of Intergroup Relations,* Winter 1960-1961, pp. 27-36.

3141. Silvers, A.H. "Urban Renewal and Black Power." *American Behavioral Scientist,* March 1969, pp. 43-46.

3142. Slayton, W.L. "Policies for Urban Renewal in the United States." *Appraisal Journal,* October 1969, pp. 587-595.

3143. Slayton, William L. "Potential of Renewal for Reducing Racial Discrimination Analyzed." *Journal of Housing,* June 1964, pp. 256-260.

3144. Slayton, William L. "State and Local Incentives and Techniques for Urban Renewal." *Law and Contemporary Problems,* Autumn 1960, pp. 793-812.

3145. Steger, Wilbur A. "Review of Analytic Techniques for the CRP." *Journal of the American Institute of Planners,* May 1965, pp. 166-172.

3146. Swanson, Bert E. "Public Efforts to Redevelop American Cities." *American Journal of Economics and Sociology,* July 1966, pp. 243-254 and October 1966, pp. 365-367.

3147. Vitullo-Martin, J. "Liberals and the Myths of Urban Renewal." *Public Policy,* Spring 1971, pp. 355-372.

3148. U.S. Commission on Civil Rights. Iowa State Advisory Committee. *Urban Renewal Programs and Their Effects on Racial Minority Group Housing in Three Iowa Cities; Report of the Iowa State Advisory Committee....* n.p., 1964. 23pp.

3149. U.S. Congress. House. Committee on Public Works. Select Subcommittee on Real Property Acquisition. *Study of Compensation and Assistance for Persons Affected by Real Property Acquisition in Federal and Federally Assisted Programs.* Washington, D.C.: Government Printing Office, 1965. 522pp.

3150. U.S. President's Task Force on Urban Renewal. *Urban Renewal: One Tool Among Many.* Washington, D.C., 1970. 15pp.

3151. Walker and Murray Associates, Inc. *Washington Square West Unit II Urban Renewal Area; Technical Report.* Philadelphia, Pa., 1964. 85pp.

3152. Walker, David M. "A New Pattern for Urban Renewal." *Law and Contemporary Problems*, Autumn 1960, pp. 633-634.

3153. Weaver, Robert C. "Current Trends in Urban Renewal." *Land Economics*, November 1963, pp. 325-341.

3154. Weicher, John C. *Urban Renewal.* Washington, D.C.: American Enterprise Institute for Public Policy Research, 1972. 96pp.

3155. Weismantel, William. "Collision of Urban Renewal with Zoning: The Boston Experience 1950-1967." Unpublished Ph.D. dissertation, Harvard University, 1969.

3156. Whelan, Robert Kendall. *Decision-making Processes and Program Goals in Urban Renewal: The Cases of Gay Street One and Inner Harbor One in Baltimore, Maryland.* Ann Arbor, Mich.: University Microfilms, 1962 (Ph.D. dissertation, University of Maryland, 1971). 262pp. (order no. 72-1696).

3157. Wilson, James Q. (ed.). *Urban Renewal: The Record and the Controversy.* Cambridge, Mass.: MIT Press. 1966.

3158. Wingo, Lowdon, Jr. "Urban Renewal: A Strategy for Information and Analysis." *Journal of the American Institute of Planners*, May 1966, pp. 143-154.

3159. Wolf, Eleanor Paperno, *et. al. Change and Renewal in an Urban Community; Five Case Studies of Detroit.* New York: Praeger, 1969. 574pp.

3160. Wolff, Carole Ann Ellis. *Urban Renewal: Patterns of Population and Housing Change.* Ann Arbor, Mich.: University Microfilms, 1967 (Ph.D. dissertation, Michigan State University, 1967). 225pp. (order no. 67-10,561).

3161. Women's City Club of New York, Inc. *When the City Takes Over: A Study of Building Maintenance and Relocation in the Bellevue South Urban Renewal Area.* New York, June 1967. 38pp.

See also: 670, 967, 1030, 3532, 3550, 3563, 3565, 3587.

b. Economic Analyses

3162. Bailey, Martin J. "Note on the Economics of Residential Zoning and Urban Renewal." In Alfred N. Page and Warren R. Seyfried (eds.). *Urban Analysis: Readings in Housing and Urban Development.* Glenview, Ill.: Scott, Foresman, 1970, pp. 316-320. (Reprinted from *Land Economics*, August 1959, pp. 288-292.)

3163. Berger, David. "Current Problems Affecting Costs of Condemnation." *Law and Contemporary Problems*, Winter 1961, pp. 85-104.

3164. Bernstein, Samuel J. "Urban Residential Renewal Investments: A Policy Analysis Employing Linear Programming." *Socio-Economic Planning Sciences*, June 1972, pp. 251-262.

3165. Citizens' Housing and Planning Council of New York. *Tax Policies and Urban Renewal in New York City*. New York, 1960. 19+pp.

3166. Davis, Otto and Andrew Whinston. "The Economics of Urban Renewal." *Law and Contemporary Problems*, Winter 1961, pp. 105-118.

3167. Ford, Edward J., Jr. *Benefit-cost Analysis and Urban Renewal in the West End of Boston.* Ann Arbor, Mich.: University Microfilms, 1971 (Ph.D. dissertation, Boston College, 1971). 118pp. (order no. 71-22,158).

3168. Lichfield, Nathaniel. *Cost Benefit Analysis in Urban Redevelopment.* Berkeley, Calif.: Real Estate Research Probram, University of California, 1962.

3169. Mace, Ruth Lowens. *Costing Urban Development and Redevelopment; Selected Readings on Costs, Revenues, Cost-benefit and Cost-revenue Analysis, in Relation to Land Use.* Chapel Hill, N.C.: Institute of Government, University of North Carolina, rev. 1964. 21pp.

3170. Mao, James C.T. *Efficiency in Public Urban Renewal Expenditures through Capital Budgeting.* Berkeley, Calif.: Center for Real Estate and Urban Economics, University of California, 1965. 118pp.

3171. Mao, James C.T. "Efficiency in Public Urban Renewal Expenditures through Benefit-Cost Analysis." *Journal of the American Institute of Planners*, March 1966, pp. 95-107. Comment (Sho Maruyama) with rejoinder, September 1966, pp. 297-299.

3172. McDonough, Edward F. *A Cost-Benefit Analysis of a Hartford, Connecticut, Urban Renewal Project.* Ann Arbor, Mich.: University Microfilms, 1968 (Ph.D. dissertation, University of Massachusetts, 1968). 266pp. (order no. 68-14,586).

3173. Messner, Stephen D. *The Application of Benefit-Cost Analysis to Selected Urban Renewal Projects in Indianapolis, Indiana.* Ann Arbor, Mich.: University Microfilms, 1966 (D.B.A. dissertation, Indiana University, 1966). 375pp. (order no. 66-11,784).

3174. Messner, Stephen D. *A Benefit-cost Analysis of Urban Redevelopment: A Case Study of the Indianapolis Program.* Bloomington, Ind.: Bureau of Business Research, Indiana University, 1967. 115pp.

3175. Nourse, Hugh O. "The Economics of Urban Renewal." *Land Economics*, February 1966, pp. 65-74.

3176. Rapkin, Chester. *The Seaver-Townsend Urban Renewal Area; A Section of the Roxbury–North Dorchester General Neighborhood Renewal Plan Area; An Analysis of the Economic, Financial, and Community Factors That Will Influence the Feasibility of Residential Renewal.* Boston, Mass.: Boston Redevelopment Authority, 1962. 114pp.

3177. Ratcliff, Richard U. *Private Investment in Urban Redevelopment.* Berkeley, Calif.: Real Estate Research Program, University of California, 1961 (Research Report no. 17).

3178. Rothenberg, Jerome. *Economic Evaluation of Urban Renewal.* Washington, D.C.: The Brookings Institution, 1967. 277pp.

3179. Schaaf, A.H. *Economic Aspects of Urban Renewal: Theory, Policy and Area Analysis.* Berkeley, Calif.: Center for Real Estate and Urban Economics, University of California, 1960. 50pp.

3180. Schaaf, A.H. "Public Policies in Urban Renewal: An Economic Analysis of Justification and Effects." *Land Economics*, February 1964, pp. 67-78.

3181. Wagner, Peter. *Scope and Financing of Urban Renewal.* Washington, D.C.: National Planning Association, 1963. 78pp.

3182. Winnick, Louis. "Economic Questions in Urban Redevelopment." *American Economic Review, Papers and Proceedings*, May 1961, pp. 290-298. Discussion (Irving Morrissett), pp. 302-304. Also in Alfred N.

Page and Warren R. Seyfried (eds.). *Urban Analysis: Readings in Housing and Urban Development.* Glenview, Ill.: Scott, Foresman, 1970, pp. 420-427.

c. Legislation and Legal Aspects

3183. Arnold, W.C. "Use of Federal Injunctive Processes to Challenge Eminent Domain: The Defenses to Requests by Community Groups for Federal Injunctions to Prohibit the Building of Freeways and Other Public Facilities." *Planning, Zoning & Eminent Domain Institute (Southwestern Legal Foundation)*, 1972, pp. 255+.

3184. "The Federal Courts and Urban Renewal." *Columbia Law Review*, March 1969, pp. 472-514.

3185. Foard, Ashley A. and Hilbert Fefferman. "Federal Urban Renewal Legislation." *Law and Contemporary Problems*, Autumn 1960, pp. 635-684.

3186. Goldston, Eli, Allen Oakley Hunter and Guido A. Rothrauff, Jr. "Urban Redevelopment–The Viewpoint of Counsel for a Private Redeveloper." *Law and Contemporary Problems*, Winter 1961, pp. 118-177.

3187. McGee, Henry W., Jr. "Urban Renewal in the Crucible of Judicial Review." *Virginia Law Review*, June 1970, pp. 826-894.

3188. Mandelker, Daniel R. "The Comprehensive Planning Requirement in Urban Renewal." *University of Pennsylvania Law Review*, November 1967, pp. 25-73.

3189. Mandelker, Daniel R. *Urban Conflict in Urban Renewal: The Milwaukee Experience.* Flagstaff, Arizona: College of Law, Arizona State University, 1971. (Reprinted from *Law and the Social Order*, no. 4, 1971, pp. 635-679.)

3190. "Real Property–Condemnation of Non-slum Area for Private Redevelopment." *De Paul Law Review*, Spring-Summer 1963, pp. 356+.

3191. U.S. Housing and Home Finance Agency. *Federal Laws Authorizing Assistance to Urban Renewal: Housing Act of 1949 as Amended Through June, 1961.* Washington, D.C.: Government Printing Office, 1961.

3192. "Urban Renewal–Essentials of the Federal Program." *Kentucky Law Journal*, Winter 1960, pp. 262+.

3193. Weinstein, L.H. "Urban Renewal in Massachusetts." *Massachusetts Law Quarterly*, March 1962, pp. 5+.

3194. Wheeler, Louise LaMothe. "Community Controlled Renewal in California: Some Proposals for Change." *Stanford Law Review*, November 1970, pp. 148-172.

d. Sociological/Political Analyses

3195. Barresi, Charles M. and John H. Lindquist. "The Urban Community: Attitudes toward Neighborhood and Urban Renewal." *Urban Affairs Quarterly*, March 1970, pp. 278-290.

3196. Brewer, G.D. *Accommodating Increased Demands for Public Participation in Urban Renewal Decisionmaking.* Santa Monica, Calif.: The Rand Corporation, July 1972. 5pp.

3197. Hawkins, Homer Chandler. *Knowledge of the Social and Emotional Implications of Urban Renewal and the Utility of this Knowledge to the Practice of Social Work.* Ann Arbor, Mich.: University Microfilms, 1972 (Ph.D. dissertation, Michigan State University, 1971). 256pp. (order no. 72-8686).

3198. Lindquist, John H. and Charles M. Barresi. "Ghetto Residents and Urban Politics: Attitudes toward Urban Renewal." *Law and Society Review*, November 1970, pp. 239-250.

3199. MacDonald, Gordon D. and Rosalind Tough. "New York: Social Action in Urban Renewal." *Land Economics*, November 1966, pp. 514-522.

3200. Greenleigh Associates, Inc. *Report of the Diagnostic Survey of Tenant Households in the West Side Urban Renewal Area of New York City.* New York: New York City Housing and Redevelopment Board, 1965. 150pp.

3201. Kaplan, Harold. *The Politics of Slum Clearance. A Study of Urban Renewal in Newark, New Jersey.* Ann Arbor, Mich.: University Microfilms, 1961 (Ph.D. dissertation, Columbia University, 1961). 450pp. (order no. 61-3442).

3202. Kaplan, Harold. *Urban Renewal Politics: Slum Clearance in Newark.* New York: Columbia University Press, 1963. 219 pp.

3203. Marris, Peter. "The Social Implications of Urban Redevelopment." *Journal of the American Institute of Planners*, August 1962, pp. 180-186.

3204. Millspaugh, Martin and Gurney Breckenfeld. *The Human Side of Urban Renewal; A Study of the Attitude Changes Produced by Neighborhood Rehabilitation.* Edited by Miles L. Colean. New York: Washburn, 1960. 233pp.

3205. New York (City) Housing and Redevelopment Board, Bureau of Planning and Program Research. *Planning for the Jumel Place Urban Renewal Area; A Social and Economic Analysis.* New York: Housing and Redevelopment Board, 1965. 40pp.

3206. New York (City) Housing and Redevelopment Board, Bureau of Planning and Program Research. *Social and Economic Analysis of the East River Urban Renewal Area.* New York: Housing and Redevelopment Board, 1965. 104pp.

3207. Rossi, Peter H. *et al. The Politics of Urban Renewal; The Chicago Findings.* New York: Free Press of Glencoe, 1961. 308pp.

3208. Wolf, Eleanor P. and Charles N. Lebeaux. "On the Destruction of Poor Neighborhoods by Urban Renewal." *Social Problems*, Summer 1965, pp. 3-8.

3209. Weaver, Robert C. "Class, Race, and Urban Renewal." *Land Economics*, August 1960, pp. 235-251. Also in Alfred N. Page and Warren R. Seyfried (eds.). *Urban Analysis: Readings in Housing and Urban Development.* Glenview, Ill.: Scott, Foresman, 1970, pp. 347-361.

See also: 3123.

e. Evaluations of the Program

3210. Anderson, Martin. *The Federal Bulldozer: A Critical Analysis of Urban Renewal, 1949-1962.* Cambridge, Mass.: MIT Press, 1964. 261pp.

3211. "The Controversy Over Federal Urban Renewal: Pro & Con." *Congressional Digest*, April 1964, pp. 97-128.

3212. Grigsby, William G. "Housing and Slum Clearance: Elusive Goals." *Annals of the American Academy of Political and Social Science*, March 1964, pp. 107-118.

3213. Grossman, David A. "The Community Renewal Program: Policy Development, Progress, and Problems." *Journal of the American Institute of Planners*, November 1963, pp. 259-269.

3214. Gruen, Claude. "Urban Renewal's Role in the Genesis of Tomorrow's Slums." *Land Economics*, August 1963, pp. 285-291.

3215. Johnson, Thomas F. "Government, Housing, and Urban Renewal: Inter-related Problems and Politics." *Michigan Business Review*, November 1967, pp. 24-29.

3216. Leach, Richard H. "The Federal Urban Renewal Program: A Ten-Year Critique." *Law and Contemporary Problems*, Autumn 1960, pp. 777-792.

3217. LeGates, Richard T. *Can the Federal Welfare Bureaucracies Control Their Programs: The Case of HUD and Urban Renewal.* Berkeley, Calif.: Institute of Urban and Regional Development, University of California, May 1972.

3218. U.S. General Accounting Office. *Premature Approval of Large-Scale Demolition for Erie-view Urban Renewal Project I, Cleveland, Ohio, by the Urban Renewal Administration, Housing and Home Finance Agency; Report to the Congress. . . .* Washington, D.C., 1963. 42 l.

3219. U.S. General Accounting Office. *Review of Slum Clearance and Urban Renewal Activities of the Atlanta Regional Office. . . .* Washington, D.C., 1961. 48 l.

## 14. VETERANS' HOUSING PROGRAMS

3220. U.S. Congress. House. Committee on Veterans Affairs. *Bills to Provide for Purchase of Mobile Homes under VA Guaranteed Loan Program.* Washington, D.C.: Government Printing Office, 1970.

3221. U.S. Congress. House. Committee on Veteran's Affairs. *Direct Housing Loans. Hearing. . . .* Washington, D.C.: Government Printing Office, 1962.

3222. U.S. Congress. House. Committee on Veteran's Affairs. *Providing Home Loans for Veterans in Housing Credit Shortage Areas. Report. . . .* Washington, D.C.: Government Printing Office, 1961. 39pp.

3223. U.S. Congress. House. Committee on Veterans' Affairs. Subcommittee on Housing. *Review of Veterans' Administration Loan Guaranty and Direct Loan Programs: Hearings. . . .* Washington, D.C., 1967. 55pp.

3224. U.S. Congress. House. Committee on Veterans' Affairs. *VA Housing Program: Bills H.R. 6652 and H.R. 7932. Hearings. . . .* Washington, D.C.: Government Printing Office, 1964.

3225. U.S. Congress. House. Committee on Veterans' Affairs. *Veterans' Housing Legislation. Hearings. . . .* Washington, D.C.: Government Printing Office, 1961.

3226. U.S. Congress. House. Committee on Veterans' Affairs. *Veterans' Housing Legislation, H.R. 9812 and H.R. 9813. Hearing. . . .* Washington, D.C.: Government Printing Office, 1964.

3227. U.S. Congress. House. Committee on Veterans' Affairs. Subcommittee on Housing. *Veterans' Housing Programs. Hearings. . . .* Washington, D.C.: Government Printing Office, 1968.

3228. U.S. Congress. Senate. Committee on Finance. *NSLI Investment Fund. Hearing . . . on S. 3008, to Increase the Availability of Guaranteed Home Loan Financing for Veterans and to Increase the Income of the National Service Life Insurance Fund.* Washington, D.C.: Government Printing Office, 1969. 95pp.

3229. U.S. Congress. Senate. Committee on Labor and Public Welfare. *Extension of Veterans' Home Loan Entitlements and Inclusion of Mobile Home Purchases. Report to Accompany S. 3656.* Washington, D.C., 1970. 57pp.

3230. U.S. Congress. Senate. Committee on Labor and Public Welfare. *Veterans Education and Training and Home Loan Programs Amendments of 1970. Hearing. . . .* Washington, D.C.: Government Printing Office, 1970. 219pp.

## 15. PROPOSED ALTERNATIVES TO PRESENT PROGRAMS: HOUSING ALLOWANCES, INCOME REDISTRIBUTION

3231. Brand, Spencer *et al. Housing Allowance Household Experiment Design: Part 6: Site Selection Strategy.* Washington, D.C.: The Urban Institute, 1971 (Urban Institute Working Paper 205-2).

3232. Brand, Spencer *et al. The Methodology of Site Selection for a Housing Allowance Experiment.* Washington, D.C.: The Urban Institute, October 1971.

3233. Buchanan, Garth and John Heinberg. *Housing Allowance Household Experiment Design: Part 1: Summary and Overview.* Washington, D.C.: The Urban Institute, 1972 (Urban Institute Working Paper 205-4). 66pp.

3234. Buchanan, Garth, Timothy Ling and Robert Tinney. *Housing Allowance Experiment Design: Part 4: Sampling Issues.* Washington, D.C.: The Urban Institute, 1972 (Urban Institute Working Paper 205-5).

3235. Cage, Roland, Bill Jukiewicz and Ammi Kohn. *Interim Report: Housing Allowance Project Evaluation: Kansas City, Missouri.* Kansas City, Missouri: Midwest Council of Model Cities, July 1971.

3236. de Leeuw, Frank. "The Housing Allowance Approach." In U.S. Congress. House. Committee on Banking and Currency. *Papers Submitted to Subcommittee on Housing Panels on Housing Production, Housing Demand, and Developing a Suitable Living Environment: Part 2.* Washington, D.C.: Government Printing Office, 1971, pp. 541-554.

3237. de Leeuw, Frank, Sam H. Leaman and Helen Blank. *The Design of a Housing Allowance.* Washington, D.C.: The Urban Institute, 1970. 42pp. (Urban Institute Working Paper 112-25).

3238. Grigsby, William G. "The Housing Effects of a Guaranteed Annual Income." In Michael A. Stegman (ed.). *Housing and Economics: The American Dilemma.* Cambridge, Mass.: MIT Press, 1970, pp. 396-422.

3239. Heinberg, John D. *Income Assistance Programs in Housing: Conceptual Issues and Benefit Patterns.* Washington, D.C.: The Urban Institute, May 1970. 45pp. (Urban Institute Working Paper 112-18).

3240. Heinberg, John D. *The Transfer Cost of a Housing Allowance: Conceptual Issues and Benefit Patterns.* Washington, D.C.: The Urban Institute, 1971. 80pp.

3241. Heinberg, John and Robert Tinney. *Housing Allowance Household Experiment Design: Part 2: Program Designs and Relation to Behavioral Responses.* Washington, D.C.: The Urban Institute, 1972 (Urban Institute Working Paper 205-1).

3242. "Housing Money that Goes to the People." *Business Week* Jan. 8, 1972, pp. 51-52.

3243. Leaman, Sam H. *Estimated Administrative Cost of a National Housing Allowance.* Washington, D.C.: The Urban Institute, 1971. (Urban Institute Working Paper 112-17).

3244. Ling, Timothy, Garth Buchanan and Larry Ozanne. *Housing Allowance Household Experiment Design: Part 5: Analysis Plan.* Washington, D.C.: The Urban Institute, 1972 (Urban Institute Working Paper 205-6).

3245. Lowry, Ira S., C. Peter Rydell and David DeFerranti. *Testing the Supply Response to Housing Allowances: An Experimental Design.* Santa Monica, Calif.: Rand Corporation, December 1971.

3246. Mattox, Joe L. "Rent Allowances Tried Out for First Time in USA in Kansas City, Missouri, Model Cities Demonstration Project." *Journal of Housing*, October 1971, pp. 482-487.

3247. McFarland, M. Carter. "The Rising Tide of Housing Allowances." *AIA Journal*, October 1972, pp. 26-28.

3248. Morris, C.N. *Considerations for a Sequential Housing Allowance Demand Experiment.* Santa Monica, Calif.: The Rand Corporation, June 1972. 20pp.

3249. Nachbaur, Elizabeth Hirsch. *An Explanatory Analysis of the Proposed National Housing Allowance Program.* Washington, D.C., 1971. 85pp. Thesis (Master of Government), George Washington University.

3250. Nourse, Hugh O. "The Effect of a Negative Income Tax on the Number of Substandard Housing Units." *Land Economics*, November 1970, pp. 435-445. Also in George Sternlieb and Lynne B. Sagalyn (eds.). *Housing: 1970-1971; An AMS Anthology.* New York: AMS Press, 1972, pp. 544-554.

3251. Nourse, Hugh O. *Income Redistribution and the Urban Housing Market.* Chicago, Ill.: Center for Urban Studies, University of Illinois, 1968. 35pp.

3252. Peabody, Malcolm E. "Housing Allowances: A New Way to House the Poor." *HUD Challenge*, July 1972, pp. 10-14.

3253. Sherer, Sam. *Housing Allowance Household Experiment Design: Part 8: Rules of Operation.* Washington, D.C.: The Urban Institute, 1972 (Urban Institute Working Paper 205-7).

3254. Sherer, Sam. *Rules of Operation for the Housing Allowance Experiment.* Washington, D.C.: The Urban Institute, April 28, 1972. (Working Paper 205-7).

3255. Sherer, Sam, Cynthia Thomas and Spencer Brand. *Housing Allowance Household Experiment Design: Part 7: Measurement and Operations Handbook.* Washington, D.C.: The Urban Institute, 1972 (Urban Institute Working Paper 205-8).

3250. Stern, David. *Housing Allowances: Some Considerations of Efficiency and Equity.* Cambridge, Mass.: Joint Center for Urban Studies of the Massachusetts Institute of Technology and Harvard University, January 1971, revised February 1972. (Joint Center Working Paper no. 6).

See also: 991, 2104, 2108, 2109, 2170, 2452-2455, 2752.

## 16. STATE AND LOCAL HOUSING PROGRAMS

3257. "An Act to Establish a Corporation for Urban Development." *Harvard Journal on Legislation*, May 1968, pp. 529-562.

3258. Alexander, Robert C. "Fifteen State Housing Finance Agencies in Review." *Journal of Housing*, January 1972, pp. 9-17.

3259. Citizens' Housing and Planning Association of Metropolitan Boston, Inc. *To Rebuild the City: A Report on the Organizational Housing Functions in Boston.* Boston, 1969.

3260. Cliff, Ursula. "UDC Scorecard." *Design & Environment*, Summer 1972, pp. 54-56+.

3261. DeSalvo, J.S. *An Economic Analysis of New York City's Mitchell-Lama Housing Program.* New York: The New York City Rand Institute, June 1971.

3262. Dreyfuss, David and Joan Hendrickson. *A Guide to Government Activities in New York City's Housing Markets.* Prepared for the City of New York. Santa Monica, Calif.: Rand Corporation, 1968. 118pp.

3263. Falk, Patricia. *Housing and Urban Development Legislation in New York State, 1972: Report.* New York: Department of Public Affairs, Community Service Society of New York, September 1972.

3264. Goldberg, Arthur Abba. "State Agencies: Housing Assistance at the Grass Roots." *Real Estate Review*, Winter 1972, pp. 14-19.

3265. Hung, Fred C. "State Housing Loan Program for Lower-middle Income Families in Hawaii." *Land Economics*, August 1963, pp. 307-313.

3266. Kozuch, James R. "State Housing Finance Agencies: Their Effect on Mortgage Banking." *Mortgage Banker*, October 1972, pp. 12+.

3267. "Legislative Solution to a Judicial Dilemma: The Pennsylvania Home Improvement Finance Act." *Villanova Law Review*, Winter 1965, pp. 309+.

3268. Michigan Commission on Housing Law Revision. *Report.* Lansing, Mich., 1969. 96pp.

3269. National Urban Coalition. *Agenda for Positive Action: State Programs in Housing and Community Development.* Washington, D.C., 1970.

3270. New York (City) Housing and Redevelopment Administration. *Report of the Task Force on Mitchell-Lama Housing.* New York, 1967. 22pp.

3271. New York State Housing Finance Agency. *New York State Housing Finance Agency and the Limited Profit Housing Companies: Organization, Operation, Financing.* New York, 1963. 27pp.

3272. New York (State) Temporary State Commission on Low Income Housing. *A Review and Appraisal of New York State's Low-income Housing Program: Report.* New York, 1963.

3273. "New York's Fair Housing Practices Law: Report of Committee on Civil Rights." *Bar Bulletin (New York County)*, March/April 1962, pp. 162-165.

3274. "Pennsylvania Housing Legislation: Proposals for Reform." *University of Pittsburgh Law Review*, Fall 1968, pp. 95+.

3275. Powledge, Fred. *New York State's Capital Grant Program: Low-income Families in Middle-income Housing.* New York: Citizen's Housing and Planning Council of New York, Inc., 1969. 39pp.

3276. Rada, Edward L. *The Cal-Vet Program; A Study of State-financed Housing in California.* Los Angeles, Calif.: Real Estate Research Program, University of California, 1962. 173pp.

3277. Rada, E.L. "Capital Cost of Cal-Vet Housing." *National Tax Journal*, March 1962, pp. 82-92. West, Richard R. "Capital Costs of Cal-Vet Financing: A Reappraisal." *National Tax Journal*, June 1966, pp. 210-214.

3278. Radisch, R. *The City's Limited-profit Housing Companies Program: An Evaluation and Projection, 1957-1970.* New York: New York City Housing and Redevelopment Board, January 1966.

3279. "Round Table Report: What Can Be Done to Get Better and More Uniform State Legislation for Housing?" *House & Home*, December 1961, pp. 130-137+.

3280. "States Try to Develop Housing." *Savings and Loan News*, July 1971, pp. 52-57.

3281a. Sullivan, A.V. "Hawaii Assists Low-income Families in Achieving Home Ownership Directed Toward the Residents of a State-Aided Program; a Nonsubsidized Operation Currently Accommodating Over 500 Families." *Journal of Housing*, January 1965, pp. 27-28.

3281b. U.S. Department of Housing and Urban Development. *State Laws Enacted in 1970 of Interest to the Department of Housing and Urban Development.* Washington, D.C., 1972.

3282. Woodfill, B.M. *New York City's Mitchell-Lama Program: Middle-Income Housing?* New York: The New York City Rand Institute, June 1971.

## C. GENERAL WORKS ON THE SOCIAL DIMENSIONS OF HOUSING

3283. Boeschenstein, Warren. "Design of Socially Mixed Housing." *Journal of the American Institute of Planners*, September 1971, pp. 311-318.

3284. Brolm, Brent C. and John Zusel. "Mass Housing: Social Research and Design." *Architectural Forum*, July 1968, pp. 66-71.

3285. Cooper, Clare. "The House as Symbol." *Design & Environment*, Fall 1972, pp. 30-37.

3286. Feldman, A.S. and C. Tilly. "Interaction of Social and Physical Space." *American Sociological Review*, December 1960, pp. 877-884.

3287. Festinger, Leon, Stanley Schachter and Kurt Back. *Social Pressures in Informal Groups; a Study of Human Factors in Housing*. Stanford, Calif.: Stanford University Press, 1963. 197pp.

3288. Fikry, Mohamed Abd-El-Rahman. *Effects of Physical Design Variables on Residents' Social Interaction in Homogeneous Communities.* Ann Arbor, Mich.: University Microfilms, 1971 (Ph.D. dissertation, University of Michigan, 1970). 258pp. (order no. 71-23,750).

3289. Gans, Herbert J. "The Balanced Community: Homogeneity or Heterogeneity in Residential Areas." *Journal of the American Institute of Planners*, August 1961, pp. 176-184.

3290. Hartman, Chester. "Social Values and Housing Orientations." *Journal of Social Issues*, April 1963, pp. 113-131.

3291. Lansing, John B. and Robert W. Marans. "Evaluation of Neighborhood Quality." *Journal of the American Institute of Planners*, May 1969, pp. 195-199.

3292. Lavanburg-Corner House. *The Utilization of Subsidized Housing in Family and Welfare Services.* New York, May 25, 1964. 90pp.

3293. MacDonald, Gordon D. and Rosalind Tough. "New York City: Changing Social Values and the New Housing." *Land Economics*, May 1963, pp. 157-165.

3294. Marcuse, Peter. "Social Indicators and Housing Policy." *Urban Affairs Quarterly* December 1971, pp. 193-217.

3295. McQueen, Phil K. *Relationships Among Selected Housing, Marital and Familial Characteristics.* Ann Arbor, Mich.: University Microfilms, 1965 (Ph.D. dissertation, Florida State University, 1964). 105pp. (order no. 65-5591).

3296. Rainwater, Lee. "Fear and the House-as-Haven in the Lower Class." *Journal of the American Institute of Planners*, January 1966, pp. 23-30. Comment (Roger Montgomery), pp. 31-37.

3297. Rosow, Irving. "The Social Effects of the Physical Environment: The Assumption of Housers that Planned Manipulation of the Physical Environment Can Change Social Patterns in Determinate Ways Seem to Be Only Selectively True." *Journal of the American Institute of Planners*, May 1961, pp. 127-133.

3298. Sanoff, Henry and Henry Burgwyn. *Social Implications of the Physical Environment with Particular Emphasis on Housing and Neighborhood Characteristics.* Monticello, Ill.: Council of Planning Librarians, 1970 (Exchange Bibliography no. 145).

3299. Sanoff, Henry and Man Sawhney. *Residential Livability: A Socio-Physical Perspective.* Raleigh, N.C.: Urban Affairs and Community Service Center, North Carolina State University, 1971. 39pp.

3300. Schermer (George) Associates. *More Than Shelter: Social Needs in Low- and Moderate-income Housing.* Prepared for the consideration of the National Commission on Urban Problems. Washington, D.C.: Government Printing Office, 1968. 213pp. (National Commission on Urban Problems Research Report no. 8).

3301. Stacey, William Arthur. *Multivariate Analysis of the Social Effects of Housing.* Ann Arbor, Mich.: University Microfilms, 1971 (Ph.D. dissertation, Florida State University, 1970). 174pp. (order no. 71-7105).

3302. Tucker, Francis Hendrick. *A Social Theory of Housing.* Ann Arbor, Mich.: University Microfilms, 1970 (Ph.D. dissertation, University of Texas at Austin, 1969). 135pp. (order no. 10,879).

See also: 1591, 1740, 2185, 3466; Public Housing–Social Aspects: 2825+; Relocation–Social/Psychological Consequences: 3072+; Urban Renewal–Sociological/Political Analyses: 3195+.

## D. HOUSING AND HEALTH

3303. Alnutt, R.F. and G. Mossinghoff. "Housing and Health Inspection: A Survey and Suggestions in Light of Recent Case Law." *George Washington Law Review*, January 1960, pp. 421+.

3304. American Public Health Association. "Basic Health Principles of Housing and Its Environment." *American Journal of Public Health*, May 1969, pp. 841-853.

3305. American Public Health Association. Committee on Hygiene of Housing. *Standards for Healthful Housing: Planning the Neighborhood.* Chicago, Ill.: Public Administration Service, 1960. 94pp.

3306. American Public Health Association. Subcommittee on Housing Regulations and Standards. *APHA-PHS Recommended Housing Maintenance and Occupancy Ordinance.* Prepared in Collaboration with Bureau of Community Environmental Management. Washington, D.C.: U.S. Bureau of Community Environmental Management, 1969. 101pp.

3307. Angevine, J.H. and G. Taube. "Enforcement of Public Health Laws—Some New Techniques." *Massachusetts Law Quarterly*, September 1967, pp. 205+.

3308. Barr, Charles W. *Housing–Health Relationships: An Annotated Bibliography.* Monticello, Ill.: Council of Planning Librarians, 1969 (Exchange Bibliography no. 82).

3309. Hackett, Phyllis (ed.). *Proceedings of Working Conference on Housing and Health, September 9-10, 1965.* Berkeley, Calif.: Center for Planning and Development Research, University of California, 1965.

3310. Male, Charles Thomas. *An Attempted Correlation of Home Accident Fatalities and Housing Quality.* Ithaca, N.Y.: Center for Housing and Environmental Studies, Division of Urban Studies, Cornell University, 1968.

3311. Teledyne Brown Engineering. *A Design Guide for Home Safety.* Prepared for the Research and Technology Division, U.S. Department of Housing and Urban Development. Huntsville, Ala., 1972.

3312. U.S. Department of Health, Education, and Welfare. Community Environmental Management Bureau. *Proceedings of 1st Invitational Conference on Health Research in Housing and Its Environment, Warrenton, Virginia, March 17-19, 1970.* Rockville, Maryland, 1970. 113pp.

3313. U.S. Department of Health, Education, and Welfare. Task Force on Health. *Housing, Urban-Rural Problems and Sanitation. Issue Study Report.* Washington, D.C., 1969. 70pp.

3314. Wilner, Daniel M. *et al. The Housing Environment and Family Life: A Longitudinal Study of the Effects of Housing on Morbidity and Mental Health.* Baltimore, Md.: Johns Hopkins Press, 1962. 338pp.

## E. HOUSING MANAGEMENT

3315. Bremner, R.H. "Iron Scepter Twined With Roses: The Octavia Hill System of Housing Management." *Social Service Review*, June 1965, pp. 222-231.

3316. Glassman, Sidney. "Managing the Resident Manager." *Journal of Property Management*, September-October 1970, pp. 224-227.

3317. Goldfarb, Karen G. "The Center for Housing Management." *Journal of Property Management*, Jan./Feb. 1972, pp. 14-18.

3318. "HUD's Philosophy for Housing Management." *HUD Challenge*, August 1971, pp. 4-7.

3319. Institute of Real Estate Management. *Experience Profile: Management of Property for Lower-Income Residents.* Chicago, Ill., 1970. 42pp.

3320a. Isler, Morton L. *et al. Housing Management: A Progress Report.* Washington, D.C.: Urban Institute, 1971. 106pp.

3320b. Kokus, John, Jr. *An Evaluation of Policies of Private Real Estate Management in Low and Moderate Income Housing.* Ann Arbor, Mich.: University Microfilms, 1971 (Ph.D. dissertation, The American University, 1971). 338pp. (order no. 71-27,258).

3321. "Maintenance: Key to Successful Housing Management." *Journal of Housing*, September 1972, pp. 379-394 (8 articles).

3322. Murray, Joseph C. "Managing Federally-Assisted Housing—Problems or Opportunities?" *Journal of Property Management*, January/February 1972, pp. 4-8.

3323. "NAHRO's Housing Management Specialist Program Moves Into Second Year." *Journal of Housing*, Jan. 1972, pp. 27-30.

3324. National Association of Housing and Redevelopment Officials. *Housing Management Bibliography*. Washington, D.C., 1971. 27pp.

3325. National Corporation for Housing Partnerships. *Needed: A Strategy for Housing Management Training*. Washington, D.C., 1971.

3326. Nonprofit Housing Center. *Critical Issues in Property Management. Report to the U.S. Department of Housing and Urban Development.* Washington, D.C.: Prepared by Nonprofit Housing Center, Inc., as consultants to Arthur D. Little, Inc. 1972. 24pp.

3327. "A Recommendation for the Management of Low-Income Housing." *Journal of Property Management*, July-August 1970, pp. 170-178.

3328. Ripps, Saul M. "Low-Income Co-Ops Need Professional Management." *Journal of Property Management*, May/June 1972, pp. 106-108.

3329. Sadacca, Robert, Morton Isler and Maragret Drury. *Housing Management: Second Progress Report.* Washington, D.C.: The Urban Institute, December 6, 1971. 124pp. (Urban Institute Working Paper no. 209-1).

3330. Sadacca, Robert and Morton Isler. *Management Performance in Multi-Family Housing Developments.* Washington, D.C.: The Urban Institute, June 1972. 47pp. (Urban Institute Working Paper no. 209-4).

3331. Sadacca, Robert, Maragret Drury and Morton Isler. *Ownership Form and Management Success in Private, Publicly-Assisted Housing.* Washington, D.C.: The Urban Institute, February 18, 1972, revised March 7, 1972. 50pp. (Urban Institute Working Paper no. 209-3).

3332. Sally, William D. "Programming Preventive Maintenance." *Journal of Property Management*, May/June 1972, pp. 102-105.

3333. Smith, J. Molton. "Managing for FHA." *Journal of Property Management*, July/August 1971, pp. 166-168.

3334. Soto, Elias. "Meeting the Challenges of Inner-City Management." *Journal of Property Management*, May/June 1972, pp. 109-110.

3335. Watson, Norman V. "Spelling Out the Management Role in Assisted Housing." *Journal of Property Management*, Jan/Feb. 1972, pp. 9-13.

See also: 1479, 1492, 1585, 1756, 2079, 2485; Public Housing—Management and Administration: 2794+.

## F. HOUSING WITHIN THE PLANNING PROCESS

### 1. GENERAL

3336. American Institute of Planners. *Housing Planning: An AIP Background Paper Prepared by an AIP Task Force.* Washington, D.C., 1971. 36pp.

3337. American Society of Planning Officials. *Planning for Apartments.* Chicago, Ill., October 1960. 44pp. (Planning Advisory Service Report no. 139).

3338. Bestor, George C. *The Challenge of Residential Land Planning.* Chicago: Mobile Home Manufacturers Association, 1967. 66pp.

3339. California Department of Housing and Community Development. *Guideline for Preparation of a Housing Element of a General Plan.* Sacramento, May 1970.

3340. California University. Graduate School of Business Administration. Housing, Real Estate and Urban Land Studies Program. *Report on the Housing Element for the General Plan of the City of Los Angeles.* Los Angeles, 1970.

3341. Carley, Judith A. *Housing: An Element of State Planning.* Monticello, Ill.: Council of Planning Librarians, 1971 (Exchange Bibliography no. 214).

3342. Inglewood, California, Department of Planning and Development. *The Housing Element of the Inglewood General Plan.* Inglewood, Calif., February 1972.

3343. Kansas State Department of Economic Development. Planning Division. *Initial Housing Element; A Study Design for the Development of a Housing Plan for Kansas; Includes a Breakthrough Operations Plan.* Topeka, 1970. 41pp.

3344. Southern California Association of Governments. Committee on Housing and Community Development. *Housing Element.* Los Angeles, Calif., 1971. 78pp.

See also: 893, 2084.

2. REGIONAL HOUSING PLANS

a. General

3345. Association of Bay Area Governments. *Regional Housing Study.* Berkeley, Calif., 1969.

3346. Connecticut University. Center for Real Estate and Urban Economic Studies. *Housing Strategy for Southeastern Connecticut: A Short-Run Projection of Housing Requirements and Problems in the Southeastern Connecticut Planning Region: 1967-80.* Prepared for the Southeastern Connecticut Regional Planning Agency. Storrs, 1968. 2 vols. (Real Estate Report no. 3).

3347. Hammer, Greene, Siler Associates. *Regional Housing Planning; A Technical Guide.* Prepared for the American Institute of Planners. Washington, D.C., 1972. 125pp.

3348. Minneapolis—St. Paul, Minn., Metropolitan Council. *Metropolitan Development Guide; Housing Policies, System Plan, Program.* Minneapolis, 1971. 32pp.

3349. National Service to Regional Councils. *National Conference on Housing: Regional Issues and Strategies: Summary of Proceedings, August 8-10, 1971, St. Louis.* Washington, D.C., 1971. 60pp.

3350. Niebanck, Paul L., Richard H. Broun, and John Pope, under the direction of Chester Rapkin. *Housing in the Greater Bridgeport Region, 1960-1980; A Study of the Regional Planning Implications of Future*

*Housing Demand and the Elimination of Substandard Housing.* Trumbull, Conn.: Greater Bridgeport Regional Planning Agency, 1965. 217pp.

3351. Southeastern Wisconsin Regional Planning Commission. *Regional Housing Study Prospectus.* Waukesha, Wisc., 1969. 66pp.

b. Planning For Low and Moderate Income Housing in the Suburbs

3352. Annett, Hugh Hunter. *The Adaptability of the NASA Planning Process to Planning for Urban Systems: A Case Study of Planning for a Low and Moderate Income Housing Program in New Castle County, Delaware.* Ann Arbor, Mich.: University Microfilms, 1972 (Ph.D. dissertation, Drexel University, 1972). 170pp. (order no. 72-24,278)

3353. Bertsch, D. F. and A. M. Shafor. *A Regional Housing Plan: The Miami Valley Regional Planning Commission Experience.* Washington, D.C.: American Institute of Planners, 1971. 8pp.

3354. Craig, Lois. "The Dayton Area's 'Fair Share' Housing Plan Enters the Implementation Phase." *City*, Jan/Feb. 1972, pp. 50-56.

3355. Dayton, Ohio, City Plan Board. *Housing Opportunities: Policies for Dispersal of Low and Moderate Income Housing.* Dayton, Ohio, 1970. 22pp.

3356. Metropolitan Council of the Twin Cities Area. *Distribution and Types of Subsidized Housing in the Twin Cities Metropolitan Area.* St. Paul, Minn., September 1971. 12pp. Updated by *Subsidized Housing Activity, July 1971-July 1972, A Supplementary Report.* St. Paul, Minn., September 1972. 13pp.

3357. Metropolitan Council of the Twin Cities Area. *Metropolitan Development Guide: Housing Policy Plan, Program.* St. Paul, Minn., 1972. 78pp.

3358. Metropolitan Dade County, Florida, Planning Department. "Housing in the Metropolitan Plan, Dade County, Florida." In U.S. Congress. House. Committee on Banking and Currency. Subcommittee on Housing. *Oversight of Federal Housing and Community Development Programs in the State of Florida. Hearing. . . .* Washington, D.C.: Government Printing Office, 1971, pp. 39-161.

3359. Metropolitan Washington Council of Governments. *A Fair Share Housing Formula for Metropolitan Washington.* Washington, D.C., January 1972. 15pp.

3360. Miami Valley Regional Planning Commission. *Housing Needs in the Miami Valley Region 1970-1975.* Dayton, Ohio, 1970.

3361. Miami Valley Regional Planning Commission. *A Housing Plan for the Miami Valley Region*. Dayton, Ohio, July 1970. 43pp.

3362. New York State Urban Development Corporation. *Fair Share: A Report on Westchester's Housing Shortage for Low- and Moderate-Income Families and the Elderly*. White Plains, N.Y., 1972.

3363. New York State Urban Development Corporation. *Five Year UDC Housing Development Program Guide for the Central New York Region*. New York, December 1971.

3364. Sacramento Regional Area Planning Commission. *An Approach to the Distribution of Low and Moderate Income Housing*. Sacramento, Calif., August 1972. 31pp.

3365. San Bernardino County, Calif., Planning Department. *Government Subsidized Housing Distribution Model for Valley Portion, San Bernardino County, California*. San Bernardino, Calif., January 20, 1972. 12pp.

3366. Southeastern Illinois Regional Planning and Development Commission. *Housing for the Disadvantaged: A Regional Assessment*. Harrisburg, Ill., 1972.

3367. Spane, Gail. *Providing Opportunity Beyond the Central City: Issues in Planning Low-Income Housing in the Suburbs*. A thesis presented to the faculty of the Graduate School of Public Administration, New York University, in partial fulfillment of the requirements for the degree of Master of Urban Planning. February 1970. 94pp.

3. DESIGN OF THE HOUSING SITE

3368. Caminos, Horacio, John F. C. Turner and John A. Steffian. *Urban Dwelling Environments; an Elementary Survey of Settlements for the Study of Design Determinants*. Cambridge, Mass.: MIT Press, 1969. 242pp.

3369. Katz, Robert D. *Design of the Housing Site; A Critique of American Practice*. Urbana, Ill.: Distributed by Small Homes Council-Building Research Council, University of Illinois, 1966. 223pp.

3370. Katz, Robert D. *Intensity of Development and Livability of Multi-Family Housing Projects; Design Qualities of European and American Housing Projects*. Prepared for the Federal Housing Administration. Washington, D.C.: Government Printing Office, 1963. 116pp.

3371. Pyron, Bernard. "Form and Diversity in Human Habitats: Judgmental and Attitude Responses." *Environment and Behavior*, March 1972, pp. 87-119.

See also: 256, 3288.

# IV. DEMOGRAPHIC FRAMEWORK

## A. RESIDENTIAL LOCATION

### 1. GENERAL

3372. Adams, J. S. "Residential Structure of Midwestern Cities." *Association of American Geographers, Annals*, March 1970, pp. 37-62.

3373. Alonso, William. *Location and Land Use: Toward a General Theory of Land Rent*. Cambridge, Mass.: Harvard University Press, 1964. 210pp.

3374. Alonso, William. *A Model of the Urban Land Market: Locations & Densities of Dwellings and Businesses*. Ann Arbor, Mich.: University Microfilms, 1960 (Ph.D. dissertation, University of Pennsylvania, 1960). 283pp. (order no. 60-3564).

3375. Alonso, William. "A Theory of the Urban Land Market." In *Papers and Proceedings of the Regional Science Association, 1960*. Philadelphia, Penn.: Regional Science Association, 1960. pp. 149-157.

3376. Anderson, Theodore R. "Social and Economic Factors Affecting the Location of Residential Neighborhoods." *Regional Science Association Papers and Proceedings, Volume Nine, 1962*. Philadelphia, Pa.: Regional Science Association, 1962, pp. 161-170.

3377. Armiger, L. Earl Jr. *Toward a Model of the Residential Location Decision Process: A Study of Recent and Prospective Buyers of New and Used Homes*. Chapel Hill, N.C.: Center for Urban and Regional Studies, University of North Carolina, 1966 (Environment Policies and Urban Development Thesis Series no. 2). 134l.

3378. Beckmann, Martin J. "Application of a Neo-classical Von Thunen Model to the Housing Market." *Annals of Regional Science*, June 1972, pp. 35-40.

3379. Beckmann, Martin J. "On the Distribution of Urban Rent and Residential Density." *Journal of Economic Theory*, June 1969, pp. 60-67. Delson, Jerome K. "Correction on the Boundary Conditions in Beckmann's Model on Urban Rent and Residential Density." September 1970, pp. 314-318. Montesano, Aldo. "A Restatement of Beckmann's Model on the Distribution of Urban Rent and Residential Density." April 1972, pp. 329-354.

3380. Bury, Richard L. *The Efficiency of Selected Site Characteristics as Predictors for Location of Land Use Shifts to Residential Purposes.* Ann Arbor, Mich.: University Microfilms, 1961 (Ph.D. dissertation, University of Connecticut, 1961). 284pp. (order no. 61-5410)

3381. Corey, Kenneth Edward. *A Spatial Analysis of Urban Houses.* Ann Arbor, Mich.: University Microfilms, 1970 (Ph.D. dissertation, University of Cincinnati, 1969). 219pp. (order no. 70-494)

3382. Cripps, E. L. and D. H. S. Foot. "The Empirical Development of an Elementary Residential Location Model for Use in Sub-regional Planning." *Environment and Planning*, Volume 1, number 1, 1969, pp. 81-90.

3383. de Leeuw, Frank. *The Distribution of Housing Services.* Washington, D.C.: Urban Institute, 1972. 121pp.

3384. de Leeuw, Frank. *The Distribution of Housing Services: A Mathematical Model.* Washington, D.C.: The Urban Institute, 1971 (Urban Institute Working Paper 208-1).

3385. de Leeuw, Frank. *The Distribution of Housing Services: First Empirical Steps.* Washington, D.C.: The Urban Institute, March 23, 1972. 56pp. (Urban Institute Working Paper no. 208-4).

3386. Dillman, Don A. and Russell P. Dobash. *Preferences for Community Living and Their Implications for Population Redistribution.* Pullman, Washington: Washington (State) Agricultural Experiment Station, November 1972. 20pp.

3387. Drennan, Matthew Paul. *Household Location Decisions and Local Public Benefits and Costs.* Ann Arbor, Mich.: University Microfilms, 1971 (Ph.D. dissertation, New York University, 1971). 213pp. (order no. 71-24,955)

3388. Drennan, Matthew P. "Household Location Decisions and Local Benefits and Costs." *The American Economist*, Spring 1969, pp. 30-39.

3389. Duncan, Beverly and Otis Dudley Duncan. "The Measurement of Intra-City Locational and Residential Patterns." *Journal of Regional Science*, Fall 1960, pp. 37-54. Also in Alfred N. Page and Warren R. Seyfried (eds.). *Urban Analysis: Readings in Housing and Urban Development.* Glenview, Ill.: Scott, Foresman, 1970, pp. 243-256.

3390. Duncan, B. *et al.* "Patterns of City Growth." *American Journal of Sociology*, January 1962, pp. 418-429.

3391. Eastin, Richard Verr. *An Entropy Maximizing Model of Urban Residential Location.* Ann Arbor, Mich.: University Microfilms, 1972

(Ph.D. dissertation, University of California at Santa Barbara, 1971). 114pp. (order no. 72-25,033)

3392. Edin, Nancy J. *Residential Location and Mode of Transportation to Work: A Model of Choice*. Chicago, Ill.: Chicago Area Transportation Study, 1966.

3393. Ellickson, Bryan C. "Metropolitan Residential Location and the Local Public Sector." Unpublished Ph.D. dissertation, Massachusetts Institute of Technology, 1970.

3394. Ellickson, Bryan. *Metropolitan Residential Location and the Local Public Sector*. Los Angeles, Calif.: Institute of Government and Public Affairs, University of California, 1969. 19pp.

3395. Ellis, Raymond H. "Modeling of Household Location: A Statistical Approach." In Highway Research Board. *Urban Land Use: Concepts and Models*. Washington, D.C., 1967 (Highway Research Record no. 207).

3396. Engle, R. F. III *et al.* "Econometric Simulation Model of Intra-Metropolitan Housing Location: Housing, Business, Transportation and Local Government." *American Economic Review, Papers and Proceedings*, May 1972, pp. 87-97.

3397. Fine, John, *et al.* "The Residential Segregation of Occupational Groups in Central Cities and Suburbs." *Demography*, February 1971, pp. 91-101.

3398. Fowler, Gary L. "The Urban Settlement Patterns of Disadvantaged Migrants." *Journal of Geography*, May 1972, pp. 275-284.

3399. Frieden, Bernard J. "Some Local Preferences in the Urban Housing Market." *Journal of the American Institute of Planners*, November 1961, pp. 316-324.

3400. Goldberg, Michael A. "Transportation, Urban Land Values, and Rents: A Synthesis." *Land Economics*, May 1970, pp. 153-162.

3401. Granfield, Michael Edward. *An Econometric Model of Residential Location*. Ann Arbor, Mich.: University Microfilms, 1971 (Ph.D. dissertation, Duke University 1970). 219pp. (order no. 71-21,540)

3402. Guest, Avery Mason. *Families and Housing in Cities*. Ann Arbor, Mich.: University Microfilms, 1971 (Ph.D. dissertation, University of Wisconsin, 1970). 307pp. (order no. 71-293)

3403. Hansen, Willard B. "An Approach to the Analysis of Metropolitan Residential Extension." *Journal of Regional Science*, Summer 1961, pp. 37-55. Also in Alfred N. Page and Warren R. Seyfried (eds.). *Urban*

*Analysis: Readings in Housing and Urban Development*. Glenview, Ill.: Scott, Foresman, 1970. pp. 226-243.

3404. Hansen, Willard Bernard. *Residential Extension in a Metropolitan Region: a Regression Analysis of Subregional Development Rates in the Philadelphia Area during the 1940-50 and 1950-55/56 Periods*. Ann Arbor, Mich.: University Microfilms, 1961 (Ph.D. dissertation, University of Pennsylvania, 1961). 351pp. (order no. 61-3520)

3405. Harris, Britton, Josef Nathanson and Louis Rosenburg. *Research on an Equilibrium Model of Metropolitan Housing and Locational Choice: Interim Report*. Philadelphia, Pa.: Planning Sciences Group, Institute for Environmental Studies, Graduate School of Fine Arts, University of Pennsylvania, March 1966.

3406. Harris, Curtis C. Jr. "A Stochastic Process Model of Residential Development." *Journal of Regional Science*, Summer 1968, pp. 29-40.

3407. Harris, R. N. S., G. S. Tolley and C. Harrell. "The Residence Site Choice." *Review of Economics and Statistics*, August 1968, pp. 241-247.

3408. Herbert, John D. and Benjamin H. Stevens. "A Model for the Distribution of Residential Activity in Urban Areas." *Journal of Regional Science*, Fall 1960, pp. 21-36.

3409. Hochman, O. and D. Pines. "Competitive Equilibrium of Transportation and Housing in the Residential Ring of an Urban Area." *Environment and Planning*, Volume 3, number 1, 1971, pp. 51-62.

3410. Hoyt, Homer. *Where the Rich and the Poor People Live; The Location of Residential Areas Occupied by the Highest and Lowest Income Families in American Cities*. Washington, D.C.: Urban Land Institute, 1966. 64pp. (ULI Technical Bulletin no. 55)

3411. James, Franklin J. and James W. Hughes. *Economic Growth and Residential Patterns: A Methodological Investigation*. New Brunswick, New Jersey: Center for Urban Policy Research, Rutgers University, 1972. 211pp.

3412. Johnston, R. J. "Activity Spaces and Residential Preferences: Some Tests of the Hypothesis of Sectoral Mental Maps." *Economic Geography*, April 1972, pp. 199-211.

3413. Johnston, Ronald John. *Urban Residential Patterns, An Introductory Review*. New York: Praeger, 1971. 382pp.

3414. Kain, John F. "A Contribution to the Urban Transportation Debate: An Econometric Model of Urban Residential and Travel Behavior." *Review of Economics and Statistics*, February 1964, pp. 55-64.

3415. Kain, John F. *Theories of Residential Location and Realities of Race*. Cambridge, Mass.: Program on Regional and Urban Economics, Harvard University, 1969. (Discussion Paper no. 47). 35pp.

3416. Katz, Albert M. "Lower Rent Costs: A Net Social Gain through the Creation of New Towns." *Land Economics*, May 1968, pp. 273-275.

3417. Lamanna, Richard A. "Value Consensus Among Urban Residents." *Journal of the American Institute of Planners*, November 1964, pp. 317-323.

3418. Lansing, John B. and Eva Mueller with Nancy Barth. *Residential Location and Urban Mobility*. Ann Arbor, Mich.: Survey Research Center, University of Michigan, 1964.

3419. Lansing, John B. and Nancy Barth. *Residential Location and Urban Mobility: A Multivariate Analysis*. Ann Arbor, Mich.: Survey Research Center, University of Michigan, 1964.

3420. Lansing, John B. *Residential Location and Urban Mobility: The Second Wave of Interviews*. Ann Arbor, Mich.: Survey Research Center, University of Michigan, 1966.

3421. Mayo, Stephen K. "An Econometric Model of Residential Location." Unpublished Ph.D. dissertation, Harvard University, 1972.

3422. Muth, Richard F. *Cities and Housing: The Spatial Pattern of Urban Residential Land Use*. Chicago, Ill.: University of Chicago Press, 1969. 355pp.

3423. Muth, Richard F. "The Spatial Structure of the Housing Market." *Regional Science Association Papers and Proceedings, Volume Seven, 1961*. Philadelphia, Pa.: Regional Science Association, 1961, pp. 207-222. Also in Alfred N. Page and Warren R. Seyfried (eds.). *Urban Analysis: Readings in Housing and Urban Development*. Glenview, Ill.: Scott, Foresman, 1970, pp. 197-207.

3424. Nelson, Robert H. "Housing Facilities, Site Advantages, and Rent." *Journal of Regional Science*, Aug. 1972, pp. 249-259.

3425. Nelson, Robert Henry. *The Theory of Residential Location*. Ann Arbor, Mich.: University Microfilms, 1971 (Ph.D. dissertation, Princeton University, 1971). 192pp. (order no. 71-25,951)

3426. Pinkerton, James R. "City-Suburban Residential Patterns by Social Class: A Review of the Literature." *Urban Affairs Quarterly*, September 1971, pp. 75-108.

3427. Richards, John M. "The Significance of Residential Preferences in Urban Areas." With comments by Jack L. Knetsch and Richard F. Muth. In Resources for the Future. *Human Resources in the Urban Economy: Proceedings, 1962*. Washington, D.C., 1963, pp. 123-136, 170-172, 175-176.

3428. Schwirian, Kent P. and Jesus Rico-Velasco. "The Residential Distribution of Status Groups in Puerto Rico's Metropolitan Areas." *Demography*, February 1971, pp. 81-90.

3429. Steffens, Roger C. *Factors Influencing Consumer Choice of Residential Location: An Exploratory Study of the Preferences of Owners of Newly Constructed Dwellings in the Greensboro Urban Fringe Area*. Chapel Hill, N.C.: Center for Urban and Regional Studies, University of North Carolina, 1964 (Environment Policies and Urban Development Thesis Series no. 3). 90pp.

3430. Stowers, Joseph Richard. *Residential Simulation Models for Urban Planning: A Methodological Study with Emphasis on Taxonomy and Location Decision Rules*. Ann Arbor, Mich.: University Microfilms, 1969 (Ph.D. dissertation, Northwestern University, 1968). 246pp. (order no. 69-6999)

3431. Straszheim, Mahlon R. *Modeling Urban Housing Markets and Metropolitan Change: An Econometric Approach*. New York, National Bureau of Economic Research, 1972.

3432. Tilly, C. "Occupational Rank and Grade of Residence in a Metropolis." *American Journal of Sociology*, November 1961, pp. 323-330.

3433. Wendt, Paul F. and William Goldner. "Land Values and the Dynamics of Residential Location." In *Essays in Urban Land Economics*. Los Angeles, Calif.: Real Estate Research Program, University of California, 1966, pp. 188-213.

3434. Wheeler, James O. "Residential Location by Occupational Status." *Urban Studies*, February 1968, pp. 24-32.

3435. Wilson, A. G. "Developments of Some Elementary Residential Location Models." *Journal of Regional Science*, December 1969, pp. 377-385.

3436. Wilson, A. G. "Disaggregating Elementary Residential Location Models." *Regional Science Association Papers and Proceedings, Volume 24, 1969*. Philadelphia, Penn.: Regional Science Association, 1969, pp. 103-125.

3437. Wingo, Lowdon, Jr. "An Economic Model of the Utilization of Urban Land for Residential Purposes." *Regional Science Association Papers and Proceedings, Volume Seven, 1961.* Philadelphia, Penn.: Regional Science Association, 1961, pp. 191-205. Also in Alfred N. Page and Warren R. Seyfried (eds.). *Urban Analysis: Readings in Housing and Urban Development.* Glenview, Ill.: Scott, Foresman, 1970, pp. 177-188.

3438. Wright, C. "Residential Location in a Three-Dimensional City." *Journal of Political Economy*, November-December 1971, pp. 1378-1387.

See also: 51-70, 3566; Land and Property Values no. 781+; Housing and Residential Land Markets no. 924+.

## 2. THE IMPACT OF EMPLOYMENT OPPORTUNITIES ON RESIDENTIAL LOCATION

3439. Brodsky, Harold. *Location Rent and Journey-to-Work Patterns in Seattle.* Ann Arbor, Mich.: University Microfilms, 1966 (Ph.D. dissertation, University of Washington, 1966), 182pp. (order no. 66-11983).

3440. Catanese, Anthony James. "Home and Workplace Separation in Four Urban Regions." *Journal of the American Institute of Planners*, September 1971, pp. 331-337.

3441. Catanese, Anthony James, Jr. *The Separation of Home and Work Place in Urban Structure and Form: A Longtudinal Analysis of Two Urban Regions.* Ann Arbor, Mich.: University Microfilms, 1969 (Ph.D. dissertation, University of Wisconsin, 1969). 394pp. (order no. 69-12,350).

3442. "Commuting & Housing in the San Francisco Bay Area." *San Francisco Business*, August 1972, pp. 19-25.

3443. Holmes, J. H. "Linkages between External Commuting and Out-Migration: Evidence from Middle-Eastern Pennsylvania." *Economic Geography*, October 1972, pp. 406-420.

3444. "Housing and Commuting." *San Francisco Business*, July 1969, pp. 25-31.

3445. Kain, John F. "The Commuting and Residential Decisions of Central Business District Workers." In *Transportation Economics.* New York: National Bureau of Economic Research, distributed by Columbia University Press, 1965, pp. 245-274.

3446. Kain, John F. *Commuting and the Residential Decisions of Chicago and Detroit Business District Workers.* Santa Monica, Calif.: The Rand Corporation, 1963.

3447. Kain, John F. *The Journey to Work as a Determinant of Residential Location*. Santa Monica, Calif.: The Rand Corporation 1961.

3448. Kain, John Forrest. "The Journey to Work as a Determinent of Residential Location." Unpublished Ph.D. dissertation, University of California, 1961. 374pp.

3449. Kain, John F. "The Journey-to-Work as a Determinant of Residential Location." *Regional Science Association Papers and Proceedings, Volume Nine, 1962*. Philadelphia, Pa.: Regional Science Association, 1962, pp. 137-160. Also in Alfred N. Page and Warren R. Seyfried (eds.). *Urban Analysis: Readings in Housing and Urban Development*. Glenview, Ill.: Scott, Foresman, 1970, pp. 207-226.

3450. Loewenstein, Louis K. *The Location of Residences and Work Places in Urban Areas*. New York: Scarecrow Press, 1965.

3451. Richards, John Marvin. *Residential Preference, Residential Location and Home-Work Separation: A Theoretical Analysis*. Ann Arbor, Mich.: University Microfilms, 1962 (Ph.D. dissertation, Louisiana State University, 1961). 289pp. (order no. 62-89)

3452. Vance, J. E., Jr. "Housing the Worker: The Employment Linkage as a Force in Urban Structure." *Economic Geography*, October 1966, pp. 294-325.

## 3. THE IMPACT OF HOUSING PATTERNS ON EMPLOYMENT OPPORTUNITIES

3453. Davies, S. and D. L. Huff. "Impact of Ghettoization on Black Employment." *Economic Geography*, October 1972, pp. 421-427.

3454. Deskins, D. R. "Race, Residence, and Workplace in Detroit, 1880 to 1965." *Economic Geography*, January 1972, pp. 79-94.

3455. Hecht, J. L. "Role of Housing in Fair Employment." *Management Review*, August 1971, pp. 31-32+.

3456. Hilaski, Harvey J. and Hazel M. Willacy. "Employment Patterns and Place of Residence." *Monthly Labor Review*, December 1969, pp. 18-25.

3457. Kain, John F. *The Effect of the Ghetto on the Distribution and Level of Nonwhite Employment in Urban Areas*. Santa Monica, Cal.: The Rand Corporation, 1965. 23pp.

3458. Kain, John F. "Housing Segregation, Negro Employment and Metropolitan Decentralization." *Quarterly Journal of Economics*, May

1968, pp. 175-197. Reply (P. Offner and D. H. Saks) with rejoinder, February 1971, pp. 47-62.

3459. Mooney, Joseph D. "Housing Segregation, Negro Employment and Metropolitan Decentralization: An Alternative Perspective." *Quarterly Journal of Economics*, May 1969, pp. 299-311.

3460. National Committee Against Discrimination in Housing. *The Impact of Housing Patterns on Job Opportunities; An Interim Report of a Study on Where People Live and Where the Jobs Are.* With an introduction by Kenneth B. Clark. New York, 1968. 38pp.

3461. National Committee Against Discrimination in Housing. *Jobs and Housing: Final Summary Report on the Housing Component.* New York, March 1972. 43pp.

3462. National Committee Against Discrimination in Housing. *Jobs and Housing: A Study of Employment and Housing Opportunities for Racial Minorities in Suburban Areas of the New York Metropolitan Region: Interim Report.* New York, March 1970. 250pp.

3463. Regional Plan Association. *Linking Skills, Jobs and Housing in the New York Urban Region.* New York, March 1972.

3464. von Furstenberg, George M. "Place of Residence and Employment Opportunities within a Metropolitan Area." *Journal of Economic Issues*, June 1971, pp. 101-116.

## B. RESIDENTIAL MOBILITY

### 1. GENERAL

3465. Birch, David L. "Toward a Stage Theory of Urban Growth." *Journal of the American Institute of Planners*, March 1971, pp. 78-87.

3466. Butler, Edgar W. *et al.* "Demographic and Social Psychological Factors in Residential Mobility." *Sociology and Social Research*, January 1964, pp. 139-154.

3467. Butler, Edgar W. *et al. Moving Behavior and Residential Choice; A National Survey.* Washington, D.C.: Highway Research Board, National Research Council, 1969. 129pp. (National Cooperative Highway Research Program Report no. 81)

3468. Chevan, Albert. *Moving in a Metropolitan Area.* Ann Arbor, Mich.: University Microfilms, 1969 (Ph.D. dissertation, University of Pennsylvania, 1968). 291pp. (order no. 69-78)

3469. Clark, A. V. "Markov Chain Analysis in Geography: An Application to the Movement of Rental Housing Areas." *Association of American Geographers, Annals*, June 1965, pp. 351-359.

3470. Copperman, M. "Residential Mobility of a Group of Public Welfare Clients." *Social Casework*, July 1964, pp. 407-412.

3471. Daniel, Robert E. *Local Residential Mobility: A Selected and Annotated Bibliography*. Monticello, Ill.: Council of Planning Librarians, 1969 (Exchange Bibliography no. 104).

3472. Diemer, Richard Dean. *Toward a Theory of Urban Residential Mobility*. Ann Arbor, Mich.: University Microfilms, 1966. (Ph.D. dissertation, Purdue University, 1966). 172pp. (order no. 66-7414)

3473. Fredland, Daniel Robert. "Residential Mobility and Choice of Tenure." Unpublished Ph.D. dissertation, Harvard University, 1970.

3474. Gilbert G. "Two Markov Models of Neighborhood Housing Turnover." *Environment and Planning*, Vol. 4, no. 2, 1972, pp. 133-146.

3475. Goldstein, Sidney and Kurt B. Mayer. *Residential Mobility, Migration and Commuting in Rhode Island*. Providence, Rhode Island: Planning Division, Rhode Island Development Council, State Planning Section, 1963. 65pp.

3476. Greenbie, Barrie B. "New House or New Neighborhood? A Survey of Priorities Among Home Owners in Madison, Wisconsin." *Land Economics*, August 1969, pp. 359-365.

3477. Kalbach, W. E. *et al.* "Metropolitan Area Mobility: A Comparative Analysis of Family Spatial Mobility in a Central City and Selected Suburbs." *Social Forces*, March 1964, pp. 310-314.

3478. Kasl, Stanislav V. and Ernest Harburg. "Research Report: Perceptions of the Neighborhood and the Desire to Move Out." *American Institute of Planners Journal*, September 1972, pp. 318-324.

3479. Leslie, G. R. and A. H. Richardson. "Life-Cycle, Career Pattern, and the Decision to Move." *American Sociological Review*, December 1961, pp. 894-902.

3480. Long, L. H. "On Measuring Geographic Mobility." *Journal of the American Statistical Association*, September 1970, pp. 1195-1203.

3481. Long, Larry Howard. *Residential Mobility: International Comparisons*. Ann Arbor, Mich.: University Microfilms, 1970 (Ph.D. dissertation, University of Texas at Austin, 1969). 219pp. (order no. 70-10,828)

3482. McAllister, Ronald J. *Neighborhood Integration and Prospective Residential Mobility*. Chapel Hill, N.C.: Center for Urban and Regional Studies, University of North Carolina, 1970 (Environment Policies and Urban Development Thesis Series no. 14). 149pp.

3483. McAllister, Ronald John. *Neighborhood Integration and Prospective Residential Mobility: A Study of the Impact of Social Relationships on Moving and Staying Plans among a National Sample of Metropolitan Area Residents*. Ann Arbor, Mich.: University Microfilms, 1971 (Ph.D. dissertation, Duke University, 1971). 195pp. (order no. 71-24,195)

3484. McAllister, Ronald J., Edward J. Kaiser and Edgar W. Butler. "Residential Mobility of Blacks and Whites: A National Longitudinal Survey." *American Journal of Sociology*, November 1971, pp. 445-456.

3485. Moore, Eric G. "Comments on the Use of Ecological Models in the Study of Residential Mobility." *Economic Geography*, January 1971, pp. 73-85.

3486. Moore, Eric G. *Residential Mobility in the City*. Washington, D.C.: Association of American Geographers, 1972. 50pp.

3487. Morrison, Peter A. "Chronic Movers and the Future Redistribution of Population: A Longitudinal Analysis." *Demography*, May 1971, pp. 171-184.

3488. Morrison, Peter Alan. *Duration of Residence and Prospective Migration: The Evaluation of a Stochastic Model*. Ann Arbor, Mich.: University Microfilms, 1968 (Ph.D. dissertation, Brown University, 1967). 103pp. (order no. 68-1482)

3489. Morrison, Peter A. *Movers and Stayers: An Analysis Based on Two Longitudinal Data Files*. Santa Monica, Cal.: Rand Corporation, December 1970. 28pp.

3490. Okraku, I. O. "Family Life-Cycle and Residential Mobility in Puerto Rico." *Sociology and Social Research*, April 1971, pp. 324-340.

3491. Orbell, J. M. and T. Uno. "Theory of Neighborhood Problem Solving: Political Action vs. Residential Mobility." *American Political Science Review*, June 1972, pp. 471-489.

3492. Prasad, S. B. and Alton C. Johnson. "Residential Mobility of the Retired Industrial Worker." *Land Economics*, May 1964, pp. 220-223.

3493. Roseman, C. C. "Migration, the Journey to Work, and Household Characteristics: An Analysis Based on Non-Areal Aggregation." *Economic Geography*, October 1971, pp. 467-474.

3494. Ross, H. L. "Reasons for Moves to and from a Central City." *Social Forces*, March 1962, pp. 261-263.

3495. Sabagh, G. *et al.* "Some Determinants of Intrametropolitan Residential Mobility: Conceptual Considerations." *Social Forces*, September 1969, pp. 88-98.

3496. Simmons, James W. "Changing Residence in the City: A Review of Intraurban Mobility." *Geographical Review*, October 1968, pp. 622-651.

3497. Smith, Wallace F. "Forecasting Neighborhood Change." *Land Economics*, August 1963, pp. 292-297.

3498. Speare, Alden, Jr. "Homeownership, Life Cycle Stage, and Residential Mobility." *Demography*, November 1970, pp. 449-458.

3499. Stockwell, Edward G. *The Population of Connecticut: Residential Mobility, 1955-1960*. Storrs, Conn.: Agricultural Experiment Station, University of Connecticut, 1964. 11pp.

3500. Straits, Bruce C. "Residential Movement among Negroes and Whites in Chicago." *Social Science Quarterly*, December 1968, pp. 573-592.

3501. Taeuber, Karl E. "Duration-of-Residence Analysis of Internal Migration in the United States." *Milbank Memorial Fund Quarterly*, January 1961, pp. 116-131.

3502. Tough, Rosalind and Gordon D. Mac Donald. "The New York Metropolitan Region: Social Forces and the Flight to Suburbia." *Land Economics*, November 1961, pp. 327-336.

3503. U.S. Bureau of the Census. *Reasons for Moving: March 1962 to March 1963*. Washington, D.C.: Government Printing Office, 1966. 14pp. (Current Population Reports, Series P-20 no. 154)

3504. U.S. Federal Housing Administration. *The Structure and Growth of Residential Neighborhoods in American Cities*. By Homer Hoyt. St. Clair Shores, Mich.: Scholarly Press, 1972 (Reprint of 1939 ed.). 178pp.

3505. Varady, David Paul. *The Household Migration Decision in Racially Changing Neighborhoods*. Ann Arbor, Mich.: University Microfilms, 1971 (Ph.D. dissertation, University of Pennsylvania, 1971). 429pp. (order no. 71-26,098)

3506. Zimmer, Basil G. and Amos H. Hawley. "Suburbanization and Some of Its Consequences." *Land Economics*, February 1961, pp. 88-93.

See also: 952, 2181, 3418-3420.

### 2. THE CONCEPT OF "FILTERING"

3507a. Guy, Donald Copeland. *An Analysis of a Filtering Hypothesis in Urban Housing Markets: An Empirical Test in Kankakee*. Ann Arbor, Mich.: University Microfilms, 1971 (Ph.D. dissertation, University of Illinois at Urbana-Champaign, 1970). 79pp. (order no. 71-14,772)

3507b. Guy, Donald and Hugh O. Nourse. "The Filtering Process: The Webster Groves and Kankakee Cases." *Papers and Proceedings of the American Real Estate and Urban Economics Association*, Vol. V, December 1970, pp. 33-49.

3508. Lansing, John B., Charles Wade Clifton and James N. Morgan. *New Homes and Poor People; A Study of Chains of Moves*. Ann Arbor, Mich.: Survey Research Center, Institute for Social Research, University of Michigan, 1969.

3509. Lowry, I. S. "Filtering and Housing Standards: A Conceptual Analysis." *Land Economics*, November 1960, pp. 362-370. Also in Alfred N. Page and Warren R. Seyfried (eds.). *Readings in Housing and Urban Development*. Glenview, Ill.: Scott, Foresman, 1970, pp. 339-347.

3510. Smith, Wallace F. *Filtering and Neighborhood Change*. Berkeley, Calif.: Center for Real Estate and Urban Economics, University of California, 1964 (Research Report no. 24).

3511. White, Harrison C. "Multipliers, Vacancy Chains, and Filtering in Housing." *Journal of the American Institute of Planners*, March 1971, pp. 88-94. Also in George Sternlieb and Lynne B. Sagalyn (eds.). *Housing: 1970-1971; An AMS Anthology*. New York: AMS Press, 1972, pp. 246-254.

See also: 2478.

## C. DENSITY

3512. "The Case for Higher Density Housing." *House and Home*, April 1962, pp. 132-141.

3513. Erb, Richard David. *Postwar Development in Urban Residential Density*. Ann Arbor, Mich.: University Microfilms, 1969 (Ph.D. dissertation, Stanford University, 1968). 155pp. (order no. 69-8176)

3514. Henry, Charles T. "Residential Occupancy Permits: University City, Missouri, Is Finding Them Effective for Controlling Neighborhood Population Density." *Journal of Housing*, August, 1970, pp. 383-386.

3515. Jensen, Rolf. *High Density Living*. New York: Praeger, 1966.

3516. Katz, Robert D. *Residential Densities*. Monticello, Ill.: Council of Planning Librarians, 1961 (Exchange Bibliography no. 18).

3517. "Land Use Intensity Rating: A New Approach to Residential Development by the Federal Housing Administration." *Urban Land*, October 1963, pp. 3-9.

3518. Lansing, John B. and Gary Hendricks. *Automobile Ownership and Residential Density*. Ann Arbor, Michigan: Survey Research Center, Institute for Social Research, University of Michigan, 1967. 230pp.

3519. "Mid-density Housing: Hottest Concept on the Market." *NAHB Journal of Homebuilding*, June 1972, pp. 40-45.

3520. Martin, Randolph Charles. *Differentials in the Intensity of Residential Land Use between Cities and Suburbs*. Ann Arbor, Mich.: University Microfilms, 1971 (Ph.D. dissertation, Washington University, 1971). 69pp. (order no. 71-19,824)

3521. Miller, J. Marshall. "Residential Density: Relating People to Space rather than to Ground Area." *Journal of the American Institute of Planners*, February 1961, pp. 77-78.

3522. Spring, Bernard P. "Is There a Habitat in Your Future?" *Journal of the American Institute of Planners*, November 1967, pp. 417-419.

3523. Sussna, Stephen. "Playing the Numbers Game: Residential Density." *HUD Challenge*, November 1972, pp. 29-30.

3524. Syracuse, Lee A. "Mid-density—Housing for a Changing America." *NAHB Journal of Homebuilding*, July 1972, pp. 54-68.

3525. U.S. Housing and Home Finance Agency. Federal Housing Administration. *Intensity of Development and Livability of Multi-family Housing Projects: Design Qualities of European and American Housing Projects*. By Robert D. Katz. Washington, D.C.: Government Printing Office, 1963 (FHA Technical Study TS 7.14). 114pp.

3526. Urban Land Institute. *Density: Five Perspectives*. Washington, D.C., 1972.

See also: 3374, 3379.

## V. INFORMATIONAL FRAMEWORK

3527. U.S. Department of Housing and Urban Development. Library and Information Division. *Information Sources in Housing and Community Development*. Washington, D.C.: Government Printing Office, 1972. 44pp.

## A. BIBLIOGRAPHIES

3528. Akin, Joy. *The Feasibility and Actuality of Modern New Towns for the Poor in the U.S.* Monticello, Ill.: Council of Planning Librarians, 1970 (Exchange Bibliography no. 167).

3529. California Department of Housing and Community Development. *Bibliography of Surveys and Studies Relating to Housing, Building, and Community Development.* Sacramento, Calif., 1968.

3530. Clapp, James A. *The New Town Concept: Private Trends and Public Response.* Monticello, Ill.: Council of Planning Librarians, 1970 (Exchange Bibliography no. 122).

3531. Connorton, John V. *Studies Completed in the City Rent and Rehabilitation Administration.* New York: New York City Office of the Mayor, Office of Administration, December 1965. 9pp.

3532. Fediuk, Simon. *Bibliography on Housing and Urban Renewal.* New York: New York State Division of Human Rights, 1970. 92pp.

3533. Freeman, E. S. "Review of the Literature on Housing and Urban Development during 1964 and 1965." *Special Libraries*, March 1966, pp. 156-166.

3534. *Housing Compendiums: Volume One.* Annandale, Va.: Modco, Inc., 1972.

3535. Howard, William A. *Concept of an Optimum Size City, A Selected Bibliography.* Monticello, Ill.: Council of Planning Librarians, 1968 (Exchange Bibliography no. 52).

3536. Howard, William A. and James B. Kracht. *Optimum City-Size and Municipal Efficiency: A Revised Version of Exchange Bibliography no. 52.* Monticello, Ill.: Council of Planning Librarians, 1971 (Exchange Bibliography no. 169).

3537. Leary, Margaret A. *Urban Housing in the United States: An Annotated Bibliography for Lawyers with Emphasis on Non-legal Sources.* Monticello, Ill.: Council of Planning Librarians, 1970 (Exchange Bibliography no. 126).

3538. Porteous, J. Douglas. *The Single-Enterprise Community in North America.* Monticello, Ill.: Council of Planning Librarians, 1971 (Exchange Bibliography no. 207).

3539. Powell, David R. *New Towns Bibliography.* Monticello, Ill.: Council of Planning Librarians, 1972 (Exchange Bibliography no. 249).

3540. Smith, Thelma E. (comp.). *Planning and Housing, 1960: A Selected Bibliography*. New York: Municipal Reference Library, 1960. 11pp.

3541. Toizer, Alfred. *Survey of Recent Housing Studies: An Annotated Guide*. Monticello, Ill.: Council of Planning Librarians, 1970 (Exchange Bibliography no. 138).

3542. U.S. Department of Housing and Urban Development. Library. *Bibliography on Housing, Building and Planning; For Use of Overseas Missions of the United States Agency for International Development*. Rev. Washington, D.C.: Division of International Affairs, U.S. Department of Housing and Urban Development, 1969. 43pp.

3543. U.S. Department of Housing and Urban Development. Library. *Books about Cities*. Washington, D.C., 1969. 24pp.

3544. U.S. Department of Housing and Urban Development. Office of Research and Technology. *A Compendium of Reports Resulting from HUD Research and Technology Funding*. Washington, D.C., 1972. 1 vol.

3545. U.S. Department of Housing and Urban Development. Library. *Films, Filmstrips, Slides, and Audio Tapes on Housing and Community Development; A Selected Bibliography*. Washington, D.C.: Government Printing Office, 1967. 38pp.

3546. U.S. Department of Housing and Urban Development. Library and Information Division. *Housing and Planning References*. Washington, D.C.: Government Printing Office, published bi-monthly.

3547. U.S. Department of Housing and Urban Development. *New Communities: A Bibliography*. Washington, D.C.: Government Printing Office, 1970. 84pp.

3548. U.S. Housing and Home Finance Agency. Library. *Bibliography on Housing, Building, and Planning*. For use of United States A.I.D. Missions. Washington, D.C.: Office of International Housing, Housing and Home Finance Agency, Rev. 1964. 52pp.

3549. U.S. Housing and Home Finance Agency. Library. *60 Books on Housing and Community Planning*. Washington, D.C.: Office of the Administrator, Housing and Home Finance Agency, 1963. 21pp.

3550. Wheaton, William L. C., William C. Baer and David M. Vetter. *Housing, Renewal and Development Bibliography*. Monticello, Ill.: Council of Planning Librarians, 1968 (Exchange Bibliography no. 46).

3551. Zeitlin, Morris. *Guide to the Literature of Cities: Abstracts and Bibliography, Part IV: Urban Housing.* Monticello, Ill.: Council of Planning Librarians, 1972 (Exchange Bibliography no. 308).

See also: 48-50, 227, 228, 305, 924, 925, 1009, 1170, 1367, 1368, 1436, 1517-1519, 1646-1650, 1761-1766, 1803-1810, 2214, 2499, 2686, 2805, 2964, 3038, 3134, 3298, 3308, 3324, 3471, 3516.

## B. DICTIONARIES

3552. Abrams, Charles. *The Language of Cities: A Glossary of Terms.* New York: Viking Press, 1971. 365pp.

3553. Markus, Marvin (comp.). *Housing and Planning Terms Commonly Used—and Misused.* New York: Citizens Housing and Planning Council of New York, 1971. 38pp.

## C. RESEARCH METHODS

3554. Becklin, Jay Reuben. *Forecasting Short-Term Local Housing Activity: An Albuquerque Example.* Ann Arbor, Mich.: University Microfilms, 1970 (D.B.A. dissertation, Graduate School of Business, Indiana University, 1969). 240pp. (order no. 70-15,566)

3555. Carman, J. M. *Rental Housing Vacancy and Turnover.* Berkeley, Calif.: Center for Real Estate and Urban Economics, University of California, 1969.

3556. Cleaver, Patrick Tracy. *The Development of an Index for Estimating Social Class Levels of City Blocks.* Ann Arbor, Mich.: University Microfilms, 1964 (Ph.D. dissertation, The Ohio State University, 1963). 88pp. (order no. 64-7002)

3557. Fisher, Dennis Udell. *Relationships between Socio-Economic and Locational Characteristics of the Occupants and Housing Condition.* Ann Arbor, Mich.: University Microfilms, 1972 (Ph.D. dissertation, Michigan State University, 1972). 305pp. (order no. 72-29,961)

3558. Gruen, Claude. *The Socio-Economic Determinants of Urban Residential Housing Quality.* Ann Arbor, Mich.: University Microfilms, 1964 (Ph.D. dissertation, University of Cincinnati, 1964). 264pp. (order no. 64-12,285)

3559. Kimbell, Larry Jack. *An Econometric Model of Residential Construction and Finance.* Ann Arbor, Mich.: University Microfilms, 1969 (Ph.D. dissertation, The University of Texas at Austin, 1968). 238pp. (order no. 69-6168).

3560. Leasure, J. W. and D. H. Stern. "Notes on Housing Segregation Indexes." *Social Forces*, March 1968, pp. 406-407.

3561. Perloff, Harvey S. *A National Program of Research in Housing and Urban Development; The Major Requirements and a Suggested Approach: Staff Study*. Washington, D.C.: Resources for the Future, Inc., 1961. 32pp.

3562. Rickert, J. E. "House Facades of the Northeastern United States: A Tool of Geographic Analysis." *Association of American Geographers, Annals*, June 1967, pp. 211-238.

3563. Robinson, Ira M., Harry B. Wolfe and Robert L. Barringer. "A Simulation Model for Renewal Programming." *Journal of the American Institute of Planners*, May 1965, pp. 126-134.

3564. Shinn, A. M. "Measuring the Utility of Housing: Demonstrating a Methodological Approach." *Social Science Quarterly*, June 1971, pp. 88-102.

3565. Steger, Wilbur A. "The Pittsburgh Urban Renewal Simulation Model." *Journal of the American Institute of Planners*, May 1965, pp. 144-150.

3566. Stegman, Michael Allen. *An Analysis and Evaluation of Urban Residential Models and Their Potential Role in City Planning*. Ann Arbor, Mich.: University Microfilms, 1966 (Ph.D. dissertation, University of Pennsylvania, 1966) 320pp. (order no. 67-7878)

3567. Sternlieb, George and Bernard Indik. "Housing Vacancy Analysis." *Land Economics*, February 1969, pp. 117-121.

3568. U.S. Department of Housing and Urban Development. *A Comparison of Two Techniques for Obtaining Housing Vacancy & Turnover Data*. Washington, D.C.: Government Printing Office, June 1969, 22+pp.

3569. U.S. Savings and Loan League. *Local Housing Research Techniques and Data. Report on a Round Table Conference Sponsored by American Marketing Association and U.S. Savings and Loan League, Palmer House, Chicago, January 26, 1965*. Chicago, Ill. U.S. Savings and Loan League, 1965. 62pp.

3570. Wolfe, Harry B. "Models for Conditioning Aging of Residential Structures." *Journal of the American Institute of Planners*, May 1967, pp. 192-196.

See also: 51, 52, 54, 55, 57-61, 65, 239, 313, 876, 883, 885, 891, 893, 894, 916, 923, 976, 977, 984, 985, 993, 1005, 1008, 2217, 3108, 3377, 3378, 3382, 3384, 3389, 3391, 3392, 3395, 3396, 3401, 3405, 3406,

3408, 3411, 3414, 3421, 3430, 3431, 3435-3437, 3469-3474, 3485; Housing Market Analysis Techniques: 1052+.

## D. HOUSING STATISTICS

3571. Advance Mortgage Corporation. *U.S. Housing Markets: A Statistical Survey of 17 Metropolitan Areas and 8 Regions*. Detroit, Mich., revised semi-annually.

3572. American Society of Planning Officials. *The 1970 Census: A Resource for Housing and City Planning Studies*. Chicago, Ill., 1971. 95pp. (Planning Advisory Service Report no. 267).

3573. Josowitz, A. "Housing Statistics: Published and Unpublished." *Monthly Labor Review*, December 1969, pp. 50-55.

3574. Kristof, Frank. "The Increased Utility of the 1960 Housing Census for Planning." *Journal of the American Institute of Planners*, February 1963, pp. 40-47.

3575. Siegelman, Leonore R. "A Technical Note on Housing Census Comparability, 1950-1960." *Journal of the American Institute of Planners*, February 1963, pp. 48-54.

3576. Smith, G. C. "Housing Forecast and Critique of Housing Data." *Commercial and Financial Chronicle*, May 1, 1969. pp. 1905+.

3577. U.S. Bureau of the Census. Social and Economic Statistics Administration. *Construction Reports: Residential Alterations and Repairs: Expenditures on Residential Additions, Alterations, Maintenance and Repairs, and Replacements*. Washington, D.C., published quarterly with annual report C50 series).

3578. U.S. Bureau of the Census. Social and Economic Statistics Administration. *Current Housing Reports: Housing Characteristics*. Washington, D.C.: Government Printing Office, published irregularly (H121 series).

3579. U.S. Bureau of the Census and U.S. Department of Housing and Urban Development. *Current Housing Reports: Market Absorption of Apartments*. Washington, D.C.: Bureau of the Census, published quarterly (H130 series).

3580. U.S. Department of Housing and Urban Development. *Housing and Urban Development Trends*. Washington, D.C., published quarterly.

3581. U.S. Department of Housing and Urban Development. *Housing Statistics: Compiled Monthly from Government and Other Sources*. Washington, D.C.: Government Printing Office, September 1966. 60pp.

3582. U.S. Department of Housing and Urban Development. *Statistical Yearbook*. Washington, D.C.: Government Printing Office, published annually.

3583. U.S. Department of Housing and Urban Development. Housing Production and Mortgage Credit—FHA. Division of Research and Statistics. Statistics Branch. *FHA Monthly Report of Operations*. In 3 parts. Washington, D.C., published monthly.

3584. U.S. Department of Housing and Urban Development. Housing Production and Mortgage Credit—FHA. Division of Research and Statistics. Statistics Branch. *FHA Trends of Home Mortgage Characteristics*. Washington, D.C., published quarterly.

3585. U.S. Department of Housing and Urban Development. Renewal and Housing Management. Office of Renewal Assistance. *Report of Urban Renewal Operations, Title I, Housing Act of 1949 as Amended*. Washington, D.C., published monthly.

3586. Wehrly, Max S. "An Advance Look at the 1970 Census of Housing." *Urban Land*, December 1969, pp. 3-8.

See for a brief description of the 1970 Census reports: U.S. Bureau of the Census. *1970 Census Users' Guide: Part I*. Washington, D.C.: Government Printing Office, 1970. See also: 129-167, 1018-1021.

## E. HOUSING DATA SYSTEMS

3587. Case, Fred E. "California Housing Information System: A Feasibility Study." *California Real Estate Magazine*, June 1972, pp. 12-13.

3588. Isler, Morton L. "Selecting Data for Community Renewal Programming." *Journal of the American Institute of Planners*, March 1967, pp. 66-77.

3589. Salkowitz, Susan M. "Data Systems: Vacant Property System." *Journal of Housing*, April 1971, pp. 187-190.

3590. Salkowitz, Susan M. "Housing Code Enforcement Data System Not Only Solves Codes Records Problems but Becomes Base for General Housing Information System." *Journal of Housing*, February 1971, pp. 79-81.

3591. Salkowitz, Susan *et al. Housing Information Systems*. Washington, D.C.: National Association of Housing and Redevelopment Officials, 1971. 24pp. (Reprint of four articles appearing in 1971 issues of the *Journal of Housing*—all listed separately here).

3592. Salkowitz, Susan M. "Why and How Philadelphia Developed Its Housing Data System." *Journal of Housing*, January 1971, pp. 28-29.

3593. Seidel, K. M. *Development of a Housing Information Base*. Eugene, Ore.: Bureau of Governmental Research and Service, University of Oregon, 1970.

3594. Tozier, Alfred, Marjorie L. McCann and Carolyn Z. Muench. "Data Systems: Housing Production Monitoring System—Its Origin, Design, Implementation, and Operation." *Journal of Housing*, March 1971, pp. 134-136.

## VI. GENERAL WORKS AND ANTHOLOGIES ON HOUSING

### A. SURVEY LISTING

3959. Abrams, Charles. *Housing in the Modern World; With an Introduction by Peter Self*. London, England: Faber, 1966. 307pp.

3596. Alpern, Robert Blair. *Pratt Guide: A Citizens' Handbook of Housing, Planning & Urban Renewal Procedures in New York City*. Brooklyn, N.Y.: Pratt Institute, 1965.

3597. American Bar Association. Special Committee on Housing and Urban Development Law. *Housing and Urban Development, a Contrast Between the Method Employed in England and the United States*. Chicago, Ill., 1972. 28pp.

3598. Beyer, Glenn H. *Housing and Society*. New York: Macmillan, 1965. 595pp.

3599. " 'Building the American City': an Early Look at Some Recommendations From The National Commission on Urban Problems" *Urban Land*. March 1969, pp. 3-13.

3600. California Governor's Advisory Commission on Housing Problems. *Report on Housing in California*. San Francisco, Calif., 1963. 78pp.

3601. California Governor's Advisory Commission on Housing Problems, *Appendix to the Report on Housing in California*. San Francisco, Calif., 1963. 817pp.

3602. California. Governor's Advisory Commission on Housing Problems. *Summary of Housing in California*. San Francisco, 1963.

3603. Congressional Quarterly Service. *Housing a Nation*. Washington, D.C., 1966. 94pp.

3604. Craig, Lois. "Housing: the Kaiser and Douglas Reports." *City*, February 1969, pp. 30-35.

3605. Duncan, Beverly and Philip M. Hauser. *Housing a Metropolis–Chicago*. Glencoe, Ill.: Free Press, 1960. 278pp.

3606. Everett, Robinson O. and John D. Johnston (eds.). *Housing*. Dobbs Ferry, N.Y.: Oceana Publications, 1968. 376 pp. (Originally published in *Law and Contemporary Problems*, Spring and Summer 1967.)

3607. Foote, Nelson N. *et al. Housing Choices and Housing Constraints*. New York: McGraw-Hill, 1960. 450pp.

3608. Fried, Joseph P. *Housing Crisis U.S.A.* New York: Praeger, 1971. 250pp.

3609. Frieden, Bernard J. and William W. Nash, Jr. (eds.). *Shaping an Urban Future; Essays in Memory of Catherine Bauer Wurster*. Cambridge, Mass.: MIT Press, 1969. 222pp.

3610. Haas, John H. *A Housing Manifesto: Residential Housing Problems–Diagnosis and Treatment*. Washington, D.C.: Workshop 221, 1964. 95pp.

3611. Meyerson, Martin, Barbara Terrett and William L. C. Wheaton. *Housing, People, and Cities*. New York: McGraw-Hill, 1962. 386pp.

3612. National Association of Housing and Redevelopment Officials. *Critical Urban Housing Issues: 1967. A Selection of Papers from NAHRC National Housing Policy Forum*. Washington, D.C., 1967. 111pp.

3613. 1952/1962: 10 Years of Progress in Housing, a 12-part Review of the Decade Illustrated by Reprints of Memorable and Still Pertinent Stories from Past Issues of House & Home and Followed by a Look into the Future." *House & Home*, March 1962, entire issue.

3614. Page, Alfred N. and Warren R. Seyfried. *Urban Analysis: Readings in Housing and Urban Development*. Glenview, Ill.: Scott, Foresman, 1970. 427pp.

3615. Princeton University School of Architecture. Research Center for Urban and Environmental Planning. *Cooperation of the Public and Private Sectors in Housing*. Princeton, N.J., 1968. 88pp.

3616. Salsich, P. W. "Housing and the States." *The Urban Lawyer*, Winter 1970, pp. 40-62.

3617. Smith, Wallace F. *Housing: the Social and Economic Elements*. Berkeley, Calif.: University of California Press, 1970. 511pp.

3618. Stegman, Michael A. (ed.) *Housing and Economics: The American Dilemma*. Cambridge, Mass.: MIT Press, 1970. 517pp.

3619. Sternlieb, George and Lynne B. Sagalyn. (eds.). *Housing: 1970-1971; An AMS Anthology*. New York: AMS Press, 1972.

3620. U.S. National Commission on Urban Problems. *Building the American City; Report to the Congress and to the President of the United States*. Washington, D.C.: Government Printing Office, 1969.

3621. U.S. National Commission on Urban Problems. *Hearings*. Washington, D.C.: Government Printing Office, 1968. 5 vols.

3622. U.S. President's Committee on Urban Housing. *A Decent Home: Report*. Washington, D.C.: Government Printing Office, 1969. 252pp.

3623. U.S. President's Committee on Urban Housing. *Report: Technical Studies, Volume I*. Washington, D.C.: Government Printing Office, 1967. 171pp.

3624. U.S. President's Committee on Urban Housing. *Report: Technical Studies, Volume II*. Washington, D.C.: Government Printing Office, 1968. 420pp.

3625. Wheaton, William L. C., Grace Milgram and Margy Ellin Meyerson (eds.). *Urban Housing*. New York: Free Press, 1966. 523pp.

# AUTHOR INDEX

Numbers following an author's name refer to entry number and not to page number

## SUBJECT FINDING GUIDE

Numbers given below refer to the entry numbers and not the page numbers.



Employment-Housing Linkage: 3439+; 3453+; See also Residential Location 3372+